Reworking Race

Moon-Kie Jung

COLUMBIA UNIVERSITY PRESS / NEW YORK

Reworking Race

The Making of Hawaii's Interracial Labor Movement

Columbia University Press
Publishers Since 1893
New York   Chichester, West Sussex
Copyright © 2006 Columbia University Press

Library of Congress Cataloging-in-Publication Data
Jung, Moon-Kie.
Reworking race : the making of Hawaii's interracial labor movement /
    Moon-Kie Jung.
    p.   cm.
    Includes bibliographical references and index.
    ISBN 0–231–13534–3 (cloth) — ISBN 0–231–50948–0
    1. Working class—Hawaii. 2. Labor—Hawaii—History. 3. Hawaii—
    Race relations. 4. International Longshoremen's and Warehouse-
    men's Union—History. 5. Diversity in the workplace—Hawaii.
    I. Title.
HD8083.H3J86   2005
305.5'62'09969—dc22
                    2005051797

Columbia University Press books are printed on permanent and durable
    acid-free paper.
Printed in the United States of America
c 10 9 8 7 6 5 4 3 2 1

Title page art: ILWU Political Action Committee Convention in Hilo,
    February 1946. Courtesy of the ILWU Local 142 Archives.

Earlier versions of parts of. this book appeared in the following articles:
"Interracialism: The Ideological Transformation of Hawaii's Working
Class," *American Sociological Review* 68 (3) © 2003 American Sociologi-
cal Association. "No Whites, No Asians: Race, Marxism, and Hawaii's
Preemergent Working Class," *Social Science History* 23 (3) © 1999 Social
Science History Association.

To Mina and Toussaint

Contents

List of Abbreviations

AFL   American Federation of Labor
AHPP   Association of Hawaiian Pineapple Packers
CALPACK   California Packing Company
CIO   Committee for Industrial Organization (from 1935 to 1938)
          Congress of Industrial Organizations (since 1938)
FJL   Federation of Japanese Labor
FLU   Filipino Labor Union
HAPCO   Hawaiian Pineapple Company
HC&S   Hawaiian Commercial and Sugar Company
HERA   Hawaii Employment Relations Act
HILA   Hilo Longshoremen's Association (predecessor to ILWU Local 1–36)
HOLA   Honolulu Longshoremen's Association (predecessor to ILWU Local
          1–37)
HSPA   Hawaiian Sugar Planters' Association
HWA   Higher Wages Association
HWM   High Wage Movement
HWWA   Honolulu Waterfront Workers' Association
IAH   Industrial Association of Hawaii
IBU   Inland Boatmen's Union
ILA   International Longshoremen's Association
ILWU   International Longshoremen's and Warehousemen's Union (Interna-
          tional Longshore and Warehouse Union since 1997)
LASSCO   Los Angeles Steamship Company
LML   Libby, McNeill & Libby
MC&S   Marine Cooks and Stewards Union

MPMWIU Maui Plantation and Mill Workers Industrial Union
MTC   Metal Trades Council
NLRB   National Labor Relations Board
PAC   Political Action Committee
PAWWA   Port Allen Waterfront Workers Association (predecessor to ILWU Local 1–35)
PCD   Pacific Coast District of the International Longshoremen's Association
PLSC   Planters' Labor and Supply Company
SUP   Sailors' Union of the Pacific
UCAPAWA United Cannery, Agricultural, Packing, and Allied Workers of America
UHW   Union of Hawaiian Workers
USED   United States Engineering Department
USES   United States Employment Service
WIA   Wage Increase Association
YMBA   Young Men's Buddhist Association

Acknowledgments

As i write these words, I realize that my professed self-image as a solitary is, if not exactly untrue, exaggerated: many people contributed in myriad ways to the making of this book. Julia Adams, Tomás Almaguer, Howard Kimeldorf, and Gail Nomura—three historical sociologists and a social historian whose scholarship I truly respect—formed an ideal dissertation committee. They provided guidance, criticism, enthusiasm, and, perhaps most importantly, freedom. Under no formal obligation to do so, Eduardo Bonilla-Silva and Donald Deskins also took an interest and gave crucial support. Although I thought I did at the time, only upon leaving did I fully appreciate the people with whom I went to graduate school: a critical mass of brilliant and progressive students of color and fellow travelers from both sides of State Street.

Its racist mascot and desolate surroundings notwithstanding, the University of Illinois has been a wonderful place to teach and write for the past five years and counting. I especially thank everyone in the Asian American Studies Program and the Department of Sociology for their collegiality, intelligence, and humor.

This book would not have been possible without the dedicated work of numerous archivists and librarians. In particular, I am grateful to Eugene Dennis Vrana at the Anne Rand Research Library of the International Longshore and Warehouse Union in San Francisco; Pam Mizukami and Rae Shiraki at the Priscilla Shishido Library of the ILWU Local 142 in Honolulu; Tab Lewis at the National Archives and Records Administration in College Park, MD; William Puette at the Center for Labor Education and Research, University of Hawai'i at West O'ahu; and James Cartwright, Joan Hori, Dore

Minatodani, Sherman Seki, and Chieko Tachihata at the University of Hawaiʻi Libraries' Special Collections. I also appreciate the assistance of many others at the Hawaiʻi State Archives, National Archives, Bryn Mawr College, and the Universities of California (Berkeley and San Diego), Hawaiʻi (Mānoa and West Oʻahu), Illinois, and Michigan. I thank labor historians Edward Beechert and Harvey Schwartz, who generously shared research material, and the officers of the ILWU, who permitted me access to the union's archival collections.

Grants and fellowships from the following institutions enabled the research, writing, and publication of this book: Department of Sociology and Rackham School of Graduate Studies at the University of Michigan; Rockefeller Foundation; Center for the Study of Race and Ethnicity at the University of California, San Diego; Center for Ethnicities, Communities and Social Policy at Bryn Mawr College; and Asian American Studies Program, Campus Research Board, and Center on Democracy in a Multiracial Society at the University of Illinois. During two lengthy stays in Honolulu, the Department of Sociology at the University of Hawaiʻi graciously extended office space and various courtesies. I owe much to the Bennett and Gutiérrez families, who warmly opened their homes to me while I carried out research in the Bay Area.

The book benefited immensely from a wide range of readers who approached it from divers disciplinary and theoretical angles. In addition to my dissertation committee, several colleagues at UCSD—Yen Le Espiritu, Ross Frank, Ramón Gutiérrez, George Lipsitz, and João H. Costa Vargas—scrutinized the earliest version of the manuscript with care and encouragement. Since then, Nancy Abelmann, Julia Adams, Augusto Espiritu, J. Kehaulani Kauanui, Amanda Lewis, Ah Quon McElrath, and Gene Vrana commented on various parts. Jim Barrett, Edward Beechert, Tyrone Forman, Tom Guglielmo, Moon-Ho Jung, Bruce Nelson, Gary Okihiro, Dave Roediger, Assata Zerai, and reviewers for Columbia University Press braved through the entire manuscript. Editors Anne Routon and Leslie Kriesel expertly guided the book to its publication, even as the series for which it was originally intended unexpectedly perished.

For wholly and blissfully unacademic reasons, my deepest gratitude is reserved for friends and family. My year in San Diego would have been a much emptier one without the trusted friendship of João Vargas that quickly became one of my best. Civilian friends of long standing who care about what I do but couldn't care less about anything else in academia shielded my sanity, such as it is: Eric Bennett, Hyun Joo Oh, and the households of Bellestri-Shih, Dapprich-Stuart, and Paul-MacDonald. My parents, Jung Woo-Hyun and Ahn Minja, grandma, Kwon Soon-Ok, and brother, Moon-Ho, have been unstinting sources of support. My dissertation was dedicated to my parents and grandmother, who took much joy in the completion of my graduate studies. Mina and Toussaint, whose births predate this book's by two years, bear the burden this time. They also agreed to assume responsibility for any errors that remain.

Reworking Race

1

Introduction

People's Republic of Hawai'i

Across the top of a two-page spread in its June 16, 1997 issue, *Forbes* magazine declared, "The People's Republic of Hawaii." This conservative journal of the economic elite bemoaned what it deemed to be an environment inhospitable to business: "At a time when even former socialist countries are going the free enterprise route, this small part of the U.S. remains mired in a half-baked form of socialism" (Lubove 1997:70). The sins of this "semisocialist welfare state" were many. Most of them stemmed from too much government and taxes: "The state's annual budget comes to around $5,270 per Hawaiian [*sic*]. That compares with $2,980 in California. It amounts to almost 19% of the islands' gross economic output. . . . Under a law passed in 1974 employers must pay virtually all of workers' [health] insurance premiums. . . . Add to this a workers' compensation system that presumes all injuries were caused on the job" (Lubove 1997:67–68). The article took Hawai'i to task for being far left of the mainstream in other areas as well. The journal feared that the state's judiciary would be amenable to demands of the Hawaiian sovereignty movement. At the time, Hawai'i also seemed to be on the verge of becoming the first state to permit same-sex marriages, stirring reactionary furor across the United States and prompting the passage of preemptive legislations in Congress and twenty-nine states.[1]

Forbes could have run off a much longer list to paint the islands red. Hawai'i instituted the first negative income tax program for the poor (Thompson 1966:29). It was the first state to legalize abortion and to ratify the ultimately failed Equal Rights Amendment. It led in abolishing the death penalty. Hawai'i was the first state to mandate prepaid health care for workers, and its workers' compensation program has had the highest payout rates. As of 1970, Hawai'i was the only state with an unemployment compensation program covering agricultural workers and 1 of only 5 states providing temporary disability insurance for illnesses or accidents unrelated to the job. Citizens of Hawai'i have continually voted overwhelmingly for Democrats, and Hawaii's Democrats have been among the most leftward leaning.[2] For example, in the 2004 Democratic primaries, Dennis Kucinich, the presidential candidate on the left fringe of the party, garnered 31 percent of the votes in Hawai'i, nearly doubling the figures for Maine, Minnesota, and Oregon, the only other so-called "blue" states in which he scored double digits.[3] While not without serious limitations—like the eventual rejection of same-sex marriage, resistance to Hawaiian sovereignty, and the Democrats' entrenched ties to wealth and power—Hawaii's politics have been arguably the most progressive in the country.

What may be even more striking about Hawaii's relatively progressive politics is its sharp break in the 1940s and 1950s with a long, resolutely conservative past: few other states or regions, if any, have traversed the political spectrum so far and so quickly. For example, increasingly dominated by a small group of *haole*[4] sugar capitalists of mostly U.S., English, and German origins, the Kingdom of Hawai'i (until 1893) and, following the illegal overthrow of the monarchy, the Republic of Hawai'i (1894–1898) sanctioned and enforced a system of indentured labor for a half century, until the U.S. territorialization of the islands in 1900.[5] The dearth of democracy, however, lasted for almost another half century, as the small group of haole sugar capitalists continued to wield virtually unfettered control over the territory's economy and politics, the latter unwaveringly through the Republican Party.

Given its long conservative past, how did Hawai'i remake itself into one of the most democratic—and Democratic—social formations in the United States? Hawaii's working class provides a necessary and essential part of the answer. Beginning in the late 1930s but not gaining much momentum until the end of World War II, the International Longshoremen's and Warehousemen's Union (ILWU) organized the islands' sugar, pineapple, and stevedoring industries, representing the vast majority of Hawaii's organized labor and becoming the generally recognized voice for the working class as a whole.[6] Leftist in its ideology and leadership, active both at the point of production and in politics, and unprecedentedly interracial, the ILWU embodied Hawaii's working class for itself. Reviewing the union's role in the swift leftward shift in Hawaii's politics, its regional director recounted in a 1968 speech: "As workers became conscious of their economic power they began to recognize that they also had political power and exercised it successfully in cooperation with other liberal sections of the community to enact in Hawaii probably the best package of social and labor legislation of any state in the union. Twenty-five years ago we were one of the most backward communities in our nation."[7] Even the harshest critics of the

ILWU concede grudgingly the union's vital role in the rapid democratization of Hawai'i, objecting to the degree to which it has succeeded, not failed, in achieving its lofty goals.

The mid-century coalescence of Hawaii's working class through the ILWU was not achieved easily. Before World War II, nobody had any realistic expectations that the workers would form a coherent, progressive social force in the foreseeable future. While employers may have feared it and the most ardent labor organizers may have aspired to it, neither anticipated the working class's actual formation in the 1940s. The employers' unremitting dominance and suppression of labor were important factors in the dismal state and prospects of prewar workers. But, as scholars agree, the most crucial factor bridling working-class formation before World War II was racial divisions.

From the middle of the nineteenth century, Native Hawaiians and migrant laborers recruited mainly from China, Portugal, Japan, and the Philippines, in overlapping succession, worked on Hawaii's sugar plantations. Following their initial contractual stints in the sugar industry, many of them moved on to work in Hawaii's other industries, including pineapple and longshoring. From U.S. annexation to World War II, there were several large-scale movements through which workers contested their poor pay and conditions and the employers' unmitigated, unilateral control. But the workers were divided racially. Then, toward the end of the war, they built, seemingly overnight, a lasting interracial movement. The protracted period of entrenched racial divisions, displaced by a protracted period of durable interracialism that continues to this day, points to the overarching research problem of this book: how to account for the historic formation of Hawaii's interracial labor movement.

Reconceptualizing Interracialism

Sociology is quiet, nearly silent, on the concept of *interracialism*, which I define as the ideology and practice of forming a political community across extant racial boundaries.[8] Instead, sociology speaks almost exclusively to racial divisions and conflicts. Despite the near silence, however, interracialism has long been present and indispensable. Since the decline of biologistic theories, a commonly shared but largely unspoken assumption has underpinned most sociological explanations of racial divisions and conflicts: the normative desirability of interracialism. A pervasive shadow presence, it functions as the analytically absent but "epistemologically structuring desire" (Kennedy and Galtz 1996:437). That is, sociology maintains its explicit focus on racial divisions and conflicts, while bracketing interracialism as something implicitly desired but rarely analyzed. A consequence of this somewhat peculiar situation is that interracialism is understood negatively, as necessitating *deracialization*.[9] In a world divided by race, interracialism happens only when race lessens in salience. Even the few studies that appear to redress this negativity through explicit analysis reproduce it.

William Julius Wilson (1999), for example, admirably aims to deal squarely with interracialism, analyzing and advocating the formation of interracial political communities mobilized against the ever growing economic inequality in the United States. Because racial ideology distorts "the real sources of our problems," building interracial coalitions requires "an adequate understanding of the social, economic, and political conditions that cause racial ideology either to flourish or subside." Emphasizing and acting upon the "race-neutral" sources of inequality are the proposed keys to interracialism (Wilson 1999:39, 7, ch. 3 passim). In other words, interracialism entails deracialization.

Wilson (1999) is hardly alone, though notably more explicit than most. Ever since the eclipse of biologistic theories of race by assimilationist ones, the same two notions concerning interracialism evident in Wilson have steadfastly held sway: that it is desirable and that it requires a retraction of race—in significance, if not in toto. From the early decades of the last century, assimilationist theorists constructed teleological explanations in which racial and ethnic conflicts and differences gave way inexorably to assimilation. As Robert E. Park ([1926] 1950:150) wrote memorably, "The race relations cycle which takes the form, to state it abstractly, of contacts, competition, accommodation and eventual assimilation, is apparently progressive and irreversible." Based "almost always [on] an implicit, if not always precisely stated, hypothesis that trends will show a moderation of differences between ethnic populations," many have proceeded productively within a broadly assimilationist approach to the present (Hirschman 1983:412; see also Niemonen 1997; Waters and Jiménez 2005).

A common assumption of assimilationism is the normative desirability of assimilation, which is, in almost all cases, the formation of a unified nation unstratified and undivided by race and ethnicity—in other words, the "imagining" of a single, interracial political community coextensive with the nation-state.[10] The path toward its realization is an evolutionary, though at times conflictual, process of deracialization by which all within a nation would eventually become raceless in their outlook and actions, save for politically amorphous celebrations of multiculturalism and diversity.

Although they developed in contradistinction to the assimilationist framework, more conflict-based approaches to race share similar assumptions concerning interracialism. A leading conflict-based alternative to assimilationism has been Marxist accounts of race.[11] Like their assimilationist counterparts, they share a largely unspoken desire for interracialism; a major difference is that the interracial political community to which Marxists aspire is not a unified nation but a unified working class in struggle against capital. Also like the assimilationists,

Marxists imply that interracialism is brought about by deracialization, as workers get beyond race and organize around their common class interests.

This implication is made explicit in the important work of Terry Boswell, Cliff Brown, and John Brueggemann.[12] Like Wilson (1999), they laudably recognize the dearth of scholarship on interracialism. But, also like Wilson, their willingness to address interracialism head-on steers them back to maintaining a racially negative conceptualization of it. Interracial working-class solidarity "requires that both cheap and higher priced labor give primacy to long-term, class-based interests" (Brueggemann and Boswell 1998:438), presumably abandoning or holding in abeyance their short-term, race-based interests. Not surprisingly, given the studies' ties to split labor market and political process theories, both of which have been criticized for objectivist biases (Omi and Winant 1994; Goodwin and Jasper 1999), their account of the ideological dimension of interracialism remains underdeveloped: racial ideologies matter when economic competition among workers corresponds to racial boundaries but do not figure centrally in structuring interracialism.

Though boasting a more substantial empirical literature on working-class interracialism than sociology, labor history also offers little theoretical help in rethinking interracialism. The study of interracialism, and race more generally, was long premised on a dichotomous understanding of race and class that privileged the latter. More recently, labor historians have sought to move beyond that understanding, although the merits of this effort remain hotly debated in the field (Arnesen 1998; Hill 1996). Regardless, even a sympathetic reviewer notes that the recent scholarship on interracial unionism, particularly with regard to the CIO unions, has been focused too narrowly on "variants of the 'how racist/ racially egalitarian were [the unions]?' question" (Arnesen 1998:156), largely overlooking the related, less metrical "how" problem of explaining the ideological formation of interracialism and the role of race in it.

Perhaps we should not view the racially negative conceptualization of interracialism as a problem. After all, that forming a political community across extant racial boundaries would require deracialization seems intuitive. The scholarship on Hawaii's working class certainly provides little reason to gainsay this: there has long been a consensus that the interracial working-class movement of the 1940s and 1950s presupposed deracialization. Seeing the historically unprecedented interracialism among the workers not as a phenomenon needing explicit analytical attention but as part of a general postwar trend toward racial democracy in Hawai'i, the more liberal, assimilationist studies presume, but do not give a clear account of, the deracialization of the working class. The more Marxist-oriented studies tend to focus on the ILWU, casting it—most pivotally its leftist leadership—in the proverbial role of the vanguard of the proletariat.[13]

There are two major weaknesses, one empirical and one theoretical, to the consensus concerning the deracialized conception of interracialism prevailing in the study of Hawaii's workers and sociology. Comparing the scholarship against the historical evidence reveals that a critical question has gone unasked: Did race in fact recede in significance for Hawaii's workers as they forged an interracial class solidarity? Current scholarship assumes that race receded in inverse relationship to the speedy ascendance of the working-class movement, but the assumption turns out to be empirically flimsy. If Hawaii's working-class interracialism had been predicated on deracialization, race should have faded from the workers' discursive and other practices. But this study's examination of primary sources demonstrates that race did not fade but instead took on altered meanings and practices.

Theoretical developments on ideology and social change over the past few decades also cast doubt on deracialization as the apposite conceptual imagery for interracialism. Deracialization, whether gradual or sudden, implies a process toward an absence or insignificance of race. In the case of Hawaii's working-class interracialism, the supposed deracialization of the class struggle entailed a seemingly straightforward retreat of racial ideology, replaced and partly actuated by a likewise straightforward diffusion of a color-blind—and hence more apt or "true"—class ideology advanced by the radical ILWU leadership. Accordingly, the workers' new class identity and politics bore ostensibly little or no relation to their old racial ones. But, more mindful of continuities, as well as discontinuities, in social change—even rapid and large-scale—social theorists argue variously against such clear-cut conceptual breaks in history, "because the concepts by which experience is organized and communicated proceed from the received cultural scheme" (Sahlins 1985:151).[14]

Labor historians and sociologists of class, among others, bear out this notion, showing how workers' ideologies and practices derive from preexisting ones.[15] In the sociology of race, Gramscian interventions, though not concerned with interracialism per se, point in a similar direction. Quoting Antonio Gramsci, Stuart Hall (1986:23) writes, "ideologies are not transformed or changed by replacing one, whole, already formed, conception of the world with another, so much as by 'renovating and making critical an already existing activity.'"[16] Therefore, the construction of new racial ideologies and practices happens through *rearticulation*, "build[ing] upon and break[ing] away from their cultural and political predecessors" (Omi and Winant 1994:89) and recombining race with other categories of practice (Hall 1980).

This theoretical development, if taken seriously, suggests an important implication for the study of interracialism: it should not be reduced to a process of deracialization. In the case of working-class interracialism, for example, rather than assuming race disappears from workers' discourse and practice, a more robust approach would be to analyze *how* workers, who perceive their interests in racially divided terms, come to rearticulate, rather than ineluctably disarticulate, race and class. In Hawai'i, ideas of class advanced by the ILWU's leadership were decisive, but not in the straightforward manner that has been suggested. Rather than unilaterally displacing race, I argue that notions of class conflict were stretched and molded to reinterpret and rework race. In other words, this study contends that working-class interracialism, and interracialism more generally, involves a transformation of race. While deracialization may indeed be a possible dimension of this transformation, it is neither necessary nor exhaustive. Hawaii's working-class interracialism offers a compelling historical case involving a transformation of race without deracialization.

In early 1944, the ILWU sent organizer Matt Meehan to Hawai'i to report on and aid the major organizing campaign that had just begun. In a passage of a report he sent from Hawai'i to the International in San Francisco, Meehan complained jokingly that he would not be able to file weekly reports, as required, because there were no "competent stenographers." He continued, "You dictate in English and it comes out pidgin, so whatthehell!"[17] Meehan's mock complaint about Hawaiian Creole English, the *lingua franca* of workers and of nonhaole more generally, provides an apt metaphor for Hawaii's working-class interracialism. If Meehan's dictations were a leftist class ideology, introduced and proselytized by radicalized militants, the stenographer's creole rendering was its rearticulation in Hawai'i, as it incorporated the workers' racialized concerns.[18] The resultant interracial working-class ideology was thereby an ideology of class that transformed and was transformed by race. It was through race, not its erasure, that Hawaii's interracial working class was made.

Scope of the Book

Since it does not always or even normally happen, under what circumstances do workers form a class? When are they likely to construct their collective interests to be distinct from or in opposition to those of the other classes, namely the capitalists? One factor that historians and sociologists find significant is the nature of employer response to workers' unionization efforts: when employers vigorously oppose the extension of economic citizenship to them, workers tend to embrace a more class-conscious orientation. Throughout the first half of the twentieth century, Hawaii's employers chose to fight unionization every step of the way, at great costs to themselves and at times with extreme force. Why and how? Chapter 2 identifies a key part of the answer in the high degree of capital concentration in a handful of corporations, commonly referred to as the "Big Five," which enabled the employers to mobilize an uncompromising, collective opposition to the workers. Examining the period from the mid-1870s to the early 1930s, the chapter analyzes how concentration of capital, collective organization of employers, and employers' opposition to workers unfolded and changed over time.

By the mid-1940s, in the face of continuing employer opposition, workers in the sugar, pineapple, and stevedoring industries cohered as a class. But, before the war, they did not mobilize against the employers interracially. The closest they came to doing so was a lengthy and bitter strike in the sugar industry in 1920, which displayed a glimmer of hope for working-class interracialism as a Japanese union and a Filipino union cooperated. However, the coalition proved to be fleeting, and the strike ended in the workers' defeat. This outcome inaugurated more than two decades of refractive racial divisions among Hawaii's workers. Japanese workers left the labor movement, not to return for two and a half decades, and Portuguese workers continued to avoid class conflict. Only Filipino workers continued to struggle collectively in the 1920s and 1930s. Critiquing prevailing approaches, chapter 3 proffers an alternative explanation for the working-class racial divisions of the prewar period. I demonstrate that Portuguese, Japanese, and Filipino workers confronted racisms based on qualitatively different assumptions, which, in turn, had material effects on their placements in the racial order. Thus differentially constrained and enabled, they constructed divergent and conflicting interests and politics, further reinforcing the racial divisions.

In the mid-1930s, the hope of an interracial working-class movement reemerged with the organization of the ILWU in Hawai'i. However, its prewar progress was laborious and limited, as the employers continued to fight independent unionism; by the time of Japan's attack on Pearl Harbor, the ILWU had gained fewer than 1,000 members, which, due to the imposition of martial law, declined over the next two years. Then, suddenly between 1944 and 1946, the ILWU's ranks expanded exponentially, taking in more than 30,000 new members. Chapter 4 shows that the ILWU movement's seemingly overnight success had long been in the making. From 1935 to the U.S. entry into World War II, two significant changes took place that, though not resulting in large immediate gains, fundamentally altered the field of class conflict: the workers' establishment of a lasting tie to the resurgent labor movement on the West Coast, most importantly through the ILWU, and the active intervention of the state, via the enforcement of the National Labor Relations Act. While martial law effectively shut down union activities, it also had the contrary, delayed effect of engendering labor organizing: having suffered under military rule, Hawaii's workers, once released from martial law restrictions, rushed into the ILWU, which, due to its prewar efforts, was in position to receive and mobilize them.

Chapter 5 explores the development of the movement's working-class ideology, specifically its quintessential and unprecedented interracialism. To date, the only explanation given in the sociological and historical literatures has been that Hawaii's workers, aided by the ILWU's leftist leadership, "realized" the importance of acting as a class rather than as separate "races"; in short, the master narrative for the postwar working class has been one of sudden deracialization whereby class effaced and replaced race. Positing a revisionist thesis, I explain how race was transformed, rather than negated, through its rearticulation with class, rendering the workers' struggles for racial and class justice coincident and mutually reinforcing. In the concluding chapter, I pull together the main findings of the study and draw out their implications.

2

Origins of Capital's Contentious Response to Labor

N THE PREFACE to *The Making of the English Working Class*, E. P. Thompson (1963:9) offered his now classic definition of class: "Class happens when some men, as a result of common experiences (inherited or shared), feel and articulate the identity of their interests as between themselves, and as against other men whose interests are different from (and usually opposed to) theirs." Hawaii's working class happened in the 1940s. Through the International Longshoremen's and Warehousemen's Union (ILWU), sugar, pineapple, and dock workers came to "feel and articulate the identity of their interests" that were "different from" and "opposed to" their employers'. But, as Thompson and many other students of labor history have noted, working-class formation is a highly contingent affair. It does not always, or even usually, happen. How did it happen in Hawai'i? Why did workers, across racial and industrial lines, conclude that they had common interests that conflicted with the interests of their employers?

Part of the explanation lies with the employers, against whom the workers struggled and formed their identity. Corroborating common sense, studies find that workers adopt a more radical, class-conflict orientation when their employers vigorously oppose the extension of economic citizenship (Eliel 1949:483–486, 488; Kimeldorf 1988; Lipset 1983).[1] In this regard, Hawai'i provides a prototypical example. In 1937, a National Labor Relations Board (NLRB) report characterized the unyielding antiunionism of Hawaii's employers in pointed, if overstated, terms: "If there is any truer picture of Fascism anywhere in the world than in the Hawaiian Islands, then I do not know the definition of it."[2]

If employer antagonism is formative in working-class consciousness and mobilization that interpret the interests of capital and labor as opposed, why do some employers, like those in Hawai'i, confront labor head-on while others seek compromise? As with innumerable facets of life in colonial Hawai'i, the question turns on the sugar industry, then the largest and oldest industry: Why did Hawaii's numerous sugar plantation companies take the path of conflict rather than one of accommodation? Why did they continually respond to workers' organizing efforts with intense opposition, at inordinate costs to themselves and at times with brutal force? Examining the period before the New Deal, this chapter traces the answer to the employers' prior coalescence as a class of actors, initially for purposes other than labor relations. In addition to propitious conditions of product market and timing, employer organization developed through an intense centralization and concentration of capital in a small group of sugar agencies known as the "Big Five," which were, in turn, controlled by a small core group of prominent haole families. Galvanized by the 1909 strike of Japanese workers, after a decade of halting, uneven responses to labor unrest, the sugar industry drew on and transposed its growing cooperation to present a united, uncompromising front against labor.

Compared with the dominant sugar industry, stevedoring and pineapple provide useful, though by no means unambiguously antipodal, studies in contrast. Like their sugar counterparts, stevedoring firms opposed unionization unbendingly, but they were able to do so without explicitly resorting to industrial organization. The concentration of capital in the sugar industry spread to the waterfront, endowing the Big Five sugar agencies with predominant control over shipping and stevedoring. Although cooperation among waterfront employers was probably possible, they did not formally join to resist unionization for the simple reason that they were individually effective. In starker contrast, the pineapple industry lacked the history of overt conflict between employers and workers evident in sugar and stevedoring. Because pineapple workers did not mount significant unionization efforts prior to the mid-1930s, how their employers would have reacted remains a matter of speculation. Within this limitation, this chapter examines the factors that may have shaped the pineapple industry's "deviant" character, including its later development, heterogeneity of ownership, seasonality of employment, and product market.

Sugar and Spite

Five Agencies Get Big

The employers' choice of conflict over accommodation began with the sugar industry, the largest and most influential industry in Hawai'i from the last quarter of the nineteenth century to statehood. As the president of the Hawaiian Sugar Planters' Association (HSPA) wrote in 1933, "It is an unquestioned truth that, economically, the entire community is to a large extent dependent on the sugar industry" (Russell 1933:55). Sugar accounted for 70 percent of the total value of Hawaii's exports that year.[3] The industry also assumed central importance because its dominant interests used their economic strength to expand into myriad other industries.

Although the commercial production of sugar began as early as the first decade of the nineteenth century (Char 1975; Glick 1980) and received a boost from the U.S. Civil War, which crippled sugar production in Louisiana, it remained relatively stunted in size and profitability until the Reciprocity Treaty of 1876. After failed attempts at similar agreements in 1855 and 1867, the treaty between the Kingdom of Hawai'i (and later the Republic of Hawai'i) and the United States permitted the duty-free entrance of unrefined sugar from Hawai'i into the U.S. market.[4] The treaty had a dramatic effect on Hawaii's sugar industry. There were only 20 plantations in 1875, compared to 79 just 8 years later (Beechert 1985:80; *Hawaiian Annual* 1883:69–71). The value of physical capital for all plantations rose from $8.43 million in 1880 to $59.75 million in 1900, a sevenfold increase (Mollett 1961:22).[5] The total area under cultivation jumped sixfold, from 26,019 acres in 1880 to 128,024 acres in 1900 (calculated from Schmitt 1977:357). The total number of plantation employees leaped nearly tenfold, from 3,786 in 1874 to 36,050 in 1900 (Schmitt 1977:359), while sugar production soared exponentially from 12,540 tons in 1875 to 289,544 tons in 1900, a 2,309 percent increase (Taylor 1935:166).

The principal drawback of the Reciprocity Treaty from the planters' perspective was its unsure future: it was subject to termination after seven years, with one year's notice by either party. The planters were at the mercy of the U.S. Congress, which could be swayed by domestic sugar interests, among others, to not renew or otherwise negate the benefits of the treaty. Faced with such opposition, the 1887 renewal of the treaty ceded to the United States the exclusive rights to enter and to maintain a naval station for coaling and repairs at Pearl Harbor (Robinson 1904; Taylor 1935).[6]

The planters' fear finally came true with the passage of the McKinley Tariff Act in 1890, which, beginning in 1891, abrogated all tariffs for unrefined sugar but provided subsidies to U.S. producers. In effect, Hawaii's sugar producers were once again, and suddenly, placed at a disadvantage in relation to domestic U.S. producers and in direct competition with other non–U.S. suppliers. Since the Reciprocity Treaty had been the primary engine for the rapid growth of Hawaii's sugar industry, its effective nullification induced a depression until the Wilson-Gorman Tariff Act of 1894 restored the earlier tariff arrangement for sugar.[7]

The U.S. annexation of Hawai'i in 1898 and its territorialization via the Hawaiian Organic Act in 1900 provided Hawaii's planters with the permanent tariff protection they desired. As the industry's journal expressed on the eve of annexation, "Hawaii is today practically an American colony, and we only ask that it may become such de facto."[8] Annexation afforded the planters the same rights as their counterparts in the metropole, as Hawai'i became an "integral" part of the United States.[9] Later, with the passage of the Jones-Costigan Sugar Act of 1934, the protection of sugar producers was accomplished through a combination of tariffs and quotas (Aller 1957:13).[10]

Under U.S. colonial rule, Hawaii's sugar production continued to grow at a rapid pace. While the number of plantations declined through consolidation, the total area under cultivation expanded, by 1933, to 254,563 acres, basically all land suitable for sugar production (Schmitt 1977:360).[11] The total value of physical capital climbed to over $105 million by 1930 (Mollett 1961:22).[12] The number of employees likewise rose, reaching its zenith in 1933 at 57,039 (*Hawaiian Annual* 1934:20).[13] They produced 517,090 tons of sugar in 1910 and topped 1 million tons 3 times during the 1930s (*Hawaiian Annual* 1940:33).

Access to the protected U.S. market was the key catalyst for the emergence of sugar as Hawaii's predominant industry.[14] In an unfettered, "free" market, each plantation—due to minimal product differentiation—would have faced a demand curve approximating perfect elasticity: a plantation could sell all of its output at the world market price but nothing above it. In this scenario, there would be a long-term trend toward zero profitability.[15] Hawaii's sugar planters, however, had a product market in the United States that deviated significantly from this ideal-typical laissez faire market. By selling their product in the United States, they enjoyed a "monopoly rent" of sorts, shielded from the harsh competition of the world market; tariffs and quotas guaranteed them robust profits, save for exceptional circumstances, such as unusually low outputs or world market prices.[16]

Does the protected U.S. market for sugar explain the planters' contentious response to the workers' organizing efforts? Studies "linking employer responses to the character of a product market" have been ambiguous on this question, according to Howard Kimeldorf (1988:53–54). Some economists and historians contend that firms in product markets that are sheltered from intense competition and hence enjoy higher rates of profit can be expected to take a more accommodating stance toward labor since they can afford to, in essence, "buy" labor peace (Kimeldorf 1988:53; Dubofsky 1994:115–116). Others, like Harold Levinson (1967:203), argue that these firms "have at their disposal substantial financial resources with which to resist union organizing efforts." Straddling the two opposing arguments, Randy Hodson (1983:16) concludes that the "expanded base of revenues" of protected product markets "operate[s] as a double-edged sword" that may be used to either accommodate or fight unionization.

In his comparative study of maritime industries of New York City and the West Coast, Kimeldorf identifies the employers' "capacity for self-organization" as the decisive factor in their differential ability to pursue a strategy of union resistance. In turn, employers' capacity for self-organization may depend on the level of capital concentration in an industry (Kimeldorf 1988:57; see also Dahl 1958; Griffin, Wallace, and Rubin 1986; Haydu 1989; Mizruchi and Koenig 1991; Olson 1965). In an industry with high capital concentration, the few large firms have the economic strength to bully the smaller firms. Moreover, the large firms' paramount position offers them the vantage point from which to consider the industry as a whole, providing the necessary leadership to "galvanize the many smaller firms around an uncompromisingly anti-union program." By contrast, in an industry with low capital concentration, the many firms, lacking a coherent leadership, may end up working out separate accommodating relationships with labor (Kimeldorf 1988:59–60; see also Dahl 1958; cf. Harris 2000; McIvor 1996).

At first glance, Hawaii's sugar industry seems to have been a clear case of an industry with low capital concentration. Even with consolidation, there were 38 sugar plantations as late as the beginning of World War II, each of which constituted a separate corporation, and every plantation—with three exceptions—was an integrated production unit, responsible for every phase of production from planting to milling.[17] Although there was a wide range in size and productivity, the plantations were fairly evenly distributed along it; no one or small group of them could be said to have held a predominant position in the industry.[18] If Kimeldorf's argument were correct, the seemingly wide dispersion of capital would have reduced the likelihood that an industrial leadership would form and mobilize the entire industry to act collectively against the workers.

Riddling this inconsistency requires taking one analytic step back for a wider view. The behavior of Hawaii's sugar industry was determined not by the plantations but by the factors, or agencies, whose relationship with the plantations critically inverted over time: the agencies became the industry's "principals" and the plantations their "agents." Besides altering the size of the industry, as described above, the Reciprocity Treaty wrought fundamental changes in its administration. Before the treaty, plantations had been relatively small-scale, proprietary firms with owner-managers presiding over the entire production process. After the treaty, the growth of the industry, previously confined to areas with adequate rainfall, necessitated bringing arid and semi-arid land under cultivation with expensive irrigation systems. It also required much larger-scale investments in milling, transportation, and labor recruitment (Beechert 1985:80). Though economically justifiable with the enactment of the treaty, the outlay of capital far exceeded the individual planters' means.

Agencies had played a limited role in the industry before the treaty. Primarily, they acted as intermediaries between the plantations and external markets, while the plantations controlled production; they charged agencies to arrange the marketing of their product and the procurement of equipment and supplies (Aller 1957:21–22; Lind 1938b:179; Taylor 1935:62). Secondarily, because sugar cane in Hawai'i had a long growing period of 18 to 24 months, and the distance to the United States meant considerable time was required for the sugar to reach its markets, the above division of tasks also involved a credit relationship: agencies provided advances for expenses against future sales.

With the Reciprocity Treaty, the credit relationship deepened as agencies supplied the considerable capital needed to fuel the industry's rapid growth. Increasingly, the plantations' mounting debts to their agencies—exacerbated by intermittent years of low production or prices and an interruption in tariff protection via the McKinley Act—were converted into ownership stakes in the plantations. Through the ownership of plantation stocks, outstanding debts owed by the plantations, and interlocking directorates between agencies and plantations, agencies tightened their authority. They progressively appropriated decisions concerning production—as well as profits and, regardless of profitability, never-ending commissions for now routine services—from their plantations (Aller 1957; Fuchs 1961:22; MacLennan 1979; Smith 1942; Sullivan 1926:171–172).[19] By the turn of the century, as Gavan Daws (1968:312) writes, "agencies, established in the nineteenth century to serve the plantations, had become the tail that wagged the dog."

TABLE 2.1 Number of Plantations and Sugar Production by Agency, 1930

AGENCY	NUMBER OF PLANTATIONS	SUGAR PRODUCTION (TONS)	PERCENTAGE OF TOTAL PRODUCTION (%)
"Big Five"	41	877,076	95.20
American Factors	10	283,775	30.80
C. Brewer & Company	13	219,071	23.78
Alexander & Baldwin	6	192,239	20.87
Castle & Cooke	6	125,825	13.66
Theo. H. Davies & Company	6	56,166	6.10
Non–"Big Five"	6	44,215	4.80
F. A. Schaefer & Company	1	19,826	2.15
J. M. Dowsett	1	7,209	0.78
Jos. Herrscher	1	5,352	0.58
H. Waterhouse Trust	1	5,240	0.57
Fred L. Waldron	1	4,467	0.48
Independent (no agency affiliation)	1	2,121	0.23
Total	47	921,291	100.00

Source: Calculated from Hawaiian Annual (1931:132–135).

Some agencies proved to be more adept than others at capitalizing on the shift in their roles, eventually dominating the industry. By annexation in 1898, 5 of the top agencies came to control 34 of 54 plantations, representing 64.5 percent of Hawaii's sugar production.[20] By 1909, these firms, widely referred to as the "Big Five"—Charles Brewer & Company, Ltd.; Alexander & Baldwin, Ltd.; Castle & Cooke, Ltd.; Theophilus H. Davies & Company, Ltd.; and Heinrich Hackfeld & Company, Ltd. (later renamed American Factors, Ltd.)—controlled 41 of 54 plantations, producing over 88 percent of Hawaii's output.[21] By 1930, the Big Five controlled 41 of 47 plantations and over 95 percent of the total output (see table 2.1).[22]

All in the Families

The missionaries came to Hawai'i to do good and did very well.

—A COMMONLY TOLD APHORISM

In addition to the intense concentration of capital, the ability of employers in the sugar industry to organize themselves as a class was further enhanced by business partnerships and familial ties among the largest shareholders of the Big Five. As early as U.S. annexation, three of the six largest sugar agencies (the Big Five and W. G. Irwin & Company) were controlled by four *kama'āina*, "missionary" families: Castle & Cooke by the Castle and Cooke families, C. Brewer & Company by the Cooke family, and Alexander & Baldwin by the Alexander, Baldwin, Castle, and Cooke families.[23]

Between 1831 and 1837, the first generation of all four families arrived in Hawai'i as missionaries from New England through the American Board of Commissioners for Foreign Missions (Dean 1950:4–5; MacLennan 1979:171; Stevens 1945:8; Taylor, Welty, and Eyre 1976:17–18). The board ordered its missions in Hawai'i to become self-supporting in 1849 and withdrew support in 1863, prompting many of the missionaries to pursue more secular endeavors, including commercial agriculture (Lind 1938b:169–170; Taylor, Welty, and Eyre 1976:45). Toward this end, the Hawaiian king and his land commission sold them government land at low prices as a special favor (Taylor 1935:10).[24]

Released from their duties, mission workers Samuel N. Castle and Amos S. Cooke formed a business partnership in 1851, which would later become Castle & Cooke, Ltd. Expanding his family's holdings, Charles M. Cooke, the second son of Amos, bought a controlling interest in C. Brewer & Company during the depression of the early 1890s and became its president in 1899 (Sullivan 1926; Taylor, Welty, and Eyre 1976). While the first generation of Alexanders and Baldwins did not take up commercial activity upon leaving missionary work, the second generation did so with vigor. Samuel T. Alexander—married to Martha E. Cooke, one of Amos's daughters—and his brother-in-law Henry

P. Baldwin formed a partnership and, with financial backing from Castle & Cooke, invested heavily in a large-scale irrigation project in 1876; the Hāmākua–Haiku irrigation ditch—the first project of its scale—fed their plantations in Pā'ia and Haiku on Maui. Building on the success of this endeavor, the two, along with a third-generation Alexander and a third-generation Cooke, started their own agency, Alexander & Baldwin, into which James Castle, of the second generation, bought later (Baldwin 1915; Day 1984; Dean 1950; MacLennan 1979; Rho 1990).

The four clans took part in family business in more than one sense, as intermarriages among them continued through the third and fourth generations and as their male members—sons and sons-in-law—assumed management positions in the agencies and related holdings (see figure 2.1). Although male in-laws could hold high offices, stock ownership stayed, on the whole, with blood-family members.[25] For each of the families, as stock ownership dispersed throughout the generational branches of the growing family tree, control of family corporate interests was decoupled from ownership to preserve a strong, coherent family voice in management.[26] As Carol Ann MacLennan (1979:179) finds, "As a result, control . . . of the large Hawaiian corporations remained in the hands of the kamaaina family leaders, who while owning only small amounts of corporate stock themselves, controlled (through the foundations and trust companies) the majority of shares."

As the four kama'āina families solidified their control of Alexander & Baldwin, C. Brewer & Company, and Castle & Cooke, these three agencies extended their influence into the other major agencies. At the turn of the century, those were controlled by families from outside Hawai'i: Heinrich Hackfeld & Company by the Hackfeld family of Germany, Theo. H. Davies & Company by the Davies family of Great Britain, and W. G. Irwin & Company by the California-based Spreckels family. In the first two decades after annexation, the agencies owned and run by the four kama'āina families obtained substantial control over the three agencies owned and run by the extra-Hawai'i families, consolidating and strengthening their position in the sugar and related industries.

Perhaps most critical to the four families', and by extension the Big Five's, ascendancy was Claus Spreckels. Heavily invested in sugar refining on the West Coast, Spreckels had been a vocal opponent of the Reciprocity Treaty prior to its passage, fearing competition from the higher grades of unrefined sugar from Hawai'i permitted under the treaty. However, not prone to wallowing in defeat, Spreckels, wealthier than anyone in Hawai'i, was one of the first to invest large amounts of capital in Hawaii's sugar production after the treaty's passage, recognizing the economic windfall (Adler 1966; Stevens 1945). Ingratiating himself with the Hawaiian monarchy, he immediately developed the islands' most technologically advanced and productive plantation, the Hawaiian Commercial and Sugar Company (HC&S), and acquired interests in a number of others.

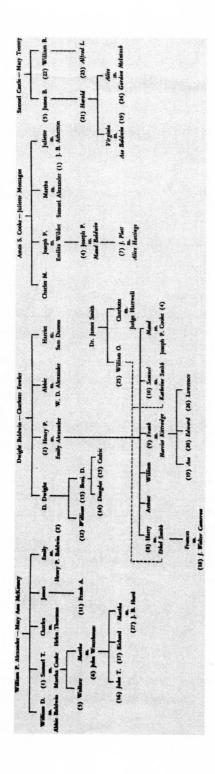

FIGURE 2.1 Intermarriages Among Alexander, Baldwin, Castle, and Cooke Families

There were three intermarriages in the second generation: Abbie Baldwin and William D. Alexander; Martha Cooke and Samuel T. Alexander; and Emily Alexander and Henry P. Baldwin. After Maud Baldwin and Joseph P. Cooke in the third generation, Virginia Castle and Asa Baldwin carried the tradition into the fourth. Those with numbers next to their names held management positions in Alexander & Baldwin or one of the companies it controlled. Those with italicized names were alive as of 1950, when Arthur Dean's history of Alexander & Baldwin, Ltd. was published.

Source: Dean (1950: 99). For other genealogies of these families, see Rho (1990) and Taylor, Welty, and Eyre (1976).

Directly controlling one third of Hawaii's sugar output at one time, Spreckels was the most influential figure in Hawaii's sugar industry between the enactment of the treaty and annexation (Kuykendall 1967:60).

Spreckels's sway waned, however, in the 1890s and 1900s. Buying up shares in secret, James B. Castle took control of the immensely productive HC&S plantation from the Spreckels family in 1898 and turned it over to Alexander & Baldwin for a 25 percent interest in the firm. In 1909, C. Brewer & Company acquired the remaining holdings of W. G. Irwin & Company, the agency in which Spreckels was a partner. A family feud and an increased focus on California's burgeoning sugar beet industry appeared to be at the root of the Spreckels family's divestment. Moreover, after the haole overthrow of the Hawaiian monarchy—which he, unlike the kama'āina families, opposed—Spreckels enjoyed little of the political influence he had commanded earlier.[27]

At the center of the four families' takeover of H. Hackfeld & Company was the prevailing anti-German sentiment before and during U.S. involvement in World War I. From 1903 onward, H. Hackfeld & Company was primarily owned, in absentia, by Johan Friedrich Hackfeld of Germany, a descendant of the corporation's founder, Heinrich Hackfeld, and run by managers sent from Germany (Joesting 1972:269; MacLennan 1979:161). In the summer of 1917, George Rodiek, who held the first vice presidency of H. Hackfeld & Company, the company's ranking office in Hawai'i, as well as the mostly ceremonial position of German Consul, and Heinrich Schroeder, a Hackfeld employee and former secretary of the German Consul, pleaded guilty to charges of violating U.S. neutrality laws. They were indirectly and, most likely unknowingly, implicated in "a grandiose and impractical German plot" for a revolution in India against the British (Joesting 1972:265). Though seemingly trivial in retrospect, Rodiek's and Schroeder's guilty pleas drew intense public scrutiny at the time, and H. Hackfeld & Company became a major focal point for World War I anti-Germanism.

In 1917, the U.S. government seized, via the terms of the Trading with the Enemy Act, 27,000 (of the 40,000 outstanding) shares of H. Hackfeld & Company held by German citizens (Joesting 1972:268). Although the law initially prescribed the seizure of German-owned properties only for the duration of the war, a representative of Hawaii's business interests went to Washington, D.C., to lobby the alien property custodian to approve and order the sale of the German shares to U.S. citizens (Joesting 1972:268; MacLennan 1979:162). Upon the 1918 passage of an amendment to the Trading with the Enemy Act—empowering the president, via the alien property custodian, to authorize the sale of "enemy" property—a newly formed, Hawai'i-based corporation bought H. Hackfeld & Company at an undervalued price. Adopting an appropriately nationalist appellation, American Factors, Ltd. was thus born.[28] The largest shareholders of the new company were Alexander & Baldwin, C. Brewer & Company, and Castle & Cooke, along with H. P. Baldwin, Ltd.,

TABLE 2.2 Officers and Directors of the "Big Five" Agencies, 1924~1927*

	ALEXANDER & BALDWIN	AMERICAN FACTORS	C. BREWER & COMPANY	CASTLE & COOKE	T. H. DAVIES & COMPANY
President	W. [M.] Alexander	A. W. T. Bottomley (m)	E. Faxon Bishop	**E. D. Tenney**	T. C. Davies
Vice Presidents	H. A. Baldwin	**C. R. Hemenway**	R. A. Cooke (m)	**F. C. Atherton**	E. H. Wodehouse
	J. Waterhouse (m)	**F. C. Atherton**	Horace Johnson	G. P. Castle	G. F. Davies
	W. O. Smith	Wm. Searby		W. R. Castle	
	C. R. Hemenway (t)				
Secretary	R. E. Mist	G. P. Wilcox	E. A. R. Ross	T. H. Petrie	
Treasurer		S. M. Lowrey		C. H. Atherton	J. E. Russell
Auditor				**A. L. Castle**	
Directors	F. F. Baldwin	W. F. Dillingham	W. Jamieson		J. N. S. Williams
	A. L. Castle	Geo. Sherman	C. H. Cooke		G. H. Angus
	J. R. Galt	J. M. Dowsett	**J. R. Galt**		**E. D. Tenney**
	J. P. Cooke	F. J. Lowrey	E. I. Spalding		Thos. Guard
		R. H. Trent	G. R. Carter		W. C. Shields
					L. M. Judd

Source: USDJ (1932:185), Exhibit No. 6. Names in bold appear in more than one column. Letters in parentheses represent additional offices held simultaneously; "m" and "t" refer to manager and treasurer, respectively.

*USDJ (1932:185) does not specify a date. Checking the above names and positions against Day (1984:51), Dean (1950:133, 199), Hoy (1983:242, 248), Sullivan (1926:192–193), and Taylor, Welty, and Eyre (1976:280) indicates that they pertain to at least one year between 1924 and 1927.

Matson Navigation Company, and Welch & Company (Sullivan 1926:179–180; Worden 1981:53).[29]

Within two years of the H. Hackfeld & Company takeover, Castle & Cooke and the Big Five–controlled Matson acquired 23.9 percent of T. H. Davies & Company under more mundane circumstances. The impetus for Davies & Company to sell major shares of its stocks appeared to have been a need for cash. At the turn of the century, the smallest of the Big Five agencies was in debt for $500,000, rendering it vulnerable to takeover attempts; no other agency carried a long-term debt of similar size. In 1930, Alexander & Baldwin joined Castle & Cooke and Matson as a major shareholder of Theo. H. Davies & Company (MacLennan 1979:163).[30] Although the Davies family, unlike the Spreckelses and the Hackfelds, did not wholly surrender its business interests in Hawai'i (Taylor 1935:81), the company became more intertwined and generally conformed with the other families and agencies.[31]

Reflecting and, in part, facilitating their cohesiveness, the Big Five had direct interlocks of officers and directors among themselves (see table 2.2). Indirect interlocks—through plantations, Matson, and other firms of mutual interest—produced knots of Gordian intricacy. Figure 2.2 charts *just one* Big Five agency's direct interlocks to the other agencies (top right corner) and its links to plantations (left side) and other companies, through many of which it had indirect interlocks to the other Big Five agencies; note that at least one officer or director of American Factors sat on the boards of a vast majority of plantations represented by the other Big Five agencies, as well as those of all but two of the plantations American Factors represented.[32]

The Big Five's Head Start

Surveying the history of labor relations in Hawai'i, an NLRB agent remarked in a 1945 speech, "The truth is they got off to a head start, for until the passage of the Organic Act in 1900, neither labor organization nor striking was possible."[33] "They" referred to the sugar plantations, and the undertaking at which they "got off to a head start" was organizing. The Organic Act marked a pivotal moment in Hawaii's labor history because it outlawed penal labor contracts, obviating the Masters and Servants Act of 1850, a fifty-year-old statute permitting indentured labor.

Although it underwent various revisions through legislative amendments and court decisions, the essence of the Masters and Servants Act remained intact: it mandated that workers under contract (and apprentices) were legally bound to perform their duties, the refusal of which was punishable by law.[34] Under the statute, workers had formal rights, for example, against physical mistreatment, nonpayment of wages, and transfer of their contracts. But, since they would have had to leave work to file complaints with the courts, workers had to

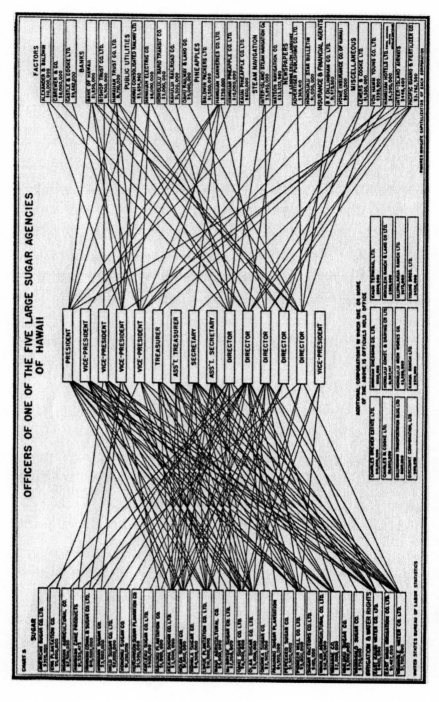

FIGURE 2.2 Interlocks of Officers and Directors Between American Factors and Other Companies

Source: USBLS (1940:197). Though not identified as such in the source, the pattern of interlocks depicted in this figure is American Factors.

violate the very statute that guaranteed their rights. Furthermore, many judges were planters themselves (Beechert 1985). Consequently, hardly any workers made claims against their employers, and almost none ever won (Merry 2000). The lack of actual protection led to widespread, if formally illegal, employer abuses, including transfers of contracts and corporal punishment that, in infrequent cases, resulted in deaths.[35] Penal contract labor effectively placed workers, as Edward Beechert notes, "in a category *outside* the law" (1985:56; emphasis in original).

Even before annexation, however, not all or even most workers were bound to such contracts. Upon the completion of their initial contracts, many refused to sign up for another term and stayed on as "day laborers"; additionally, some plantations chose to employ day laborers exclusively. By 1895, 53.6 percent of men and 40.2 percent of women were day laborers, the balance working under penal labor contracts.[36] The coercive effect of the contracts on labor organizing was, however, more complete than these percentages may suggest. When a large percentage of workers could not de jure withdraw their labor and when they could not de facto assert their limited contractual rights through a heavily biased legal system, labor resistance was seriously circumscribed with regard to structure, scale, and duration.[37]

This is not to suggest that workers did not put up serious resistance; quite the contrary. Rather, the existence of penal contract labor winnowed their repertoire of resistance to acts of individual defiance (e.g., violence against *lunas* or straw bosses) or, if collective, to short-lived strikes ignited by, for example, a work gang's conflict with a supervisor over piecework rates or abuse. In the 10 years before annexation, there were 48 such labor "disturbances" reported in the sugar industry (Beechert 1985:161).[38] Perhaps most significantly, workers protested with their feet, deserting their bound service and flooding the court dockets. From 1876 to 1898, the number of desertion cases grew from 2,099 to 5,876, even as acquittal rates plummeted from 64.3 percent in 1876 to 14.3 percent in 1878 to 13.3 percent in 1880, the last year reported (Beechert 1985:47–48; see also Kotani 1985:19).

The restraining effect of penal contract labor on collective labor organizing can be seen, in relief, in the actions taken by workers after its abolition.[39] There were 18 strikes by plantation workers in 1900, in the immediate aftermath of the Organic Act, and 32 within 5 years, a significant increase over the previous period (USBL 1906:401). The release of all workers from indentured servitude also transformed the quality of the labor actions: they became progressively larger in scale and more organized, with the workers formulating their demands ahead of time and withdrawing their labor if the employers did not meet them (Beechert 1985:161; Coman 1903:47–48; USBL 1906).[40]

Given the severe limitations imposed on labor organizing by the existence of indentured labor and its enforcement by the state, the sugar industry did not need to mount an organized response before the Organic Act. Nevertheless, the industry did get a "head start" in organizing itself as a class. In 1882, six years after the passage of the Reciprocity Treaty, sugar planters formed an industry-wide cooperative association, the Planters' Labor and Supply Company (PLSC). Notably, the main impetus for its formation was not labor struggles but the tenuous future of the Reciprocity Treaty, which was up for renewal in 1884. The initial invitation sent out to sugar agencies and plantations read:

> It must be evident to you and others who own property in this Kingdom, that the most energetic and united action is now required to protect it. Prudence and forethought require that there be no delay. We are threatened with a serious check, if not great disaster, to our prosperity under the reciprocity treaty. The period is near by in which the Government of the United States may, by treaty provision, terminate it. A powerful opposition to its continuance is manifested throughout the United States, so far as it is possible to judge from the newspapers.... What is needed then at this critical period is a prompt and full gathering of all who are interested in these subjects that may confer together and take such united measures as may bring mutual prosperity.[41]

"Another equally serious matter, the labor question" topped the agenda, but the question was one of labor supply (i.e., labor recruitment), not labor relations.[42] Under the Masters and Servants Act, labor "disturbances" were handled foremost by and through the state, specifically the police and the courts, and required little direct, much less concerted, effort on the part of sugar interests: "with penal contracts... [giving] them many of the advantages of slavery without its disadvantages, they were free from the perplexities of the labor problem as employers know it in a free country" (USBL 1906:375). Cultivation, machinery, legislation, transportation, and refining were other matters concerning sugar production to be discussed by the new organization, membership in which was confined to "actual owners of sugar-planting interests" (*Hawaiian Annual* 1935:74).

What is noteworthy about the industry's effort at organizing was that it was initiated by the then influential sugar agencies: the invitational letter quoted above was signed by Castle & Cooke, Bishop & Company, H. Hackfeld & Company, C. Brewer & Company, Theo. H. Davies & Company, G. W. Macfarlane & Company, W. G. Irwin & Company, F. A. Schaefer & Company, and E. P. Adams. Handling the affairs of multiple plantations and accruing increasing influence over them, agencies—not individual plantations—recognized the benefits of pooling the industry's efforts in lobbying, recruiting labor, and developing technology (Taylor 1935:64). Gaining control of a rapidly growing industry, the agencies began to acquire an industrywide perspective.

The PLSC, however, was not initially efficacious. During its first eight years, as William Taylor (1935:22) observes, it "published a monthly journal and held annual meetings" but "seemingly was not very active or powerful." In fact, dissolution of the association was seriously considered, because too many sugar planters had not joined or were not paying their dues, and lingered as a possibility.[43] Against the centripetal pull of industrial cooperation, significant centrifugal forces tore at their solidarity. Agencies had not yet fully secured their hold on plantations; the concentration of capital had begun with the Reciprocity Treaty but was still at a relatively early stage in the 1880s. Agencies still competed to represent the plantations: if a plantation could get a better deal from a different agency, it would and did switch.[44] As the PLSC stated in 1884, "When the sugar business of these islands began to receive the impetus which the treaty gave it in 1876, the supply of agencies really seemed to exceed the demand—so much so that the agent sometimes feared to demand security for his advances lest the planter might get another agent."[45] Consequently, the 1880s was a decade of keen competition among agencies (Taylor 1935:64).

Beyond interagency competition, Claus Spreckels proved to be a singularly divisive force in the industry. Perhaps above all, his monopoly of sugar refining set him at odds with the other agencies and their affiliated plantations. Dominating the business on the West Coast by the 1880s, his California Sugar Refinery forced Hawaii's other sugar producers to sell at unfavorable terms.[46] After briefly managing to escape Spreckels's grip in the late 1880s, the Honolulu sugar agencies found themselves back in it, and in that of the formidable Sugar Trust, by 1891.[47]

The 1890s and the early 1900s brought dramatic changes that enabled the agencies to become more cooperative and tightly organized. In retrospect, the McKinley Act may have been a "blessing in disguise." It was during the four years of its obtainment that plantations became deeply indebted to agencies, as well as more efficient (Taylor 1935:24; see also USBLS 1940:27–28). Beholden to their respective agencies, plantations could no longer readily switch representation (Smith 1942). As agency-plantation relationships thereby stabilized, interagency competition dissipated.

In 1895, the year after the Wilson-Gorman Act neutralized the McKinley Act, the PLSC reorganized itself as the Hawaiian Sugar Planters' Association (HSPA).[48] More significant than the change in legal status from a corporation to an unincorporated association, the newly formed HSPA signaled a decisive turn toward true industrial cooperation on all matters concerning the production of sugar; this time around, the agencies not only provided the necessary industrywide vision but also held the requisite control of the plantations to carry it out. One visible manifestation of this renewed effort was the creation of the HSPA Experiment Station, which was patterned after the Louisiana Sugar Experiment Station and conducted agricultural research to improve productivity (Beechert 1989).[49] The undertaking, like the HSPA, was spearheaded by the agencies.[50]

By the end of the first decade of the twentieth century, the Spreckels family had also withdrawn from the industry in Hawai'i, eliminating a longtime source of division. Even more significantly, the Spreckels family's monopoly of sugar refining on the West Coast was broken in 1898–1899 when Castle & Cooke, C. Brewer & Company, and Alexander & Baldwin, along with the head of a Kaua'i plantation, took over a former flour mill in Crockett, California, and turned it into a sugar refinery. The ownership of the California and Hawaiian Sugar Refining Company was subsequently transferred to Hawaii's plantations in 1905, but it was vested in its trustees, heads of the plantations' agencies.[51]

The HSPA was organized along similar lines as the Crockett refinery: nominally made up of member plantations and individuals, but actually controlled by the agencies. The association was funded by a production tonnage tax assessed against member plantations, and each plantation was entitled to a number of votes in proportion to its sugar production. Belying this appearance of diffuse control, the individual plantations did not actually cast their own votes. Instead, each was "represented...through duly authorized Powers of Attorney, together with the number of votes to which each is entitled."[52] Not surprisingly, an officer from its agency was the "duly authorized" representative of the plantation.[53] The HSPA was a transparently oligarchic organization led by the Big Five agencies (see table 2.3). Comparing tables 2.1 and 2.3 readily illustrates the nearly isomorphic translation of their economic power into political power within the HSPA.[54]

The trustees, elected according to the above voting scheme, provided the leadership of the HSPA and, by extension, the industry. They were to "exercise full control and management of the business and affairs of the Association and have all the powers and perform all the acts which the Association can legally exercise and perform."[55] There were originally nine trustees, eventually reduced to six as the number of agencies dwindled;[56] they were invariably the "duly authorized" representatives of the plantations, top officers from the agencies. The presidency and the two vice presidencies of the association were rotated annually among the trustees. The treasurer and the secretary were appointed by them. Each trustee was entitled to one vote, and "all questions [were] decided by the majority of the votes cast." Every year, the trustees met frequently to decide on all relevant matters concerning the industry.[57] Reflecting and, in part, facilitating this tight network, headquarters of the agencies all sat within a hundred yards of the HSPA offices in Honolulu and, "on a few minutes' notice," as A. L. Dean (1933:17) remarks, "the trustees [could] come together and make decisions for the whole industry."

Thus, by the end of the second decade of the twentieth century, the sugar industry, through the HSPA, was firmly in the hands of the Big Five agencies. There were no longer any major rifts in the leadership. Several agencies

TABLE 2.3 Votes in the Hawaiian Sugar Planters' Association by Agency, 1930

VOTERS	NUMBER OF VOTES	PERCENTAGE OF VOTES (%)
Big Five "Plantation" Votes	8,769	95.62
American Factors	2,865	31.24
C. Brewer & Company	2,183	23.80
Alexander & Baldwin	1,920	20.94
Castle & Cooke	1,243	13.55
Theo. H. Davies & Company	558	6.08
Non–Big Five "Plantation" Votes	323	3.52
F. A. Schaefer & Company	198	2.16
J. M. Dowsett	72	0.79
Jos. Herrscher	53	0.58
"Individual" Member Votes	79	0.86
Total	9,171	100.00

Source: Proceedings of the Fiftieth Annual Meeting of the Hawaiian Sugar Planters' Association, November 17–21, 1930, pp. 5–7, HC.

had faltered during the competitive 1880s and the economically lean early 1890s, and the surviving ones were no longer competing for plantation business. The Spreckels family had withdrawn from the islands, and its refining monopoly of Hawai'i-produced sugar had been broken. H. Hackfeld & Company and Theo. H. Davies & Company—two Big Five agencies originally headed by extra-Hawai'i interests that had been in disagreement with the three kama'aina-led Big Five agencies over, for example, U.S. annexation—had been almost wholly or substantially taken over by them. Consequently, the Big Five—closely allied through business partnerships, family ties, stock ownership, and interlocking directorates—emerged as the unquestioned and united leaders of the industry.[58]

The few smaller agencies that survived the nineteenth century posed no serious threat to this leadership. They were simply too small. Although their chosen representatives were perfunctorily voted in as trustees of the HSPA and included in the decision making, the smaller agencies would have had an impossible time opposing the Big Five, even if they had perceived their interests as being opposed (see table 2.3).[59] It must have been obvious to them that their formal inclusion in the HSPA leadership and decisions was at the largest of the Big Five.[60]

Monolithic, Efficient, and Ruthless

Although the industry had not been wholly unfamiliar with labor conflicts before the Organic Act, dealing with labor in the absence of penal contracts and the coercive force of the state behind them posed a new challenge. In the months before the law took effect on June 14, 1900, plantations already had an alarming glimpse into their uncertain future, as strikes grew to unprecedented size, three of them involving 700, 1,160, and 1,350 workers.[61]

Bracing for "the doing away of the contract system by the United States Government on June 14," the HSPA convened a "special meeting" ten days prior, "result[ing] in the formation of Central Committee and labor bureaus in the various districts on the Islands, and the adoption of the pass book system, whereby the plantation managers might act in unison and prevent united action on the part of the laborers in demanding excessive wages."[62] Still, the industry was caught off guard. To the employers' dismay, workers—almost exclusively the most numerous Japanese—disrupted operations on every plantation except one, as soon as the Organic Act went into effect.[63] No longer bound to particular plantations, they also "drift[ed]" to certain districts for better conditions and higher pay, leading to labor shortages in others. Appalled that they would not honor their no-longer-valid contracts, the HSPA's committee on labor complained, "Amongst these Japanese laborers there seems to be an entire absence of any appreciation of the moral compulsion of a promise."[64]

The first decade of the twentieth century was a period of transition, no less for the employers than for the workers. While workers exercised their newly obtained rights to move freely and withdraw their labor, as well as to relocate to the metropole, the sugar industry strove to figure out how to cope, how much to relent. The U.S. commissioner of labor observed in 1906: "plantation administration in Hawaii is at present passing through a stage of transition from the methods adopted and used successfully when the laborers were contract coolies, without many rights that employers were bound to respect compared with those of free laborers at the present time, to the methods which changed conditions following annexation demand" (USBL 1906:498). By the end of the decade, the employers' transition would be complete, as they found their bearings and indurated their stance.

In the meantime, with mixed results, the industry drew on its prior mobilization—its "head start"—to face its novel labor problems: "As soon as these difficulties [of labor unrest] became apparent, joint action was taken through the Hawaiian Sugar Planters' Association to meet them."[65] In other words, the industry transposed its schemas and resources of industrial cooperation to the new arena of labor conflict (Haydu 2002; Sewell 1992). Initial joint actions variously attempted to bind workers to plantations to which they were no longer legally bound. As noted above, in anticipation of annexation, the HSPA attempted to institute a "pass-book system," something that the industry had tried already in 1894 to curb "desertion of contract men."[66] The territorial government also revived a vagrancy statute from 1869 for the same purpose, though likely without much enforcement (Beechert 1985:133). And, as with other political matters in the past, the HSPA lobbied, with others, to halt the migration of Japanese laborers to the U.S. metropole, successfully leading to an immigration law and an executive order in February and March 1907, respectively (Okihiro 1991:37; INS 1935; Wakukawa 1938:141–143). Other practices that the HSPA pursued—and would continue to pursue—to retain and discipline the labor force were the establishment of common wage rates, evictions from plantation housing for not working regularly, recruitment of new workers from abroad, bonus schemes, and labor contracts without penal sanctions.[67]

The various measures failed to deliver labor peace, as strikes, with decreasing frequency but increasing organization, erupted on various plantations. For much of the first decade after the Organic Act's passage, the industry's response was neither completely collective nor consistent. Though setting guidelines and sharing information through the HSPA, as well as planters' associations on each island, the industry as a whole did not directly contend with the strikes, leaving the affected plantations and agencies to do so.[68] Consequently, in stark contrast to periods before and after, this decade saw plantations negotiating and, in a substantial minority of strikes, making concessions according to their own particular exigencies, especially on nonwage issues.[69]

The "Great Strike" of Japanese workers in 1909 was a major turning point (Takaki 1983:152; Beechert 1985:ch. 8). The threat and actuality of a multiplantation strike triggered the industry to harden its antiunion position by fully extending the power and reach of the HSPA. From then on, the employers' overall strategy would be simple and straightforward: do not recognize or negotiate with labor unions, particularly in response to strikes. Even when the plantations, through the HSPA, eventually adopted many of the changes demanded by striking workers, they did so only *after* the strikes had been uncompromisingly defeated, allowing them to claim that any ameliorative changes in working and living conditions were acts of altruistic paternalism rather than of capitulation. Concerning the industry's outlook, a journalist remarked in 1911, "I have rarely visited a place where there was as much charity and little democracy as in Hawaii."[70]

The seed for the 1909 strike was planted by a series of essays, written by Motoyuki Negoro, a Honolulu attorney, appearing in the widely read Japanese newspaper *Nippu Jiji*.[71] As the title of his inaugural piece of July 31, 1908— "How about the Higher Wages" (USBL 1911:63)—indicates, the primary focus of his articles was the wages of Japanese workers, who accounted for 31,477 of Hawaii's 44,789 sugar workers in 1908 (*Hawaiian Annual* 1910:27): their wages were too low vis-à-vis the large profits reaped by the industry and the rising costs of living and were racially discriminatory vis-à-vis those of the higher-paid Portuguese and Puerto Rican workers. In one of his articles, Negoro reasoned, "The prosperity enjoyed by the sugar industry does not extend to the Japanese who are suffering from the steadily rising living cost and weighted down by a practice of a discriminatory wage system." The topic of higher wages gathered momentum for the remainder of the year, as other Japanese papers and mainstream English-language papers entered the increasingly acrimonious debate (Okihiro 1991:46–47).

Meeting in Honolulu on December 1, 1908, 42 Japanese individuals—mostly urban and educated men, not sugar laborers—organized *Zokyu Kisei Kai* or the Higher Wages Association (HWA) (Okihiro 1991:47; Takaki 1983:153–154). Initiated by the Japanese urban elite, the putative "union" had to actually recruit workers around whose interests it had been formed. Plantation managers were less than receptive. Yasutarō Sōga, a founding member of the HWA and the editor of *Nippu Jiji*, recounted, "The night we stumped the Ewa Plantation Honouliuli area, the plantation police all carried pistols. It is said that an order had been given that if any of us were to as much as put one foot in the cane-fields, they were free to shoot the intruder dead." Even against such threats, real or imagined, the HWA quickly gained support among Japanese workers on the sugar plantations of Oʻahu, holding "mass meeting after mass meeting" (USBL 1911:83; see also Takaki 1983:154). On December 12, 1908, 1,700 Japanese attended a rally in Honolulu. As a result, the HWA sent a formal letter to the HSPA on December 19, requesting a meeting between representatives of the two organizations. Not even deigning to refuse, the HSPA acknowledged the receipt of the HWA request and then conspicuously ignored it (Okihiro 1991:47; USBL 1911:83).

Undeterred, the HWA drafted a meticulously crafted letter of demands to the HSPA, accompanied by copious supporting documents. The letter requested an increase in the basic monthly wage, from $18 to $22.50, which would have brought the pay up to that of the Portuguese and Puerto Ricans. The HWA also asked for improvements in housing for families and a reduction in the workday to 10 hours, with Sundays paid double time. Avoiding the appearance of an ultimatum and seeking dialogue, the letter stated, "Our demand is not unreasonable. We are not thinking what we will do if our request be not heard by the planters. We are trusting to the planters' good sense and sense of justice and equity, and trusting that they will listen to the voice of reason and justice." The HWA further assured the HSPA that it "[is] not, as alleged by the press, appealing to force or violence."[72]

As with the HWA's earlier request for a meeting, the HSPA did not offer a direct response. Adumbrating subsequent strikes, the major English-language dailies communicated the HSPA's position that the proponents of the HWA were outside agitators and had no support among the workers. The conservative factions of the Japanese press also fell in line with the HSPA's viewpoint.

Although the HWA was clearly initiated by those outside the sugar plantations, the HSPA either underestimated or, more likely, purposely misstated the extent of grassroots support among the workers. Japanese sugar workers on the outer islands of Kaua'i, Maui, and Hawai'i promised aid to their fellow workers on O'ahu, as did many Japanese business and social organizations (Okihiro 1991:49). Rebuffed by the planters, Japanese workers on O'ahu plantations walked out in May 1909. The strike began with 1,500 workers at 'Aiea on May 9, followed by those at Waipahū on May 10 and 12, Waialua on May 19, Wai'anae on May 20, Kahuku on May 21, and 'Ewa on May 23 (USBL 1911:86).[73] By the end of May, 7,000 workers from all the O'ahu plantations were on strike (Takaki 1983:154).

With the organizational infrastructure of the HSPA in place, the response of the sugar industry to the strike was unified and unyielding, if not entirely devoid of internal doubts at times.[74] Anticipating the prospect of an islandwide, possibly industrywide, strike with substantial financial losses, trustees of the HSPA met on May 10, the day after the walkout at 'Aiea, to solidify their ranks for an all-out fight. At the meeting, they passed a resolution by which all HSPA member plantations, not just the struck ones, would pay for strike costs on a prorated tonnage basis. On May 17, they agreed on another resolution that stated clearly that the association would pay for strike costs "only when the plantations concerned adhere to [its] policy."[75] The HSPA's policy, as an agency informed one of its plantations, was to "absolutely refuse to recognize, or negotiate with men that are out on strike and in answer to any demands to inform the men that should they return to work their grievances will be listened to and be adjucated [sic] upon."[76]

Confident of its own unity, the HSPA announced on May 22 that it would not enter discussions with any organization concerning wages and working and living conditions (Beechert 1985:172–173).[77] Urged by the HSPA, the struck plantations evicted the strikers and their families. Aside from causing obvious hardship, the intention of the "extreme course of ordering the strikers out of the plantation quarters has been . . . for the purpose of making a larger demand on the strike funds which have been gathered for use in Honolulu."[78] Following the lead of the plantation managers at 'Aiea and Waipahū, who began evictions on May 22, those at 'Ewa, Kahuku, and Waialua initiated them on June 7. By the end of June, over 5,000 evicted strikers and family members lived in makeshift homes in Honolulu (Okihiro 1991:50–52; Takaki 1983:160).

Another tactic of the HSPA was to hire strikebreakers to maintain the appearance of normal operations, although production never actually approached prestrike levels (Beechert 1985:173–174). Hawaiians, Chinese, and Portuguese from Honolulu were hired at $1.50 per day, twice the wage of Japanese workers.[79] The planters also introduced espionage to Hawaii's labor history during the strike, perhaps most effectively by receiving information and disseminating disinformation through two Japanese newspapers.[80]

With the territorial government firmly behind the sugar industry, a final tactic used by the HSPA was legal harassment. As early as February 26, 1909, Sōga of *Nippu Jiji* was arrested for allegedly inciting unrest—but was released shortly thereafter (Okihiro 1991:49). After the strike began, 3 leaders of the HWA and 6 men from *Nippu Jiji* were arrested on conspiracy charges on June 10. William Henry, the high sheriff of the Territory of Hawai'i, later reported to the territorial attorney general, "I took the position in making these arrests, that the Higher Wages Association, together with its organ, the Nippu Jiji, was a criminal organization, organized in the first instance with the deliberate plan to violate the law in carrying out the purposes of that organization" (as quoted in Okihiro 1991:53). Although the arrests had been made on evidence collected from homes and offices without proper warrants, the 9 men were convicted on all counts and sentenced to 10 months in prison and $300 in fines. In addition to going after the leadership, Henry on June 11 banned all mass meetings and public speeches for the duration of the strike (Beechert 1985:173; Okihiro 1991:53).

The relentless assault of the HSPA wore down the workers, who had a limited strike fund and little previous experience with large-scale actions. As the strike progressed, they trickled back to work. On August 5, 1909, HWA representatives met and voted to officially end the strike (Okihiro 1991:53). Within several months, the HSPA made it plainly clear that what had provoked its ire had not been the workers' demands per se but the workers' *demanding*: on November 29, 1909, the HSPA decided to raise the wages of Japanese workers to "a day wage basis of $20 per month... and a [turnout] bonus at the end of the year... to be paid to all such laborers who for 12 months average 20 days and more per month."[81]

The 1909 strike is instructive for a couple of reasons. It established a pattern of response by the sugar industry to be followed repeatedly in subsequent strikes. The entire industry fell in line behind the HSPA's position of no compromise, no concession, no negotiation, and no recognition; under the leadership of the agencies via the HSPA, the employers resolved to fight and bear the costs of strikes on an industrywide basis. Whereas the struck plantations on their own might have opted to cut their losses—an estimated $2 million (USBL 1911:62; Wakukawa 1938:170)—at some point during the strike and negotiate with the HWA, they remained adamantly antiunion, assured that the entire industry supported them. In fact, according to the U.S. Bureau of Labor (1911:91), "at the outset of the strike some of the managers affected were insistent that concessions be made the Japanese, but under the strict organization of all sugar employers in the Territory they could not take individual action." After the strike, Beechert (1985:175) concludes, "increasingly, the basic pattern of labor relations came to be dominated by the HSPA. In times of labor unrest, this domination amounted to complete direction of the labor policies of the individual plantations."

The strike also showed that the conflictual response of the sugar industry to workers' inchoate attempts at unionization had less to do with the combativeness of the workers, as some scholars claim, than with the employers' ability to organize themselves and act as a unified class (Kimeldorf 1988:52–53). The workers took pains to demonstrate that they were not looking for conflict, in fact not even for explicit recognition of the HWA as a union. In the period before and even after the start of the strike, they carefully maintained unconfrontational language toward the HSPA and the plantations.[82] For example, on the day they walked out, the strikers at the Oahu Sugar Company in Waipahū wrote a letter to the plantation manager explaining their position. After expressing gratitude for the opportunity to partake in the development of the plantation and the territory, they wrote, "it has become our painful burden to hereby respectfully present to you our request for [a] reasonable increase of wages."[83] Certainly, the hostile response of the sugar industry did not reflect the anterior posture of the workers.

The "Dual Union Strike of 1920" was the next major test of the HSPA's resolve in dealing with labor. As in the metropole, the inflated cost of living and relative labor scarcity induced by World War I provided the context for labor's insurgence (Reinecke 1979:90).[84] In 1911, the sugar industry paid turnout bonuses in the following manner: "Day workers receiving less than twenty-four dollars per month and working an average of twenty days per month were paid a bonus of one percent of their annual earnings for each dollar of the price of sugar above seventy dollars per ton (three and a half cents per pound)[, which was].... paid in November or December." In response to rapid inflation, the bonus system was revised in 1916 to include contract workers, and the bonus was increased half a percentage point.[85] But, to ensure a more uniform turnout from one month to the next, bonuses were calculated on a monthly basis rather than on an yearly average; one fifth of the bonuses were paid monthly, the remainder paid semiannually. But, in 1917, a year of high sugar prices, the HSPA suddenly lowered the bonus rate, fearful that large bonuses resulting from high sugar prices would raise workers' expectations permanently. Moreover, the industry withheld half of the bonus until the end of the year in an effort to reduce worker turnover (Beechert 1985:196). Meanwhile, the basic wage remained unchanged between 1916 and 1920 at 77¢ per 10-hour day for men and 58¢ per 10-hour day for women (Reinecke 1979:94).

Beginning in 1916, there were renewed efforts in the Japanese community, especially through the Japanese press, to increase plantation wages. The 1916 change in the payment of wages was reported to be an indirect response to such efforts. However, when Japanese editors and businessmen in Honolulu formed the Wage Increase Association (WIA) and submitted proposals for higher wages and changes in the bonus system directly to the HSPA, the latter predictably rejected them, after which the WIA faded out of existence (Reinecke 1979:98).

After the WIA's demise, Japanese workers curtailed the involvement of the elite, preventing them from direct participation and limiting them to supporting roles. Unlike in 1909, they chose to build a labor movement themselves from the ground up. Another notable, and related, change between 1909 and 1920 was the appearance of Young Men's Buddhist Associations (YMBA) on nearly all plantations (Reinecke 1979:98–99). Organically tied to plantation communities, they served a function similar to that of black churches in the civil rights movement, as preexisting grassroots fora for discussing grievances and politics, breeding grounds for local leadership, and network nodes of communication among dispersed plantation communities (Morris 1984; Beechert 1985:197–198; Okihiro 1991:68).

By December 1919, local plantation unions had sprouted from the YMBAs throughout the four sugar-producing islands—Hawai'i, Kaua'i, Maui, and O'ahu—and together formed the Federation of Japanese Labor (FJL) (Okihiro 1991:68). Formalizing its federated structure, the FJL chose its leaders at the plantation, island, and territory levels, with the "ultimate power rest[ing] in the hands of the individual plantation unions" (Reinecke 1979:100; see also Beechert 1985:199).

In the meantime, Filipino workers were also becoming active in union organizing. The Gentlemen's Agreement of 1907–1908 between the United States and Japan had halted the migration of Japanese laborers. From then on, the sugar industry turned mainly to the Philippines, a U.S. colony, for migrant labor. At the end of 1909, there were 644 Filipino sugar workers in Hawai'i, comprising a mere 1.54 percent of the sugar labor force of 41,748 (*Hawaiian Annual* 1912:29).[86] A decade later in 1919, they numbered 10,354, representing 22.9 percent of the sugar labor force of 45,311. They were already second only to the Japanese, who made up 54.7 percent of the sugar labor force with 24,791 workers (*Hawaiian Annual* 1920:18).

In August 1919, after four months of "agitation," representatives of Filipino workers met in Honolulu and formed the Filipino Labor Union (FLU). However, unlike its Japanese counterpart, the FLU did not have preexisting community organizations to draw upon, as its members were relative newcomers to Hawai'i and were overwhelmingly young men without families (Reinecke 1979:100). As a result, the FLU formed more haphazardly and unevenly than the FJL. Vaguely reminiscent of the urban elite leadership of the HWA in 1909, the charismatic leadership of Pablo Manlapit, a former sugar and dock worker turned lawyer, and a few others substituted for an effective grassroots organization. As one historian notes, Manlapit "was primarily an agitator, not an organizer. . . . But for all his faults, Manlapit had bravura and courage which won the hearts of thousands of Filipino laborers, to whom he symbolized their resentment and resistance against the lowly status they were assigned" (Reinecke 1996:6; see also Beechert 1985; Kerkvliet 2002).

From December 1 to 4, 1919, FJL representatives from throughout the islands met and formulated their demands. At the top of their list of concerns was the bonus system. The workers realized that their current pay was temporarily bloated from an unusually high price for sugar, to which their turnout bonuses were pegged. Anticipating the inevitable downward turn in the sugar market, they were bracing for and trying to stave off a pay cut.[87] Toward this end, the virtual elimination of the bonus system by increasing the daily wage from 77¢ to $3.00 was proposed and fiercely debated. In the end, suspecting that neither the planters nor the public would support such a drastic increase, the delegates voted to ask instead for a raise in the daily wage to $1.25 and a modified bonus system, whereby 75 percent of the turnout bonus would be paid monthly and only 25 percent of it would be held until the end of the year. Furthermore, the bonus would be based on 15 days of turnout per month for men and 10 days for women (Beechert 1985:199). The union also sought "an eight-hour day in place of the prevailing ten hours in the fields and twelve hours in the mills, double pay for overtime, paid maternity leave, increases in payments to cane-growing contractors, and improved health and recreational facilities." The FLU quickly adopted the same set of demands, partly because it needed the support of the Japanese (Reinecke 1979:95, 102).

The two unions submitted their demands to the HSPA on December 6, two days before the HSPA's annual meeting. Presumably without directly referring to the unions' demands, the HSPA at its meeting decided to withhold only 25 percent of the turnout bonus until the end of the year, as the unions had proposed, and to set up a social welfare bureau to improve living conditions on the plantations (Beechert 1985:201). To the unions' other demands, the HSPA responded on December 11 with a flat rejection (Reinecke 1979:102).

While the FLU wanted to react by initiating a strike on December 20, the FJL convinced its Filipino counterpart, as a temporary measure, to postpone until January 19, 1920. Ideally, the Japanese union wanted to schedule the strike in the late spring or early summer, both to coincide with the harvest season and to allow itself time to amass an adequate strike fund. Sensing the FLU's growing impatience, the FJL decided on December 19 to act independently to avoid a strike and negotiate a settlement. The Japanese union submitted a second "petition" to the HSPA on December 27, re-arguing its case. Replying nearly two weeks later, the HSPA again rejected the workers' demands. On January 17, the Japanese asked Manlapit to have the FLU once again postpone the strike, which was to begin two days later. Manlapit agreed but found that he could not pull Filipino workers back in time, perhaps betraying his union's underdeveloped organization. On January 19, Filipino workers on the island of O'ahu went out on strike (Reinecke 1979:102–103; Beechert 1985:201–202).

As in 1909, the strike made clear that the employers' rigid and combative opposition had not been provoked by the workers. While the FLU was arguably more willing to go out on strike and less conciliatory toward the employers, the FJL was, at least for a while, effective in moderating that stance (Reinecke 1979). Meanwhile, the FJL tried repeatedly to avoid even the appearance of inciting class conflict. Its goal was to win the workers' demands, preferably through dialogue. Anticipating a rejection from the HSPA to the second petition, the FJL nevertheless sent the following, temperate letter to its constituent local unions on January 10:

> Federation expects to receive second reply from Planters Association around 15th of this month. We have an idea that it will not bring any satisfaction to us. Therefore we wish that the third negotiation for wage-increase be most effectively carried out. We believe we can accomplish this by having all laborers on each plantation go before the manager on the 20th this month, explain their reasons for wage demands in calm and humble attitude, and present him the enclosed petition for wage-increase. We want to have the capitalists understand the real desire of laborers. Please do not misunderstand. We wish earnestly that you would be calm, reasonable and humble. (as quoted in Reinecke 1979:104)

After receiving the HSPA's rejection of its second petition as anticipated, the FJL followed the above plan and submitted a third petition on January 17. Even as Filipino workers walked out on January 19, the FJL still sought a negotiated settlement, sending a delegation to the HSPA the next day. But, as in 1909, the industry denied the unions any voice. Refusing to acknowledge any union as representing the workers, the secretary of the HSPA tersely rejected the FJL delegation: "The HSPA will settle its own industrial troubles." The FJL still hesitated, because it had not wanted to strike until late spring and because it was still willing to find a compromised solution (Reinecke 1979:103–105).

When Filipino workers went out on strike, many Japanese workers, as well as some 300 Puerto Rican and Portuguese workers, followed suit without the FJL's official endorsement, alleging or actually fearing Filipino strikers' intimidation.[88] On January 26, the FJL publicly announced a strike for February 1.[89] On that date, Japanese workers on the island of O'ahu officially joined the Filipino strikers. On the outer islands, Japanese workers remained at their jobs and funneled strike funds to O'ahu. Similarly, FLU members on the outer islands sent funds, but the effort was much more uneven (Reinecke 1979:104–105). Given the FJL's better overall planning, including the collection of a substantial strike fund, it subsidized the FLU throughout much of the strike.

The response of the sugar industry was unified and unyielding. Through the HSPA, the industry did not waver from its previous, battle-tested plan of fighting unionization. At times of labor shortage, the plantations were known to violate their own HSPA uniform wage policies and compete against one another for labor. "At the first sign of worker resistance, however," as Beechert (1985:211) observes, "the ranks closed and labor was confronted with a monolithic, efficient, and ruthless organization." At the start of the strike, the head of a Big Five agency wrote,

> I am glad to say that the sentiment is of the very strongest that we should fight this out to a finish and beat them, no matter how long it takes, nor what it costs. We shall probably never have a better opportunity and to give in now would simply mean the control of our plantations handed over to the so-called Federation of Labor, an utterly irresponsible body.[90]

The planters deployed espionage on a larger scale than in 1909 (Beechert 1985:200–207).[91] The four largest struck plantations—Ewa Plantation Company, Honolulu Plantation Company, Oahu Sugar Company, and Waialua Agriculture Company—employed significant numbers of strikebreakers, averaging 1,759 and peaking at 2,206 (Beechert 1985:204; *Hawaiian Annual* 1920:161). The sugar industry also revived its tactic of legally harassing union leaders, the most dramatic example of which involved a "dynamite plot." In June 1920, the home of a Japanese plantation official on the island of Hawai'i was dynamited. The two men who confessed to actually setting off the explosives, who were also conveniently the only eyewitnesses, testified that the entire Japanese union leadership on the islands of O'ahu and Hawai'i had planned the bombing. Although there was little credible evidence against them, 15 union leaders were nonetheless charged and convicted of conspiracy. The industry's other attempts at contriving criminal violations were less successful, though not due to lack of effort or inventiveness. At one point, the HSPA even tried to construe the workers' sometimes crude language as a criminal offense (Beechert 1985; Duus 1999).

The most effective weapons wielded by the sugar industry were racial vilification of the strikers, mass evictions, and the loss-sharing agreement. From the beginning of the strike, the sugar industry adopted the interpretation that the strike was not just a labor conflict but an imperialist attempt by the Japanese to take over Hawai'i. Invoking and exacerbating deeply held racial suspicions of the Japanese, the industry and the mainstream press effectively posed the strike as a racial war. Portrayed as unthinking followers of the Japanese, Filipino strikers were ignored (see chapter 3).

On February 14, the HSPA announced that all workers not at work on the 18th, along with their families, would be evicted from their plantation homes.

Coinciding with the height of a severe flu epidemic, the timing was particularly malevolent. Often forcibly, 12,020 people, including 4,137 children, were evicted (Beechert 1985:204). According to an estimate made two months later, 1,056 Japanese and 1,440 Filipinos fell ill, and 55 Japanese and 95 Filipinos died as a result (Reinecke 1979:109). The HSPA was unavoidably culpable, since it had been forewarned by both the acting governor and the president of Hawaii's board of health. Implicitly acknowledging the possible consequences, the HSPA had even tried to justify its draconian action beforehand: "We are sorry that the good men must suffer with the bad, but there can be no compromise or deviation from the lines that we have laid down" (as quoted in Reinecke 1979:108–109).

As in the 1909 strike, the sine qua non of the industry's various bellicose tactics was its internal solidarity, the most important manifestation of which was its continued commitment to the loss-sharing agreement. Exclusive of direct strike expenses, the six struck plantations lost a staggering $11,483,358.[92] Left to their own devices, one or more certainly would have broken down and negotiated with the unions at some point.[93] But, with the losses shared by all, the industry stood firm to the end.

Faced with the employers' "monolithic" opposition, the strike gradually lost momentum. In addition to those workers who never participated, mostly non-Filipinos and non-Japanese, several hundred Filipinos, lacking resources, returned to work in the course of the strike.[94] At the same time, newly recruited Filipino workers arrived from the Philippines. By the end of April, sugar production had returned almost to normal, and the HSPA announced unilaterally that it considered the strike to be over. The Japanese union held out until the end of June. But, when outer island union members refused to send further contributions to O'ahu, the union formally conceded defeat on July 1 (Reinecke 1979:115–116). The strike ended with the sugar industry pronouncing that it made "no concessions whatsoever, either direct or implied."[95] But, as after the 1909 strike, the HSPA considered the workers' demands privately and adopted changes, including a 50 percent increase in wages, formal elimination of racial disparities in wages, and monthly payments of bonuses.[96]

The strike's defeat effectively marked the end of Japanese participation in the labor movement for the next two decades (see chapter 3). Spared the kind of direct racial attack mounted against the Japanese, Filipino workers regrouped and, in 1924 and 1925, undertook another long, drawn-out strike. It was the most disorganized organizing campaign in Hawai'i history, prompting Reinecke (1996) to dub it the "Filipino Piecemeal Sugar Strike." It began on the island of O'ahu in April 1924 and meandered haltingly through the island of Hawai'i beginning in June and the islands of Maui and Kaua'i beginning in July (Manlapit 1933:65; Reinecke 1996:32–34).[97] Illustrative of the indeterminate character of the strike, it ended sometime in 1925, but an exact date cannot be placed. It directly involved 34 of the islands' 49 plantations and up to three fifths of the Filipino workforce (Reinecke 1996:30–33).[98]

As the workers had predicted before the 1920 strike, the wholesale price of sugar fell precipitously, from a record high of 12.33¢ per pound in 1920 to 4.76¢ per pound in 1921 and to 4.63¢ per pound in 1922 (Taylor 1935:168). The turnout bonus was consequently worth only about a penny an hour in 1922 (Beechert 1985:217). The daily wage of a day laborer was, for all intents and purposes, the industry's minimum of one dollar, the sugar industry's repeated protestations about the "average" wage being much higher notwithstanding.[99] And, if all workers fell ill with the proverbial cold of the sugar price drop, Filipino workers caught pneumonia, being largely confined to minimum-wage unskilled jobs.

In fall 1922, Filipino workers held a series of meetings on various plantations. Many participants were veterans of the FLU. Another series of meetings followed in early 1923. Led by Manlapit and George Wright, a college-educated, haole head of an AFL local with a sharp disdain for the sugar planters as well as a fast-fading dream of building an interracial "One Big Union" (Reinecke 1996:11), the workers drafted a petition with a list of their "requests," on which more than 6,000 signatures were collected (Manlapit 1933:34).[100] As indicated by the name they adopted for the union and the movement, the primary "requests" or demands of the High Wage Movement (HWM) were the raising of the minimum wage to two dollars and the elimination of the bonus system. Other demands included a reduction of the workday to eight hours, time and a half for overtime and double time for work on Sundays and legal holidays, "equal compensation for men and women engaged in the same kind of work," "proportionate increase in the wages paid to skilled and semi-skilled employees," and "recognition of the principle of collective bargaining and the rights of employees to organize for their mutual benefit and protection."[101]

The petition, along with a letter, was sent to the HSPA on April 10, 1923. The HSPA characteristically ignored it. The HWM sent another letter and a second copy of the petition early in November, which the HSPA again ignored. A third attempt was made on December 20, with the same result.[102] Reasoning that the HSPA was legally not an incorporated body but a "purely voluntary clique" with no legal standing, the HWM then made a last-ditch effort by presenting the petition to the "individual plantation companies, which [were] incorporated and legally responsible."[103] Neither the HSPA nor the individual plantations responded (Manlapit 1933:61).

As outlined in the HWM manifesto of January 1924, the HSPA's refusals led the union to proceed with its intention to strike. In March, its executive committee drafted a "Strike Proclamation," calling for the strike to begin on April 1. Workers on some plantations would engage in a "direct strike," while those on others would "go on a silent strike," essentially a slowdown.[104] Whether nonstriking Filipino workers actually engaged in a slowdown is unclear, but the "direct strike" commenced its erratic career as scheduled, though with minimal organizational structure, strike fund, or means of communication (Beechert 1985:219).

Like its predecessor, the FLU, the HWM lacked infrastructure, which was not surprising. Filipino workers were almost exclusively young men without families, working in the worst jobs and living in the worst housing: "Unlike the plantation Japanese with their temples, language schools, young men's associations, and neighborhood stores, the Filipinos had no community roots." Adding to the lack of stability was the high turnover rate among Filipinos, who moved from one plantation to another in search of higher wages. In 1923, the rate of turnover was 80 percent (Reinecke 1996:3).[105]

As much as the strike's lack of infrastructure proved to be a liability, its improvisational, tortuous tour of the islands proved to be an unpredicted asset as well. The employers never knew when, where, or for how long the workers were going to strike. Nonetheless, the sugar industry coalesced to confront the amorphous action and did not hesitate to apply all due force. Once again, compromise was not entertained. Ten days before the strike, the HSPA set up a claims committee to deal with strike losses, again vowing to diffuse the costs to the entire industry. The plantations evicted strikers, forcibly if necessary (Beechert 1985:220).[106] Espionage through informants and agents provocateur was a standard practice; reminiscent of the 1920 strike, there was even a poorly executed bomb plot on O'ahu.[107] At this time of labor scarcity, the industry's main source of strikebreakers was newly arriving Filipino workers, a thousand of whom, according to Manlapit, joined the strike (1933:67–68).

Though certainly not new, collusion between the industry and the territorial government was particularly pronounced during the strike. Begun before but prompted more proximately by the rancorous 1920 strike, the territorial legislature had passed a series of antilabor laws. The government therefore had a wider array of legal weapons with which to criminalize labor activism. Patterned after similar legislative efforts on the continent, a broad criminal syndicalism law, passed in 1919, prohibited not only "crime, sabotage, violence or other unlawful means of terrorism as a means of accomplishing industrial or political ends" but also "word of mouth, writings or teaching the duty, necessity or propriety of those actions."[108] In reaction to Japanese newspapers that had been sympathetic to the 1920 strike, another piece of legislation, the anarchistic publications statute of 1921, forbade the publishing not only of material "for the purpose of restraining or coercing or intimidating any person from freely engaging in lawful business or employment" but also, more broadly, of material intended "to create or have the effect of creating distrust or dissention [sic]."[109] In 1923, the picketing and protection of labor statute, a combination of a right-to-work bill and an antipicketing bill, was passed. The law made it a misdemeanor to interfere with a person's right to work or pursue employment and to "loiter about, beset, patrol, or picket in any manner the place of business or occupation of any person."[110] So broadly conceived and interpreted, it could be used against a single peaceful picketer. The 1923 law also contained a provision allowing the police to hold a suspect for up to 48 hours after arrest without charge (Reinecke 1996:35).

Another reason for the close cooperation between the industry and the territorial government was that they, and most non-Filipinos, expected the strike to be violent, based on the dominant belief that Filipinos were a violent "race." Financed by the HSPA, the government hired hundreds of "special police" in preparation. Both the industry and the government stockpiled weapons and braced for violence, even as the strike turned out to be generally free of violence in the first five months. The panic over anticipated violence became a self-fulfilling prophecy. In Hanapēpē, on the island of Kaua'i, the police, bloated with newly hired special deputies, clashed with a crowd of strikers on September 9, 1924. Of the incident, later known as the Hanapēpē Massacre, Beechert writes:

> Who or what precipitated the violence is not known. The special deputies, armed with hunting rifles and positioned above the exit road on a bluff, fired repeatedly into the massed strikers, *killing sixteen and wounding others.* Four policemen were killed in the melee. One hundred and sixty-one strikers were rounded up and jailed. Subsequently, seventy-six Filipinos were indicted for rioting; fifty-seven others pled guilty to charges of assault and battery. A single counsel was provided for the seventy-two men tried and convicted. The county attorney was assisted by two special deputy attorney generals hired and paid for by the HSPA. (1985:222; emphasis added)[111]

In a much more mundane manner, the authorities also invoked the various antilabor laws at their disposal, especially the 1923 antipicketing law, to harass and arrest innumerable strikers; as of November 1925, fifty Filipinos were still in prison for strike-related convictions, while many more had already served out their terms (Reinecke 1996:35).[112] In particular, the authorities sought ways to arrest the leadership of the HWM, Manlapit being their most prized target. In June 1924, an HSPA bulletin instructed plantation managers, "If there are any violent speeches made, or any threats, or actions violative of the antipicketing statute, it is hoped that the plantation managers will be able to cause the civil authorities to arrest Manlapit at once and prosecute him or any of his gang." The secretary of the HSPA went on to lament, "It is unfortunately true that despite our surveillance we have not been able to get a good case against him. This would be highly desirable because there is no question of his many violations of law."[113] Eventually, most leaders, including Manlapit, were convicted of various charges. For example, in September 1924, Manlapit was charged with suborning perjury. Although the government's case was highly suspect—based on perjured and purchased testimony—Manlapit was convicted and imprisoned until 1927 (Beechert 1985:223).

Like the strikes of 1909 and 1920, the 1924 strike ended with the HSPA making no concessions. As the HWM was internally disorganized, the outlook of the strike had been less than auspicious from the start. But even had the movement been a paragon of efficiency, its chances of overcoming the opposition were slim. What remained clear was the combined determination of the sugar industry in resisting unionization. Organized top-down by a small clique of agencies, the plantations did not fracture into struck and nonstruck factions and stayed committed to a unified, unyielding position.[114]

In response to each of the three major strikes, though publicly disavowing any direct links, the sugar industry, like many employers in the metropole, rationalized and intensified its "program of welfare capitalism" to preempt future unionization efforts (Beechert 1985:195). The HSPA continually established committees and programs to make improvements in housing, medical care, recreation, sanitation, and other areas. For example, after the 1920 strike, the plantations implemented an extensive, though highly uneven, project of repairing and building houses. In 1925, befuddled by the 1924 strike, the HSPA commissioned an outside firm to investigate conditions on the plantations and make recommendations. Along with wages, hiring, promotions, and hours, the investigation exposed continuing deficiencies in housing, medical care, sanitation, education, and recreation.[115] Though originally finding the study's recommendations "quite radical," the industry, by early 1937, had accepted them and was satisfied with the progress it had made.[116] The workers would shortly disabuse the employers of their misconception, as 1937 proved to be a particularly eventful year for Hawaii's labor movement.

Longshoring: Opposition Without Much Organization

Throughout the territorial period from annexation to statehood, the Big Five parlayed their stranglehold on the sugar industry to penetrate myriad sectors of the economy. Given Hawaii's geography, the maritime industry was of obvious importance and drew their attention. Sugar and pineapple produced in Hawai'i had to be shipped to the U.S. metropole, and with almost all arable land earmarked for the production of these crops, Hawai'i depended on imports for nearly all of its necessities.[117]

Until the turn of the century, shipping in Hawai'i was a competitive industry with a number of carriers (Worden 1981:24, 40). But, by the end of World War I, Matson Navigation Company had beaten out all others, thereby "alone maintain[ing] Hawaii's lifeline" to the West Coast (Worden 1981:47; see also

Thomas 1983:167). Not only resembling the prior concentration of capital in the sugar industry, the concentration of capital in shipping was an extension of the same process, involving the same group of agencies.

One of the pivotal moments in the history of Matson's good fortune in Hawai'i was its choice of Castle & Cooke as its Honolulu agency in 1907. Mostly confined to Hilo on the island of Hawai'i until then, Matson sought to expand its operation into Honolulu, the islands' main port. Matson had been represented by W. G. Irwin & Company, but concluding that the agency favored its other shipping client, the Oceanic Steamship Company, Matson turned to Castle & Cooke to "drum up more business" and finance its ambitious expansion plans (Taylor, Welty, and Eyre 1976:139–140; Worden 1981:31).

In the nineteenth century, sugar had been transported mainly aboard sailing ships owned by plantations or agencies. At the turn of the century, Castle & Cooke and C. Brewer & Company, among others, combined their fleets and formed the Planters Line (Sullivan 1926:165; Worden 1981:4). As the volume of freight increased, larger, faster, and more reliable steamships replaced their sailing counterparts (Beechert 1991:125).[118] Recognizing this trend, Matson's new agency, Castle & Cooke, exchanged its shares in the Planters Line for Matson stock and also invested $100,000 in additional shares to finance the construction of a new steamship. Other Planters Line investors, including C. Brewer & Company, also swapped their shares for Matson stock. The shipping company's goal was to remove competition; it soon sold or otherwise disposed of the ships acquired in the Planters Line deal. In 1908, Castle & Cooke and C. Brewer & Company enlarged their stakes in Matson, while Alexander & Baldwin bought a substantial number of shares (Dean 1950:86–89; Rho 1990:45–47; Sullivan 1926:165; Smith 1942:ch. 10; Taylor, Welty, and Eyre 1976:140–142; Worden 1981:31–36). Continually increasing their ownership in Matson, these Big Five firms, along with American Factors, owned 41.29 percent of Matson by 1946 (see table 2.4); in addition to direct corporate investments, individual directors, officers, and principal stockholders of the Big Five agencies also had significant holdings of Matson stock.[119] The Big Five's control over Matson stretched to its management. In the early 1930s, two members of the five-member executive committee, the controlling body of the company, were executives of Big Five sugar agencies, and an additional member was the president of Welch & Company, a subsidiary of C. Brewer & Company (Taylor 1935:79; *Walker's Manual* 1930:177).

Even the foregoing ownership and management ties do not fully capture the Big Five's influence over Matson. These firms were not only the company's principal owners and managers but also agents and customers; by 1919, Matson transported Hawaii's entire sugar crop to the metropole (Taylor, Welty, and Eyre 1976:142–143; Worden 1981:58). This monopoly of the sugar trade, in turn, warded off potential competitors for Hawai'i-bound cargo from the West Coast (Beechert 1991:119); other companies' ships would essentially have had

TABLE 2.4 Stock Ownership of Matson Navigation Company by Agency, 1946

AGENCY	NUMBER OF SHARES	PERCENTAGE (%)
Big Five	679,488	41.29
Alexander & Baldwin	276,380	16.79
Castle & Cooke	208,413	12.66
C. Brewer & Company	154,712	10.46
Welch & Company	17,363	
American Factors	22,620	1.37
Theo. H. Davies & Company	0	0.00
Non–Big Five	966,155	58.71
Total	1,645,643	100.00

Source: Calculated from Hawaiian Economic Foundation, "A Study of Ownership of Corporations in Hawaii," 1948, p. 35, and "Direct Holdings of Big Five and Welch & Co.," October 4, 1949, file Companies/Hawaii/Big Five, ILWUSF.

to sail empty from Hawai'i to the continent, since sugar comprised the bulk of Hawaii's outbound freight.

In 1922, the Los Angeles Steamship Company (LASSCO) attempted to penetrate this Hawai'i-metropole trade. It held its own in the transportation of passengers for a number of years. But, locked out of the profitable business of transporting cargo, LASSCO finally gave in and accepted Matson's bid for a merger in 1930, once again leaving Matson without serious competition (Worden 1981:54, 70–71).[120] Tightening its grip on Hawaii's shipping, Matson had also acquired, in 1925, controlling shares of Inter-Island Steam Navigation Company, the principal carrier of freight and passengers between the Hawaiian islands.[121] Not surprisingly, seven of its twelve directors in 1935 were Big Five executives (Taylor 1935:78).[122]

The Big Five's web of control in the maritime industry extended to stevedoring; stevedoring companies were essentially labor contractors that employed longshoremen and were contracted by shipping companies to load and unload their cargoes. By the 1920s and 1930s, the Big Five either owned outright or had controlling interests in all but one of the seven largest companies.[123] Castle & Cooke bought out Matson Terminals from the shipping company and later renamed it Honolulu Stevedores; it was the larger of the two stevedoring companies operating in Honolulu, by far the islands' largest and busiest port.[124] Castle & Cooke also controlled Mahukona Terminals, operating on the island of Hawai'i. C. Brewer & Company owned Hilo Transportation & Terminals, the only stevedoring operation in Hilo, the islands' second largest port. Alexander & Baldwin was in charge of Kahului Railroad Company on the island of Maui and Kauai Terminal in Port Allen, Kaua'i. American Factors controlled Ahukini Terminals, also on the island of Kaua'i. The Inter-Island Steam Navigation Company also employed a small number of longshoremen. The only stevedoring company not affiliated with a Big Five agency was McCabe, Hamilton & Renny in Honolulu. Handling mostly international and governmental freight, it did not pose a competitive threat to Castle & Cooke operating in the same harbor (Brooks 1952:58–59).[125]

Given the close relationship between the agencies and the waterfront employers, the staunch opposition to unionization evinced in the sugar industry spilled over into stevedoring. Firmly anchored to the sugar industry, it was viewed by the Big Five as less an autonomous economic enterprise than a subsidiary extension: "longshoring was, in money terms, an insignificant part of their interests" (Brooks 1952:251).[126]

Although the waterfront employers undoubtedly shared with their corporate relatives in the sugar industry a penchant for vigorous opposition to unions, their resistance was more straightforward: they did not require an explicit, industrywide employer organization analogous to the HSPA. This difference did not arise from differing levels of competition in the industries. Like sugar, neither shipping nor stevedoring was a competitive industry in Hawai'i; Matson and Inter-Island were virtual monopolies in Hawai'i-metropole and interisland shipping, respectively, and only Honolulu was home to more than one stevedoring firm, the noncompetitive Castle & Cooke and McCabe, Hamilton & Renny.

Although concentration of capital and lack of economic competition provided the possibility of industrial cooperation, there was simply little need for it. Unlike sugar, stevedoring in Hawai'i did not rely on government protection through tariffs and quotas requiring a united political voice. It did not call for technical innovations analogous to those developed by the HSPA Experiment Station; from the adoption of winches in the late nineteenth century to containerization in the late 1950s, there was fairly little change in how longshoring was performed (Wellman 1995). Also, due to limited employment opportunities outside agriculture, labor recruitment, like that undertaken by the HSPA, was unnecessary. In fact, continually recruiting labor from overseas, the sugar industry indirectly supplied an ample number of workers to all other industries in Hawai'i.

In addition, stevedoring in Hawai'i lacked the element that inspired the formation of most employer organizations: a large-scale labor movement affecting multiple employers. In contrast to the sugar workers' multiplantation unionization efforts—culminating, for example, in the strikes of 1909, 1920, and 1924—no similar efforts took place in stevedoring until the late 1930s. The one exception was the 1916 longshore strike in Honolulu, which involved all of the stevedoring firms operating there; intimating the cooperative potential of the industry, the struck firms joined informally and faced the strikers in tandem (Beechert 1985:157–158). Otherwise, with little coordination in the workers' unionization efforts, the firms suppressed them effectively on their own, with the backing of their respective agencies.

Longshoremen in Honolulu took part in short-lived strikes in 1867, 1869, 1880, 1886, and 1889, primarily for higher wages (Beechert 1985:155–156). After annexation, a local of the International Longshoremen's Association (ILA), the AFL-affiliated progenitor of the ILWU on the West Coast, was established and had a sporadic, tenuous existence on the Honolulu waterfront from 1901 to 1905 and again from 1912 to 1916. During the 1910s, the ILA also had smaller locals on the outer islands that were even more "ephemeral" than their Honolulu counterpart (Reinecke 1966:3–6). Workers of the new century engaged in a few additional, brief strikes: in Honolulu in 1901 and 1905 and Hilo in 1904 (Beechert 1985:156–157). In the aforementioned 1916 strike in Honolulu, a more substantial job action involving 300 longshoremen for nearly a month, the ILA local demanded union recognition, union shop, establishment of a joint employer-union board of arbitration, and higher wages (Beechert 1985:157–158).[127]

As in the sugar industry, the strikes ended in defeat. No labor unions gained recognition from employers, although the strikes, as in the sugar industry, did have the mostly unacknowledged effect of pushing up wages. But, unlike in sugar, the employers did not draw from an elaborate repertoire of antiunion tactics: "the vulnerability of the workers was a function of the sharply limited employment opportunities in the cities" (Beechert 1985:158). Accordingly, all of the strikes were broken through the use of strikebreakers, usually of different racial groups. Since the ILA excluded Asian-origin workers from membership, this proved to be even more effective, as the firms usually hired Japanese workers as strikebreakers.

After repeated defeats, the ILA locals in Hawai'i gained special permission from their International in 1912 to admit Asian "aliens" into their ranks, but with the proviso that those new members could not then transfer their membership to locals in the metropole as normally permitted (Reinecke 1979:31–32). The 1916 longshore strike was, as a result, an interracial effort. Moreover, because the workers' basic daily wage of $2 was the same as it had been 30 years prior, many in the community were initially sympathetic to their demand for a raise— 40¢ per hour for a 9-hour day and 50¢ per hour for overtime—prompting the mayor of Honolulu and the chamber of commerce to attempt mediation. Even under this unprecedented public pressure, the employers refused to meet with the union and proceeded with their tried and true tactic of hiring strikebreakers, leading to numerous physical confrontations between them and the strikers. In the end, the strikers gained a partial wage increase—to 30¢ per hour for a 9-hour day plus 40¢ per hour for overtime—but no official acknowledgment of the union (Beechert 1985:158; 1991:149–150). Within four years, the union disappeared altogether, attesting to the employers' strength and the workers' disadvantaged position in an urban labor market with limited opportunities.

One thing that could have shifted the balance of power toward the union in 1916 was an effective sympathy boycott of scab-loaded cargo by the West Coast longshoremen, a strategy that would later become important for the ILWU. Although they supposedly promised, via the Sailors Union of the Pacific (SUP), to carry out such a boycott, longshoremen on the West Coast—similarly struggling against hostile employers—turned out to be in no position to offer such help (Beechert 1985:158; 1991:149). Following their own strike defeats in 1916 and 1919, they were compelled to join the infamous "Blue Book" company union, as independent unionism was crushed. Similarly, the ILA was completely driven out of Hawai'i by 1920, and a company union took its place in Honolulu.[128]

As on the West Coast, unionization in stevedoring reached its nadir in the 1920s and early 1930s.[129] Employers unquestionably dominated. The imbalance of power was most evident in hiring practices. "Through a process of selection and elimination based in part on fitness for the work, adaptability,...ability to work with others and *in part on loyalty*," stevedoring companies employed a core group of "regulars" and "regular transients" (those filling in for absent regulars), who received steady paychecks. Beyond this core group, foremen hired "casuals" as they were needed through the "shape-up" system: "Every morning about six o'clock," those "hoping to be selected" gathered before the foremen and "mill[ed] around, yelling, shouting, kicking, punching, trying to attract attention." Given Hawaii's narrow economy, there was no shortage of men at these daily shape-ups, a situation that grew worse with the onset of the Great Depression. For example, at the largest stevedoring outfit, Castle & Cooke Terminals, only slightly more than 500 of the 2,154 longshoremen who received pay from the company in 1936 were regulars or regular transients, the remainder having been hired through the shape-up. Such open-shop conditions on the docks served to constantly remind the "regular" workers that they were easily replaceable and effectively checked unionization for over a decade and a half.[130]

Pineapple: Without Much Opposition or Organization

Before the New Deal, the relationship between employers and workers in the pineapple industry differed markedly from those in sugar and stevedoring. There was little overt conflict. In 1914, workers at a cannery engaged in a one-day strike over wages, described vaguely as a "riot" in a local paper. In 1917, skilled workers at one cannery engaged in a five-day strike for higher wages, apparently with a modicum of success. In neither case did there seem to be a sustained drive toward unionization.[131] Aside from these isolated incidents, the industry was notably free of conflict.

Although the pineapple industry certainly diverged from the conflictual pattern of sugar and stevedoring, it does not lend itself readily to a comparison. The research question guiding the preceding sections of this chapter—if employer antagonism abets a working-class consciousness that interprets the interests of capital and labor as fundamentally opposed, why do some employers choose to fight rather than accommodate unionization?—does not pertain to the pineapple industry. The lack of conflict was not, in the final analysis, due to a more accommodating employer stance toward unions. Rather, examining the lack of conflict in the pineapple industry requires asking a question that logically precedes the employers' response to unionization efforts: Why did these workers, on the whole, not organize collectively in the first place?

A principal reason was the industry's relative youth. "Of later development and coming after the abolition of indentured labor," the pineapple industry did not experience the long gestational period of contentious class relations of the penal labor contract era (Adams and Kai 1928:43–44). The sugar industry's pattern of continual, spontaneous labor actions on the job during that era followed by a surge of increasingly better planned and mass-based unionization efforts thereafter had no parallel in the pineapple industry.

The industry's virtual nonexistence in pre-annexation Hawai'i was primarily due to the high tariffs imposed by the United States. Along with other fruits, pineapple was not one of the commodities exempted from tariffs through the Reciprocity Treaty of 1876. Subject to a prohibitive 35 percent duty, pineapples remained insignificant before annexation (Marques 1908:59). The only pineapple firm of any size in the nineteenth century was the Hawaiian Fruit and Packing Company, which closed in 1898 after only six years in business (ESOHP 1979:A25). During its entire existence, the company produced 13,798 cases of pineapple (Morgan 1917:36).[132]

Eliminating all tariffs, U.S. annexation had a dramatic effect on the pineapple industry, similar to the Reciprocity Treaty's earlier effect on the sugar industry. In 1901, James D. Dole established the Hawaiian Pineapple Company (Hapco) on the island of O'ahu. Following the fruit's two-year period of maturation, Hapco's first harvest in 1903 resulted in a modest pack of 1,893 cases. The establishment in 1906 of the American Can Company, which supplied locally produced tin cans, and the invention in 1913 of the Ginaca machine, which peeled and cored pineapples automatically, by Hapco engineer Henry A. Ginaca accelerated the industry's productive capabilities and growth (ESOHP 1979:A26, A28; Morgan 1917:41–42; Taylor, Welty, and Eyre 1976:164; White 1957:9, 16, 18). By 1915, merely 12 years after the initial Hapco crop, there were 11 pineapple companies with plantations on 3 islands—Kaua'i, Maui and O'ahu—producing 2,669,616 cases (*Hawaiian Annual* 1918:46a). The number of companies reached a high mark of 13 between 1924 and 1926, declining thereafter through consolidation. In 1930, 9 companies with plantations on 5 islands—Kaua'i, Lana'i, Maui, Moloka'i, and O'ahu—produced over 12.6 million cases (see table 2.5). The total acreage owned or leased by pineapple plantations increased from 5,360 acres in 1909 to 46,845 acres in 1920 to 50,124 acres in 1937 (USBLS 1940:83).

Another probable reason for the pineapple workers' quiescence, especially in contrast to sugar workers' activism, was the higher wages and better overall working conditions prevailing in the industry. This comparison of conditions in the two agricultural industries is highly relevant, and not only analytically, since workers themselves must have made similar comparisons. Unlike the sugar industry, the pineapple industry did not recruit labor from overseas: whereas the former's policy was to continually recruit new workers to Hawai'i on labor contracts with low, preset wages, the latter drew its workforce from those who were already in Hawai'i, primarily from sugar plantations (USBLS 1916:42). In order to attract former, current, or potential sugar workers, the pineapple industry consistently paid slightly higher wages: for example, around a dollar per day for field work, when the sugar industry paid 80¢ (Beechert 1985:182). In 1940, the average annual income of full-time pineapple workers was $955, while the average annual income of full-time sugar workers was $767 (Matsumoto 1958:33).[133]

Although working in the pineapple industry had its own set of drawbacks—principally uneven housing and other living conditions due to the industry's later development—working conditions on pineapple plantations were, overall, less onerous than on sugar plantations. Requiring no irrigation, pineapples "naturally thrive[d]" at higher elevations and in a cooler and drier climate than sugar cane. They were also easier to cultivate and handle (USBLS 1916:42; also Beechert 1985:182).[134] The main advantage of pineapple cannery work was its

TABLE 2.5 Pineapple Production by Company, 1930

COMPANIES	NUMBER OF CASES	PERCENTAGE OF TOTAL PRODUCTION (%)
Hawaiian Pineapple Company	4,577,091	36.12
Libby, McNeill & Libby	3,289,501	25.96
California Packing Corporation	2,227,566	17.58
Haiku Fruit & Packing Company	740,700	5.85
Hawaiian Canneries Company	601,179	4.74
Kauai Fruit and Land Company	573,215	4.52
Baldwin Packers	434,045	3.43
Honolulu Fruit Company	148,896	1.17
Kohala Pineapple Company	80,103	0.63
Total	12,672,296	100.00

Source: Calculated from Hawaiian Annual (1932:22). One case contains two dozen cans of pineapple.

proximity to urban areas, given the generally limited job opportunities in cities (Beechert 1985:158). Furthermore, there seems to have been a distinctly more favorable feeling among pineapple workers toward their employers than among sugar workers: "Apparently, there [was] less race discrimination. They [got] along without a plantation policeman. The discipline [was] less rigid. The opportunities for promotion [were] better" (Adams and Kai 1928:44).

Perhaps the most decisive factor in pineapple workers' lack of unionization was the irregularity and seasonality of the work (Brooks 1952:108). Both on the plantations and in the canneries, there were three major classes of workers: "regular" workers, who worked full-time on a year-round basis; "nonregular" (plantation) and "intermittent" (cannery) workers, who worked all year but on a part-time, as-needed basis during the off-peak months; and "seasonal" workers, who worked only during the peak harvest months of the summer (ESOHP 1979:xiii). A 1929 survey of "a representative cannery and...two representative plantations" by the U.S. Department of Labor documented the extent of the seasonality of pineapple work. At the cannery, the average number of workers was 4,378 during the peak months of June, July, August, and September, dropping to an average of 1,107 for the remaining "slack" period. On the plantations, the average numbers of workers for peak and slack seasons were 4,248 and 2,017, respectively (USBLS 1931:77–79). Describing the sources of the canneries' seasonal labor, a 1940 report of the Women's Bureau of the U.S. Department of Labor found,

> When cannery employment skyrockets in midsummer, the extra seasonal labor is not recruited to any extent from the usual industrial or agricultural sources. Managers reported that housewives, maids, and high-school and college girls make up most of the extra female supply. Maids flock from their regular jobs to the canneries, and during the canning season many openings for domestics go unfilled. Wives who do not seek employment outside the home at any other time report to the cannery year after year for a few weeks of work to help swell the family budget. For the extra men, the young Filipinos who work at odd jobs in the towns and have irregular employment on the sugar and pineapple plantations serve as one important source. Most of the other males are young men without regular jobs or students who are a part of the surplus labor supply seeking employment whenever it may be forthcoming. (USWB 1940:14)

Since most nonregular, intermittent, and seasonal pineapple workers "look[ed] upon the work as a temporary source of additional income each year" (USBLS 1940:101), labor organizing for long-term gains was hard to achieve.

In one sense, the absence of labor activism among pineapple workers before the mid-1930s could be seen as a missed opportunity. Compared to their sugar and stevedoring counterparts, the pineapple employers' had limited ability to fend off unionization. If they had faced the kind of mobilization exhibited by sugar workers in 1909, 1920, and 1924, the pineapple companies' response and the ultimate outcome of the strikes would have been much more in doubt due to their relative inability to organize themselves. This was, in turn, due to two key factors: a competitive product market and heterogeneity of ownership.

From the beginning, there was a high concentration of capital in the pineapple industry: "From 1903 to 1933, three of the largest companies have controlled from seventy to eighty-five per cent of the total pack of the Hawaiian Islands" (Chapman 1933:6). For example, the three largest companies—Hapco, California Packing Company (Calpack), and Libby, McNeill & Libby (LML)—produced 80 percent of Hawaii's pineapple pack in 1930. The fourth largest company—Haiku Fruit & Packing Company, which Hapco later bought out in 1935[135]—produced only a third of what the third largest produced (see table 2.5). The three largest companies' predominance reached far beyond Hawai'i, as the islands' pineapple industry enjoyed an approximately 85 percent share of the world market in 1930 (Chapman 1933:5).

One might expect the high concentration of capital in the industry to have led to relatively easy cooperation among the firms, as in the sugar industry. But the "fact that the Hawaiian pineapple industry is confined to a relatively small area and to a few individuals [did] not mean that cooperation has been either general or easily brought about." Unlike in the sugar industry, Royal Chapman (1933:5, 11) pointed out, there was "wide-open competition...through the twenties and up to 1931."

Although sugar and pineapple were both agricultural products, their markets were vastly different. The product market for sugar provided little incentive for direct competition among Hawaii's producers. Sugar was an undifferentiated, homogenous product. Moreover, since there were many sugar producers around the world, each had very little control over the price; for Hawaii's sugar producers, the price of their product was basically the world price plus the size of the tariff protection. Therefore, because every sugar plantation in Hawai'i was producing the same product and selling at the same price, there was little incentive for price or production secrets (Brooks 1952:79).[136]

The product market for pineapple deviated significantly. Accounting for over 80 percent of the world market, Hawaii's pineapple companies acted as an oligopoly. With so few producers, each company, especially the larger ones, could palpably alter the market and competed in a much more conscious way than did sugar producers. The market demand for pineapple was also much more elastic than for sugar. Consumers did not view pineapple as a necessity. The market was therefore more fickle, and downturns in the economy hurt pineapple producers more. In addition, pineapple had more viable "substitutes": consumers would more readily replace pineapple with other fruits than sugar with other sweeteners. Finally, despite appearances, pineapples were not as homogeneous as sugar. Due to the elasticity of market demand, each company tried to differentiate its product, through advertising, to cultivate brand loyalty. Consumers purchased not just pineapples but "Dole" (Hapco) or "Del Monte" (Calpack) pineapples. All of the preceding factors made Hawaii's pineapple companies much more competitive with one another than their sugar counterparts, thereby discouraging industrywide cooperation (Brooks 1952; USBLS 1940).

The structure of ownership also distinguished the pineapple industry from the sugar industry. The Big Five agencies, which came to dominate Hawaii's sugar industry, were controlled by kamaʻāina families of missionary background, who were allied through business partnerships, family ties, stock ownership, and interlocking directorates. The ownership of Hawaii's pineapple industry was much less homogeneous and interrelated. For the first three decades of the twentieth century, the Big Five had a relatively minor presence. In 1930, Alexander & Baldwin controlled Kauai Fruit and Land Company and Baldwin Packers, which together produced around 8 percent of Hawaii's pack, and American Factors controlled Hawaiian Canneries Company, which produced 4.7 percent (see table 2.5). While Castle & Cooke gained a substantial share of Hapco, the largest pineapple company, in 1922 when the Waialua Agricultural Company, a Castle & Cooke sugar plantation, bought a one-third interest (White 1957:22), Hapco's founder and principal owner, James Dole, retained control. Two of the other top three producers, Calpack and LML, were local branches of U.S. corporations. Although the degree to which this heterogeneity of ownership in the pineapple industry accounted for its lack of cohesion is hard to ascertain, it certainly did nothing to abate competition among the companies.

Until the early 1930s, Hawaii's pineapple companies competed fiercely and only cooperated when the industry teetered on the brink of disaster. Due to the competitiveness and the elasticity of demand, overproduction was a recurrent source of peril. Between 1906 and 1907, the companies more than doubled their pack, from 74,245 to 168,205 cases. Between 1907 and 1908, they again more than doubled their output to 340,726 cases (calculated from *Hawaiian Annual* 1918:46a; see also Chapman 1933:7). As the U.S. economy took a downturn in 1907, the rapid gains in production resulted in low prices and excess inventories. As of February 1909, the companies still had around 70 percent of their 1908 pack in inventory. Only when faced with this huge carryover did the companies pull together reluctantly and form the Hawaiian Pineapple Growers Association, to undertake a joint advertising campaign to spur demand. But, attesting to the centrifugal tendencies of the industry, the companies soon abandoned this cooperative venture and returned to their competitive ways. In 1912, the first year that the industry produced over 1 million cases, the companies faced a similar dilemma. In response, they formed the Association of

Hawaiian Pineapple Packers (AHPP), which carried out another advertising campaign (Chapman 1933:7–8).[137]

In addition to joint advertising, the pineapple companies began to gradually engage in joint research and experimentation to combat pests and diseases. In 1914, the AHPP contracted the HSPA Experiment Station to do some work. In 1922, two years after the industry reorganized under its original appellation, the Pineapple Growers Association expanded its research efforts, cooperatively leasing 100 acres for the purpose. In 1924, the industry withdrew from the HSPA Experiment Station altogether and formed its own research unit (Chapman 1933:8–9; USBLS 1940:85; ESOHP 1979:A30–A31).

The pineapple industry still did not achieve a level of cohesion comparable to the sugar industry. Whereas the experiment station of the HSPA emblematized the sugar industry's cooperation in all matters concerning production, the experimental ventures of the pineapple industry represented a survival strategy of an otherwise highly competitive and secretive industry (USBLS 1940:85). Even as they enlarged the proverbial pie through joint advertising campaigns, the companies went on vying for their own slices through individual ones (ESOHP 1979:A–31). They also fought over land to expand cultivation, often exacerbating the danger of overproduction (Chapman 1933:11). In fact, except for joint advertising and research, forced upon them by economic and natural exigencies, the pineapple companies refused to cooperate.

Although the pineapple industry's vulnerabilities were patent, particularly compared to the sugar industry, they should also not be overstated. The companies were clearly reluctant to cooperate, but when they were confronted with conditions disastrous to the industry as a whole, they did pull together, if only temporarily and hesitantly. Later the Depression forced more lasting changes, bringing the industry, structurally and philosophically, into closer alignment with the sugar industry. In 1932, Castle & Cooke wrested control of Hapco from Dole, its founder. As Hapco suffocated under large debts and distended inventory, Castle & Cooke "rescued" it from bankruptcy, becoming, together with Waialua Agricultural Company, the majority shareholder in the process.[138] With this takeover, combined with the other Big Five agencies' holdings in the smaller pineapple companies, the Big Five suddenly controlled a majority share of the industry.[139]

More extensive and damaging than previous economic downturns, the Depression also compelled the pineapple companies to cooperate more closely. Unlike in the past, advertising did not sufficiently increase demand. The companies formed the Pineapple Producers' Cooperative Association; "an important factor in forcing the companies to come together was the realization that if one of the large companies were to pass through bankruptcy and creditors were to throw its stock of pineapple on the market, the rest of the companies would face financial ruin" (Chapman 1933:12). In addition to a $1 million advertising campaign, the new organization assumed the character of a cartel. Through the cooperative association, the companies negotiated a reduction in the total pack produced and a quota on each member's output (Chapman 1933:12–13; 1934:87–88; Dean 1950:193–196). The industry recovered to healthy profitability, and the association continued to operate until 1942 (USBLS 1948:76).[140]

Although its "deviant" character would reverberate into the postwar era, the pineapple industry had become more like the sugar industry by the end of the Depression—largely controlled by the Big Five and united in its outlook and actions. Hence, when the ILWU began its organizing campaign in the mid-1930s, it found employers in the sugar and stevedoring industries that had long been ready and willing to fight unionization and employers in the pineapple industry that were potentially more ready to do so. As the NLRB discovered in 1937, "The mores of the Territory provide no place for a union of any of its employed inhabitants, and consequently activity in looking toward such union organization and moves made toward it which are commonplace on the mainland become endowed with portentous and revolutionary significance when seen through island eyes."[141]

3

Race and Labor in Prewar Hawai'i

BY THE CLOSE of the nineteenth century, Hawai'i had become a colony of the United States, presided over by a cohesive oligarchy of haole capitalists. The "enormous concentration of wealth and power" held by the Big Five in the first half of the twentieth century had no parallel in the metropole (Cooper and Daws 1985:3–4). By contrast, Hawaii's workers endured low wages and poor working and living conditions paradigmatic of agricultural-export regions. In the 1940s, they would organize themselves into one large, left-led union and engage in an interracial class struggle in the sugar mills and in the pineapple canneries, on the plantations and on the docks.

Before World War II, however, workers did not struggle against the Big Five employers interracially. The long and bitterly fought 1920 sugar strike of Japanese and Filipino workers evinced hints of such possibilities, convincing some to conclude hastily that the working class had been made.[1] But the cooperation between Japanese and Filipino workers during the strike proved to be fleeting, a temporary marriage of convenience between two unfamiliar parties that ended in a quick annulment after their sound defeat by the sugar plantations. Perhaps, had the strike ended more favorably for the workers, they might have tried to build a more permanent interracial union. Instead, the strike ushered in more than two decades of racial divisions among Hawaii's workers.

Though throwing light on many aspects of working-class formation, studies of the past two decades have been less illuminating with regard to race. In fact, their misapprehension of race in relation to the postwar formation of Hawaii's interracial labor movement is largely prefigured by their misapprehension of race in relation to its prewar absence, the specific focus of this chapter. Why and how were workers racially divided, not seeking to form an interracial working class before the 1940s? I begin with a review of recent theoretical approaches, discuss an alternative approach, and empirically analyze the prewar divisions.

Rethinking Race, Nation, and Class

In the last twenty years, the scholarship on Hawaii's working class took a much needed critical turn toward the study of social inequalities and conflicts, challenging the long-standing predominance of the assimilationist school. Leading the challenge were two overlapping literatures: Asian American studies, which explicitly fixed on the islands' largely Asian-origin workers, and Marxism, which provided a vital class-based critique of capitalism. While qualitatively advancing our knowledge, this critical scholarship presented its own limitations to understanding the persistent racial inequalities and divisions among prewar workers.

Taking the salience of an "Asian" or "Asian American" category for granted, much of the scholarship, particularly by Asian Americanists, inadvertently effects a double conceptual overextension—from the present onto the past and from the metropole onto Hawai'i. As Yen Le Espiritu (1992) and Jonathan Okamura (1994) remind us, respectively, "Asian American" as a panethnic racial category is a postwar and a continental U.S. construct that, to this day, enjoys little currency in Hawai'i.[2] An important consequence of such conceptual overextension is the obscuration of racialized inequalities and divisions *among* Hawaii's Asian-origin workers.

Rather than "Asian," categories like "Japanese" and "Filipino" exhibited the requisite qualities of *panethnicity* in prewar Hawai'i: the assumption of a supraethnic identity whose boundaries were initially shaped by societal discrimination and state practices.[3] Japanese from different prefectures were categorized together as the Japanese "race" by the colonial state, haole, and other non-Japanese; Visayans, Ilocanos, and Tagalogs were categorized together as the Filipino "race."[4] These preconstructed, ascribed racial identities thereby gained salience for the people thus categorized, even if regional and ethnic differences did not disappear altogether. In other words, the Japanese and Filipinos came to see themselves as Japanese and Filipino "races."[5] But they did not see themselves, nor were they seen by others, as together belonging to *one* Asian "race."

Reducing questions of race to answers of class, much of the critical scholarship, particularly by Marxists, also obscures racialized inequalities and divisions among prewar workers. Adhering to a classic Marxist formulation, some portray the history of Hawaii's working class as having followed the predicted path from "class in itself" to "class for itself." Racial divisions are seen as having been obstacles on this "true" path of working-class formation but not *of* the path itself: "The responses of the working class, as they perceive their situation, are often incorrect. The problem of 'false consciousness' is one which recurs with dismal frequency" (Beechert 1984:158). While race is empirically recognized as an all-too-real impediment, it is at the same time theoretically placed outside working-class formation, acknowledged but inadequately analyzed.

Most other Marxist studies shift the analytic focus from workers' "false consciousness" to capitalists' class interests to explain working-class racial inequalities and divisions. Specifically, they argue that haole capitalists pursued their economic interests by dividing and ruling racially through the recruitment of workers of diverse origins, selective hiring of strikebreakers, occupational stratification, and differential pay.[6] This explanation certainly holds a measure of cogency, but there are good reasons to doubt its adequacy: frequent unavailability, especially after the 1910s, of workers of diverse origins for recruitment and strikebreaking due to immigration restrictions; insufficient account, or even recognition, of the relative positions of workers, who were not *horizontally* but *vertically* divided; and minimization of workers' agency.[7] Above all, by reducing race to class and class to the economic, the prevailing divide-and-rule explanation ignores the taken-for-granted racial notions and dispositions that underlie and enable even the most deliberately divisive practices. Even if race were a tool wielded by haole capitalists, it had to be, and was, always much more.

Far from unique to the study of Hawai'i, class reductionism has come to be perceived in recent decades as perhaps *the* Achilles' heel for theories of race and class, especially Marxist ones. It has led many in the social sciences to disengage from, disregard, and even disdain not only Marxism but also class analysis altogether.[8] For others, it has provided a focal point for retheorizing. One promising approach within, or in close conversation with, Marxism has centered on innovative readings of Antonio Gramsci by scholars in the United States and Britain.[9] Most influential in U.S. sociology and adjacent disciplines of the past two decades has been the racial formation theory of Michael Omi and Howard Winant.

Breaking with various reductionist theories of race, Omi and Winant argue for the "treatment of race as a *central axis* of social relations which cannot be subsumed under or reduced to some broader category or conception" (1986:61–62, emphasis in original; see also Hall 1980, 1986). The project of assaying how race is or can be central to class formation is of critical importance to this argument, since the theory, as one of its principal aims, seeks to undermine class reductionism without undermining the continuing relevance of class and its relation to race. In essence, the theory turns previous Marxist thought on its side: "racial dynamics must be understood as determinants of class relationships and indeed class identities, not as mere consequences of these relationships" (1986:37).

However, perhaps because they develop and illustrate their theory by empirically examining the past four decades of U.S. racial history, around the civil
rights movement and its denouement, Omi and Winant train their analytic gaze
almost exclusively at the state, which they argue to be "increasingly the preemi-
nent site of racial conflict" (1994:82). Moreover, they likely aim to counter the
general absence of race in the sociology of the state and the general absence of
the state in the sociology of race. Whatever the reason, their rapt focus curiously
results in an analysis that adroitly critiques class reductionist theories of race
but, aside from the programmatic statement above, provides little direction, theoretically or empirically, toward a new understanding of race and class.

Omi and Winant also offer a sweeping critique of nation-based theories of
race similar to the one they direct toward class-based theories.[10] They argue
that nation-based theories ultimately analogize and reduce race to nation
and hence "neglect the specificity of race as an autonomous field" (Omi and
Winant 1994:48). Furthermore, beyond critiquing these theories' ineffective-
ness as sociological explanations, Omi and Winant take them to task as failed
political ideologies: "Considered critically, none of these political projects
succeeded even remotely in forging an oppositional racial ideology or movement capable of radically transforming the U.S. racial order" (1994:111). Just as
nation-based theories of race falter as sociological theories because they reduce
race to nation, nationalist racial movements falter as social movements largely
because the theories around which they mobilize reduce race to nation.[11] But
this hasty dismissal of nation-based theories—not only as sociological theories
but also as political ideologies—prevents Omi and Winant from attempting to
analyze the historically recurrent nationalist impulse in racial practices and
discourses—both dominant and subaltern. Why are "the discourses of race and
nation...never very far apart" (Balibar 1991:37)?

What are "race," "nation," and "class," and why do they—in prewar Hawai'i
and in countless other historical moments—articulate continually and in the
ways that they do? All three are forms of *categorical* identity. They differ from,
for example, kinship in that they do not refer to concrete networks of interper-
sonal social relations. Beyond this, each is notoriously hard to pin down with
an exact definition. The more satisfactory definitions implicitly or explicitly
acknowledge this difficulty by being expansive—nearly to the brink of vacuity.
Omi and Winant (1986:68) define race as "an unstable and 'decentered' complex of social meanings constantly being transformed by political struggle."[12] As
quoted previously, Thompson (1963:9) writes, "Class happens when some men,
as a result of common experiences (inherited or shared), feel and articulate
the identity of their interests as between themselves, and as against other men
whose interests are different from (and usually opposed to) theirs." Recognizing
the impossibility of a "precise definition of nation," Craig Calhoun (1997:4–5)
lists ten "features of the rhetoric of nation [that] seem most important, though

none of them is precisely definitive and each may be present in greater or lesser degree in any nation. It is the pattern formed by having a preponderance of them that is crucial."[13]

From these definitions, as accepted and acceptable as any, we can draw some implications. Race, nation, and class are not transcendental categories: they are, above all, historical—meaningless outside history. They are also far from mutually exclusive. Omi and Winant's definition of race is more or less the same as Thompson's definition of class, and Calhoun's definition of nation—the most specified of the three—aptly fits many "rhetorics" that claim racial or class identities. They are all, per Benedict Anderson's (1991:6) definition of nation, forms of "imagined political community." In other words, each refers to the construction of an *identity* of interests, in both senses.[14] To recognize the categories' imbrications is to recognize the condition of possibility and probability for their articulations. It is also to recognize the condition of possibility for the rampant theoretical reductions of race to nation or class that Omi and Winant, among others, critique, as well as theoretical reductions in other directions.

Whether race, nation, and class—in pairs or a trio—actually articulate is a historical question. How, when, where, and why they articulate in the ways that they do are likewise historical questions. But if race, nation, and class are "largely empty receptacles" to be filled with lived history (Goldberg 1993:79),[15] the receptacles themselves possess particular "styles" that enable them to receive and carry certain matters of history, and not others, and that render them recognizable as themselves across different historical moments. I propose that stylistic affinities of the categories instill tendencies toward recurrent articulations in history. That is, if these forms of "communities are to be distinguished, not by their falsity/genuineness, but by the style in which they are imagined" (Anderson 1991:6), they bear largely overlapping styles. Moreover, at least for prewar Hawai'i—but I suspect for far more cases—race was, to paraphrase Stuart Hall (1980), the modality in which class and nation were lived: of the three, race was the fulcrum, as it hinged the other two.

Anderson (1991:11) is, I think, right to note, "If nation-states are widely conceded to be 'new' and 'historical', the nations to which they give political expression always loom out of an immemorial past, and, still more important, glide into a limitless future." In the accompanying footnote, he gives the example of President Sukarno's speaking earnestly of his nation having endured 350 years of colonialism, although Indonesia had had no precolonial existence. But Anderson is wrong to think that this characteristic differentiates nation from race—that nation is a way of fashioning history into destiny whereas race is imagined "outside history" (1991:149). To the contrary, I suggest that it is a point of similarity and a key to the articulatability of race and nation.

Although I am mostly in agreement with Omi and Winant's (1986) wide-open definition of race that "decenters," or empties, the category of any transhistorically stable meaning, I contend that the stylistic feature that makes race recognizable as race across space and time is the deeply held—though, of course, biologically untenable—schema of "separati[ng] human populations by *some* notion of stock or collective heredity of traits" (Anthias and Yuval-Davis 1992:2; emphasis added). I emphasize "some" to underscore the idea that this schema, if always implicitly or explicitly present, is itself historically variable, for example, with regard to whether and to what extent religion and contemporary science are invoked. Not unlike vernacular language in Anderson's discussion of nation, this schema infixes race with a sense of belonging to a pseudo-kinship or a common descent, intimating a shared history with a "horizonless past" (Anderson 1991:144). Like Sukarno's anachronistic projection of his nation, people project race onto history to speculate on and argue about, for example, the appropriate racial category for Jesus Christ, never mind that race as a category of practice would not appear on the historical stage for over a millennium and a half after his crucifixion.[16] The imagined antiquity of both nation and race—modern ways of peoplehood that invent, presume deep roots in, and are thus seemingly sanctioned by history—allows national claims and practices to conjoin seamlessly with racial ones, and vice versa.[17]

Class claims, in contrast, are less able and wont to assert historical depth. Class *feels* historically shallower. The degree to which particular class formations assume historical—and, in part, emotional—depth may be related to the extent to which they articulate with and draw from other, seemingly deeper forms of community, like those based on race, religion, ethnicity, nation, clan, village, and neighborhood. Jesus Christ may have been a carpenter, but today's carpenters, even Christian ones, do not search or find in this coincidence the historical continuity of a *people*.

Then what, if anything, can we say about the insistent articulations of race and class—in lived history and in social theories? Class is distinguished from other styles of political community by its central concern with the economic. More specifically, class discourses and practices produce, institutionalize, justify, naturalize, contest, subvert, and otherwise relate to economic inequalities, although they can be and always are about much more. From the very beginning, racial discourses and practices have also been about the production, institutionalization, justification, naturalization, contestation, and subversion of inequalities—not only, but almost always including, economic inequalities.[18] This overlap in relation to material inequalities allows class claims and practices to conjoin seamlessly with racial ones, and vice versa. It is also how, today, many across the political spectrum—ranging from the far right to neoconservatives and neoliberals to socialists and others on the left—can choose to see or emphasize one side of this articulation, subsuming racial inequalities and dynamics to class ones (Roediger 1991:6–11; Steinberg 1995:ch. 6), as class inequalities and dynamics have been subsumed to racial ones at other historical moments.

Recognizing that the structuration of race by class and nation, and vice versa, is contingent on not only historical specificity but also durable stylistic affinities of those categories allows insight into one of the most widely misrecognized features of racism. It is not unidimensional. It can be, as commonly thought, about the presumption of superiority/inferiority that produces and rationalizes inequalities. But it can also be about presumed suitability/unsuitability for civic inclusion, and this dimension does not necessarily bear a consistent relationship to the presumed superiority/inferiority dimension.[19]

In prewar Hawaiʻi—an overseas U.S. colony, beyond the nation-state but within the empire, with a small elite ruling over colonized natives and migrant laborers—questions of national belonging were prominent and persistent. In prewar Hawaiʻi, a capitalist society with extreme economic inequalities, so were questions of class. And both sets of questions turned, above all, on race. Referring to *class* both in its specific sense of social class and in the generic sense of categorical differentiation, Pierre Bourdieu writes, "struggle for classification...is a dimension of every kind of struggle between classes" (1990a:180). In other words, all social struggles—even those thought of in the most materialist terms, like those between social classes—are at once symbolic struggles, struggles over "principles of construction and evaluation of the social world" (Bourdieu 1984:466; also 1991). In prewar Hawaiʻi, workers struggled, with their employers and among themselves, over classifications like "coolie," "cheap labor," "citizen," "haole," and "American," defining what these categories meant and determining who belonged to them and how. Conceptualizing Portuguese, Japanese, Filipino, and other migrant laborers in racially disparate ways, haole capitalists set the initial terms of these struggles and wielded preponderant influence. Facing qualitatively different racisms that articulated with class and nation differentially, workers responded in incompatible ways, in the process contributing to the reproduction of working-class racial inequalities and divisions.

Racial Hierarchy of Portuguese, Japanese, and Filipino Labor

From 1910 onward, Portuguese, Japanese, and Filipino workers were the most numerous in the sugar industry, with Filipinos overtaking the Portuguese by 1912 and the Japanese by 1922 (*Hawaiian Annual* 1912:29; 1913:35; 1923:14). The industry employed 2,533 Portuguese, 16,992 Japanese, and 18,189 Filipinos in 1922; together they made up 84.9 percent of the plantation workforce. Filling 92.8 percent of the plantation payrolls 10 years later, there were 2,022 Portuguese, 9,395 Japanese, and 34,915 Filipino sugar workers. And in 1942,

2,673 Portuguese, 10,397 Japanese, and 18,135 Filipinos accounted for 94.4 percent of sugar workers (Lind 1980:82).

With haole almost exclusively in top managerial and professional positions (Lind 1938b:252), a consistent pattern emerged among the three main groups of workers: a racial hierarchy with Portuguese, Japanese, and Filipinos occupying positions in descending order of status and power. Filipinos were almost entirely confined to unskilled labor positions, while a sizable number of Portuguese and Japanese, to different degrees, could be found in supervisory, skilled, and semi-skilled jobs. Table 3.1 illustrates the stability of this hierarchical order, evincing significant disparities in the odds of securing supervisory and skilled positions in the sugar industry in 1915 and fifteen years later. For example, as in 1915, haole had more than 10 times their proportionate share of supervisory positions in 1930, while Filipinos still had not reached 20 percent of their "fair" share. At both time points, the Portuguese and the Japanese, in that order, fell in between.[20] In the less prestigious category of skilled jobs, Portuguese and especially haole were not as highly overrepresented as they were in supervisory positions, but the overall pattern among the groups still obtained.

A fairly large and representative plantation on the island of Hawai'i, the Olaa Sugar Company affords an opportunity for closer examination of the industry's employment practices from the late 1920s onward.[21] In raw numbers and odds

TABLE 3.1 Odds and Pay Rate of Supervisory and Skilled Employment in the Sugar Industry by Year and Racial Category

| Racial Category | ODDS | | | |
| | 1915 | | 1930 | |
	Supervisory (Mo. Salary)	Skilled (Daily Wage)	Supervisory	Skilled
Haole	10.91 ($104.95)	4.54 ($3.98)	12.06	4.94
Portuguese	4.29 ($46.91)	1.91 ($1.67)	7.73	4.34
Japanese	0.34 ($36.60)	1.04 ($1.21)	1.19	2.04
Filipino	0.04 (N/A)	0.22 (N/A)	0.18	0.16

Source: Based on Lind (1938b:255–256). Odds refers to the percentage in supervisory or skilled positions in the sugar industry divided by the percentage in all occupations in Hawai'i. A score of 1.00 signifies proportionate representation.

TABLE 3.2 Number of Employees by Year, Skill, Gender, Minor Status, and Racial Category, Olaa Sugar Company

Racial Ancestry[a]	AUG. 1929		SEPT. 1935		SEPT. 1938		SEPT. 1941		SEPT. 1944	
	Skilled	Total	Skilled	Total	Skilled	Total	Skilled	Total	Skilled	Total
Men										
Haole[b]	34	34	33	37	41	48	33	35	31	32
Portuguese	43	109	41	119	61	121	18	88	32	83
Japanese	29	510	39	701	76	672	32	604	58	647
Filipinos	6	1760	4	1365	11	1050	4	837	16	687
Others[c]	26	92	29	113	40	128	4	68	6	39
Women	0	114	0	126	0	158	3	154	8	103
Minors	0	344	0	15	0	117	0	58	0	349
Total	138	2963	146	2476	229	2294	94	1844	151	1940

Source: Form 111, August 1929, PSC34/1, and Forms 54, September 1935, September 1938, September 1941, and September 1944, PSC40/7, HSPAP. No data for August or September 1932 found.

[a] Labeled as "Nationalities" in 1929 and as "Racial Ancestry" in the other years.

[b] Labeled as "American" in 1929 and as "Anglo-Saxon" in the other years.

[c] Includes categories "Chinese," "Puerto Rican," "Hawaiian," and "All Others" for 1941 and 1944; additional categories "Spanish" and "Korean" for 1935 and 1938; and additional category "Russian" for 1929.

respectively, tables 3.2 and 3.3 show that the hierarchical pattern continued to hold into the mid-1940s, the tables' somewhat indistinct and inconstant category of "skilled" notwithstanding.[22] As seen in table 3.3, haole men took 8.5 to 21.47 times more than their proportionate percentage of the plantation's most preferred jobs. Portuguese men's portion of these "skilled" positions fluctuated between 4.01 and 8.47 times their share. At all 5 time points, Japanese men were more or less proportionately represented in the "skilled" category, hovering around the 1.00 odds mark. Filipino men were vastly underrepresented, failing to hold more than 10 percent of their proportionate share of skilled jobs until 1944, even as their overall numbers fell dramatically during the 1930s and the early 1940s (see table 3.2).[23] The only groups faring worse were minors and, before 1941, women, who were both, in all probability, mostly Japanese.[24] No woman held a "skilled" job until 1941, although women quickly reached proportional representation in the early 1940s partly because of their small overall numbers and strict job segregation.

Within the broad categories of "skilled" and "unskilled," a fractal racial pattern prevailed in terms of jobs and pay. At ʻŌlaʻa, for example, the mean monthly salaries of skilled and semiskilled haole men far surpassed those of others and never dropped below $200 from the mid-1920s to the early 1940s,

TABLE 3.3 Odds of Skilled Employment by Year, Gender, Minor Status, and Racial Category, Olaa Sugar Company

Racial Ancestry[a]	ODDS OF SKILLED EMPLOYMENT				
	Aug. 1929	Sept. 1935	Sept. 1938	Sept. 1941	Sept. 1944
Men					
Haole[b]	21.47	15.13	8.56	18.50	12.45
Portuguese	8.47	5.84	5.05	4.01	4.95
Japanese	1.22	0.94	1.13	1.04	1.15
Filipinos	0.07	0.05	0.10	0.09	0.30
Others[c]	6.07	4.35	3.13	1.15	1.98
Women	0.00	0.00	0.00	0.38	1.00
Minors	0.00	0.00	0.00	0.00	0.00

Source: Form 111, August 1929, PSC34/1, and Forms 54, September 1935, September 1938, September 1941, and September 1944, PSC40/7, HSPAP. No data for August or September 1932 found.

Odds refers to the percentage in skilled positions divided by the percentage in all positions. A score of 1.00 signifies proportionate representation.
[a]Labeled as "Nationalities" in 1929 and as "Racial Ancestry" in the other years.
[b]Labeled as "American" in 1929 and as "Anglo-Saxon" in the other years.
[c]Includes categories "Chinese," "Puerto Rican," "Hawaiian," and "All Others" for 1941 and 1944; additional categories "Spanish" and "Korean" for 1935 and 1938; and additional category "Russian" for 1929.

as they were securely ensconced in top management (see table 3.4); the most "typical" job—defined here as the most numerous position at the median salary of haole men—was section overseer in 1934.[25] Among the major groups of workers, Portuguese, Japanese, and Filipino men followed the usual descending order at each time point on table 3.4. As shown in figure 3.1, their mean salaries shifted in lockstep over time, demonstrating the durability of the racial hierarchy. Among Portuguese men in skilled and semiskilled positions, the most typical job in 1934 was *luna* (straw boss or foreman). It was blacksmith, luna, or store clerk for the Japanese and store clerk for the Filipinos.[26] Women's mean monthly salary plummeted from a high of $150.00 to a low of $60.08, as the lone woman in a skilled or semiskilled job, a nurse, in 1926 was joined by 23 others, mostly clerical workers, by 1942 (see table 3.4 and figure 3.1).[27]

A similar pattern seems to have existed among "unskilled" laborers in the sugar industry, according to available data. A study by the U.S. Department of Labor, based on a sample of 8 plantations, found that the mean monthly earnings in 1939 for Portuguese, Japanese, and Filipino men in unskilled positions were $56.23, $50.94, and $46.92, respectively (USBLS 1940:52). The same study noted that women in unskilled jobs, most of whom were Japanese, earned on average $1.10 per day, 6 cents below the average daily wage of minors and only 5 cents above the minimum mean mandated by the Agricultural Adjustment Administration (USBLS 1940:56).[28]

For both skilled and unskilled workers, differential "perquisites," especially housing, correlated with and magnified the racial inequalities stemming from disparities in occupation. Even if there had been no "independent" effect of race on perquisites, racial imbalances in jobs meant racial imbalances in perquisites, as those in higher positions were assigned better housing, given access

TABLE 3.4 Mean Monthly Salaries of Skilled and Semiskilled Employees by Year, Gender, and Racial Category, Olaa Sugar Company

Racial Category	MEAN MONTHLY SALARY ($)				
	1926	1930	1934	1938	1942
Men					
Haole	207.94	240.56	221.90	236.88	305.38
Portuguese	76.22	83.13	79.17	89.59	102.93
Japanese	68.65	75.75	70.96	83.50	93.01
Filipinos	51.43	56.50	51.36	66.62	76.21
Others	80.26	79.02	71.60	79.56	83.97
Women	150.00	N/A	85.00	61.89	60.08

Source: Calculations based on payroll records in PSCPV.45, HSPAP.

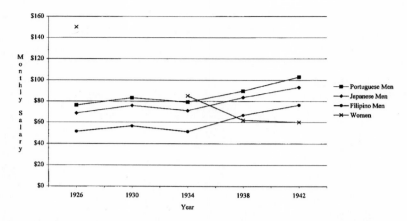

FIGURE 3.1 Mean Monthly Salaries of Skilled and Semiskilled Employees by Year, Gender, and Racial Category, Olaa Sugar Company

Source: Calculations based on payroll records in PSCPV.45, HSPAP.

to better recreational facilities, etc. The inequities were particularly acute for Filipinos, who were disproportionately men without wives or children in Hawai'i. For example, in 1930, 13,685 Filipino men, women, and children lived in marital family units on Hawaii's sugar plantations, compared to 30,624 living as "single[s]."[29] In contrast, among the Portuguese, the respective numbers were 7,289 and 497. Similarly, 34,842 Japanese lived in marital family units, while only 3,453 lived as "single[s]."[30] For the two groups at the bottom, the Filipinos and the Japanese, this difference in living arrangement alone meant "that the real income of the Japanese [was], on the average, considerably higher than that of the Filipinos since the total value of perquisites [was] two to three times as great for married as for unmarried workers" (USBLS 1940:52).

Much less is known, and knowable, about the pineapple and longshoring industries than the extensively archived and studied sugar industry. In the exclusively male longshoring industry, the 3 largest groups of workers in 1937 were the Japanese, Filipinos, and Hawaiians, who accounted for 34.8 percent, 30.2 percent, and 24.9 percent of the labor force, respectively; into the 1930s, especially in the main ports of Honolulu and Hilo, a disproportionate number of Hawaiians worked in longshoring, a typical subsequent occupation for sailors among whose ranks, since the nineteenth century, large numbers of Hawaiians could be found.[31] Unfortunately, there is little systematic data concerning racial disparities among longshoremen. There was one suggestive, if flawed, finding: using an unrepresentative sample, the U.S. Department of Labor reported, "Among the salaried workers [in 1939], exactly one-third (33.3 percent) were Caucasians and one-quarter Japanese. Filipinos had an extremely small representation in the salaried group"

(USBLS 1940:171); how Hawaiians fared was not reported.[32] Given the paucity of documentary evidence for the period before 1935, the year when the labor movement was revived on the waterfront after a long period of dormancy, analysis of the racial dynamics among longshoremen is taken up in later chapters; on the whole, the analysis reveals that the racial dynamics were consistent with those in the sugar industry.

The pineapple industry deviated from, or at least tempered, the pattern set by Hawaii's predominant agricultural industry, sugar. For a number of reasons discussed in the previous chapter, the pineapple industry treated its workers better overall. With regard to race, the workers apparently perceived less discrimination (Adams and Kai 1928:44). Two studies carried out by the U.S. Department of Labor in 1938 confirmed this perception. Summarizing its investigation of pineapple canneries, the department's Women's Bureau concluded, "Earnings by race, in unpublished figures, indicate that racial equality where earning opportunity is concerned is a practice as well as a policy. In the four groups where numbers are large enough to show a normal distribution—Caucasian, Hawaiian, Chinese, and Japanese—there is no significant variation" (USWB 1940:14). Similarly, concerning pineapple plantations—on which men outnumbered women 14 to 1, unlike in the more evenly split canneries—the report by the labor department's Bureau of Labor Statistics stated, "The distribution of hourly earnings of nonsalaried workers indicated very little difference in racial earnings of males" (USBLS 1940:91).[33] The biggest disparity was between men and women: on average, men received 1.91 times, in the canneries, and 1.93 times, on the plantations, more in wages than women.[34]

According to both studies, the overall lack of racial disparities in earnings had to do with the industry's lack of demand for skilled workers and minimal differentiation among the unskilled. There was indeed little difference in pay between Filipino and Japanese men on the plantations, who made up 60.4 percent and 25.3 percent of the male labor force, respectively (USBLS 1940:92).[35] No earnings data were collected by race for female plantation workers, 79.9 percent of whom were Japanese (USBLS 1940:95). One major source of racial inequality on pineapple plantations was perquisites. As on sugar plantations, a "careful estimate indicate[d] that married men received three times as much in the way of perquisites as unmarried," adversely affecting Filipino men, who tended to be either unmarried or without their wives in Hawai'i (USBLS 1940:99).

In the canneries, located in urban areas to attract seasonal and intermittent workers, no one racial group predominated among women; Japanese, Chinese, and Hawaiians were the most numerous. There was, again, little difference in pay among these groups (USBLS 1940:111). Men in the canneries were the exception proving the rule that the lack of racial disparities stemmed from a lack of skill-differentiated jobs: "among the men a higher proportion of the lunas (foremen) are Caucasian, which tends to place this group at the top for men, and this is true also of the mechanics" (USWB 1940:14). With a higher proportion of supervisory and skilled positions, and consequently more hierarchical divisions, male cannery workers showed significant imparity. In "4 representative canneries...a sample of about 60 percent of the total employment in the [territory's] canneries," the 4 largest groups of regular, year-round male workers in 1938 were Japanese, Filipinos, Chinese, and "Caucasians," who made up 28.8 percent, 23.4 percent, 10.6 percent, and 8.7 percent of the labor force, respectively.[36] Following a pattern similar to the sugar industry's, the mean annual earnings were $1,295 for "Caucasians," $1,094 for the Japanese, $848 for the Chinese, and $665 for Filipinos (USBLS 1940:111).[37]

Overall, the pineapple industry displayed less of the racial inequalities evident in the sugar industry, although, when it did, they followed a similar pattern. For the 1920s, in addition to the relative equality prevailing in the industry, the scantiness of available evidence does not allow for a close examination of racial dynamics. The strain of the Depression in the 1930s, however, caused or exposed deeper racial inequalities, particularly in relation to Filipinos. In the process, as discussed below, the story of racial inequalities and divisions in the pineapple industry became an inextricable part of the larger story of racial inequalities and divisions in the sugar industry.

Chinese "Coolies": First Migrant Labor

Long before the 1930s, Hawaiians and then the Chinese had formed the bulk of the sugar plantation labor force. In 1872, when 35 plantations employed 3,786 laborers, 2,627 of them were Hawaiian men, and 364 were Hawaiian women (Kuykendall 1953:178). But the declining population of Hawaiians—from a fairly conservative estimate of 250,000 at the time of initial contact with Westerners, and their diseases, in 1778 to 47,508 in 1878 to an all-time low of 37,656 in 1900—could not meet the exploding demand for labor ignited by the Reciprocity Treaty (Nordyke 1977:table 2). By the early 1880s, the Chinese had filled much of the new demand. In 1882, 5,037 of the booming industry's 10,243 laborers were Chinese, while 2,575 were Hawaiian (*Hawaiian Annual* 1890:87; Takaki 1983:28).

Sally Engle Merry (2000:128) argues that the haole elite, based on their very different relationships, projected two "very different images" onto Hawaiians and migrant laborers from abroad. Exemplifying a "classic colonial relationship," haole sought to reform and transform Hawaiian society as they assumed political and economic control over it. They assigned themselves the mission of civilizing Hawaiians, who were to be taught and assimilated into the colonial order. From the mid-nineteenth century onward, haole "infantilized and sexualized," as well as "feminized," their image of Hawaiians, construing any resistance to the imposition of Christian and capitalist discipline as signs of intrinsic racial character: "The Native Hawaiians were regarded as 'our' natives by the whites and treated as childlike but benign, lazy, irresponsible with money, and friendly, although too sensuous" (Merry 2000:127–131).[38] In a study done in the 1920s, plantation managers and other haole elite identified similar, faulty traits: "the worst defects of the Hawaiian temperament are his deficiency of planning capacity, extreme suggestibility, and instability of interest" (Porteus and Babcock 1926:102). The authors of the study noted that longtime haole residents "regard[ed Hawaiians] with the utmost friendliness and affection," but the "easy-going good nature of the Hawaiian render[ed] him today somewhat amenable to unhealthy social influences, just as it did in the early days of his first contact with civilization." Pointing to larceny, gambling, and female "sex offenders," the researchers wrote that the criminal "offenses [Hawaiians] were prone to commit were faults of irresponsibility rather than viciousness" (Porteus and Babcock 1926:29–30).[39]

Rather than the "classic colonial relationship" between haole and Hawaiians, Merry (2000:128) contends that "the immigrant sugar workers had a typical immigrant relationship to the haole/Hawaiian leadership of the Hawaiian kingdom and later Territory of Hawai'i":

As the demand for sugar plantation labor escalated, American and European landowners imported vast numbers of immigrant sugar workers from Europe and Asia. These groups were largely labor units in the imagination of the dominant groups, both white and Native Hawaiian, never the target of a reformist gaze. They remained an alien "other" while the Native Hawaiians were assimilated into a category of "us" by the economically and politically dominant whites. (Merry 2000:7)

Among the migrant workers from Europe and Asia, Merry (2000:131) trains her attention on "immigrant groups from Asia," leaving Portuguese workers in analytic ambiguity and abeyance with regard to the "typical immigrant relationship." This ambiguity already hints at the diversity within the migrant labor category. Indeed, within the narrower realm of Asian-origin migrant labor, the "typical immigrant relationship" proved to be likewise elusive, especially beyond the nineteenth century. By the 1920s and 1930s, there was arguably as much difference in racialization between the Japanese and Filipinos as between Hawaiians and "Asians."[40]

For the late nineteenth century, however, Merry's distinction between Hawaiians and Asian-origin migrants mostly held, particularly in relation to the Chinese. Coming from China and, later and in smaller numbers, California and other parts of the U.S. West Coast, Chinese laborers were synonymous with "coolies."[41] Beyond its identical relation to Chinese labor, the term "coolie" never had a fixed meaning in Hawai'i, not unlike in the United States or elsewhere (Jung forthcoming). There were occasional objections to the term for its suggestion of slavery; for example, the president of the Board of Immigration, the governmental agency that regulated immigration and labor importation, argued in 1886, "The coolie system known as such has never existed here" (as quoted in Coman 1903:50).[42] But the category, with its legal and cultural uncertainty in relation to "free labor," was probably less fraught in Hawai'i than in the United States, as its "unfree" status was less debatable and problematic under the Masters and Servants Act. Nonetheless, whenever "coolies" were disparaged as "slave" or "involuntary" labor, Hawaii's planters and government officials were quick to insist that, like the planters, the laborers entered their penal contracts voluntarily (Coman 1903:50; Kuykendall 1953:188), even though this was not always the case (Dye 1997; Yen 1985).[43] In fact, the planters formed the Planters' Labor and Supply Company in large measure to collectively counter charges of "maintaining a species of human bondage" that threatened the renewal of the Reciprocity Treaty.[44]

From their first arrival in 1852 but increasingly with their growing numbers, Chinese "coolies" drew intense political opposition in Hawai'i, pitting sugar planters against other haole and Hawaiians. Characteristic of exclusion movements, though often unremarked in studies thereof, the opposing sides shared basic racist beliefs about "coolies": they were constructed as "servile," "cheap labor" unfit for permanent settlement and citizenship, precisely for which they were at once desired and disdained.[45] Many Hawaiians objected that "coolies" had a morally corrupting influence on their population, blaming the Chinese for bringing disease, opium, gambling, violence, and, given the extreme gender imbalance, sexual depravity (Glick 1980; Lydon 1975; Merry 2000). Concerned with offsetting the decline in the Hawaiian population with immigrants suitable for permanent settlement, preferably "of a cognate race...to increase the population of our group," they saw the "uncivilizable coolies" as undesirable and sought "a new infusion of good blood."[46] Adding to these objections, haole and Hawaiian merchants, peddlers, and skilled workers complained of unfair competition from former Chinese plantation laborers (Glick 1980:15–17; Kuykendall 1953:190; 1967:175; Lydon 1975:37, 52, 56–58). Haole planters did not consider "coolies" any more acceptable as citizens and were as alarmed as anyone whenever Chinese laborers arrived in Hawai'i not under contract and thus "pass[ed] unchecked into our community."[47] Despite the undesirability of "coolies" as permanent members of the community, the planters argued that Chinese labor and the penal contract system were necessary for the prosperity of Hawaii's main industry and overall economy. Against their objections, which abated temporarily with the ready availability of Japanese laborers, the Hawaiian government instituted a series of restrictions between 1883 and 1886—regulating steamship lines, quotas, and visas—that slowed the rate of Chinese labor migration to Hawai'i considerably (Lydon 1975:ch. 6).

In 1887, frustrated with the Hawaiian monarchy on a wide range of issues, not the least of which was the king's patronage of Spreckels to the disadvantage of the islands' other sugar interests, a secret and almost entirely haole organization by the name of the Hawaiian League—allied with Honolulu Rifles, a voluntary militia that was originally a part of the kingdom's armed forces—compelled King Kalākaua to accept a new constitution under threat of violence. This so-called "Bayonet Constitution" variously limited the king's and Hawaiians' rights and expanded those of haole, especially in relation to elections and the franchise. It stripped the king of all important independent powers other than those to veto legislation and to appoint cabinet members. The House of Nobles, the legislative upper chamber, was made into an elective body rather than one appointed by the king, and a steep property requirement effectively prevented the vast majority of Hawaiians from running and voting for its offices. The constitution extended the right to vote to adult male *residents*—no longer necessarily *subjects* of the kingdom—of Hawaiian, American, or European ancestry who could read Hawaiian, English, or some other European language. In relation to those of Asian origin, it underscored in the most explicit terms that they were not and would not be part of the political community: while male, *nonsubject* residents of American and European ancestry could vote and run for office, male *subjects* of Asian ancestry could do neither (Kuykendall 1967: ch. 14; Rowland 1943). When the haole elite, with the backing of the U.S. minister to Hawai'i and U.S. troops, overthrew the monarchy in 1893 and set up the "republic" the following year, the new government essentially reinforced the racialized political hierarchy and, albeit without explicit reference to race or nationality, continued the wholesale disenfranchisement of Asian-origin peoples (Russ 1991:31–36). With annexation, haole planters pleaded unsuccessfully with the U.S. government to retain their restrictive system of citizenship and franchise, wishing to exceed existing U.S. law that already denied naturalization to Asians.[48]

The racist consensus against "coolies" reached its legislative apotheosis in 1890 and 1892, making Chinese laborers' entry and stay contingent on being limited to work unwanted by others.[49] Under the 1890 law, Chinese laborers, applied for by employers and approved by the government, were given permits to enter Hawai'i on the condition that they stayed no longer than five years and worked only in agricultural labor. Violations or unemployment led to arrest and deportation to China. In 1892, Hawaii's Supreme Court invalidated the law, finding unconstitutional its provision for the withholding of wages to pay for the laborers' return trip to China upon the completion of employment. Later that year, a constitutional amendment overrode the court decision, thereby allowing the legislature to pass a similar law confining Chinese migrant laborers to domestic service or agricultural labor and, in the absence of such employment, forcing them to leave Hawai'i. Combined with the Masters and Servants

Act, the law created a coercive form of labor that came the closest to slavery in Hawaii's history (Beechert 1985:92–93; Kuykendall 1967:184–185).

Even before the development of the sugar industry and the importation of "coolies," Chinese had been in Hawai'i as merchants and entrepreneurs, whose ranks expanded rapidly in the second half of the nineteenth century. In fact, whether from the start or after initial stints in sugar, many Chinese laborers worked for other Chinese, not haole, who owned and operated rice plantations and myriad other businesses; many went on to start their own enterprises. Leaving Hawai'i for China or the United States—departures numbered more than half of arrivals[50]—or finding a niche in the growing ethnic and "middleman" sectors of the economy that enabled upward mobility without threatening the haole elite, Chinese laborers continued their exodus from sugar plantations after U.S. annexation. When Hawai'i became a U.S. territory in 1900, exclusion laws barred further influx of laborers from China. Increasingly emptied of bodies, the "coolie" category that had contained Chinese laborers fell into disuse (Glick 1980; McKeown 2001).

Differential Racisms and Reactions

The Portuguese: Model Minority

From the Reciprocity Treaty and its renewal to annexation, the penal contract system and its cheap "coolie" labor came under continual criticism from the United States, particularly its sugar interests: "Sandwich Islands sugar crop produced by Chinese and semislave labor, and introduced into our country free of duty, under the conditions of the Hawaiian treaty without reduction in price to the consumers is each year injuring and unfairly competing with our sugars."[51] In response to this pressure from without and the pressure of the homegrown anti-Chinese movement from within, Hawaii's planters and government sought to find laborers fit for citizenship and permanent settlement. During the last decades of the monarchy, a variety of peoples were considered, including Europeans, Polynesians, Malaysians, and even Japanese. With the demise of the monarchy and the unrivaled rise of haole and U.S. dominance, the list soon shortened to Europeans and Americans.[52] Consequent labor recruitment efforts found most, and arguably sole, success in Portugal, specifically its economically depressed islands of Madeira and the Azores. Between 1878 and annexation, 10,926 Portuguese landed in Hawai'i, their numbers peaking in the early 1880s (Schmitt 1977:97–98). Another 5,392 arrived between 1901 and 1924, nearly all of them in the late 1900s and early 1910s (Schmitt 1977:100).[53] By 1930, there were 27,588 Portuguese in Hawai'i, accounting for 7.5 percent of the population (Nordyke 1977:table 3).

A major motivation for the planters' recruitment of Portuguese workers, as with other workers, was to check the numerical predominance of any one group. As the planters explained, "We need them especially as an *offset* to the Chinese; not that the Chinese are undesirable,—far from it,—but we lay great stress on the necessity of having our labor *mixed*. By employing different nationalities, there is less danger of collusion among laborers, and the employer, on the whole, secures better discipline."[54] Later, the planters expressed the need for additional Portuguese laborers to offset the Japanese, who had become the most populous. In the wake of Japanese labor activism after annexation that culminated in the 1909 strike, the planters redoubled their effort: "One of the immediate results of the [1909] labor disturbance was to cause [HSPA's trustees] to take in hand very vigorously the question of obtaining supplies of fresh labor from every available source."[55] This effort supplied the last of the Portuguese migrant labor.

Portuguese laborers were, however, qualitatively different from Chinese "coolies." They were also qualitatively different from Japanese laborers, who began to arrive in large numbers at the tail end of the pre-annexation wave of Portuguese migration and whose recruitment was also partly an antidote to the Chinese, and from Filipino laborers, who began to arrive in the middle of the postannexation wave of Portuguese migration and whose recruitment was also partly an antidote to the Japanese.[56] As already indicated in the discussions of the Bayonet Constitution, the republic, and U.S. naturalization law, being of European descent carried the crucial significance of conferring citizenship, membership in Hawaii's political community. To be sure, Portuguese were brought for their labor. But, like other, if less successful, labor recruits from Europe, they were also always deemed desirable as "citizens" and "permanent settlers."[57] The haole elite continually extolled the Portuguese as embodying the ideal of being "both good laborers and good citizens, a combination devoutly to be desired."[58] They were distinguished from Asian-origin workers, whose only purpose was to provide labor: "Portuguese laborers are under a different engagement, as they are designed to form the basis of a permanent population."[59] Consequently, the planters and the government actively promoted the migration of families rather than individual men.[60] The Portuguese exceeded the planters' expectations and, probably, wishes in this regard: of the 10,177 arrivals between 1879 and 1886, 30.7 percent were men, while 22.5 percent and 46.8 percent were women and children, respectively.[61] In contrast, the frequent and ardent calls for, and less frequent and ardent efforts toward, obtaining a higher proportion of women among Chinese migrants were not about nurturing a permanent population of citizens but about mitigating the various perceived dangers posed by the preponderance of Chinese men.[62]

Consistent with the unquestioned categorization of the Portuguese as "citizens," potential and actual, nobody in Hawai'i classified them, or other Europeans, as "cheap labor." For the planters and the government, who shared the recruitment costs, this dissociation was literally true.[63] In 1886, the planters estimated that a Portuguese male laborer cost them "$100 or more each," while a Japanese male laborer cost "about $55."[64] With their families, the planters figured that the cost per male laborer, during the mid-1860s, was $263.88 for Portuguese and $92.75 for Japanese.[65] Though it lowered somewhat over time, the cost of recruiting Portuguese labor remained high into the twentieth century—"$207.32 per adult male" in 1907.[66] Moreover, as one plantation manager put it, "The Portuguese have always been paid more than either the Japs or Chinese for doing exactly the same work."[67] Of course, they rarely did exactly the same work, being favored for skilled and especially low supervisory positions (USBLS 1916:19–21; Lind 1938b:255). As shown previously, this pattern of higher pay and preferential jobs persisted into the 1940s.

The abiding willingness of the planters and the government to bear the much higher cost of Portuguese labor, however, betrayed much more than a literal dissociation of the Portuguese and "cheap labor." It was predicated on a taken-for-granted symbolic dissociation that rested on race. Praising Portuguese labor on the one hand and pleading for more Chinese labor on the other, the planters stated in 1886: "Providence did not intend that the white man should do field work in the tropics. . . . the experience of sugar growing, the world over, goes to prove that cheap labor, which means in plain words, *servile* labor, must be employed in order to render this enterprize [sic] successful."[68] The planters knew that they neither would nor could fill all of their labor needs with Portuguese workers: "During the coming year, we shall want all the Portuguese we can obtain. They are first-class laborers, and though high priced, it is not likely that we will obtain too many of them." The planters intended to meet their much greater need for cheap, servile labor with the 6,000 Chinese they were seeking at the same time.[69] In the ensuing decades, Japanese and Filipino workers replaced the Chinese in—and, in turn, resisted—the category of "cheap labor," while the Portuguese remained out of danger of inclusion.

The Portuguese were nevertheless identified with *plantation* labor. Like other Europeans and, to varying degrees, those from Asia, most Portuguese left the plantations for better opportunities in Honolulu and the U.S. metropole. But, like the Japanese and the Filipinos but unlike all others, the Portuguese maintained a sizable presence on the plantations from their first arrival in Hawai'i to the 1940s and beyond. As the territorial governor wrote in 1904, "So far as the Europeans and Americans are concerned, it has, with one exception, been found that they were unfitted for tropical field work. . . . The one exception noted is that of the Portuguese from Madeira and the Azores."[70] This was likely because three fourths of the recruits had been illiterate peasants from islands in the Atlantic with roughly a similar climate (Fuchs 1961:56), as opposed to, for example, unemployed skilled workers from Norwegian cities (Beechert 1985:86–87). And, because the planters deemed the pre-annexation importation of Portuguese labor a success, they renewed it after annexation, thereby prolonging and reinforcing the symbolic link between the Portuguese and plantations.

With each failed experiment of bringing in and keeping European labor to advance "industrial welfare" and "civic development," only the former of which was a consideration for Asian-origin labor, Portuguese persistent presence on the plantations, initially as unfree indentured labor no less, stood as a counterpoint that took on racial significance.[71] For example, while discussing its "strong desire for a further supply of Portuguese laborers," the planters' labor committee in 1894 was cautious about "turn[ing] to Belgium for our labor supply," reasoning "Northern Europeans are unsuited both by constitution and inclination."[72] Evidently without much conscious intention, the planters drew an increasingly rigid racial distinction among Europeans, seeing the "Portuguese as a race."[73] They were considered the proverbial "model minority" among Hawaii's migrant laborers, which was, not surprisingly, a racialized and racializing status with certain, if often misrecognized, barriers to full equality.

By the turn of the century, the Portuguese had become a "race" separate from haole. Sometime shortly before 1898, a leading haole advocate of U.S. annexation felt the need to declare "unjust and incorrect" the fact that the Portuguese were "even [being] spoken of as not being Europeans," adding that they "constitute the best laboring element in Hawaii" (Thurston n.d.:32).[74] By the end of the first decade of the twentieth century, expressions like "white men or Portuguese" and "Anglo-Saxons and Latins," in addition to haole and Portuguese, were commonplace and required no explanation.[75] Though consonant with similar turn-of-the-century distinctions of race among "whites" in the continental United States, the distinction in Hawai'i between haole and Portuguese ran deeper and longer, lasting to this day (Baganha 1991; Estep 1941a, 1941b; Fuchs 1961; Geschwender et al. 1988). Adopting separate racial categories for haole and Portuguese, the territorial government and the Big Five employers ratified and rendered *fait accompli* the distinction.[76]

The Portuguese became a "race" that was ascribed to be related to haole but distinctly inferior to them and even to some nonhaole, a racialization accepted without much question or comment by not only haole but also everyone other than the Portuguese themselves. A survey of haole plantation managers, along with several plantation doctors and educators, conducted by psychologists Stanley Porteus and Marjorie Babcock at the University of Hawai'i in the 1920s, unintentionally offered a telling assessment of haole beliefs about the Portuguese and Hawaii's other "races," although the original intention was to provide unbiased ratings of those groups by ostensibly objective haole arbiters. The exclusion of haole and the inclusion of Portuguese as study subjects to be assessed by haole raters already marked the Portuguese as distinct from and inferior to haole, the unremarked and unmarked standard. For the eight racial traits rated—"planning capacity," "self determination," "inhibition of impulse," "resolution," "self control," "stability of interest," "tact," and "dependability"—the Portuguese fell in the middle of the pack, markedly below the Japanese, except with regard to tact, and markedly above Filipinos, again except with regard to tact (Porteus and Babcock 1926:96–97).[77] The Japanese and the Chinese, and likely others, did not disagree with the haole appraisal of the Portuguese "race" (Masuoka 1931; McKeown 2001).

By the early decades of the twentieth century, haole treated the Portuguese like a distant relative who was hired and favored, even over certain nonkin deemed more able, but could climb only so far. On the plantations, Portuguese were kept out of top managerial and professional positions, rarely appearing on the first page of company payrolls.[78] At the same time, they maintained their advantage over Japanese and Filipino workers (see earlier section). Above all, they were the "lunas," the job category that became inextricably racialized as Portuguese, although most Portuguese were not lunas and most lunas were not Portuguese (USBLS 1916:20; Lind 1938b:255).[79] More than the always dispropor-tionate number of Portuguese lunas, the racialized figure of the "luna" fit and stuck with the Portuguese because it resonated with their general position in the social order—as the "day-to-day buffers" between haole and Asian-origin peoples (Fuchs 1961:57).

Portuguese "middleman" status engendered a singular racial identity, not only among laborers on the plantations but also across class lines. The "slighted race" resented the exclusion from the haole category, especially since the Portuguese were aware of their fuller whiteness in the metropole.[80] According to a third-generation Portuguese woman, "a university graduate and a social worker":

> It is a shame that just because our ancestors came here as laborers, with low economic status, that their children, for generations, have been made to feel keenly inferior through prejudicial practices in the Islands.
>
> The year and a half I spent in California proved to me that prejudice against the Portuguese is very slight there as compared with here. Neither there, nor in any other states, do prejudicial "Other Caucasians" and "haole" classifications exist. There we are "Caucasian," and as such, are accepted in accordance with individual merits. (as quoted in Estep 1941b:12)

In a study that was itself an appeal to erase the racial boundary between haole and Portuguese, Gerald Allan Estep (1941b:12) wrote that this woman's "feeling of inferiority, so prevalent in the Portuguese, no matter of what generation, [was] so widespread among them that it might almost be referred to as a group inferiority complex."[81] No doubt a source of perplexity and perturbation for Hawaii's Portuguese, a paradox of their prewar racial identity was that they, in an effort not to be distinguished from haole, "assimilated" and rid themselves of markers of "otherness" (e.g., newspapers, social organizations) much more than their counterparts in California, who were more readily accepted as, and by, "whites" (Baganha 1991; Estep 1941a).

The racial aspirations and frustrations of Hawaii's Portuguese, as well as the incongruity between the racial categories of Hawai'i and the metropole, were also captured appositely in the following letter to the editor. Having recently registered for the draft, a Portuguese man wrote that he had identified himself as "Portuguese" to the registrar, who had asked him the origin of his last name. On the registration card, a document issued by the federal government and employing metropolitan racial categories, the choices were limited to "White," "Negro," "Oriental," "Indian," and "Filipino." The registrar resolved the apparent dilemma by "cross[ing] out 'Indian' and insert[ing] above it, in precise handwriting, 'Portuguese.'" His "ire rising like the hackles of a game cock," the writer concluded his letter by insisting "that the Portuguese are of the Caucasian race, and therefore white."[82] Estep (1941b) found similar sentiments among his study's subjects with regard to the territorial government's use of separate categories for "Portuguese" and "Other Caucasians," the official designation for haole.

Workers were not exempt from this conflicted racial identity, providing a piece of the explanation for the lack of an interracial working-class identity or movement before the 1940s. The most notable feature of the Portuguese in relation to prewar labor history is their absence from major organizing efforts or labor disputes. As George Martin, a Portuguese leader of the postwar labor movement, joked about the prewar period, "Japanese strike, Filipinos worked. Filipinos strike, Japanese worked. Portuguese all the time working."[83] The principal ambition of Portuguese workers on the plantations was not to engage in class conflict against the haole planters but to be accepted as haole; thus, they de-emphasized any perceived differences with haole and emphasized any perceived differences with other nonhaole (Estep 1941a; Kimura 1955:46–47).[84] As Lawrence Fuchs (1961:58) put it, "Non-acceptance [as haole] by the Hawaiians and haoles constantly forced the Portuguese to show their superiority over the Orientals. Time after time, Portuguese insisted they were haole." As a Portuguese laborer exclaimed to a rude immigration officer upon his 1911 arrival, "See my arm? See the skin? It's white. I did not come here to be driven as a slave in this free country of America."[85] From the 1880s, almost as soon as the Portuguese laborers had begun to land in Hawai'i, they joined haole and Hawaiians in movements to keep out Chinese and then Japanese laborers (Kuykendall 1967:172–175; Reinecke 1979:6).[86] On the plantations, Portuguese workers' racial identity manifested perhaps most visibly in the behavior of the lunas, who supervised Japanese and Filipino workers. Regarding the straw bosses of the late 1920s and 1930s, a retired half-Portuguese sugar worker recalled, "They[, the Portuguese,] were the lunas. And they were the slavedrivers. And they were the worst you could get on the sugar plantation." Explaining how the Portuguese lunas had strongly identified with the haole management and not with labor, he recounted reprovingly, "Everything would be for the plantation. Nothing for the work-men."[87] In the 1909 and 1920 strikes, Portuguese, along with Chinese, Hawaiians, Koreans, and, in 1920, Puerto Ricans, worked as strikebreakers, which, needless to say, did not bode well for interracialism (Takaki 1983:161, 170). The permanent "substitution" of Japanese with Portuguese in skilled positions on at least some plantations after the 1909 strike also did not help in this regard.[88]

The Japanese: Fear and Loathing

As the Portuguese were never intended to replace the disappearing "cheap labor" of the Chinese, the planters turned to Japan for this purpose. Known as *gannenmono*, or people of the first year of the Meiji era, 148 Japanese arrived as contract laborers in 1868.[89] However, departure from Japan without proper authorization and reports of worker mistreatment in Hawai'i quickly led to interventions by the Japanese government, return of some workers, and, more lastingly, cessation of further labor migration (Conroy [1949] 1973:ch. 3; Kotani 1985:8; Kuykendall 1953:183–184; Odo and Sinoto 1985:13–16). Only after much negotiation, and political-economic changes in Japan, did the Japanese government allow the emigration of contract laborers to Hawai'i.[90] Between 1885 and 1894, 29,069 Japanese migrated to Hawai'i under direct supervision of the Japanese government. Some 57,000 more landed between 1894, when the Japanese government licensed and ceded control to private emigration companies, and 1900. Between 1900, when penal labor contracts were prohib-ited, and the Gentlemen's Agreement of 1907–1908, there were around 71,000 additional arrivals. Finally, from then to the Immigration Act of 1924, during which only immediate relatives or returning migrants were permitted, another 61,000 Japanese, including more than 20,000 so-called "picture brides," dis-embarked in Hawai'i (Odo and Sinoto 1985:43, 49). With departures to Japan and the metropole partly offsetting arrivals and births, Japanese made up around 40 percent of the population by 1900 and for the next 4 decades, peak-ing a little above it around 1920 and declining slightly thereafter (Nordyke 1977:table 3).[91] By 1890, Japanese laborers already outnumbered the Chinese in the sugar industry (*Hawaiian Annual* 1891:62).

Making a case for retaining the penal contract labor system they would lose in two years, the planters contended in 1898, "Now as regards the labor contract service on Hawaii, it is not a 'system of slavery.' It serves chiefly as a convenient plan to identify laborers. The Asiatics all look very much alike, and it is often difficult to identify them if they leave a plantation on one island and remove to another island."[92] If absurd and desperate, this contention did illustrate one initial cultural logic by which the haole planters and others in Hawai'i comprehended

Japanese migrant laborers: they were the new "cheap labor," symbolic and cor-
poreal replacements for Chinese labor.[93] Albeit infrequently, the Japanese were
at times referred to as "coolies."[94] Seemingly regarding them as interchangeable
"cheap labor," the planters intermittently sought to discipline or replace Japanese
laborers with renewed importation of Chinese laborers. Even after annexation,
alarmed over escalating Japanese labor activism, they periodically lobbied Congress, never successfully, for an exception to the ban on Chinese labor migration
(Duus 1999; Okihiro 1991; Reinecke 1979; USBL 1906).

As in the United States, the anti-Chinese movement in Hawai'i likewise saw
Japanese laborers as analogical extensions of Chinese "coolies," that is, as an
additional target of its ire. A formal embodiment of this outlook was the 1888
organization of the Hawaiian Anti-Asiatic Union that sought to restrict both
Chinese and Japanese labor migration (Kuykendall 1967:178). The "anti-Asiatic" movement also continually agitated to keep both groups out of preferred
occupations. In 1903, it helped secure the passage of a territorial law that mandated "no person shall be employed as a mechanic or a laborer upon any public work carried on by this Territory, or by any political subdivision thereof,
whether the work is done by contract or otherwise, unless such person is a
citizen of the United States or eligible to become a citizen" (as quoted in USBL
1906:402–403). The law left public sector employment "open to all whites and
natives, excluding practically only the Orientals" (USBL 1906:403). A year later,
the HSPA passed a resolution to hire exclusively "American citizens, or those
eligible for citizenship" for skilled positions.[95]

Though real and significant, continuities between the racialization of Chinese labor and that of Japanese labor should not be overstated. Everyone,
including the Japanese themselves, understood the Japanese to be racially different from the Chinese and later, to a considerably greater degree, from Filipinos. In Asian American studies, it has long been recognized, rightly, that the
history of the Japanese in Hawai'i and the United States differed in certain ways
from those of other Asian-origin peoples, because the Japanese state could and,
at times, did assert the rights of its citizens abroad. However, even more important than, though inextricably bound up with, the actual protections sought
or secured by the Japanese state—which was as likely in practice to disregard
or contravene the wishes of Japanese laborers in Hawai'i (Okihiro 1991)—was
the symbolic value of the state itself. In this "age of empire" (Hobsbawm 1989),
states were a key index of national and racial rank and worth. Political sovereignty was a minimum requirement for respectability. To be a colonial power
or, more rarefied, a "great power" was a sign of superiority; to be colonized was
a sign of inferiority and self-evidence of its justness. In the late nineteenth and
twentieth centuries, Japan was a rapidly and self-consciously modernizing state
that, alone outside the West, became a "great power" (Shimazu 1998), which
figured centrally in the singular racialization of the Japanese in Hawai'i.

Up to the Bayonet Constitution, the Japanese were considered by Hawaiian state officials as a people "resembl[ing] our native race very much" and therefore as potential permanent settlers who could "readily amalgamate" with and augment the native population.[96] As the Hawaiian envoy to Japan communicated to the Japanese minister of foreign affairs in 1882, "We believe that Japanese and Hawaiians spring from a cognate race and that Japanese children growing up and amalgamating with our population will produce a new and vigorous race, which will repeople our Islands. If we simply wanted coolies or laborers we could obtain Chinese but we seek more than that; we wish to repeople our country with an orderly, laborious, civilized, law abiding and cognate race."[97] The notion that Japanese and Hawaiians were of a "cognate race" was based on Hawaiians' malleable racial classification scheme of the day and, relatedly, on their perception of cognate political interests. Wishing to forestall U.S. absorption, some among the Hawaiian elite sought a potential ally and ballast in the rising power in Asia. To this end, King Kalākaua, during the Japanese leg of his world tour in 1881, even proposed to Emperor Meiji the formation of a "Union and Federation of the Asiatic nations and sovereigns," with the Japanese emperor as its head (Conroy [1949] 1973:74–76; Kuykendall 1953:182, 1967:228–230).[98]

For its part, the Japanese state consciously strove to prevent its citizens' being associated with the globally denigrated "coolies" (Conroy [1949] 1973:99; Kuykendall 1967:154, 167–168). With the Treaty of Friendship and Commerce in 1871, Japan and Hawai'i agreed that the "subjects of each…[were entitled to] at all times the same privileges as may have been, or may hereafter be granted to the citizens or subjects of any other nation."[99] In other words, Japanese in Hawai'i were to be accorded the same rights as immigrants from the United States and Europe, including rights of naturalization and franchise. The Japanese government also carried on long, elaborate negotiations that culminated in the Convention of 1886. Governing Japanese migration to and employment in Hawai'i, it specified rights and obligations of the two governments that, in theory and to a much lesser extent in practice, safeguarded the well-being of Japanese laborers (Kuykendall 1967:ch. 6). Leading up to the convention, the Japanese government also secured an agreement for 30 percent of the migrants to be women (Conroy [1949] 1973:106; Odo 2004:20). In a further effort to distinguish Japanese laborers from "coolies," those selected for emigration by the Japanese government were not from the poorest classes, who could potentially have reflected badly on the Japanese state, nation, and "race" (Kuykendall 1967:154; see also Azuma 2005:28, 227).

The planters did not see the Japanese in the same light as the Hawaiian elite did, of course, but they did see them as different from the Chinese or any others of Asian origin. After the Bayonet Constitution, with the government now firmly in haole control, talk of the Japanese as a "cognate race" and potential settlers, which the planters had tolerated but not subscribed to, subsided. As discussed above, the planters understood the Japanese primarily as their much needed "cheap labor." At the same time, even the planters could not but recognize and treat with due care the increasingly powerful Japanese state from which this labor was recruited. Although the 1871 and 1886 agreements were violated, blatantly at times (e.g., the Bayonet Constitution), the haole elite in power took Japanese protests against the violations with seriousness and consternation not accorded the Chinese, who lacked the backing of a strong state (Conroy [1949] 1973; Okahata and PCUJSH 1971; Rowland 1943).

"Behind the Japanese stood Japan in a vague, undefined, yet potentially threatening, position," Hilary Conroy ([1949] 1973:175) observes of the 1890s. "In one sense a fear of Japan among the governors of Hawaii made antagonism to the Japanese run deeper; yet it also made them cautious." For example, however much they desired to, the planters and the Hawaiian government in the 1890s did not dare impose the same restriction on Japanese laborers as on Chinese laborers—making their stay contingent on employment in agricultural labor or domestic service.[100] Instead, to resolve their contradictory concerns—needing Japanese labor, worrying about the large and growing presence of the Japanese, and fearing Japan's imperialist intentions—the planters continually pleaded for the security of U.S. annexation: "[Japanese migration] is now threatening, if not soon stayed, to swamp the whole Hawaiian group and by the natural law of survival of fittest, to control the destinies of Hawaii from now onward, unless Uncle Sam should hoist over us his broad flag, and declare that Hawaii ought and from henceforth shall be American soil."[101] Lorrin A. Thurston (n.d.:6–7), a prominent missionary descendent, advocated similarly for U.S. annexation:

> The awakening of Japan has introduced a new element into the politics of the world, and more especially the Pacific.... Under the existing constitution of Hawaii, the Japanese are not citizens and are ineligible to citizenship; but it goes without saying, that an energetic, ambitious, warlike, and progressive people like the Japanese can not indefinitely be prevented from participating in the government of a country in which they become dominant in numbers, and the ownership of property... and unless radical action is taken to stay the process there can be but one logical result, viz: the ultimate supremacy of the Japanese, and thereby of Japan, in Hawaii.[102]

Temporarily ebbing with annexation, this anti-Japanese discourse of race, nation, and empire would flow and grow, from Japan's defeat of Russia in the Russo-Japanese War of 1905 forward.

In the social sciences, the presumed inferiority of a racial group has long been considered to be the overriding, essential quality of racism (Jung 2002). But, as evidenced here, anti-Japanese racism in Hawai'i was not fundamentally about the presumed inferiority of the Japanese. The core schema of anti-Japanese racism concerned national loyalty: the imagined, potential hostility of an increasingly powerful Japanese state was projected onto the Japanese population in Hawai'i by the haole elite, territorial and federal governments, and eventually, nearly everyone in Hawai'i. The Japanese were constructed as an inscrutable people beholden racially, and therefore inherently, to their nation of origin and carrying out its imperialist ambitions from within. Coherently, anti-Japanese racism was not based on an assured belief that the Japanese were inferior but on a fear that they were *not*.

Not surprisingly, then, the survey of the haole elite by Porteus and Babcock (1926:96–97) from the 1920s rated the Japanese highly on a variety of racial "traits": first in "planning capacity," "resolution," "stability of interest," and "self control" and second in "prudence," "self determination," and "dependability." Only in the wild-card category of "tact"—which, across the 6 racial groups rated, did not correlate much with the other categories—did the Japanese rate low, in fact, the lowest; this ostensibly indicated their overly aggressive and ambitious nature (Porteus and Babcock 1926:94–95). Despite that low score, the study's composite rating had the Japanese at the top with a score of 85.5 on a 100-point scale; the unrated haole presumably merited the full 100.[103] The 25 haole judges, 16 of whom were plantation managers, rated the Japanese significantly higher than the Portuguese, who had a composite score of 60 (Porteus and Babcock 1926:108–111).[104] Thus deemed by haole to be considerably inferior to the Japanese, the Portuguese were nonetheless favored and more highly placed on the plantations. In other words, it paid to be "Caucasian," even if not "Other Caucasian."

Interpreting the above ratings, and other "objective" psychological and physiological measurements, Porteus and Babcock linked them to past and future trajectories of the Japanese state and to practical implications for dealing with the Japanese. While projecting their fears of a strong Japanese state onto the Japanese in Hawai'i, the authors also projected their suspicions of the Japanese in Hawai'i back onto the Japanese state, reflecting the cycle of fear and loathing of Japan and the Japanese that obtained generally in prewar Hawai'i. Although their study was not exclusively about the Japanese, the authors' conclusions regarding "racial futures" were nearly so:

> Having drawn together all our various lines of investigation we find them all pointing to the fact of superior endowment in the Japanese over all the other races studied. What then is the conclusion that we should reach as to the bearing of these advantages on inter-racial competition and especially with regard to our own relations with Japan.... While we are not alarmists we recognize that a serious situation confronts the dominant white race....perhaps the heaviest handicap that western civilization still carries is the humanitarian impulse. Side by side with the growth of medical science

has been the development of this impulse towards preserving and perpetuating the unfit.... Knowing nothing of all this much vaunted progress [of the West], she [Japan] was conserving her national strength through the elimination of her unfit by natural eugenics. Now at one stride she steps forward into the front rank of nations, inheritor of all the fruits of the effort and wisdom of the Western mind.... Despite all of Japan's protestations we believe that her ambition is by no means dormant, and that her policies are very shrewdly shaped and hidden behind a mask of inscrutability.... Our personal opinion of the inherent advantages that the Japanese race enjoys is so high that we could entirely favour a policy of rigid exclusion from Canada, United States and Australia. (Porteus and Babcock 1926:326–327, 329, 331, 334–335)

Also evident in the study was that the haole elite found the Japanese threatening, because they, as a "race," were imputed to possess the ideal qualities of manhood that haole, implicitly male, admired and by which they defined themselves: forethought, discipline, self-determination, assertiveness, courage, virility, and so on.[105] The ostensible masculinity of the Japanese was, for example, what separated them from the other "Oriental race":

On the one hand was the Chinaman plodding away at his allotted task, accepting the burden which centuries of use had laid upon his shoulders, unwilling or unable to follow new leads or fearing to face new situations, hating notoriety and the unaccustomed, and clinging fast to the old traditions and ways—essentially the feminine temperament. On the other hand we get a picture of the Japanese—self-assertive and anxious for a larger place in the sun, eager for any adaptation that will advance his ambitions, selfish in outlook and not given to over-scrupulousness, sensitive as regards his self-conceit, yet exhibiting wonderful tenacity of purpose and self-control in meeting new difficulties—essentially masculine characteristics. (Porteus and Babcock 1926:48)

Similarly, note the masculine imagery, as well as the admixture of admiration and apprehension, in Admiral Yates Stirling Jr.'s remarks to an audience of *nisei*[106]:

As you know, I am on record in an official report published by Congress in which I question... [your loyalty to] a nation different in many fundamental respects from the nation of your forefathers. In reaching this conclusion, my thoughts have reviewed the virility, pride, efficiency, and determination of the Japanese nation from which you have sprung....

What other nation in modern times can point to the distinction of having risen from a small feudal island kingdom to one of the greatest commercial, military, and naval empires of the world in less than three quarters of a century?...

Gentlemen, I do not intend to discourage the determination you all must have of proving your loyalty to your new country, but only to point out how much more difficult is your task than if you were not the descendants of a powerful militaristic people, whose ambitions have carried them so far in Empire building in such an incredible short span of time.[107]

Recent scholars have insightfully pointed to the gendered character of haole racism that constructed the other "races" as unmanly.[108] The Japanese proved to be an exception to this argument—and increasingly more so as fears and suspicions of them grew during the first half of the twentieth century.

The Filipinos: Colonized Labor

In contrast to the Japanese, Filipinos were believed by haole and nearly all non-Filipinos in prewar Hawai'i to be unequivocally inferior. Just as the Japanese imperial state, rival to Western "great powers," served as a national and racial index of its people, so too did the U.S.-colonized Philippines in relation to Filipinos. Almost by definition, colonialism—the usurpation of political sovereignty of another people—necessitated and produced a presumption of inferiority of the colonized, and the establishment of the U.S. colonial state in the Philippines was no exception.[109] Between military and civilian officials, there were conflicting opinions, with consequential implications for colonial policies, concerning whether and which Filipinos could be taught to govern themselves. At the same time, these conflicting opinions of U.S. colonizers were built on a broad, taken-for-granted agreement: Filipinos were racially inferior and, at best, not yet capable of self-government (Go 2004; Hoganson 1998; Jacobson 2000; Kramer 1998; Love 2004; Rafael 2000; Salman 2001; Welch 1979; Worcester 1930). In Hawai'i, anti-Filipino racism was even flatter and internally less conflicted, for it applied to a less heterogeneous population of migrant laborers. Most of them hailed from a similar peasant background, and although haole occasionally spoke of regional differences among Filipinos in racial terms, those occasions were uncommon, as the Filipinos, like the Japanese and the Chinese, were categorized as one, if hybrid, "race."[110]

Plantation managers and other haole in the Porteus and Babcock study judged Filipinos to be exceedingly inferior. Filipinos rated a mere 33 on the study's 100-point composite scale—dead last and polar opposite of the Japanese. Filipinos ranked either last or second to last on 7 of the 8 traits, "tact" again being the exception (Porteus and Babcock 1926:92–97, 109). In other words, Filipinos were considered to be extremely short-sighted, suggestible, impulsive, irresolute, overemotional, unstable in their interests, and undependable, although of average tactfulness. The study concluded, "Summing up these characteristics we may say that the Filipinos represent a fine example of a race in an adolescent stage of development" (Porteus and Babcock 1926:67). As an agency executive explained to a plantation manager, "They are so like children."[111] Not only making them childlike, the supposed absence of traits valued by haole also marked Filipinos as unmanly. Evincing the circulation of racist discourses, along with labor, within the U.S. empire, a very similar racialization had taken place earlier in relation to Filipinos in the Philippines. As Kristin Hoganson (1998:134–137; see also Kramer 1998) writes of the initial colonial moment at the turn of the century, "Imperialists based their assertions that the Filipinos were unfit for independence on three stereotypes that gave meaning to racial prejudices by drawing on ideas about gender. All three presented the Filipinos as lacking the manly character seen as necessary for self-government." The three stereotypes were that they were "savages," "childlike," and "feminine."

There were obvious parallels between the racialization of Filipinos and that of Hawaiians. U.S. colonialism entailed the representation of both "races" as childlike and unmanly. But there was also a striking difference that placed Filipinos in a more inferior and menacing position in the racial imagination of haole. Unlike the supposedly gentle Hawaiians, Filipinos were deemed volatile and violent by nature: "highly emotional, impulsive, and almost explosive in temperament" (Porteus and Babcock 1926:64; see also Anderson 1984; Fuchs 1961; Reinecke 1979). As with the presumption of Filipino inferiority in general, the belief in their violent disposition was shared by most non-Filipinos in Hawai'i. A contemporary observer as well as historian of prewar Hawai'i, John Reinecke (1996:3) writes, "Between the Filipinos and other ethnic groups there was a wide social distance.... A great part of the population stereotyped them as hotheaded, knife-wielding, overdressed, sex-hungry young men." They were commonly subjected to slurs like "poke poke" and "poke knife" for their putative propensity to engage in violence, especially with knives, and feared as sexual predators.[112]

The divergent beliefs occasioned by U.S. colonialism that Hawaiians were childlike, unmanly, and benign and that Filipinos were childlike, unmanly, but malign were rooted in different modes of colonial incorporation. Though not completely free of violence, U.S. colonization of Hawai'i did not involve violence on the order of the brutally waged Philippine-American War, during which an estimated 16,000 to 20,000 Filipinos were killed in battle and perhaps another 200,000 died of war-related causes; though far fewer in comparison, of the 126,468 soldiers who served on the U.S. side, 4,234 died, and more than 2,800 were wounded, comprising one of the highest casualty rates in U.S. military history (Hoganson 1998:7; Welch 1979:42; see also Franco 1987). The United States fought a ruthless war—routinely employing torture and killing civilians—and then attributed its ruthlessness to the Filipinos themselves, who supposedly, in the words of U.S. Secretary of War Elihu Root, "conducted [the war] with barbarous cruelty common among uncivilized races" (Jacobson

2000:243–245; see also Kramer 1998). Characterization of Filipinos as "savages" survived the war and migrated to Hawai'i, along with Filipino labor. It is worth noting that the racist epithet "goo goo," antecedent to the more infamous "gook," that U.S. soldiers likely originated during the war was taken up by plantation supervisors and others in Hawai'i.[113] As E. San Juan Jr. (1992:47) reminds us, "the context [of Filipino migration] then was the violent colonization of six million Filipinos."

If haole judgments of Filipinos were a product and reflection of U.S. colonialism in the Philippines, they also served as arguments for the necessity of its continuation:

> At present their characteristics have a decided bearing on their fitness for independence. If the traits that we have found to be characteristic of the Filipinos in Hawaii are also typical of the Filipino at home then we are forced to the conclusion that they are a long way from the stage of development at which they could be safely entrusted with self-government. A single glance at their list of racial defects should be sufficient to demonstrate the wisdom of this conclusion. (Porteus and Babcock 1926:68)

The planters, in fact, saw Filipino labor migration as an extension of the U.S. colonial project in the Philippines:

> Has not the opportunity been offered to us to assist the home government [U.S. colonial government in the Philippines] in Americanizing the Filipinos?...The Hawaiian Islands have earned the reputation of conducting their political affairs in accordance with the methods practiced on the mainland. If the Filipino in his sojourn here on the different islands becomes acquainted with these methods, he returns to his country a better man physically and intellectually, and, we hope, politically.[114]

But, as this passage suggests, political tutelage was to be an incidental and passive byproduct of the planters' primary, "possibly selfish" purpose of Filipino migration to Hawai'i: providing "a very necessary supply of labor."[115]

Filipinos were the new "cheap labor" in Hawai'i. Begun a mere four years after the official, though not actual, end of the Philippine-American War, the first effort to recruit Filipino labor in 1906 and 1907 failed miserably. But the Gentlemen's Agreement of 1907–1908 and the major strike of Japanese sugar workers in 1909 stirred the planters to intensify their effort.[116] As U.S. "nationals," though not "citizens," Filipinos were unaffected by various immigration restrictions placed on "aliens," including the Johnson-Reed Act of 1924. The planters had renewed the importation of Portuguese labor in the first decade of the twentieth century as well, but it could not slake their thirst for cheap labor. Because they regarded Filipino laborers as "poor material for good citizenship," the planters had initial hopes that they would "at best be a stop gap to meet a difficult labor situation."[117] But the planters' "possibly selfish" motive of securing plentiful, cheap labor outweighed their sense of civic duty: the Philippines continued to be the only major source of additional labor, and the HSPA consciously tried to weed out the literate and the educated, though not always successfully.[118]

Shifting its attention away from agricultural-export regions with labor shortages, where not coincidentally a substantial amount of capital from Hawai'i was invested, and pouring more resources into recruitment and incentives, like free return passage upon the completion of a three-year contract, the HSPA made fast progress in the 1910s and 1920s. The flow of labor migration from the Philippines continued to grow, even when the HSPA discontinued active recruitment and stopped paying transportation costs in the mid-1920s. From 1907 to 1924, 57,675 Filipinos arrived in Hawai'i from the Philippines, with 12,513 returning; in the same period, 6,036 moved on to the metropole, while 130 moved back to Hawai'i from there. Between 1925 and 1929, 44,404 arrivals from the Philippines outnumbered the 17,982 returnees; 9,786 left for the metropole from Hawai'i, and 689 came back. In the first half of the 1930s, departures to the Philippines far outnumbered arrivals, 27,862 to 19,513; the number of Filipinos going on to the continent decreased to 2,864, while the number coming the other way increased to 864. In 1934, the Philippine Independence Act (Tydings-McDuffie Act) cut Filipino migration to the United States to 50 per year and turned Filipinos into "aliens ineligible to citizenship." Among the 121,744 Filipinos who arrived in Hawai'i from the Philippines between 1907 and 1935, there were only about 9,000 women and 4,000 children (Cariaga [1936] 1974:4; Platt 1950; Sharma 1984a, 1984b; Teodoro 1981: ch. 2). In 1930, there were 63,052 Filipinos in Hawai'i, about 17 percent of the population (Nordyke 1977:table 3). After an initial wave of Tagalogs, Visayans formed the bulk of labor migration up to 1915, after which Ilocanos predominated. By the 1930s, a clear majority of Filipino workers were of Ilocano origin (Cariaga [1936] 1974:9; Sharma 1984b; Teodoro 1981:13–14).

Tale of Two Strikes

The dual union strike of 1920 crystallized how the haole planters and the larger public conceived of Japanese and Filipino workers in racially dissimilar terms. The hitherto largest strike, undertaken by more than one major "race" of workers, signaled an unmistakable inflection point in Hawaii's racial and labor histories. Reflecting on its profound impact, Reinecke (1979:87) writes, "The Oahu sugar plantation strike of 1920 was a traumatic episode in Hawaiian history. It can best be compared with the dock strike of 1949.... A later generation in Hawaii, witness to how the fears and resentments aroused by that strike had not wholly subsided fifteen years later, can appreciate how emotions aroused by the strike of 1920 influenced the thinking and emotions of islanders long afterward." The 5-month strike involved 8,300 Japanese and Filipino workers on Oʻahu, representing 77 percent of the island's workforce. It was conducted by Oʻahu members of 2 separate unions, the Federation of Japanese Labor and the Filipino Labor Union, with outer island members continuing to work and contributing their wages to the strikers (Reinecke 1979:95). As noted in the last chapter, the strike ended in the workers' defeat, with the planters sticking to an uncompromising position.

From the beginning of the strike, the HSPA adopted the interpretation that the "action taken by the Japanese Federation of Labor is, as we see it, an anti-American movement designed to obtain control of the sugar business of the Hawaiian islands" (as quoted in Okihiro 1991:78). The two mainstream dailies agreed zealously with the industry's assessment. Drawing on the public's pre-existing fear of an imperialist takeover by the Japanese "alien race," the *Pacific Commercial Advertiser* editorialized:

> The strike is an attempt on the part of the Japanese to obtain control of the sugar industry. It is in line with Japanese policy wherever they colonize. It is of a part with the Japanization of Korea, Manchuria, Eastern Inner Mongolia, Shantung, and Formosa.... The Japanese evidently think that they can use [their methods] with equal success in Hawaii. They evidently fail to realize that it is one thing to bluff, bulldoze and bamboozle weak oriental peoples and another thing to try to coerce Americans.[119]

Depicting Hawaiʻi as "a buffer outpost on the border line" between the United States and Japan, the same paper later urged its readers to "fight...until all of Hawaii is unquestionably American."[120] The *Honolulu Star-Bulletin* asked rhetorically, "Never lose sight of the real issue: Is Hawaii to remain American or become Japanese?"[121] Centered on the Japanese supposed "blind loyalty to an autocratic government," the *Honolulu Star-Bulletin* opined more broadly two months into the strike, foreshadowing the various manifestations that anti-Japanese attacks would assume in the next two decades:

> We come now to a fundamental and practical phase of the situation: Why does there exist, not only in Hawaii but throughout the greater part of the United States, a deep-running but unmistakable under-current of suspicion and distrust of the Japanese? Is it not largely because of the form, actions and attitudes of the Japanese government and the characteristics of the Japanese people themselves?... The Portuguese and other nationals who have come here quickly accepted the American ideals and became good citizens of this country. Japanese who have been here for years and years are still as Japanese in manners, customs and thoughts as they were when they left the motherland.... It becomes the duty of the Japanese in Hawaii,

if they are really sincere in their protestations, to make an active effort to show themselves capable of becoming Americans, entitled to the manifold blessings of American citizenship....So long as they cling to their own language schools, give every evidence of first allegiance to their mother country, transplant and foster their own religion, many of whose tenets are in direct conflict with American ideals and principles, and show a disinclination to break away from many of their racial customs, so long will they be looked upon with suspicion and distrust and be counted a potential menace instead of being welcomed as worthy to be true sons and daughters of this republic.[122]

Holding the Portuguese up as the model minority among laborers, the paper anathematized the Japanese for not being "good citizens of this country," unreflexively fortifying the tautological barrier between the "American" nation and the Japanese.

The HSPA's and the press's racialization of the strike has primarily been interpreted as a conscious ruse to steer attention away from the workers' class demands.[123] No doubt, there is an element of truth to this interpretation. For example, Acting Governor Curtis 'Iaukea reckoned at the time that "the racial issue [had] been deliberately emphasized to cloud the economic issue," drawing quick criticisms from the HSPA and the mainstream dailies (as quoted in Duus 1999:73). In a letter to his agency, even a plantation manager questioned the inflammatory nature of the HSPA's "propaganda."[124] But the extent to which the planters, along with the larger public, actually believed the Japanese to be a racial threat to the community should not be underestimated. However consciously invoked by the planters, the dominant anti-Japanese discourse during the strike drew on a preexisting, enduring racist imagery of the Japanese that was widely taken for granted; otherwise, the deep and lasting effects of the strike described by Reinecke would make little sense. Intelligence shared between the military and the planters also argues against viewing anti-Japanese racism as having been merely utilitarian subterfuge. "Highly confidential" letters from military intelligence with warnings about "agents of the Japanese Consulate General" were probably not taken lightly by plantation managers and no doubt fueled their racial imaginations.[125]

The characterization of the Filipino strikers contrasted sharply. The planters and the press responded to them with conspicuous silence. When not being ignored, they were portrayed as the misled followers of the Japanese, even though Filipino workers had been more eager to go out on strike and did so before Japanese workers. Casually calling them "ignorant," one paper wrote, "As regards to the Filipinos, there is good reason to think that they are mere catspaws, used by wily Japanese agitators to further the interests of the subjects of the Mikado."[126] Accordingly, while the mainstream press ran numerous cartoons depicting the impending Japanese takeover of the "American" sugar industry and territory, there were no comparable ones of Filipinos (see figures 3.2 and 3.3). With the Philippines under U.S. colonial rule, such depictions of Filipinos would have been unthinkable and nonsensical. In the "chess match" for Hawai'i between imperial powers conjured by haole, Filipinos and the Philippines were not players but implicitly the chessboard of an earlier match against Spain already won by the United States (see figure 3.4).

The 1924 strike, in which only Filipino workers took part, underscored the difference. Based on the previously noted beliefs that Filipinos lacked self-control and were violent by nature, there was a near consensus: "Everyone," according to Reinecke (1996:35), "expected a Filipino strike to be a violent one." This expectation was not confined to haole. A Japanese newspaper that *supported* the Filipino workers editorialized, "If the strike is once commenced, violent deeds would be

FIGURE 3.2 "The New Ruler" by E. J. Catton

Source: *Pacific Commercial Advertiser,* February 13, 1920, p. 1.

FIGURE 3.3 "Shall This Be Our Flag?" by Salonga

Source: *Pacific Commercial Advertiser*, February 22, 1920, p. 4.

FIGURE 3.4 "The Language School Game" by Salonga

Source: *Pacific Commercial Advertiser*, November 2, 1919, p. 4.

perpetrated everywhere. We may witness nearly every day the arson and mur-
der."[127] George Wright, the sympathetic haole progressive who helped organize the
strike and lost his job at the Pearl Harbor Navy Yard as a result, later referred to
Filipinos as a "primitive people" whom he had tried to steer away from violence
(Reinecke 1996:158).

The public fears, however, had little factual foundation in the High Wages
Movement's (HWM) words and actions before and during the strike. Aware
of the general perception, Filipino workers explicitly and repeatedly called for
nonviolence. For example, their "Strike Proclamation" declared typically, "Let
us stand together, avoid violence, use every lawful means to gain our ends, and
we will WIN THE FIGHT." In an addendum titled "WARNING," it went on to
state,

> The Executive Committee of the High Wages Movement hereby warns all strikers
> against committing acts of violence and breaking the laws.... Strikers who deliber-
> ately violate the law must expect punishment and need not look to this committee for
> defense or protection.... Watch out for traps set for you by stool pigeons and traitors.
> In every strike there are always some of the skunks who mix with the strikers and
> try to stir up trouble. When you catch any of these fellows, don't be rough or cruel to
> them, that would be against the law. Be orderly, cheerful, quiet and patient. You are
> fighting for justice and a square deal, and for American ideals. Get the sympathy of
> the public by your good behavior.[128]

According to the wife of a striker, the discourse of the workers emphasized nonviolence: "That was really the understanding, that the strike would be won and
would be pursued by the strikers not through a troublesome kind of way, but it
would be done through a peaceful way. They really didn't want to use arms."[129]
The discourse of nonviolence also circulated through the union newspaper, *Ang
Batay* (Beechert 1985:219). True to the workers' word, the strike was indeed notably free of violence in its initial months (Jung 2004).

Unable to fathom Filipino nonviolence, the HSPA and the territorial government disregarded the strikers' actual discourse and practice. Instead, they
prepared, quite literally, for battle: the former funded the latter to hire "special
police," and both stockpiled weapons. A week after the HWM's "Strike Proclamation" and 10 days before the start of the strike, the HSPA, in establishing
a strike claims committee, set up funds for "hiring special policemen." With
these funds, the HSPA paid the government to hire more police for the express
purpose of quelling the strike, all but erasing the line between corporate interests and the state.[130] On Oʻahu, more than 100 special police officers were hired.
On Kauaʻi, 110 would be paid off at the end of 1924. On the Big Island, the number on active duty reached over 300. At the strike's peak in Lāhainā, Maui, 107

police officers patrolled 600 strikers; at one particularly absurd point, 95 kept watch over 230 strikers (Reinecke 1996:36).[131] Two rather uneventful weeks into the strike on O'ahu, the executive secretary of the HSPA sent out a directive to the plantations on the outer islands, ordering that "arms, ammunition, belts, badges, etc. which are able to be recovered and salvaged will be brought out to Honolulu, put in condition for use and ready for immediate distribution, if necessity should arise."[132] Two days before the directive, the HSPA had assessed each plantation 40¢ for each ton of the average produced for the years 1921 to 1923 to pay the premiums for insurance against arson and violence (Beechert 1985:220).

A comparison to the 1920 strike highlights the specifically anti-Filipino racism structuring the foregoing frantic preparation for physical violence. As bitter and contentious as it had been, the earlier strike had not prompted a comparable call to arms, even with Filipinos as major participants. In 1920, Filipino strikers had not drawn the bellicose response they would four years later, presumably because they had been thought to be "mere catspaws" under the firm, if misguided, control of the Japanese (Duus 1999; Jung 1999). In 1924, the HSPA and the territorial government themselves took on the task of disciplining Filipino strikers and their supposedly "primitive temperament" (Porteus and Babcock 1926:65).

As noted in the previous chapter, the arms buildup in anticipation of violence was a self-fulfilling prophecy that culminated in the Hanapēpē Massacre. Not only the Filipino workers themselves but even those on the industry's side would, much later, fault the police: "It wasn't a real battle, it was a slaughter really."[133] At the time, however, the killing of sixteen strikers by the police failed to elicit scrutiny, much less censure. Instead, scores of strikers were arrested, tried, convicted, and imprisoned; many were also deported. The police violence against Filipinos simply did not raise questions of legitimacy. For the haole elite and, as far as is known, the public at large, the massacre only served to confirm preexisting beliefs about Filipinos.[134]

As suggested by the absence of Japanese workers in the 1924 effort, an enduring consequence of the 1920 strike was the hasty splintering of the labor movement. If the politics of Japanese and Filipino workers coincided for the duration of that strike, they quickly diverged afterward. The workers' defeat and the employers' seemingly unshaken antiunion posture dashed any hopes of sustaining the interracial coalition that was weak from the start. Even after overhauling its leadership, the Japanese union quickly fell out of favor with its constituency and never recovered (Duus 1999). For the better part of the next two decades, the Japanese on the plantations stayed clear of the labor movement. In contrast, Filipino workers went on to organize the 1924 strike and, later, to reignite the labor movement in the 1930s.

Americanizing Labor in Interwar Hawai'i

The divergence between Japanese and Filipino workers had a number of causes beyond the 1920 strike. They did not share the same structural position in the plantation economy. Filipinos were relegated to the most labor-intensive, unskilled jobs, while the Japanese could increasingly be found in supervisory, skilled, and semiskilled positions; even among the unskilled, the Japanese were more likely to benefit from the plantations' effort to rely less on lunas, who caused much discontent among workers, through the use of short-term and long-term contracts (Beechert 1985).[135] The Japanese were also increasingly leaving the plantation economy, resulting in the number of nonplantation workers equaling the number of plantation workers by 1920 (Tamura 1994:211). Foreseeing a limited future on the plantations for themselves and their children, they left to join the ranks of the petty bourgeoisie, nonplantation skilled labor, and independent farmers (Lind 1946:17). More circumscribed in their opportunities, Filipinos remained overwhelmingly tied to the plantation economy as unskilled labor. Compared to 30.0 percent of the Japanese, 76.5 percent of the Filipinos in Hawai'i were living on sugar plantations in 1928.[136] Similarly, while Japanese made up 29 percent, Filipinos constituted 57 percent of all pineapple plantation workers in 1939 (USBLS 1940:86). At the same time, having migrated earlier and with a higher proportion of women, the Japanese were fast becoming a second-generation population and consequently a citizen population, while the more recently arrived and more male Filipino population continued to be disenfranchised. By 1920, 44.5 percent of the Japanese were already Hawai'i-born, and 58.2 percent were by 1930. Only 11.2 percent of the Filipinos were Hawai'i-born in 1920, and just 16.6 percent ten years later (Lind 1938b:120).

Though certainly significant, the various differences in and of themselves do not sufficiently explain the interwar racial division between Japanese and Filipino workers. After all, the differences largely persisted into the 1940s, when an interracial working-class movement took shape. Moreover, why did the remaining Japanese workers, but not Filipino workers, leave the labor movement? How did the growing number of nisei figure into the division?

The ubiquitous anti-Japanese Americanization movement proved to be decisive in deterring Japanese involvement in the labor movement. Although the conclusion of World War I ushered in a period of nativist American nationalism throughout the United States, Hawaii's version was unique in its single-minded focus on the Japanese (Weinberg 1967). From the mid-1920s onward, the primary target of the Americanization movement shifted from the *issei* to the nisei.[137] If the issei's anti-Americanism was taken for granted by the haole elite, the nisei's national allegiance appeared more pliable, if never above suspicion. Thoroughly melding race, class, and nation, as evidenced during the 1920 strike, the haole-led movement effectively narrowed the range of politics in which the Japanese could engage, leading the increasingly nisei citizen popula-tion away from class conflict and toward assimilationist politics.

In the name of Americanization, Japanese newspapers, Japanese language schools, and virtually anything else Japanese came under intensified attack after the 1920 strike, resulting in a series of territorial laws regulating their operations (Harada 1927; Kotani 1985; Monobe 2004; Nomura 1987; Odo 2004; Okihiro 1991). With the number of registered Japanese voters increasing from 658 in 1920 to 27,107 in 1940, constituting the largest racial group of voters, vot-ing behavior of the nisei was also carefully monitored, and any deviations from the haole elite's Republican politics were construed as racially motivated and anti-American. For the most part, the nisei did not deviate, but this had little mitigating effect on the continuing stream of accusations of anti-Americanism (Kotani 1985:131; Lind 1980:99–102). Their dual citizenship, the default status resulting from the principle of *jus sanguinis* governing Japanese citizenship and the principle of *jus soli* governing U.S. citizenship, drew intense scrutiny and calls for expatriation (Odo 2004; Wakukawa 1938).[138] While the assimilation of the Japanese was the purported goal of the Americanization movement, its ideology was also adapted to segregate public schools racially. Haole parents who could not afford to send their children to elite private schools success-fully mobilized to set up publicly funded "English standard schools," thereby preserving the "pure Americanism" of haole children (Okihiro 1991:139–140; see also Tamura 1994). At the first of these schools, only 19 Japanese children passed the English standard examination compared to 572 haole children for the first year, replicating the racial segregation pattern of Hawaii's elite private schools (Fuchs 1961:276–277).[139]

With the racially charged 1920 strike as the backdrop, issues concerning Americanization rapidly supplanted worker-led movements as the focal point of Japanese politics in the interwar period. Indicative of this sea change, the Japanese union spent its last gasps on proposing to Americanize itself with the plantations' support. The planters declined, seeing no role for unions in their vision of Americanization.[140] For the haole planters, who along with other haole "thought of themselves as the only real Americans in Hawaii" (Reinecke 1979:19), a central aspect of "Americanizing" the sugar industry was to induce the nisei to stay on or head back to the plantations as loyal, tractable workers. In the mid-1920s, confronted with declining numbers of Japanese workers, the planters began to voice concerns about the "rising generation" of Japanese who "show[ed] no inclination of returning to the soil."[141] Such concerns grew more urgent toward the end of the 1920s, as exclusion movements in the metropole continually placed their only outside source of labor from the Philippines "in jeopardy."[142]

The annual Conferences of New Americans, organized by the Reverend Takie Okumura and his son Umetaro, fervent advocates of assimilation, and supported by the HSPA and other like-minded haole and Japanese (Kotani 1985; Monobe 2004; Okihiro 1991), embodied the planters' interfused interests in nisei Americanization and nisei labor.[143] If the Okumuras and other Japanese elite had a slightly ulterior objective at the start—envisaging independent farming rather than plantation work as the nisei's route to Americanization—it would perish with the Depression (Monobe 2004).[144] Presumably representing "old Americans," invited haole speakers from industry, government, military, and education lectured the gathered "new Americans"—nisei delegates assembled from throughout Hawai'i—on how to be properly American and propagated their "back-to-the-soil" message.[145] Both explicitly and implicitly cooperating with the islands' agricultural industries, Hawaii's public schools conveyed the same message.[146] Sounding a note that would be heard continually for the next two decades, the superintendent for public instruction opined in 1919, "The mass of Hawaii's population must be trained to live successfully and happily in the country; to earn their living through agriculture, and to develop a self-respecting citizenry on the land."[147] Producing the next generation of plantation laborers and stamping out middle-class ambitions were, quite explicitly, the principal objectives of Hawaii's schools in the interwar period (Glenn 2002:229–231; Okihiro 1991:ch. 7; Tamura 1994:ch. 6).

Initially, certain segments of the Japanese community criticized the planters' "back-to-the-soil" message, rejecting the idea that the nisei should temper their middle-class aspirations and rightly viewing the plantations as not giving them an equal opportunity to reach the higher echelons of management.[148] As the Depression and unemployment took hold, however, criticisms eventually gave way to endorsement.[149] While the pineapple industry—producing what was considered a luxury fruit—was crippled in the early 1930s and dramatically reduced its labor force, the sugar industry was relatively unscathed and continued to encourage the nisei to look to it for employment. Initially focused on unemployed citizens, the industry expanded its hiring program and guaranteed jobs to "all youths who leave school for work on our plantations."[150] Faced with shrinking opportunities in other industries, the nisei turned to the sugar industry in growing numbers. The percentage of "citizen" sugar workers jumped from about 13 percent in January 1931 to over 32 percent in January 1937 to 45 percent in 1939.[151] Among Japanese workers, citizens outnumbered noncitizens by 1937 (Okahata and PCUJSH 1971:249).[152]

The always laden category "citizen" underwent a semantic transformation in the late 1920s and 1930s. The Japanese had hitherto been excluded from the category, which had long been defined in opposition to "cheap labor." "Citizen" had referred simultaneously, and without much ambiguity, to formal membership in the U.S. nation-state and to informal membership in the "American" nation. Racially discriminatory naturalization law had barred the Japanese from the former, and racialization as an anti-American "race" had kept them out of the latter. The rising number and maturation of nisei unsettled this iso-morphism. The planters, and other haole, were forced to recognize and deal with the fact that the nisei were U.S. citizens by birth, even as they denied or at least doubted the possibility of the nisei being fully acceptable as Americans. Hence, the planters began to regard and refer to the nisei as "citizens," acknowledging their legal status and also their distinction from the issei and, as will be discussed later, the Filipinos. At the same time, the category's ambiguity in relation to the nation—that one could legally be a U.S. citizen without *really* being an American—allowed for the continued racialization of the Japanese, issei and nisei alike, as anti-American. For the haole elite, the fact that the nisei had citizenship rights, including the franchise, made them seem in some ways potentially more dangerous than the issei, requiring vigilant Americanization (Harada 1927:10; Odo 2004:70; Okihiro 1991:138).

On the plantations, vigilance entailed close surveillance of the transformed "citizen" category.[153] Starting in 1928, the HSPA carried out an annual census on all its member plantations, collecting information on the number of men, women, and children by race, island, marital status, housing type, and so on. After the 1930 census, the HSPA began to collect systematic data on the citizenship status of its labor force.[154] In doing so, it delineated explicit conceptual distinctions between race, nation, and citizenship, unintentionally betraying their implicit imbrications. On the first page of the census reports for 1928, 1929, and 1930, there was a point of clarification for readers: "Note: Grouping is racial, not by citizenship." In relation to "Japanese," "Filipino," "Chinese," "Korean," "Porto Rican," "Portuguese," "Hawaiian," and "All Other Races," the note indicated that people in these categories could in fact be U.S. citizens. The one final "grouping" made this note more necessary but also more confusing: the racial category for haole was "Americans," which, in all probability, included non–U.S. citizens.[155] As the HSPA intensified and found more success in the recruitment of nisei and, secondarily, other citizen labor, interest in citizenship became more overt with the 1931 census. "Racial Ancestry" information was still collected, but each of the categories was subdivided into "Citizens" and "Non Citizens." The only "ancestry" category to change its label as a result of adding citizenship information was that of haole, who became "Anglo Saxon."[156] Other HSPA forms went through similar modifications that embodied the planters' increasing fixation on the "citizen" category and also their attempts to disentangle race, nation, and citizenship.[157]

The Americanization movement on the plantations had an indirect but dire effect on Filipino workers. In relation to the U.S. state, Filipinos were, until the Tydings-McDuffie Act, legally "nationals," which permitted their migration within the U.S. empire but did not confer rights of U.S. citizenship. In relation to the "American" nation, Filipinos were unmistakably excluded. But, unlike the Japanese, Filipinos were not perceived by haole and others as an imperialist threat and therefore escaped the scrutinizing and reformist gaze of the Americanization movement. They were seen as simply "un-American," not "anti-American." They were also unquestioningly categorized as an inferior people whose natural place was at the bottom of the racial order. Always considered "cheap labor," Filipinos were now singularly synonymous with it and would remain so into the postwar period. That they were employed exclusively as unskilled labor and were not seriously considered for advancement into higher positions hardly needed to be justified, which was made acutely obvious during the Depression.

As the pressure of unemployment mounted, the sugar and pineapple industries targeted Filipino workers as the release valve.[158] For its part in dealing with the territory's growing unemployment problem, the HSPA repatriated 11,670 workers to the Philippines between October 1931 and February 1934. As William Taylor (1935:115) notes, "that this shifted the burdens of unemployment [to the Philippines] interested the planters not at all." Nor were they concerned that the most vulnerable were sent back first and foremost: "any incapacitated, sick or unfit" and "those with large families."[159] In addition to former sugar workers, many of the repatriated were "indigents, mostly being those thrown out of work by the pineapple companies."[160] About 3,100 in that time span fell into this category (Taylor 1935:115).

The unemployment and repatriation of Filipino workers did not result from their lack of seniority on the job, at least not in the sugar industry. With the unquestioned understanding that the Depression's effects should be minimized for "citizens," the Filipino labor force in the industry was reduced, as a matter of explicitly stated policy, at the same time nisei and other citizens were newly hired.[161] For example, a plantation manager on the Big Island reported, "As a matter of policy Honokaa Sugar Co. has accepted all graduates from the local schools, whether we had work for them or not—feeling that they belonged to the plantation and should be given an opportunity to work on completion of their schooling." He added, "Some times we have had to lay off men, after engaging these additional laborers."[162] Filipinos were the ones laid off. Citizens replaced those who completed their current contracts—which "earned" them their HSPA-paid trips back to the Philippines—or who were dismissed from their jobs for being "unsatisfactory" for one reason or another—which made them jobless and, not being "bonafide unemployed," also tripless. The looseness with which plantations dismissed Filipino workers exacerbated an already discriminatory practice, which the HSPA admitted to itself at one point.[163] Even among "satisfactory" Filipino workers, the HSPA and the plantations could afford to be extremely selective, given the surplus of "hale, able-bodied and industrious" Filipinos without employment.[164] Later, figuring that the direct costs of repatriation would be "far less expensive" than the indirect costs of "indigent Filipinos" in towns and "undesirables" on the plantations, the HSPA loosened its policy in March 1934 and decided to repatriate any "surplus back to the Philippines."[165]

Of the citizens newly employed, the "largest increase numerically was in men of Japanese descent,"[166] with the Portuguese in second.[167] In the year preceding June 1932, the number of Filipino male workers decreased by 700 while the number of Japanese male workers increased by the same number.[168] A year later, the HSPA reported, "During the period from February 1 to September 30, 1933, a total of 2,600 citizens were newly employed on sugar plantations. During the same period 2,700 Filipino men returned to the Philippine Islands through the Association."[169] Likewise, table 3.2 shows a substantial decline in the number of Filipino workers and a substantial rise in the number of Japanese workers at the 'Ōla'a plantation between 1929 and 1935, along with smaller increases in the number of Portuguese and other workers.

Given limited numbers of skilled and semiskilled jobs, the HSPA emphasized the need for the newly hired citizens to take up unskilled field work. But, with the unquestioned understanding that "citizens" should be favored, the planters—again as a matter of explicitly stated policy—expedited their advancement, finding it "highly important to place qualified citizens in 'preferred' and semi-skilled jobs wherever possible."[170] As one plantation manager reported in 1932, "Most of our present force of lunas, office assistants, store assistants, scale men, locomotive men and truck drivers, as well as the important positions of machinist, sugar boilers, clarification housemen, and surveyors we have recruited from local boys, mostly of Oriental and Portuguese blood."[171] The "Oriental" category did not include Filipinos. Consequently, Filipino workers who did not lose their jobs found themselves being passed over for promotions and confined to the bottom of the plantation hierarchy. It is telling that a study of Filipino sugar workers in the mid-1930s found no relationship between length of residence in Hawai'i and pay (Wentworth 1941:37). Table 3.3 shows that the odds of skilled employment for the Japanese remained relatively stable as their overall numbers were augmented with inexperienced workers, while Filipinos continued to be grossly underrepresented.

Not despite, but partly because of, the racism they faced themselves, the Japanese were not merely passive observers in the marginalization of Filipinos. Ensnared in the discourse of Americanism, most Japanese shared with haole and others the assumption that citizenship should entail privileges. But, unlike the dominant discourse that produced and played on the ambiguity of the citizen category to cast doubt on the national loyalty of the nisei in spite of their legal status as U.S. citizens, the discourse of the Japanese insisted on the coincidence of national and state belonging in relation to the nisei. At the same time, this discourse set the nisei apart from and above those regarded as clearly not worthy of belonging to the community: the Filipinos. With their racial identity firmly linked to claiming their Americanness, the nisei—"Japanese by race and

Americans by birth and citizenship and nationality"[172]—not only formed a racial identity vis-à-vis haole, who assailed their rightful place in the imagined community of Americans, but also vis-à-vis Filipinos, who were imagined, and at times literally displaced, out of the community. Japanese racial formation during the 1920s and 1930s was a collective project of both longing and rebuffing.

Interwar anti-Filipino discourse of the Japanese did not develop *ex nihilo*. From their initial arrival, the issei had been far from immune to the racial nationalism of modern Japan that impelled its colonial projects. The issei followed, celebrated, and, at times, contributed to Japan's imperial and military exploits.[173] Like the dominant racial discourse in Hawai'i, issei nationalism measured the racial character of nations by the power and status of their corresponding states. As Ernest Wakukawa (1938:167–168) writes,

> Japan's victory over both China and Russia within a brief period of ten years, necessarily raised her prestige and made her power felt in the counsels and contests of the nations. This in turn strengthened the self-confidence and self-respect of the Japanese residents of Hawaii. As subjects of a new world power, they no longer hesitated to assert their just rights in their effort to improve their economic and social status.... The labor disputes and strikes which were quite common in the early years of the twentieth century were largely the concrete expressions of their new consciousness as subjects of one of the first rate powers and of their new outlook on international affairs based on that consciousness.

By this metric, most issei considered as inferior those nations and peoples under Japanese colonial rule, including Okinawans and Koreans, and under the colonial rule of other powers, including Filipinos and Puerto Ricans (Duus 1999; ESOHP and UOAH 1981; Kaneshiro 1999; Kerkvliet 2002; Kotani 1985; Iwata 2003; Odo 2004; Sakamaki 1928; Stephan 1984; Toyoma and Ikeda 1950; Wakukawa 1938; Yamamoto 1976). For example, the Japanese fight against racially discriminatory wages in the 1909 strike was based less on a universalist principle of racial equality than on the conviction that the Japanese should not be considered or treated as racially inferior to the Portuguese or the Puerto Ricans. As Motoyuki Negoro, one of the strike leaders, proclaimed, "We are first-rate nationals [*ittō kokumin*]. Therefore we have the right to demand equal pay with stateless Puerto Ricans and the so-called white laborers of the Portuguese" (as translated and quoted in Iwata 2003:99). Expressed openly in Japanese and muted in English, Japanese nationalism held sway among the issei up to World War II (Iwata 2003; Monobe 2004; Odo 2004; Stephan 1984). In the 1920s and 1930s, racial discourse of the issei was then rearticulated in relation to and, in part, by the nisei, who were less concerned with Japan's place in the world than with their own racially precarious place in Hawai'i. Inflected by different, though overlapping, concerns, Japanese estimations of Filipinos and other "races" none-theless showed striking intergenerational continuity (Masuoka 1931; Odo 2004).

When the HSPA announced its policies of favoring citizens for employment and promotions, *Hawaii Hōchi*—a widely read newspaper that claimed to speak to and for Japanese workers and progressive causes—questioned only the association's sincerity.[174] As in the mainstream press, the negative impact that such policies would have on Filipino workers who were already living and working in Hawai'i was not of vital concern. And, although discussions of citizen labor should logically have marginalized other noncitizen workers, like the issei, only Filipinos were isolated as the category of workers to be defined as "alien," revealing a distinctly racial, as well as paradoxical, logic.[175] As in the past, "citizen" was defined in contradistinction to "cheap labor." For example, later convinced that the entire sugar industry fully supported citizen labor policies, *Nippu Jiji* commented, "We are also happy that sugar plantations are bent on attracting better types of citizen labor with better living and working conditions, and not with the conditions like today's which are fit only for cheap imported labor."[176]

Understandably most evident between the beginning of the Depression and the passage of the Tydings-McDuffie Act, *Hawaii Hōchi* intermittently produced a racist discourse that combined arguments regarding the nisei's and others' prerogatives as American citizens and the Filipinos' inferiority, alienness, and cheap labor:

Filipinos will eagerly avail themselves of every opportunity to grab jobs by under-bidding the citizen labor.... That is the reason that thousands of our own people, Portuguese, Hawaiians, Japanese and Chinese are unable to work.... [They] herd together in little tenement rooms like sardines in a can, living in the barest squalor... [and] save money on wages that would mean starvation to any American.... Things have come to a point where American citizens, born and raised here in what is assumed to be an American community, find that there is not any room for them in their own land because it has been flooded with recruited labor from an alien country!... Filipinos are of an alien race, of a stock that does not fit in with our social system.[177]

Accordingly, when Filipino workers at the Honolulu Plantation Company in 'Aiea walked out briefly in June 1933, *Hawaii Hōchi* took a stand against them, while insisting that the paper "has always supported labor in its rightful demand for a square deal." Applauding the plantation and the police for making "it evident to the agitators that such activities would be dealt with summarily," the editorial continued:

We do not know just what complaints, real or imaginary, the discontented Filipinos claim to have against the plantations. But we do know that this is no time for defiant agitation and threats of strikes or direct action. And we believe that those who assume such an attitude should be promptly deported to the Philippines as undesirable members of our community....Much of the distress due to unemployment and the burden of cost that it places on the community has been due to presence here of a surplus of unwanted Filipinos, many of whom came over at their own expense and on their own initiative. Hawaii is not responsible for their presence and it is certainly bad taste for them to stir up additional trouble that will cause greater inconvenience to the industries of the territory.[178]

Four years later, in reaction to a much larger strike of Filipino workers on Maui and Molokaʻi, *Hawaii Hōchi* again opposed the Filipinos, provoking *Yōen Jihō*, a relatively small Japanese paper with a Marxist orientation, to declare *Hawaii Hōchi*'s position "all wrong" and, given haole's racist claims against the Japanese during the 1920 strike, to point out the irony of its making similar statements.[179] *Yōen Jihō* was, however, taking the minority position of the Japanese community. *Maui Shinbun* advised its readers: "Filipinos in this strike are very peaceful and orderly....But we can not tell what they may do. The best and safest thing is not to go near them, and have nothing to do with them. After sunset, every woman and girl should never go out of the house without a male guardian."[180]

Another Japanese paper saw the strike as an opportunity for nisei workers, observing that the plantations were replacing unskilled positions with machinery necessitating fewer workers overall but more skilled ones.[181] Indeed, since the first decade of the twentieth century, the sugar industry had intensively researched various mechanical means of reducing unskilled manual labor, especially in harvesting, prompted by continual uncertainties of labor supply from abroad. In the late 1920s and 1930s, after years of experimentation, the industry began to find success and "save" labor through mechanization (Beechert 1988, 1989). Regardless of whether the nisei took advantage of the strike in this manner, "citizens," not Filipinos, were in fact the primary beneficiaries of new opportunities in skilled work.[182]

Expressions of Japanese dissociation from Filipinos were not confined to editorial pages. As noted above, anti-Filipino racism was not a marginal phenomenon among the Japanese—issei and nisei alike (Masuoka 1931). Even in a highly publicized forum like the annual Conferences of New Americans, some of the nisei delegates characterized Filipino workers as befitting their lowly status on the plantations and the Japanese as being superior to the Filipinos. One delegate from Wailuku, a sugar plantation on Maui, stated, "We have certain types of work that must be handled by [Filipinos]; we Japanese citizens cannot handle those jobs." He further asserted, "[The Filipinos'] living conditions are not on a par with those of the Japanese....Naturally until the Filipinos improve their conditions or get out[, social distance between the two groups] will be a problem for the Japanese citizens to tackle."[183]

Anti-Filipino discourse of the Japanese resembled anti-Filipino discourse of white workers in the metropole and haole and Portuguese workers in Hawai'i. For example, *New Freedom*—a newspaper that catered to "Caucasian" workers, most likely including Portuguese workers, and purported to be "devoted to progressive democracy" (Chapin 1996:143)—argued for cutting off Filipino migration by similarly counterposing Filipino cheap labor to unemployed citizens. Freely employing colonialist expressions, like "little brown brothers and sisters," the paper suggested an intimate connection between Hawaii's being "flooded" with Filipino workers and their supposedly voluntary propensity to leave the plantations shortly thereafter. While others could not find jobs due to the constant influx of Filipinos, the Filipinos themselves left their jobs to pursue their vices:

> Every week, we are reliably informed, a steamer arrives here bringing from 600 to 2000 Filipinos into this [Honolulu] port. The new arrivals are shipped to the different plantations as fast as transportation can be obtained and in the meantime the tenement houses, the billiard parlors and the "merry-go-rounds,"...are filled to overflowing with Filipinos who have left the plantations after a brief period of work with their wages intact in their pockets—plus what was gained in the gambling dens or cock-fighting pens on the sugar estates.
>
> A generous Congress which prevents our little brown brothers and sisters from landing in California or on the mainland in general offered no objection to having Hawaii flooded with these Asiatics.[184]

Not unexpectedly, then, Filipino workers did not attempt to align themselves with other workers. Hit hardest by the Depression—the first to be laid off in the pineapple industry and cast aside as the Americanization of the sugar industry favored citizens—many of them responded by resurrecting the territory's labor movement, which had been moribund since the 1924 strike. As in that strike, active repression by employers and the state, among other factors, hampered participation and solid organization. Driven into secrecy, the movement also left behind relatively little documentary evidence. But one thing is certain: Filipino workers felt themselves to be uniquely discriminated against in relation to "citizens." Brief strikes on three sugar plantations in June 1933 made this point clear to the employers.[185] Shortly after, the HSPA shared with all the sugar agencies its "analy[sis of] the happenings of the past few days in connection with the so-called strikes or walkouts on Honolulu Plantation, Waialua Agricultural Co., and Waimanalo Plantation":

> It is quite apparent that in each group involved in this walkout or strike, a shaky feeling has grown up that the Filipino is to be discriminated against in favor of the native born citizen.

In one instance, particularly, there was a very fixed view that the plantation was displacing Filipinos with native born and that the Filipinos would get the worst of it in that native born would be given preference and better jobs even where the Filipinos were not actually eliminated.

There was in all instances the feeling that the management was hasty and unjust in its discharge of the Filipinos, which, coupled with the basic favor to citizens, unified the Filipinos to resistance.[186]

The HSPA also reported that lunas in charge of Filipino workers—likely Portuguese or Japanese in most cases—exacerbated the situation: "It has been reported several times from several places that lunas have made remarks to laborers in the tenor of: 'If you don't like your work, get out— there are citizens willing to take your place.' Of course, such an attitude will only breed trouble."[187]

In the same report, the HSPA warned that "the intown [sic] predatory gang of agitators led by the so-called President of the Labor Union, [E. A.] Taok, seized upon the disturbances of the plantations to attempt a more general disturbance and acquisition of leadership."[188] This union had begun to form the year before. Decrying the high rate of unemployment, the high cost of living, and the lack of opportunities, over a thousand Filipinos gathered for a mass protest in Honolulu in 1932, at which there was a public announcement calling for the rebirth of the Filipino Labor Union (Beechert 1985:219), followed by a series of mass meetings.[189]

A vigorous attack by the Big Five subsequently forced the union underground, as it transformed into a secret organization by the name of Vibora Luviminda.[190] "Luviminda"—the nominal contraction of the three main groups of the Philippine Islands: Luzon, Visayas, and Mindanao—suggested racial and national unity among Filipino workers. Also suggestive, "Vibora" was the nickname of the Filipino general Artemio Ricarte, a nationalist who had resolutely resisted U.S. colonization of the Philippines. If the planters had conceived plantation work in Hawai'i as an extension of U.S. colonial rule and political tutelage of Filipinos, Filipino unionists seemed to suggest that their struggle as plantation laborers was an extension of Filipino anticolonial resistance; after all, according to a 1929 U.S. military intelligence report, "it [was] an undisputed fact that the majority of Filipinos in Hawaii [were] in favor of complete independence" of the Philippines.[191] Rounding out this colonial dynamic, and further isolating Filipino labor over the years, were the miniscule Filipino petty bourgeoisie, including clergy and an ever ephemeral press, and a string of colonial state officials from the Philippines investigating labor conditions in Hawai'i. Most of the former received support from and sided with the plantations, and the latter, though variable in their levels of criticism of and collusion with the sugar industry, invariably opposed unionization (ESOHP 1979; Kerkvliet 2002; Lind 1980; Reinecke 1996; Sharma 1984a).

The movement protested Filipinos' being singled out for the worst treatment and "placed the responsibility for the unemployment situation in the Territory of Hawaii upon the sugar barons."[192] In 1933, several months after the three aforementioned strikes, E. A. Taok echoed the strikers' grievances in a letter to the territorial legislature, pointing out how Filipinos "fac[ed] a miserable condition due to the fact that they [were] not citizens."[193] Later, he wrote to the president of the Philippine Senate that Filipinos in Hawai'i were "all the time subject of discrimination" and were treated worse than other groups.[194] At a meeting on the island of Hawai'i, an organizer spoke to the same theme: "The plantations should not treat the Filipinos lower than the other laborers, because we are just as good as they are."[195] Among the specific lower treatments, Filipino workers cited lack of promotions, poor housing, and discrimination in law enforcement.[196] Representing the unemployed as well as plantation laborers, the union demanded "employment or repatriation" from the HSPA for the former; they were the "un-bona fide" unemployed for whose plight the HSPA denied any responsibility at the time.[197] The isolation of Filipinos as *the* expendable "cheap labor" led the movement to build "an organization leaded [sic] by the Filipinos and not the other races."[198] Explaining why they needed to join an exclusively Filipino union, an organizer received applause of approval from the workers when he averred, "We Filipinos are capable of organizing our own union without the help of others.... There are many Managers who treat the Filipinos different from others. Why can't these Managers treat us right, when we are just as good as the other nationalities. These people are treating us like mules."[199]

In 1937, Vibora Luviminda went out on strike on a Maui sugar plantation; the action later escalated into a general strike of Filipino sugar and pineapple workers on Maui and Moloka'i. It ended with minimal material gains for the workers. The strike nevertheless served as a significant point of transition and transformation for the labor movement in Hawai'i. Vibora Luviminda became the first plantation union to obtain a negotiated settlement. And it had found novel allies during the strike: the National Labor Relations Board and the organizers of what would become the ILWU. Not only the last racial strike, as it is often reductively portrayed, the 1937 strike of Filipino sugar and pineapple workers was also a precursor of the interracial movement that followed.

4

Shifting Terrains of the New Deal and World War II

FROM THE WORKERS' vantage point before World War II, the present state and future prospects of Hawaii's labor movement appeared rather bleak. From the last quarter of the nineteenth century to the 1930s, they witnessed the Big Five sugar agencies obtaining ownership and management control of the sugar industry. Spurred by this concentration of capital, the Big Five also organized the industry into a cohesive, cooperative association, the Hawaiian Sugar Planters' Association (HSPA). When workers began to build a labor movement following the abolition of penal contract labor in 1900, they were continually met by the combined opposition of the Big Five and their plantations, which—emboldened by their organized strength and aided by the repressive mechanisms of the territorial government—sought to stamp out, rather than accommodate, organized labor. Even though strikes caused substantial losses to the industry over the years, the employers adhered steadfastly to their uncompromising stance, with inarguable success.

Having established themselves in Hawaii's largest basic industry, the Big Five extended their holdings to numerous other industries, most importantly to shipping and pineapple. Not surprisingly, employers in these industries proceeded to adopt the antiunion position of their elder corporate siblings. As the soon-to-be appointed CIO director of Hawai'i wrote in 1937, "Since annexation days ([year] 1900) up to the latter part of 1935, the territory of Hawaii was as viciously and completely anti-union as the company controlled steel towns or certain regions of the deep south. The oligarchy of shipping, sugar, and pineapple interests known as the 'big 5' frowned on the idea of labor unions and ruthlessly exerted dictatorial powers to eradicate any semblance of organization among island workers."[1]

The U.S. entry into World War II did nothing to ameliorate the dismal situation of labor in Hawai'i. The initial impact of the war on labor unions in Hawai'i was quite different from its impact on labor unions in the metropole, including the ILWU on the West Coast. Assessing the general predicament of organized labor in 1944, a frustrated group of unionists observed accurately, "While on the mainland the past two years have been a period of phenomenal growth in union membership, the number of active union members in Hawaii today is probably less than it was on the eve of Pearl Harbor."[2] This difference derived from the imposition of martial law in Hawai'i that placed tight strictures on labor and effectively halted union activities for the better part of the war.

In view of these developments, Hawai'i seemed to offer an improbable setting for the large-scale interracial labor movement of the mid and late 1940s. Its estimated membership of 900 frozen and declining from the beginning of the war to the end of martial law in 1944, the ILWU ballooned to over 33,000 members by 1946, accounting for almost the entire union membership in the islands (McElrath 1946:17; Schmitt 1977:138). As the U.S. Department of Labor (USBLS 1948:188) reported, "Until 1944 Hawaii was one of the least organized areas in the United States, but within 2 years it had become one of the most highly organized areas."

Although this upsurge in working-class mobilization at the tail end of and immediately after the war may have been sudden, it was not, in retrospect, inexplicable. Beneath the seemingly unperturbed surface of employer dominance and labor suppression, significant but largely unregistered changes took place from the mid-1930s to the mid-1940s that facilitated the post–martial law organization of workers into one militant, interracial union. In other words, the "overnight" success of Hawaii's working-class movement had long been in the making, which is the focus of this chapter.

In the language of the literature on social movements, "mobilizing structures" and "political opportunities" available to Hawaii's workers were reconfigured from the mid-1930s to World War II (McAdam, McCarthy, and Zald 1996). Later than in the metropole, the New Deal era arrived, providing Hawaii's workers with both access to new mobilizing structures and wider political opportunities. Hawaii's labor movement became "de-isolated," as local unions grew institutionally tied to unions in the metropole, most significantly the ILWU. Meanwhile, the passage of the National Labor Relations Act (Wagner Act) and its enforcement by the National Labor Relations Board (NLRB) gave workers a measure of protection from the employers' most egregious antiunion tactics for a time, until the enactment of the Taft-Hartley Act.

Though it stalled these promising developments, the imposition of martial law during World War II, specifically its strict controls on labor, also created a breeding ground for worker discontent. Advised by employers, the military government shut most workers, especially plantation workers, out of lucrative opportunities in the defense industry and throttled union activities. Like the period of indentured labor, the period of martial law proved to be a time of festering worker grievances and latent class conflict, and like the effect of the abolition of indentured labor, the relaxation of military restrictions re-expanded political opportunities and had the effect of unleashing and pushing workers toward unionization.

Those familiar with the literature on Hawaii's labor history may recognize that numerous authors have suggested broadly similar arguments over the years: the significance of the Wagner Act and the ILWU/CIO to the rebirth of Hawaii's labor movement and the significance of martial law in "readying" the workers for the rapid postwar mobilization. But most previous studies have not ventured much beyond these general statements and are alarmingly scant on evidence.[3] They do not probe in depth or offer evidence for how the ILWU/CIO's network of unions and organizers spread in Hawai'i; how employers and unions interpreted, mediated, and interacted with the NLRB; how far-reaching, or limited, the effects of the NLRB's enforcement of the Wagner Act were in regulating labor relations; how the ILWU/CIO's slow prewar organizing prefigured its rapid post–martial law organizing; how the workers' discontent grew under martial law; and why they directed that discontent toward the employers. Therefore, this chapter specifies and traces the processes through which class relations were qualitatively transformed from the mid-1930s to the mid-1940s.

New Unions and New Law

Discussing class capacities, Göran Therborn (1983:46–47) argues that the relative strength of the capitalist class—and concomitantly, the relative weakness of the working class—depends, in part, on capital concentration and on a "friendly" state "directly centralized into [the capitalist class's] own hands within an otherwise weak state structure." Higher levels of the former enable the capitalist class to marshal its resources against workers, and the latter "allows the capitalist class to pursue its opposition to the workers unfettered." Therborn suggests that the class capacities of workers and capitalists also depend partly on the degree of "isolation" from possible allies. He is concerned with the propensity of the other classes in a given society (e.g., peasantry, petty bourgeoisie) to become the workers' allies against the capitalists—or, inversely, become the capitalists' allies against the workers.

In this section, my main argument is that during the latter half of the 1930s, the class capacity of Hawaii's workers in relation to their Big Five employers grew significantly in two principal ways: metropolitan state intervention and de-isolation. First, up to the mid-1930s, the Big Five's concentrated stranglehold on Hawaii's economy was facilitated by a "friendly" government: Hawaii's

territorial government intervened consistently on behalf of powerful employers and against workers, most of whom were either disenfranchised or, in the
case of the nisei and the Portuguese, pressured by the haole elite into Republican consent (Fuchs 1961:179–181). There were virtually no countervailing state
mechanisms to temper the employers' aggressive antiunion tactics: "Every
previous attempt to organize has been broken—mostly with the aid of the
[territorial] Government."[4]

But, while capital remained concentrated in the hands of the Big Five, the
role of the state took a decided turn beginning in the mid-1930s, as the metropolitan state veered from its previously laissez-faire course. The metropolitan
state had had little presence in mediating class relations in Hawai'i: aside from
intermittent congressional hearings on immigration restrictions and periodic
reports produced by the Department of Labor and its predecessor Department
of Commerce and Labor, it had basically left the islands' employers and the territorial government to their own devices. However, with the passage of New
Deal legislation, most notably the Wagner Act in 1935, the metropolitan state
took a decisive step toward intervening in class relations, even in the remote
colony of Hawai'i, curbing the rampant abuses of employers and enabling
workers to confront them on a less skewed field of struggle.

Second, neither before nor after the 1930s did "isolation," as conceived by
Therborn, play a significant role in the formation of Hawaii's working class;
there is little historical evidence to suggest that the other classes in Hawai'i,
which were relatively small due to the islands' narrow economy, were consistent or important allies to either employers or workers. However, I propose
that Therborn's notion of isolation, if expanded, can still be useful in analyzing
Hawaii's workers. Because he treats societies—nation-states, in his analysis—as
discrete, independent, and comparable cases, Therborn considers working-
class isolation in terms of *intrasocietal* class allies. He does not explore the possibilities of allies from without. Extending his discussion, I propose that the
class capacity of workers depends partly on their degree of "isolation" from
potential allies from outside their "society."

During the second half of the 1930s, Hawaii's workers became *de-isolated*
and formed lasting institutional ties to the resurgent labor movement on the
U.S. West Coast. As seen in the preceding chapters, only the longshoremen,
who had belonged to the short-lived International Longshoremen's Association
(ILA) locals during the first two decades of the twentieth century, had had formal links to labor unions or other possible allies on the continent. And even
they had had a tenuous existence and had received little support through their
affiliation. In any case, the ILA, both in Hawai'i and on the West Coast, all but
disappeared during the 1920s and early 1930s, replaced by company unions and
the shape-up. But, through the establishment of ties to West Coast maritime
workers, Hawaii's workers gained access to limited but vital support in the early

stages of unionization in the late 1930s and to expanded, full-fledged support during the formative struggles of the 1940s.

Though not immediately resulting in a dramatic increase in the number of union members in sugar, pineapple, and stevedoring, the two changes—the intervention of the metropolitan state and the de-isolation of Hawai'i's workers—enlarged the class capacity of workers to mobilize collectively and thereby transformed the field on which class conflict would henceforth take place. In other words, these less visible developments of the late 1930s set the stage for the more visible and dramatic developments of the 1940s.

Some Hope for a Victory

Even in the 1920s and 1930s, when independent unionism languished both in Hawai'i and on the West Coast, the constant shipping traffic circulated news, ideas, and workers across the ocean. So it was not surprising that a sizable number of maritime workers from Hawai'i actively participated in the revitalized labor movement on the West Coast in the 1930s, including the historic, bloody 1934 strike in San Francisco. Attesting to their active involvement, workers from Hawai'i gained, according to one account, the reputation of being the "toughest" on the waterfront in "going after scabs."[5]

Sparked by this explosive activism on the West Coast, especially the revival and radicalization of the Pacific Coast District of the ILA (PCD), many of the participants returned to Hawai'i to catalyze its inert labor movement; given their high numbers in the maritime industry since the nineteenth century, they were disproportionately Hawaiian. In relation to received historical narratives, these returnees dispel, from the outset, the deeply held misconception that labor radicalism in Hawai'i was a "foreign" and haole concept (Beechert 1985; Puette 1988). They were soon joined by other participants of the West Coast movement, who passed through or relocated in Hawai'i.[6]

Among those originally from Hawai'i were two seamen, Harry Kamoku and Levi Kealoha, who returned to organize longshoremen (Beechert 1985:255). From them and a number of others grew interwoven networks of organizers and unions that would eventually spread throughout the islands. As two early converts to his organizing mission on the Hilo waterfront recalled, Kamoku arrived on the Big Island in 1935 after having "lived through the rough days on the Mainland," including the 1934 strike, and having "learned a lot."[7] "Preaching labor union to the longshoremen . . . [and telling] them what unions were doing for the people on the Mainland,"[8] Kamoku "started to organize the longshoremen with the blessings of the Mainland people" (i.e., PCD).[9] With Kamoku and Harry Kealoha, Levi's cousin and another returning seaman, assuming leadership positions in Hilo and Honolulu, respectively, the newly formed Hilo Longshoremen's Association (HiLA) and Honolulu Longshoremen's

Association (HoLA) applied for ILA charters in 1935 to formalize their ties to the West Coast longshoremen.

In this way, returning seamen who turned to longshoring established the initial link between Hawaii's longshoremen and their West Coast counterparts.[10] The influence of sailors on Hawaii's longshoremen continued, as the new unions received support from their fellow maritime unions, most notably the Sailors' Union of the Pacific (SUP). Established in 1935 for seamen circulating through the islands, the SUP union hall in Honolulu became the central hub for much of the labor organizing that took place in Hawai'i in the next two years.[11] As SUP's business agent in Hawai'i, Maxie Weisbarth, a part-Hawaiian, was pivotal in these early years as coordinator, receiving news and requests for organizing assistance from throughout the islands and dispatching any available organizers and other aid to those locales.[12] One such organizer was Jack Hall, another sailor who had participated in the 1934 strike and moved to Hawai'i in 1935. Speaking as the regional director of the ILWU in 1955, Hall recalled:

> Twenty Labor Days have passed in the history of these islands since a small group of American seamen, fresh from the great 1934 maritime strike, came off the ships, joined a few courageous workers and their friends to take on the seemingly impossible task of changing Hawaii from a feudal community.... I had the good fortune to be one of those seamen who piled off the ships—young, eager and optimistic enough to believe that if American seamen could overcome all of the obstacles that faced them in 1934, then the same job could be done for Hawaii's workers.[13]

For the fledgling longshore unions in Hilo and Honolulu, connection to the reinvigorated and radical PCD represented the prospect of external support in myriad forms. It implied financial help, technical expertise, and backing of fellow longshoremen, particularly in cases of labor actions. In addition to these material resources, it held the larger promise of being part of a progressive, militant working-class movement.[14]

Although the two longshore unions' eagerness to become ILA locals was almost palpable, institutionalizing the linkage did not proceed smoothly. The Honolulu and Hilo Longshoremen's Associations did not receive the ILA charters they applied for in 1935—not immediately and, as it would turn out, not ever.[15] Their applications were ensnared in a bitter intra-ILA feud between the left-led PCD and the corrupt, conservative International. Because the longshore unions of Hawai'i had been closely aligned with the PCD from their inception, the International of the ILA resisted strengthening the district further by chartering new locals under its aegis.[16]

Despite their continual frustrations in obtaining formal admittance into the ILA, the longshore unions of Hawai'i attempted to demonstrate their solidarity with their Pacific Coast brethren by staging a sympathy strike when a second large-scale strike broke out on the West Coast in 1936.[17] But, not yet tightly organized, particularly in the main port of Honolulu, they were largely ineffectual in shutting down shipping traffic. According to the secretary-treasurer of the HoLA, "when the strike of 1936 was called[,] half of the Longshore workers or two thirds of the Longshoremens [sic] were not organized, and even some of our members did go to work."[18]

Although employer opposition kept many longshoremen out of unions, the ILA's refusal to grant charters was also a contributing, demoralizing factor. Two weeks before the beginning of the strike on October 29, there were approximately 140 "real union longshoremen" in Honolulu, according to the ILA organizer from Seattle reluctantly sent by the International to determine whether the islands' longshore unions should be chartered. When the organizer quickly recommended to ILA president Joseph Ryan that "they are absolutely entitled to be chartered," an additional 300 longshoremen joined the Honolulu union, buoyed by the "possibility of being chartered."[19] However, as Ryan continued to rebuff the union—in the middle of the strike, no less—a "majority of the men . . . elapsed [in their membership] . . . due to the lack of the Charter."[20] Not having the charters "killed the spirit of the members."[21]

In the meantime, the stevedoring firms, especially in Honolulu, had stepped up their antiunion activities. Passed in 1935, the Wagner Act guaranteed workers' right to "self-organization, to form, join, or assist labor organizations, to bargain collectively through representatives of their own choosing, and to engage in concerted activities for the purpose of collective bargaining or other mutual aid or protection."[22] Although Hawaii's labor organizers and workers found optimism in the new law, it held little meaning for the employers initially. Rather than curtailing their antiunion activities and recognizing the workers' right to unionize, the stevedoring firms baldly defied the Wagner Act and escalated their antiunion efforts: "It [was] apparent on the whole record that intimidation and coercion, interference [was] ingrained in the entire longshoremen's situation and that it not only preceded but followed all attempts at organization."[23]

Initially, the stevedoring firms simply fired and blacklisted active union members.[24] Later, in September 1935, the Industrial Association of Hawaii (IAH) was formed, an antiunion organization that sought to "check and eradicate communism [and] radicalism."[25] Frank C. Atherton—the head of Castle & Cooke, the agency that owned Honolulu Stevedores and had the largest stake in Matson Navigation Company, which, in turn, controlled Inter-Island Steam Navigation Company—was among its prominent incorporators. Its members included all of the Big Five, as well as Matson and Inter-Island.[26] Managed by the Castle & Cooke attorney Frank Thompson, with cooperation of the police and military intelligence, the organization identified and intimidated labor activists; earlier in his career, Thompson had been instrumental in carrying out espionage for the HSPA during the 1920 sugar strike.[27] Intimidation tactics included orchestrated acts of violence against suspected union organizers, Weisbarth being one target.[28]

Faced with the employers' open disregard for the Wagner Act, the longshoremen sent two representatives to San Francisco in late August 1936 to file charges with the NLRB on their behalf.[29] With the longshore unions in Hawai'i, as well as the PCD, continuing to exert pressure, the NLRB agreed, in March 1937, to investigate labor conditions on the Honolulu waterfront.[30] Edward J. Eagen, regional director of the NLRB in Seattle, arrived later that month.[31] His investigation began in stevedoring and continued later in sugar, pineapple, and other industries. At the end, he authored a scathing report on the Big Five's fierce antiunionism, at the conclusion of which he recommended the maintenance of NLRB presence. Eagen's wish to have the NLRB "remain in the Islands long enough to convince the Sugar Trust that the Board does intend to enforce the National Labor Relations Act" was heeded, as the board intervened continually in subsequent labor conflicts.[32]

Between April 5 and 29, 1937, the NLRB held its first hearing in the islands to adjudicate the various charges of unfair labor practices filed by the HoLA against the territory's largest stevedoring firm—known successively as Matson Terminals, Castle & Cooke, Honolulu Stevedores, and later as Castle & Cooke Terminals.[33] During the eighteen-day hearing, trial examiner George O. Pratt gathered evidence and heard testimonies concerning the following charges:

> [The company] had refused to bargain collectively with Honolulu Longshoremen's Association. The complaint further alleged that the respondents had at various times during 1936 and 1937 discharged and refused to employ many stevedores, numbering 54 in all, for the reason that said stevedores were members of and had assisted Honolulu Longshoremen's Association. The complaint further charged [the company] with the maintenance and support of a labor organization known as Matson Athletic Club and generally with acts of intimidation, coercion and interference with their employees in their effort to form, join and assist Honolulu Longshoremen's Association.[34]

Exemplifying the employers' disregard of the Wagner Act and the NLRB, Lawrence Judd—IAH president and a former territorial governor of Hawai'i—testified famously at the hearing that he had seen no need for the IAH to attend to the "obey[ing] of the Wagner Act any more than the Desha Bathing Suit Law," a seldom enforced local statute that forbade people from appearing publicly in Honolulu in an uncovered bathing suit.[35] Hawaii's employers were not alone in their defiance. As Melvyn Dubofsky writes, corporations across the United States were advised to ignore NLRB orders by their corporate

lawyers and constitutional law experts, most of whom insisted on the uncon-
stitutionality of the Wagner Act (1994:142; see also Gross 1981; Tomlins 1985;
Zieger 1995).

By the conclusion of the Castle & Cooke hearing, however, Hawaii's employers could no longer be so dismissive. On the sixth day of the hearing, April 12,
the Supreme Court upheld the constitutionality of the Wagner Act and the
operations of the NLRB, confounding not only learned expectations but also
the Court's earlier rulings (Dubofsky 1994:144).[36] On the same day, the *Honolulu
Star-Bulletin* carried the news in two front-page articles, in one of which Eagen
urged all Hawaii's employers to comply with the Wagner Act.[37]

Although he did not feel there was enough evidence for or otherwise did
not agree with some of the longshoremen's charges, NLRB trial examiner Pratt
found, importantly, that Castle & Cooke had indeed violated the Wagner Act
and ordered the company to reinstate, with back pay, eleven union members
unfairly dismissed before or during the 1936 strike.[38] More generally, the trial
examiner concluded that the various "actions of respondent [Castle & Cooke
between 1935 and 1937] . . . were all calculated to instill in the minds of the
longshoremen that a union was not desired, that trouble would follow the organization of such a union; and there is no question that all these things taken
together have had that effect." He further ordered the company to post conspicuous notices informing its workers that it would

1. . . . cease and desist from interfering with, restraining or coercing their employees
in the exercise of the right of self-organizing, to form, to join or assist labor organizations, to bargain collectively with representatives of their own choosing, and
to engage in concerted activities for the purpose of collective bargaining or other
mutual aid of protection.

2. . . . cease and desist from discouraging representation in any labor organization
by discrimination in regard to hire or tenure of employment or any term of condition
of employment.[39]

The hearing marked an unmistakable inflection point in the trajectory of
Hawaii's working class. Both employers and workers perceived the hearing as a
certain harbinger of a fundamental change in their relations. The metropolitan
state intervened actively in local labor relations for the first time, and it would
continue to do so for the next decade. Two years after the law's passage, the
NLRB hearing and ruling on the Castle & Cooke case had finally, as Beechert
(1985:258) notes, "brought the National Labor Relations Act to Hawaii and
served notice on all corporate employers that the law did apply to Hawaii and
workers now had an avenue of appeal."

Though by no means giving up their fight against unions, Hawaii's employers stopped violating the Wagner Act with impunity, signaled by the immediate

dissolution of the notorious IAH.[40] Inversely, union organizers were encouraged by the NLRB's intervention and planned to "launch an extensive unionization program."[41] In a letter to PCD president Harry Bridges, Weisbarth and Edward Berman—editor of the *Voice of Labor*, a small pro-labor paper begun in 1935, and Hawaii's CIO director-to-be—described the qualitative transformation in the "atmosphere" since the NLRB hearing that had concluded only one and a half months prior:

> Now that the hearings of the National Labor Relations Board are over and we have been afforded a breathing spell, I feel that a brief resume of the local situation would be timely. As you may recall . . . the whole Honolulu waterfront was in a pretty sorry state.
>
> But to-day I am happy to report that a completely changed atmosphere exists in this island "paradise." The Labor Board investigation of waterfront conditions and the startling disclosures of attempts to form company unions, of company spy outfits and actual gangster and terroristic methods to curb unionism in Hawaii has been an eye-opener for a lot of our "respectable" citizens. The anti-union forces have temporarily, at least, sneaked back into their hiding places. And the workers, for the first time, have come out into the open.[42]

Quickly after the hearing, key developments in Hilo, Port Allen, and Maui confirmed the fundamental shift in relations between capital and labor that had just taken place.[43] In Hilo, C. Brewer & Company, owner of the port's lone stevedoring outfit, formally recognized the HiLA as the sole and exclusive bargaining representative of its workers. That the Hilo longshore union, and not the one in Honolulu, obtained employer recognition first was not surprising. From the beginning, "there [has been] no doubt the Port of Hilo has [had] the strongest Longshore Union in the Territory."[44] There were many fewer longshoremen in Hilo than in Honolulu for the initial core group of radicalized ex-seamen to organize.[45] For example, in Hilo, C. Brewer & Company employed 170 "regular" longshoremen in 1937. By contrast, in Honolulu, Castle & Cooke alone employed 659 "regular" longshoremen; in fact, McCabe, Hamilton & Renny, Honolulu's second largest stevedoring firm, employed nearly twice as many workers as C. Brewer & Company did in Hilo.[46] Furthermore, the longshore union in Hilo had fewer "casuals" hired through the shape-up with whom to contend. Hilo's longshoremen were also all employed by a single company, C. Brewer & Company. The longshoremen of Honolulu had to deal with three separate hostile employers, Castle & Cooke, McCabe, Hamilton & Renny, and Inter-Island, spreading thin and requiring more of the fledgling union's resources.[47] Finally, as the NLRB hearing against Castle & Cooke intimated, the employers in Honolulu put up more of a fight than did C. Brewer & Company in Hilo. While many similarities in conditions could be found in the two ports, the most virulent forms of antiunionism in Honolulu, like the IAH, were not as prevalent in Hilo.[48]

Beginning in December 1935, a month after it applied for an ILA charter, the HiLA engaged in a series of strikes, usually to restore members who had been unjustly dismissed from their jobs. Each time, the union was effective in tying up a ship or shutting down the port and having the dismissed workers reinstated. Faced with a solid, cohesive union, C. Brewer & Company arrived at an informal agreement with it (Beechert 1985:256). Not comparable to conditions won on the West Coast but remarkable for Hawai'i, the informally negotiated terms of the agreement included an 8-hour day, 60¢ per hour, overtime guidelines including 80¢ per hour, and load restrictions. However, although it settled with the workers, C. Brewer & Company insistently kept the settlement informal and "repeatedly refused to recognize [the union] as a collective body and to sign an agreement."[49]

Strategically capitalizing on the NLRB's arrival in the islands, the HiLA moved quickly to hold an NLRB election, seeking to have the company officially recognize the union as the workers' sole bargaining agent. In an April 23, 1937 response, NLRB representative Eagen wrote that he had been discussing the logistics of the representation election with the officers of C. Brewer & Company in Honolulu. He suggested that the union meet with the company's manager in Hilo and come to an agreement on the list of workers eligible to vote. Eagen proposed that the NLRB then "could hold just a short hearing and stipulate as to most of the facts" before the vote.[50] But on May 5, just six days after the end of the NLRB hearing in Honolulu, C. Brewer & Company decided suddenly not to contest the union in a representation election:

> On the matter of determining representation for collective bargaining purposes among our stevedore employees, it is our opinion that there exists no necessity for such an election at the present time. We are informed and believe that the majority of our stevedore employees are members of the Hilo Longshoremen's Association. With that in mind, we have been bargaining with representatives of that association in all matters covered by the National Labor Relations Act, as well as other matters. . . . If this meets with your [Eagen's] approval, we will agree to continue bargaining in good faith with representatives of the Hilo Longshoremen's Association as the exclusive representative of our stevedore employees as long as we believe that it continues to represent a majority of our employees.[51]

What accounted for this unanticipated decision? Despite the company's denials, the prospect of an NLRB investigation and hearing in Hilo, like the ones in Honolulu, seems to have been the stimulus. The union reasoned that the company's decision "clearly show[ed] that C. Brewer & Co. dislike the National

Labor Relations Board."[52] NLRB representative Eagen concurred: "Labor unions had been unable to make any headway in the Hawaiian Islands prior to the time of the Castle and Cooke hearing. Not a single employer had entered into a contract with a labor union. Subsequent to our hearing [in Honolulu], above referred to, the first employer, C. Brewer and Company, Ltd., recognized the Hilo Longshoremen's Association as the exclusive bargaining agency for its waterfront employes [sic]."[53] Although the recognition would not lead to a signed contract until 1941 or to easy relations between the company and the union, C. Brewer & Company's unexampled recognition of the HiLA affirmed the shifting balance of power induced by the Wagner Act and its enforcement by the NLRB.

Overlapping chronologically with the developments in Hilo, the waterfront of Port Allen, on the island of Kaua'i, furnished further indication that labor relations had entered a distinctly new phase with the arrival of the NLRB. On April 22, 1937, longshoremen in Port Allen went out on strike and shut down the port.[54] At the outset, the action did not differ from other more or less spontaneous strikes of the past. A group of longshoremen at the port's lone stevedoring firm, Kauai Terminal, objected to the company's treatment of an "old-time stevedore supervisor." Employed by the company for more than 25 years, he had recently assumed the "pilot" duties of an ill port captain. But the company's 2 newly appointed acting managers attempted to discharge him of his new duties and replace him with a recently hired tug captain. In support of the apparently popular old-time supervisor, 7 longshoremen formed a strike committee. Going door-to-door to all of the longshoremen's homes, they solicited support for the strike, the principal objective of which would be to have the new managers fired. In the process, the list of strike demands grew to include a wage hike, improved working conditions, secure overtime pay, and free meals after 10 hours of work. Though hastily organized, 95 percent of the workers went out on strike (Izuka 1974:30–32).

Two characteristics set this strike apart from previous ones in Port Allen. For the first time, the strikers reached out for assistance to the maritime unions in Honolulu, likely having heard about the increased union activities and the NLRB hearing there. Up until then, "there had never been any direct contact, [as Port Allen] was more or less a closed plantation community with a port."[55] Not knowing much about the Wagner Act and inexperienced at building a union, Port Allen's strikers sought "expertise." William Makanui, one of the strike organizers, called Weisbarth for help. Upon receiving the phone call, Weisbarth dispatched Hall and George Goto, a *kibei* Communist, to Port Allen; they arrived on the first day of the strike.[56] According to Goto, Weisbarth instructed simply, "You go to Kauai. Port Allen is on strike. Here's the [plane] tickets. Go see what you can do down there."[57] By the second day, the strikers, with the help of Goto and Hall, formed the Port Allen Waterfront Workers Association (PAWWA).[58]

The second characteristic that set the strike apart was the employer's response. Whereas the Big Five-related employers had preferred to ignore independent unions and to quash strikes completely, Kauai Terminal did neither. John Waterhouse—vice president of Alexander & Baldwin, the corporate parent of Kauai Terminal—arrived in Port Allen from Honolulu on the same day as Goto and Hall. With astonishing alacrity, he and the newly formed union agreed on a settlement and signed a contract, the terms of which did not discharge the two acting managers but did increase the workers' wages and establish an eight-hour day. Like C. Brewer & Company in Hilo, Kauai Terminal recognized the PAWWA as the exclusive bargaining agency of the workers.[59]

Deviating from the Big Five's past practices, Alexander & Baldwin recognized, negotiated with, and even signed a nominal contract with an independent union—and quickly. Why? Unlike in Hilo, the NLRB did not have a direct hand in the matter. Nevertheless, circumstantial evidence suggests that, as in Hilo, sidestepping the board's unfriendly gaze was the major impetus.[60] The strike and the settlement overlapped with the end of Castle & Cooke's NLRB hearing in Honolulu and with C. Brewer & Company's dealings with the NLRB in Hilo. Moreover, as discussed later, Alexander & Baldwin itself took a similarly untrodden path in dealing with the Vibora Luviminda strike on Maui at about the same time, in which the NLRB had a more direct presence.

Following the signing of the contract, the PAWWA proceeded to strengthen its ties to the maritime workers in Honolulu, namely the HoLA, and, through this association, to the West Coast longshoremen. Shortly after the strike, on April 28, 1937, George Goto and Jack Hall gave a report to the HoLA on the state of affairs in Port Allen.[61] After a period of informal ties, the PAWWA affiliated formally with the HoLA during the first week of June 1937.[62]

At this time, the PCD was voting to bolt from the conservative ILA and form a separate union that would be affiliated with the CIO. Since none of Hawaii's longshore unions had ever been chartered by the AFL-affiliated ILA and since they had been closely tied to the West Coast from their beginnings, their decisions to join the West Coast longshoremen in organizing a CIO union were foregone conclusions. Even the PAWWA, scarcely a month after its formal affiliation with the HoLA, wrote to the PCD to express its desire to affiliate with the CIO.[63] On October 5, 1937, the PAWWA, along with the Longshoremen's Associations of Hilo and Honolulu, received their charters from the newly formed International Longshoremen's and Warehousemen's Union; the three unions became Locals 1–35, 1–36, and 1–37, respectively. Finally, two long years later than they had expected, Hawaii's longshoremen were formally united with their West Coast counterparts.

Overlapping with the developments in Hilo and Port Allen, another indication of the NLRB's immediate impact involved Vibora Luviminda, the exclusively Filipino union of plantation workers. As discussed in the last chapter, the Filipino Labor Union (FLU) was revived in 1932 in reaction to the uniquely unfair treatment of Filipino workers. Trying to build the union, the FLU's three principal leaders—Antonio Fagel, Epifanio Taok, and the 1924 strike leader Pablo Manlapit—trekked through the four major islands, beginning on Oʻahu and continuing to Hawaiʻi, Maui, and Kauaʻi. Almost immediately, the union faced stiff employer opposition. As in the past, the HSPA and its member plantations used the local police and the courts to have the union leaders arrested, convicted, and imprisoned. On the island of Kauaʻi, in 1934, Fagel was arrested for trespassing and banished to Honolulu for thirteen months, later reduced to five months upon appeal. In 1935, Taok and Manlapit were arrested and convicted on two separate counts related to union dues. Betraying the weaknesses of the cases against them, Taok's conviction was later overturned on appeal, and Manlapit's conviction was won based on testimony of a highly suspect witness who had also been the principal witness in the rigged case against Manlapit in 1924.[64] Not confining its attention to the union's top leadership, the HSPA also cracked down on any "agitators" it identified, routinely discharging and blacklisting them.[65]

To deflect the attention of employers, the FLU became an underground organization, which Fagel renamed Vibora Luviminda.[66] On November 12, 1935, having served out his sentence in Honolulu, Fagel went to Maui and gathered support for the union in secret, but it was nevertheless closely monitored by labor spies. On June 2, 1936, Vibora Luviminda resurfaced and started holding open meetings on public roads, thereby skirting Hawaii's strict trespassing laws (Felipe 1970b:5). On January 2, 1937, Vibora Luviminda held one of these meetings near HC&S, an Alexander & Baldwin plantation in central Maui. The group was violently "dispersed by a gang of company agents" who severely beat Fagel and many of the gathered workers.[67]

Whereas such an incident in the past would have merely faded with time, as no government action would have been taken against the plantation, subsequent turns of events set this one apart. On April 1, 1937, soon after Eagen's arrival in Honolulu, Fagel filed unfair labor practice charges with the NLRB against HC&S, which would eventually lead Eagen to visit Maui.[68] While in Honolulu, Fagel also went to Weisbarth at the SUP union hall for assistance. Weisbarth referred Fagel to Hall and Bill Bailey, a seaman who had taken part in the 1936 maritime strike on the West Coast and was subsequently sent to Hawaiʻi by the Communist Party.[69] Between April 8 and 19, Fagel, Hall, and Bailey held Vibora Luviminda meetings at numerous Maui sugar and pineapple plantations, drawing large, enthusiastic crowds.[70]

On April 20, a day after Bailey and Hall returned to Honolulu, an unplanned strike broke out at HC&S. It began when a group of Filipino cane cutters demanded a pay hike for the harvesting of thick cane they were about to begin and the dismissal of 4 Japanese lunas whom they suspected of cheating them.

Likely emboldened by the momentum Vibora Luviminda had generated in the preceding 2 weeks, the workers refused to back down. Quickly, this confrontation grew to a prolonged strike as most Filipino workers, approximately 1,000 to 1,200, walked out.[71]

Following the familiar script of the sugar industry, the plantation refused to negotiate, funded the hiring of 100 special county deputies, employed strikebreakers, and evicted strike leaders.[72] But this strike also offered unfamiliar plot twists. On May 9, Fagel asked Berman, an elected adviser and member of the HoLA, for assistance. The next day, Berman flew to Maui with Eagen, who had recently concluded the Castle & Cooke hearing in Honolulu; although the NLRB's jurisdictional authority was murky at best, Eagen went to Maui ostensibly to investigate the charge Fagel had filed earlier.[73] Upon arrival, Eagen quickly found, "The Company had refused to meet the union committee, and had taken the position which indicated that it intended to starve the strikers into submission." He contacted and met with HC&S manager Frank Baldwin and his two lawyers and "went over the demands of the union." By the end of the meeting, Eagen had "secured from the manager the first written proposition that has ever been made by a plantation relative to a Filipino strike," or any strike, for that matter.[74] In this "statement of policy," the company relented on some of the strikers' demands, though mostly in noncommittal language. HC&S agreed to increase pay slightly, discharge lunas found to be cheating or mistreating workers, and meet with strike representatives to settle any future grievances or disputes; moreover, the company agreed to fire the newly hired strikebreakers and reconsider the dismissals and evictions of strike leaders. But, not allowed to meet among themselves to discuss the "statement" without the presence of the police or company spies, the strikers voted to reject the offer.[75]

After a month and a half, during which the escalated to involve all five sugar plantations on Maui, the strike ended with another historic precedent: between July 1 and 10, 1937, representatives of the HSPA and the three sugar plantations of central Maui met with the leaders of Vibora Luviminda six times and negotiated a settlement. Both sides signed the agreement on July 15. Fagel subsequently reached nearly identical agreements with the two remaining sugar plantations, and the strikers returned to work on July 17.[76]

In terms of Hawai'i class relations, that the HSPA and the plantations negotiated and settled with a striking union was of far greater significance than the actual terms of the agreement. The workers gained only a slight raise through a new pay scale for cutting and loading cane and the reinstatement of 22 of 26 strike leaders discharged by HC&S. The secretary of the HSPA also agreed to ask the territorial prosecutors for leniency in a pending criminal case against 9 strikers. Critically, the plantations refused to recognize Vibora Luviminda, and accordingly, the union was not even mentioned in the agreement.[77] Glibly, the secretary-treasurer of the HSPA later summarized the agreement in a letter to a Kaua'i sugar plantation manager: "We did not recognize any union, did not yield to any of their numerous propositions of any importance."[78]

But why did HC&S and the other plantations decide to deviate from past practice and negotiate with the strikers at all? A couple of factors stand out, each of which was likely necessary but not sufficient. The strike grew large in scale.[79] The initially small, spontaneous action at HC&S spread throughout Maui and even to the neighboring island of Moloka'i. Between the HC&S strikers' rejection of the company's offer on May 10 and the negotiated settlement in July, Filipino workers staged sympathy strikes at every sugar and pineapple plantation on Maui. At the end of June, 700 pineapple workers at the Libby, McNeill, & Libby plantation on Moloka'i also went out on strike for 3 days.[80]

The size of the strike and its cost implications, however, could not have been enough to convince the HSPA and the plantations to go to the bargaining table for the first time. After all, the strikes of 1909, 1920, and 1924 had been larger, longer, and costlier for the industry.[81] The crucial factor that set this plantation strike apart from all previous ones was the intervention of the NLRB. As seen above, Eagen's appearance on Maui had already provoked an unprecedented reaction from HC&S on May 10; although it had not been willing to negotiate directly with the strikers at that time, the company had not summarily dismissed their demands but had actually addressed them through its proposed "statement of policy."

When the strikers rejected its NLRB-induced overture, the company, with the backing of the HSPA, reverted to its hard-line tactics. After meeting with a representative of the HSPA, HC&S manager Baldwin came to see the strike as a "test for the Hawaii sugar industry."[82] As in the past, the entire industry, not just the struck plantations, would bear the cost of the strike.[83] Thus, on May 19, Baldwin declared firmly that the company's "statement of policy" had been its final offer: HC&S would not be the first domino to fall. He averred, "They [the strikers] can tear down the mill, but I won't give in."[84]

Without damage to the mill, the company's reversion to the hard line did not last. In the end, as described above, the company and the HSPA backed down, met with representatives of the strikers, and negotiated a settlement. In addition to the strike's growing size, the NLRB appears to have played a pivotal role. After the strikers rejected the company's "statement of policy," Berman filed NLRB charges against HC&S and the HSPA for unlawfully interfering with unionization through espionage, control over governmental agencies, and intimidation (Felipe 1970b:13). Eagen found the charges to be "very interesting, and, to [his] knowledge, true and correct." In fact, he saw them as an entry point into investigating "the entire set-up in the Islands" and eventually "break[ing] the backbone of the entire anti-labor set-up and the anti-democratic policies now existing."[85] A month later, on June 26, 1937, the strikers filed NLRB petitions for representation elections at the struck sugar plantations. The petitions asserted that the Wagner Act, though it excluded agricultural workers, applied to the strikers because "a large number" of them worked in the sugar mills and were thus industrial workers.[86] Just five days later, representatives of the HSPA and the three central Maui plantations met with strike leaders for the first time.

On the basis of the preceding evidence, it seems reasonable to infer that the risks of a thorough investigation and/or a representation election conducted by an unfriendly NLRB figured into the sugar industry's calculus. Further supporting the inference, the HSPA, in the month after the strike, conferred with its attorneys and sent out a memo to all sugar plantation managers concerning the and the NLRB. Explaining that unions tended to abuse the law and that the NLRB was prone to place the burden of proof on employers, the memo outlined the precise steps managers should take to forestall such "abuses."[87]

Thus, in a brief four-month span in 1937, from the NLRB's arrival in April to the conclusion of the Vibora Luviminda strike in July, the terms of class struggle in Hawai'i had been indelibly altered. The NLRB hearing on the case brought by the HoLA against Castle & Cooke alerted both employers and workers that the Wagner Act would be enforced in Hawai'i—it was no longer comparable to the Desha Bathing Suit Law. This change was then affirmed quickly by three nearly simultaneous developments involving longshoremen in Hilo and Port Allen and Filipino plantation workers on Maui. Accordingly optimistic about the future of labor in Hawai'i, Berman wrote, in October 1937, "Heretofore, isolated from the mainland, it was very difficult for us to get any action on violations of the Wagner Act, but now with the Labor Board right at hand, organization can move ahead swiftly and the fight against Company Unions, discrimination, intimidation and the 'black-list' is beginning to show some hope for a victory."[88]

Reverses Yet Continued Struggle

The ensuing four years, however, would not fully bear out Berman's optimism: organization was seldom swift, and victories were rarely unambiguous and often punctuated with defeats. On the halting rhythm of progress, a Honolulu longshoreman wrote in 1940, "Since the beginning of organization on the Honolulu waterfront in September of 1937, the history [of ILWU] Local 1–37 (formerly the Honolulu Longshoremen's Association) has been one of reverses, yet, continued struggle in the face of the determined opposition."[89] The interventions of the NLRB in 1937 undoubtedly heralded the beginning of a *new* era in class relations, but they heralded no less the *beginning* of a new era. Although they recognized that their opposition to unions could no longer operate "unfettered," Hawaii's Big Five-related employers were not about to give up.[90]

In Port Allen, almost as soon as the first contract was signed, Kauai Terminal tried promptly to split the union (Izuka 1974:34). When the workers had gone out on strike and initially formed the PAWWA, according to Ichiro Izuka, one of the original members, the "strikers [had] represented all racial groups: Chinese, Hawaiian, Portuguese, Filipino, Koreans, and Japanese" (Izuka 1974:30–31). But, as Hall would later recall, "The company went to work [thereafter] and caused some very serious racial splits."[91] According to a similar account by a PAWWA member, "[By] about the fifteenth of July, 1937, the company succeeded in splitting the union by using racial propaganda and other splitting tactics, such as favoritism. After the split the company backed up its puppet union openly and placed the bona fide union [PAWWA] in danger."[92]

If the PAWWA had started out with widespread, interracial support of the workers, how did this racial split arise? Not unlike the sugar industry during and after the 1920 strike, Kauai Terminal portrayed the PAWWA as a Japanese-dominated organization, drawing on the deeply ingrained racist trope of the Japanese as inherently anti-American and loyal to Japan. The management apparently told the workers that the union was "a Japanese union [and] even said some of the members were Lt. Comdr[s]. in [the] Japanese navy."[93] Subsequently, PAWWA members—including Makanui, one of the organizers of the foundational strike—defected in increasing numbers and formed a separate union that was close to and favored by the company.[94]

According to those who remained in the PAWWA, "the only excuse [the defectors] gave in splitting up the union was because only the Japanese were running the union."[95] Although almost all of its officers were indeed Japanese, the PAWWA's Japanese members seemed somewhat dumbfounded by the criticism, since everyone had voted in the election.[96] But the defectors' *perception* that the Japanese had seized control was made plausible by the racial demographics of the port: a majority of the workers at Kauai Terminal were Japanese. In August 1937, 125 of the company's 223 employees were Japanese; in contrast, there were 35 Filipinos, 5 Hawaiians, and 58 "others."[97]

In an effort to undermine the PAWWA's claim to sole and exclusive bargaining agency, Kauai Terminal "constantly support[ed] the other union. . . . The Company started hiring dozens of new hands and recruiting them into their union in order to gain the majority for that union."[98] Of course, such direct interference by the company, if true, was clearly in violation of the Wagner Act, of which Kauai Terminal was no doubt aware. Consequently, in early 1938, notably after a visit by an NLRB investigator in autumn 1937, Kauai Terminal tried to avoid the appearance of supporting a company union by urging the "puppet union" to affiliate with the Honolulu Waterfront Workers' Association, an AFL-affiliated upstart, which it subsequently did (Izuka 1974:35).[99]

Throughout 1938, Kauai Terminal used this tactic of favoring the newly formed AFL union to undercut ILWU Local 1–35 (successor to the PAWWA).[100]

During the same year, an AFL-ILWU dispute also affected the nearby port of Ahukini, operated by The Lihue Plantation Company, an American Factors sugar plantation. At both Kaua'i ports, the ensuing struggles for majorities were bitterly contested, as the employers favored the AFL unions and the NLRB supported the ILWU. Finally, in early 1940, the ILWU emerged victorious, and the AFL unions faded out of existence.[101] But this victory also proved to be fleeting, as the employers refused to scale back their opposition. In 1940–1941, the two Kaua'i employers and the ILWU clashed again, resulting in a strike that began in Ahukini and spread to Port Allen. With no clear winner, the strike lasted for 298 days, making it the longest in Hawaii's history.[102] As most strikers were Filipino in Ahukini and Japanese in Port Allen, their cooperation did give organizers, like Hall, some hope that interracialism could take hold in Hawai'i (Beechert 1985, 1991; Zalburg 1979).[103]

In Honolulu, the plight of the fledgling longshore union was considerably, albeit expectedly, worse. The April 1937 NLRB hearing had exposed the blatant antiunion practices at Castle & Cooke. But the reaction of Castle & Cooke and the other two stevedoring firms on the Honolulu waterfront—McCabe, Hamilton & Renny and Inter-Island—was not to become immediately accommodating toward the union or the NLRB. The NLRB-ordered reinstatement of eleven union members was momentous, but it was also the only part of the ruling with any real bite.

As a result of the hearing, the stevedoring firms tempered and modified their opposition to the HoLA, as the heavy-handed IAH and company unions soon disappeared. But even before the NLRB had issued its official ruling on the case, Castle & Cooke, along with the other stevedoring firms, reverted to many of its erstwhile practices. As in the past, but not as openly, Castle & Cooke fired and blacklisted workers who were found to be active in promoting the HoLA. A Castle & Cooke longshoreman in 1937, Jack Kawano recalled, "I used to attend [union] meetings regularly, and I was one of those crazy ones that used to stand up in front and participate in job action[s]. And, so it didn't take long before the company got their eye on me and finally got me off the job. . . . I was bringing up too many grievances."[104] Three years later, as the president of ILWU Local 1–37, Kawano continued to witness similar treatment of union members: "The Company, knowing that our membership were increasing, laid off, suspended, and demoted many workers, many of them union members. This situation put a complete stop on our recruiting; even our own members were getting annoyed and demoralized."[105] So while the threat of being physically intimidated may have receded with the NLRB and the dissolution of the IAH, Honolulu's longshoremen continued to fear antiunion discrimination.[106] Moreover, as in the past, the shape-up and the sheer size of the "casual" work force in Honolulu rendered these fears more acute. Hence, as a historian of the ILWU notes, membership in the union fluctuated wildly: "the longshoremen were afraid to join a union . . . sign[ing] up one week and dropp[ing] out the next" (Zalburg 1979:16).[107]

The threat of loss of employment was, as in the past, coupled with paternalistic measures: "At the present time [in 1939], the weakest spot in the Islands is the port of Honolulu. . . . Intimidation of workers, threats and the inevitable blacklists are still the weapons being used to keep the workers apart. Company paternalism is another weapon employed to defeat unionism."[108] Before the NLRB hearing, in response to the formation of the HoLA in fall 1935, Castle & Cooke had passed out turkeys to all of its employees on Christmas and had paid them bonuses, "which had not been done for some years." Two months later, in February 1936, the company had institutionalized its paternalism and formed a "Personnel Department which would handle recreation and other personnel work."[109] Although it acknowledged that the company, through such tactics, had been aiming to lure the workers away from the union and that the union membership had declined as a result, the NLRB hearing in 1937 did not find these activities to be in legal violation of the Wagner Act. Consequently, a year later, ILWU Local 1–37 found that the "Company [Castle & Cooke] through the Personnel Department [was still] doing everything in their power to discredit and discourage Unionism in Honolulu."[110] Without many details, Local 1–37 reported, in 1938, that McCabe, Hamilton & Renny was likewise "spend[ing] a lot of money to break unions and to keep the men from joining the ILWU."[111]

As mentioned earlier, in anticipation of Hawaii's already existing longshore unions' imminent affiliation with the CIO, an AFL longshore union by the name of the Honolulu Waterfront Workers' Association (HWWA) was organized in July 1937. Whether the Honolulu stevedoring firms had a direct hand in the HWWA or not, it was clear to the longshoremen that the new union was favored by the employers and was undermining the HoLA's efforts. One HoLA member explained, "Several of the 'Big Five,' knowing that unions in Hawaii can't be prevented, are trying to use Ryan's AFL charter to wreck the CIO movement. If they succeed, it will be Company Union under the guise of the so-called AFL 'industrial' charter."[112] In an effort to steer longshoremen toward the HWWA and away from the HoLA/ILWU, Inter-Island preemptively recognized the former as the bargaining agent of its longshoremen. Despite such company interference, the ILWU eventually prevailed at Inter-Island, as it decisively defeated the HWWA in an NLRB representation election held on March 31, 1938.[113]

Struggles for recognition were much harder won at the port's two much larger firms, Castle & Cooke and McCabe, Hamilton & Renny. Although it never surpassed HoLA/ILWU Local 1–37 in numbers and disappeared from the Honolulu waterfront by the end of 1938, the HWWA, along with the companies' coercive and paternalistic measures, was effective in preventing the HoLA/ILWU from gaining early majorities. At McCabe, Hamilton & Renny, the HoLA/ILWU lost NLRB elections in 1937 and 1938; even worse off at Castle & Cooke and certain to lose, the union did not seek elections there at the time.

But Local 1–37 slowly tightened its ranks and built up its membership. Especially effective was a secret organizing campaign, through which the union gained strength without the companies' immediate knowledge, followed by a couple of bold job actions to protest unfair labor practices. Castle & Cooke reacted by instituting "a *wage cutting*, and *speed-up* plan, titled the 40 hour plan, just to kill the morale of the workers, so that when the election comes along the workers will not vote for the union."[114] Unlike in the past, the company's effort at intimidation backfired. Attesting to the union's firmer standing, the company's unpopular plan pushed more workers into the union rather than pulling them away.[115] Finally, on January 24 and February 26, 1941, Local 1–37 won NLRB representation elections at Castle & Cooke and McCabe, Hamilton & Renny, respectively, both by comfortable three-to-one margins.[116]

Between its recognition by C. Brewer & Company in 1937 and World War II, HiLA/ILWU Local 1–36 remained the most solidly organized union for the reasons stated earlier: a single employer to contend with, less effectual employer resistance than in Honolulu, and a high concentration of radical ex-seamen as organizers. Although C. Brewer & Company managed to keep the terms of its agreement with the union informal (i.e., not codified in a written contract) for a few years, the union enforced them vigilantly through numerous job actions. Though it tried, the company simply could not sway the port's longshoremen away from the union.

The most serious test of unity for Local 1–36 occurred in 1938. From the end of May to mid-August, Local 1–37 at Inter-Island—along with members of the Inland Boatmen's Union (IBU) and the Metal Trades Council (MTC), an amalgam of three craft unions—went out on strike, primarily to obtain wage parity with the West Coast and a union hiring hall. The strike eventually ended in the unions' defeat, gaining almost nothing.

From the fourth week of the strike, Inter-Island hired and tried to sail with strikebreakers, which instigated a series of violent clashes in Honolulu.[117] On two occasions, Inter-Island attempted to restore shipping service to Hilo. Both times, Local 1–36 longshoremen of Hilo, joined by other local residents, staged sympathy protests and prevented the unloading of cargo. At the first protest on July 22, the police almost set off a violent confrontation when an overanxious lieutenant threw tear gas into the crowd, injuring an eleven-year-old boy. Improbably, the union leaders held the crowd back from retaliating, *and* the union succeeded in preventing the ship from unloading.[118]

After Inter-Island's failed first attempt, the sheriff, pressured by the Hilo Chamber of Commerce, "gave [his] guarantee and assurance" of protection for another try, after which Inter-Island scheduled to dock once again in Hilo on August 1.[119] In response, Local 1–36 members and sympathizers planned to meet the ship with another peaceful but confrontational protest (Beechert 1991:154; Puette 1988:30–31).[120] The sheriff, on the other hand, readied for a battle. On August 1, he met the demonstrators with sixty-eight policemen in a three-line formation. The lines were armed, respectively, with tear-gas grenades, shotguns with bayonets, and fire-water hoses (Beechert 1991:154). As the unarmed demonstrators executed their plan of occupying the pier, the police, without provocation, bayoneted, clubbed, and shot at the crowd. Not counting those with minor injuries, fifty-one people were treated later at Hilo Hospital. Attacked as they were fleeing, a majority received their wounds from behind (Beechert 1985:266). Bert Nakano, a Local 1–36 leader, "barely escaped with his life" after being shot four times.[121]

Miraculously, nobody died in what has since come to be known as the Hilo Massacre. The only other incident in which an employer-backed police force opened fire against workers in Hawai'i had occurred fourteen years earlier in Hanapēpē during the 1924 sugar strike. But, whereas the violence then had led to the defeat and decline of the Filipino labor union, the Hilo Massacre had a contrary effect. While Local 1–37 and the other two unions lost the Inter-Island strike, the sympathy strike mounted by Local 1–36 and the violence it faced on August 1 only steeled its unity.

Living up to its reputation as the most militant and solid union in the islands, Local 1–36 shut down the port a year later to commemorate "Bloody Monday": "On August 1, a 24-hour stoppage of work was called by our local, in commemoration of Bloody Monday, in respect to those workers who were shot down and wounded in a peaceful labor demonstration in 1938. The howls of the company were very great in their mud press, in trying to turn public sentiment against the workers, in saying that no cargo would be unloaded that day since a ship was to be scheduled in port but we won our 24 hour stoppage of work."[122] Another year later, Local 1–36 president Kamoku summarized the union's steadfast solidarity: "Hilo local has held its own against many company attacks in [the] past four years. . . . [They] have maintained their favorable working conditions despite company attempts to increase sling-loads, etc. Dues payments are good. . . . Approximately 90% are in good standing."[123] While wage rates, as in other ports of Hawai'i, remained considerably lower than on the West Coast, Local 1–36's syndicalist impulse on the job "brought working conditions much into line with West Coast practices and enforced a virtual closed-shop, rotary hiring and equalization of earnings."[124]

For years, Hawaii's longshoremen recognized intuitively that the port of Honolulu, the "Crossroads of the Pacific," was the linchpin of their future. In particular, unless Castle & Cooke, the unquestioned industrial leader, were organized, the ILWU realized that its goal of obtaining a territorywide agreement was unattainable.[125] In 1941, this theory would be proven correct. After it finally won the NLRB election at Castle & Cooke, Local 1–37 negotiated and signed its first contract with the company, on June 12, 1941, "with the assistance of William T. Guerts, Mediator, U.S. Maritime Labor Board, and ILWU International Representative, Clifford O'Brien."[126] In quick succession, McCabe, Hamilton & Renny in Honolulu and the stevedoring firms on Kaua'i and in Hilo followed suit and signed almost identical contracts with the ILWU (Brooks 1952:68–69).[127]

As on the waterfront but even more so, labor organizing on the plantations during the period between the NLRB's initial intervention and World War II was "one of reverses, yet, continued struggle in the face of the determined opposition."[128] In the aftermath of the 1937 strike, Vibora Luviminda deteriorated rapidly for three reasons. First, having formed mostly in secret and under intense interference by the plantations, Vibora Luviminda never developed much of a structure. Even when the union emerged from underground and obtained the help of additional organizers from Honolulu, the campaign consisted mainly of speech making, soliciting membership, and haphazard dues collecting.[129] While there was certainly commitment on the part of the Filipino workers, as exemplified by the duration and eventual size of the strike, "they didn't have the organizational structure to continue," according to Hall[130] Second, partly related to the first reason, the union could not survive the employers' criminal prosecutions and blacklisting of its members; in addition, some of its leaders apparently "sold out" to the employers.[131]

Finally, there was an eventual split between the Vibora Luviminda leadership and the organizers from the Honolulu waterfront. From the beginning, when Fagel enlisted the help of Hall and Bailey, there was an openly acknowledged difference between Vibora Luviminda and the Honolulu organizers concerning race: Vibora Luviminda insisted on Filipino exclusivity, wanting to "strengthen [its] movement first," and the CIO-oriented Honolulu organizers advocated including non-Filipino workers, "trying to get them to move toward a multi-racial union."[132]

Despite this disagreement, Bailey and Hall supported the union's organizing effort, as did several other organizers from Honolulu who joined them after the strike began. However, the ideological difference resurfaced intermittently during the strike. For example, by June 1937, there was a move, at least on the part of the Honolulu organizers, to turn Vibora Luviminda into a HoLA affiliate.[133] On June 24, this effort culminated in the formation of the Maui Plantation and Mill Workers Industrial Union (MPMWIU); as a unit of the HoLA, it planned to "eventually unite itself" with the CIO. The union would organize "along industrial lines, including all the workers engaged in the sugar and pineapple industries regardless of craft or skill" and "regardless of race, color, or religion."[134] It sought, in effect, to subsume the preexisting Vibora Luviminda and add non-Filipino workers.

Probably because MPMWIU was launched by Grover Johnson, a radical labor lawyer from California whose services the HoLA's Berman procured to defend indicted Filipino strike leaders, including Fagel (Beechert 1977:10; 1985:230), Vibora Luviminda leaders did not object to the proposed transformation of their union—at least not immediately. For example, four Vibora Luviminda leaders, *as* the MPMWIU Strike Defense Committee, signed a letter of appeal for financial assistance that was sent to unions in the metropole.[135] However, even at that point, there does not seem to have been a genuine, long-term intention on the part of Vibora Luviminda to open up its membership to non-Filipinos or to merge with MPMWIU, causing "confusion between the Vibora Luviminda and the new [MPMWIU] CIO constitution."[136] Consequently, organization of non-Filipino workers was not seriously attempted.[137]

Not earnestly supported by the Vibora Luviminda leadership, MPMWIU was never much more than a paper union and disappeared altogether after the strike. Not recognized by the struck plantations, with much of its leadership either under criminal indictment or bought off by the employers, and without a durable structure, Vibora Luviminda also waned on Maui after the strike, although it tried to regroup the next year.[138] Vibora Luviminda, unwaveringly exclusive to Filipino workers, and Hawaii's CIO-oriented unions, clearly aligned with the industrial and interracial direction of the CIO, did not cooperate again.

The Vibora Luviminda strike of 1937 should not be interpreted, however, as a dead end, merely the "last racial strike" (Zalburg 1979:19). Through this action and the attendant publicity, the desire for unionization among Maui's plantation workers became widely known and had a ripple effect on plantation workers on the other islands: "there was such a demand for organization among these people that word got throughout the state [territory]."[139] Although Vibora Luviminda and the CIO-oriented unions did not collaborate again, the split was not, on the whole, rancorous; they basically went their separate ways. Accordingly, there was no subsequent backlash for the CIO-oriented, interracial unions vis-à-vis Filipino workers' support. On the contrary, the CIO-oriented organizers had made a positive connection with Filipino workers, which the organizers would invoke.[140] After all, it was the message of the Honolulu organizers—highlighting the external support they could expect from West Coast workers—that had revived the tremendous interest in Vibora Luviminda among Maui's plantation workers.[141] It was also through the HoLA that Johnson, a lawyer with the leftist International Labor Defense, had been brought to Hawai'i to defend Filipino strikers in court. Since no lawyer in Hawai'i dared to go up against the sugar industry, Filipino workers received him with enthusiasm.[142] Furthermore, some leaders of Vibora Luviminda later joined the

ILWU/CIO movement.[143] In these ways, the Filipino union's "strike helped lay the basis for the aggressive, inter-racial organizations that followed."[144]

Upon its demise on Maui, what remained of Vibora Luviminda turned its attention to the islands of Hawai'i, Kaua'i, and, to a lesser extent, O'ahu. Beginning in fall 1937, the HSPA, the Big Five agencies, and the plantations collected and exchanged information on the whereabouts and activities of Vibora Luviminda's leaders, especially those who had taken part in the Maui strike.[145] The plantations predictably refused to hire them and otherwise tried to block their organizing efforts. Four short, unsuccessful strikes and a demonstration resulted from the union's activities on the three islands in the following year (Beechert 1985:231). Producing no gains, they turned out to be the denouement of a story that had clearly passed its climax. As early as December 1937, the manager of the Kaiwiki Sugar Company on the island of Hawai'i reported on the union's withering support: "The Maui, Filipino strike agitators, who have been holding regular scheduled meetings on this island during the past two months, were scheduled to have a meeting here yesterday evening. The agitators arrived in their cars and after waiting around for an hour-and-a-half returned to Hilo owing to the complete absence of any Filipino attendance."[146] According to surveillance records of the HSPA and its plantations, Vibora Luviminda's activities dropped off and ended in 1938, although the union did not officially cease to exist until 1939, according to Reinecke (1966:10).

Meanwhile, the CIO-oriented organizers opened their "aggressive, interracial organization" of agricultural workers, focusing on the island of Kaua'i.[147] Not much evidence exists of this prewar drive, of which the mainstream press in Honolulu barely took notice. In some ways, the lack of attention is understandable: Kaua'i was the smallest of the 4 sugar-producing islands, and none of the top 3 pineapple companies owned a plantation or a cannery there. The prewar campaign also netted only 500 employer-recognized union members in sugar and pineapple combined.[148]

In retrospect, however, the relatively insignificant numbers belied the significance of prewar Kaua'i as a model for the future. In several important ways, the organizing of workers on Kaua'i before World War II prefigured the organizing of workers throughout Hawai'i in the mid-1940s. The unionization of sugar and pineapple workers in prewar Kaua'i was initiated and supported by longshoremen; the more established longshore union acted as a beachhead for the "march inland" to the plantations.[149] Not long after its own start and before its own future existence was secure, the PAWWA, along with organizers from Honolulu, reached out to Kauai's sugar and pineapple workers. As an original PAWWA organizer, Goto "convinced Port Allen [longshoremen] that [they] alone cannot survive. [They] have to give . . . a hand in organizing the plantations."[150] The longshoremen concurred. As early as July 1937, PAWWA leaders joined the Honolulu organizers, holding meetings on Kaua'i plantations.[151]

On September 30, 1937, *Hawaii Hōchi* reported that the United Cannery, Agricultural, Packing, and Allied Workers of America (UCAPAWA) had issued a charter for the "organization of Hawaii's vast army of agricultural and cannery workers." James Cooley and Calixto Piano, along with Hall and Goto, were named as "official CIO organizers to assist Edward Berman," the newly appointed CIO director for Hawai'i.[152] Though welcome, the charter was misleading. Although the organizers "set [Kaua'i] up as a CIO organization, with UCAPAWA Local 76," they "got nothing" from the national union.[153] Rather, they were financed by the PAWWA/ILWU Local 1–35 (Zalburg 1979:28). Upon receiving the charter, the official UCAPAWA organizers and Local 1–35 members held countless organizational meetings on Kauai's sugar and pineapple plantations, fanning out from their base of support in Port Allen. The nearby McBryde Sugar Company and Kauai Pineapple Company were early targets. From there, the UCAPAWA "branched off into the adjoining [sugar] plantations, Olekele, Kekaha, to the west, and Koloa and Lihue, to some extent, toward the east."[154]

As throughout Hawai'i in the mid-1940s, organizers in prewar Kaua'i, in their effort to incorporate all racial groups, held their meetings in multiple languages—at least in English, Japanese, and Ilocano, but at times in other Filipino dialects as needed. Accordingly, the meetings were conducted by teams with at least one organizer per language.[155] As Hall described the early days on Kaua'i, "And, of course, the union [meetings] used to go on for five and six hours. I guess in those days they had to be conducted in 3 and sometimes 4 languages. . . . you had to have a lot of discussion in Japanese and Ilocano, and English for the younger workers. And, somewhere, I guess still Visayan."[156]

Organizers not only recruited workers into the union but also persuaded them to become politically active. Comprised mostly of Local 1–35 and UCAPAWA members, "the Progressive League of Kauai was founded in the autumn of 1938, to support progressive delegates to the Territorial Legislature," both by having union members run for office and by endorsing other progressive candidates.[157] In plantation communities throughout Hawai'i, only Republican candidates sanctioned by the plantations had been allowed to campaign on their premises, and workers had become convinced that the employers knew how they voted and had been genuinely fearful of reprisals for voting against the plantations.[158] But as support for the unions grew, support for the Progressive League grew. Its first success came in 1939, when its endorsed Democratic candidate, J. B. Fernandez, beat the Republican candidate, L. A. Faye, manager of the Kekaha Sugar Company, for a seat in the territorial senate.[159]

Finally, as throughout Hawai'i in the mid-1940s, organizers were aided by Arnold L. Wills, the conscientious head of the NLRB in Hawai'i with socialist leanings, who diligently investigated charges of unfair labor practices, efficiently held representation elections, and even gave useful advice to some of the neophyte unionists (Zalburg 1979:72–75). The plantations on Kaua'i closely monitored the organizers' activities and attempted to thwart their efforts through familiar means: "The workers were afraid to be seen with you," an organizer at McBryde recalled. "They thought you had cancer."[160] But the UCAPAWA made steady progress, in large part because the NLRB's active presence on the island tempered the plantations' antiunion tactics.[161] The attorney of a Kaua'i plantation advised his client,

> I come to feel that Mr. Wills is perhaps, partly from his experience as a coal miner in New Zealand, absolutely sold on the idea that it is pretty hard for labor to do anything wrong and that it is equally hard for the employer to do anything right when the employer's acts conflict with the desires of labor. . . . every plantation manager . . . has got to watch his step, and that wherever there is the slightest question as to the propriety of his actions, he has got to assume that they will be construed as in some way a violation of the [Wagner Act].[162]

On June 3, 1939, "nonagricultural" workers, mostly cannery workers, at Kauai Pineapple voted in an NLRB election to have the UCAPAWA be their sole and exclusive bargaining agent by a 162 to 10 margin; on June 29, 1939, UCAPAWA Local 76, Unit 6 signed a contract with the company. Both were firsts for the pineapple industry.[163] On October 24, 1940, "nonagricultural" workers, mostly sugar mill workers, at McBryde voted to have the UCAPAWA be their sole and exclusive bargaining agent by a 200 to 40 margin; on August 26, 1941, UCAPAWA Local 76, Unit 1 signed a contract with the company. Both were firsts for the sugar industry (Brooks 1952:83).[164]

Martial Law: Innervating Interregnum

By the end of August 1941, the CIO had gained a foothold in stevedoring, sugar, and pineapple. The ILWU had signed contracts with stevedoring firms on three of the four major islands, and the UCAPAWA had signed contracts with one sugar company and one pineapple company. Although a vast majority of Hawaii's workers, particularly in sugar and pineapple, were not yet organized, the hard-won successes appeared replicable, and the CIO unions were cautiously optimistic. But a little over three months later, on December 7, 1941, the future was abruptly held in abeyance.

Although Japan's attack on Pearl Harbor came as a surprise to Hawaii's residents, the war with Japan did not, for preparations had long been under way. From the late 1930s, there had been a conspicuous military buildup in Hawai'i. If not before, residents were alerted to the probability of war in 1939, when all of Honolulu participated in a complete blackout exercise. One-time territorial attorney general

J. Garner Anthony noted, "It would have been odd if the people of Hawaii had witnessed the feverish activity that took place in the Islands for more than a year prior to Pearl Harbor without being aware of the imminence of war" (1955:1).

For its part, the territorial legislature, in a special session called by Governor Joseph B. Pointdexter, had passed the Hawaii Defense Act in October 1941. Advocated by Lieutenant General Walter C. Short, commanding general of the U.S. Army's Hawaiian Department, the law outlined, in effect, a plan for "civilian martial law," granting far-reaching legislative powers to the territorial governor in the eventuality of a military emergency (Okihiro 1991:200). One of the selling points of the immoderate law, as advanced by General Short, was that it would "delay or even render unnecessary a declaration of martial law."[165] In other words, heavy-handed civilian authority would be the lesser of two evils.

At 11:30 on the morning of the bombing, Pointdexter issued a proclamation stating that he was assuming the new powers granted him by the Hawaii Defense Act. But just four hours later, he effectively negated the law with a second proclamation, ironically at the behest of Short, who had urged the act's passage. Pointdexter declared martial law and suspended the privilege of writ of habeas corpus, invoking his powers under the Hawaiian Organic Act. Moreover, pushed by Short to venture far beyond the Organic Act into constitutional incertitude, Pointdexter ceded to the commanding general "all of the powers normally exercised by [him] as governor . . . and by judicial officers and employees of this territory and of the counties and cities therein, and such other and further powers as the emergency may require."[166] In turn, as the newly anointed "military governor," a position with no legal basis, General Short issued a companion proclamation: "I announce to the people of Hawaii, that, in compliance with the above requests of the Governor of Hawaii, I have this day assumed the position of military governor of Hawaii, and have taken charge of the government of the Territory. . . . good citizens will cheerfully obey this proclamation and the ordinances to be published; others will be required to do so. Offenders will be severely punished by military tribunals or will be held in custody until such time as the civil courts are able to function."[167]

Thus, on December 7, 1941, Hawaii's civilian government ceased to function, and a military government commanded by a military governor assumed power. On March 10, 1943, the military government partly acceded to civilian authority, but not until October 24, 1944 was martial law fully terminated. Although federal courts, including the Supreme Court, would eventually find the imposition of martial law in Hawai'i to have been unconstitutional, their rulings were handed down after the fact. In the meantime, the military governor issued a continual flow of general orders, in lieu of laws passed by the legislature, all of which involved criminal sanctions. Military provost courts and, for the most serious cases, military commissions supplanted the territory's courts, resulting in few acquittals and harsh sentences (Anthony 1955).

Martial law penetrated virtually every aspect of life in wartime Hawai'i, and labor was one of its primary concerns. Promulgated on December 20, 1941, General Order 38, the first order concerning labor, froze all "employees of the Federal Government and its contractors . . . [including] City and County of Honolulu, Territorial agencies, their contractors and subcontractors and utilities and sources of supply controlled by the Army and Navy" to their current employers. The order retroactively forced workers who had left any such employers between December 7 and 20, 1941 to return to them. Terms of labor contracts with these employers that "restrict or specify the nature of work to be performed" were suspended. All "men employed hereafter [had to] report to the job for which they [were] ordered by the Military Governor," and on the island of O'ahu, where labor shortages were the most acute, wages for all jobs were frozen at the December 7 rate.[168] The military government did not consult any labor unions prior to issuing this order, and the order did not establish any avenues for appeal (Van Zwalenburg 1961:26).

On January 1, 1942, the military governor, via the U.S. Army Corps of Engineers, set down the terms with sugar and pineapple companies under which the military government would "obtain for military purposes and, if necessary . . . commandeer such *labor*, material, supplies and equipment as . . . required in order to properly carry out orders issued or which may hereafter be issued."[169] Through the agreement, made retroactive to December 7, 1941, Hawaii's sugar and pineapple companies became, in effect, the largest labor contractors for the military. As compensation for the "loaned labor," those companies received from the military government the direct cost of wages, 9¢ per hour per worker to cover the cost of perquisites, the indirect costs of overhead and taxes, and an additional 8 percent as profit.[170] The loaned workers themselves, however, received their prewar plantation wages, well below wages paid to nonplantation workers for the same jobs performed. Attesting to the extent to which the military relied on loaned plantation labor, the HSPA reported at the war's end that, from December 1941 to the end of 1944, Hawaii's sugar and pineapple plantations had loaned out 514,130 person-days of labor to the military, 456,212 person-days of which had been before 1943.[171]

On the outer islands, where local commanders had relative autonomy in interpreting the military governor's general orders to apply to local conditions, the above labor-loan arrangement was construed to mean that plantation workers fell within the purview of General Order 38. Hence, they were bound to their employers and could not seek higher-paying jobs in the defense industry. On O'ahu, the authorities did not formally apply General Order 38 to plantation workers. However, they accomplished the same result via a "gentlemen's agreement": the plantations agreed to make their workers available to the military, and the military agreed, in return, not to "pirate" workers away.[172]

On January 26, 1942, the military government supplemented General Order 38 with General Order 56. It established the United States Employment Service (USES) as the "central employment agency for the procurement and distribution of civilian labor." The order required "every able-bodied male person" 18 years of age or older who was unemployed to register with USES, and those who became unemployed were required to re-register within 72 hours; all employers—public and private—were also required to report to USES all additions to and subtractions from their payrolls. Violators of these requirements were subject to fines and/or jail terms.[173]

The other major provision of General Order 56 concerning labor was the appointment of Douglas Bond to the position of director of labor control, whose functions were to "recommend to the Military Governor" rules and regulations for the "procurement, augmentation and distribution of labor" and to "investigate and mediate such labor disputes as are referred to him by the Military Governor."[174] Bond was the manager of the Ewa Plantation Company, a Castle & Cooke sugar plantation on O'ahu. The director was assisted by a nine-member labor advisory council, the head of which had been the industrial relations director at the 'Ewa plantation. Only two of the members were labor representatives, one from the AFL and one from the CIO; Clifford O'Brien, the ILWU representative from the West Coast who had facilitated the 1941 longshore contract negotiations, represented the CIO.

Before the public issuance of General Order 56, members of the council, notably the labor representatives, advocated for the inclusion of measures moderating the harshness of the military's control of labor: a return to collective bargaining, unfreezing of labor in nondefense industries, and payment of prevailing wages to loaned plantation workers. The head of the council ignored the recommendations (Van Zwalenburg 1961:27–30). On organized labor's lack of voice and the plantations' undue influence in the military government, O'Brien observed, "For a time it looked as if we'd get taken into the councils of government, at least as they directly concerned labor, but the Labor Advisory Council to Military Governor of which I'm the CIO member is a joke, and the persistent plantation people are being more and more heard."[175]

On March 31, 1942, General Order 91 replaced General Order 38. The new labor restrictions were similar to the previous ones, except employers, rather than the government, held more direct power over the fate of workers. Paragraph 2c(1) of the order read:

No Army or Navy agencies, their contractors or subcontractors, Federal agencies, Territorial agencies, City and County of Honolulu agencies, their contractors or subcontractors, hospitals, public utilities, stevedoring companies and sources of supply controlled by the Army and/or the Navy, shall employ or offer to employ, any individual formerly or now in the employment of the above mentioned employers unless and until such individual shall have presented to the employing agency a bona fide release without prejudice, in writing, from his last previous employer.[176]

The order prohibited the specified employers from hiring workers away from other employers unless the workers received permission from them to leave. In other words, workers were frozen to their employers unless the employers, at their discretion, gave them releases "without prejudice."

Workers attempting to obtain employment without such a release were subject to fines and/or jail terms. If released "with prejudice," a worker could appeal. However, the existence of the appeal mechanism was not widely known. In contrast, employers found to be in violation of the general order did not face punitive measures. The inordinate imbalance of power led to frequent abuses by employers, which would not be forgotten by the workers. Employers used release "with prejudice," and likely threats of it, to discipline workers. They also instituted "conditional releases" to temporarily permit employees to work elsewhere until the employers needed them again (Van Zwalenburg 1961:37–41).

Not unlike the nineteenth-century penal labor contracts, General Order 91 also legally *compelled* workers at the aforementioned employers to work regularly. That is, it forbade absenteeism and, by extension, strikes. Whereas absenteeism would normally have been grounds for termination, under martial law it led to fines and/or jail time. The military government's threat to try and sentence alleged violators in provost courts was not idle; arrests, fines, and jail sentences for absenteeism were frequent (Van Zwalenburg 1961:39–41). The territorial attorney general noted sardonically, "Those in command here seem to lose sight of the fact that the Civil War and the Thirteenth Amendment are generally considered to have put at rest involuntary servitude in the United States 'or any place subject to their jurisdiction.'"[177]

On the outer islands, plantation laborers continued to be bound to their jobs, and everyone was compelled to work at least twenty days a month or face prosecution in provost courts. They were also subject to severe travel restrictions, which prevented them from seeking higher wages on Oʻahu, where most defense jobs were located. On the island of Kauaʻi, plantation laborers also had to obtain releases from their employers to travel off the island (Fuchs 1961:354).[178]

On March 10, 1943, martial law was relaxed, and civilian rule—territorial and federal—was partly restored. All existing general orders were revoked, and the military governor commenced issuing a new series of general orders in line with the military's more delimited role.[179] The new order concerning labor, General Order 10, did not differ much from its predecessor General Order 91 except in one important way: only those working for the army or the navy, stevedoring companies, and public utilities remained under its direct control, reducing the number of affected employers from 171 to 41 (Allen 1950:312). So, while longshoremen and others subject to General Order 10 stayed under military restrictions, all other workers were now under the civilian control of the War Manpower Commission and no longer subject to military provost courts.

Restrictions on labor loosened, though by no means at once. From October 1943, agricultural workers were finally permitted to change jobs but were still limited to other agricultural employers unless they received permission from USES. Military restrictions on interisland travel, especially from the outer islands to O'ahu, were somewhat relaxed, as the manpower director tended to be more permissive. His criterion for granting a permit was whether the worker would be more valuable to the war effort if she or he remained on the outer island. Nonetheless, plantation workers were almost always deemed more valuable to the war effort at their current positions and continued to have a hard time obtaining travel permits to work on O'ahu (Allen 1950:313).

Under pressure by the War Manpower Commission from early 1944, the military governor agreed to place all workers under civilian control. Put into effect on August 21, 1944, the new program "was in accord with national War Manpower Commission policies and provided ceilings on manpower for each employer as well as for a system of priority referrals through the U.S. Employment Service" (Van Zwalenburg 1961:48). Thus, though not officially for another two months, martial law in regard to labor ended.

One overall effect of martial law was to stifle unions and labor organizing. Terms of labor contracts were suspended. Large numbers of workers were bound to their employers; they were legally compelled to work; and their ability to move about was restricted. And these restrictions were ultimately enforced by unforgiving military provost courts. A month and a half into martial law, the ILWU's O'Brien anticipated accurately, "I had thought we might develop some plan to further the Hawaiian organizing program and to build greater membership during the war, but I've thought the thing through and am now convinced that under the present form of Military Government we will do well to hold our own and keep the locals together."[180] As predicted, the ILWU and other unions had a hard time just maintaining their membership under martial law, particularly on Kaua'i, the focal point of the CIO's prewar efforts and, during the war, the island with the most overtly antiunion authorities.[181]

Countervailing this first effect of labor suppression, a second overall effect of martial law on labor was to foment discontent among workers, making them receptive to the ILWU's subsequent organizing campaign. Laborers, most notably the unorganized thousands in sugar and pineapple, bristled under the military's regime of coerced peace and stability: "They were plenty pissed off about the manner in which they were treated during the war."[182] Explaining the ILWU's rapid progress in mobilizing workers toward the end of the war, Bob Robertson, the International's vice president in charge of organizing, similarly identified the period of martial law as having been crucial: "The populace in the islands had been under military control for a long time and American military [was] pretty rough, and they had been subjected to the discipline of military control."[183] "People wanted to organize," Hall concluded. "They were resentful of labor controls."[184]

Of course, in wartime, particularly prior to the relaxation of martial law, workers seldom expressed their discontent openly. In addition to military orders incapacitating union activities, heightened nationalism and fear discouraged public expressions, let alone actions, that could be construed as unpatriotic, subversive, or merely disruptive.[185] And what was true for all workers was more profoundly so for Japanese workers (see chapter 5).

Nonetheless, employers, especially sugar and pineapple companies, detected the muffled dissatisfaction mounting among workers under martial law. The most frequent complaint concerned the plantation workers' low, prewar wages stemming from being frozen to their jobs. Their income kept up with neither the wages of defense workers, many of whom had been fellow plantation workers, nor wartime inflation. As a department head on a Big Island plantation wrote to his manager, "There is much unrest and general dissatisfaction throughout caused chiefly by rising living costs and the reports, true and otherwise, of the huge sums being earned by defense workers."[186] A department head on an Oʻahu plantation similarly reported, "The unprecidented [sic] rate of pay and the effort and desire of the defense contractors, USED [U.S. Engineering Department], and other military and naval units to aquire [sic] our men, caused the loss of a great number of our crew. . . . The lost employees return to the plantation frequently and boast of their new wealth and of the ease and small physical effort with which it can be obtained. This causes discontent, loss of interest and the lack of cooperation of the present crew."[187] Sensing the discontent, another plantation supervisor predicted, "After this war is over, the problem of the plantation will not be in raising sugar, it will be placating labor."[188] The ILWU tapped into this unrest and dissatisfaction when it renewed its organizing effort at the end of martial law.[189] One of the union's arguments, which found ready and enthusiastic audiences, was, "You poor fellows should get more money like the USED, etc. [workers] to compensate you for being frozen."[190]

Nothing made the inequities of martial law more baldly and immediately apparent to the workers than the "labor loan" program. As sugar and pineapple companies contracted out labor to the military for profit, frozen sugar and pineapple workers, earning their prewar wages, went to work alongside defense employees earning much higher wages for the same jobs. One study found that loaned plantation workers from one of the "higher-paying plantations" earned 34.3¢ per hour, while the pay for "common laborers" hired directly by the military was 65¢ (Van Zwalenburg 1961:34). Recognizing the discord such differentials could cause, the military made at least some effort to prevent its workers from discussing wages with the loaned plantation workers: "In accordance with Department [USED] regulations, all employees are directed not to hold conversation with unauthorized persons regarding work projects or labor conditions including hours of work and rates of pay; and particularly with Plantation laborers."[191] But of course, word got out. Haruo Nakamoto, an ILWU organizer on the island of Kaua'i at the end of the war, remembered that loaned plantation workers were well aware that while they were receiving only 25¢ per hour, the military was paying its workers 60¢ to 75¢, and as much as $1.25 for skilled jobs. Echoing the sentiment of many others within the ILWU, Nakamoto concluded that such wartime conditions provided workers with compelling "incentives to organize."[192]

Trying to make sense of the swelling dissatisfaction, an O'ahu plantation supervisor could not figure out why the *employers* were being blamed for the wartime conditions: "Many of [the workers] seem to forget there is a war on and blame the Plantation for any inconveniences they may have to endure."[193] Why did the employers become the target of the workers' anger? That is, how was the workers' discontent so easily directed at the employers? After all, was the military not responsible for the workers' plight?

Given the Big Five employers' intimate relationship with the military before and during martial law, it is not surprising that the workers would channel their subsequent activism against the employers. As mentioned earlier, the Big Five and the military enjoyed a long prewar history of mutual assistance; most important, they both surveilled and kept each other abreast of "subversive" activities, focusing on the Japanese in particular.[194] Of course, there were always tensions, for example, over land use (Stirling 1939). But the overall relationship was one of cooperation, if sometimes reluctant.

Leading up to and during the war, that relationship grew more intimate, as the military exercised much of its power through Hawaii's preexisting industrial structures. There was an affinity of interests: for the military, utilizing those structures to prepare for war and, later, to carry out orders maximized its efficiency; for the employers, cooperating with the military meant that they could have much more direct input into the military's decision-making processes and minimize the war's inevitable disruptions to their operations. Again, this cooperation did not preclude—and perhaps enabled—the companies' lodging complaints to the military about the diversion of labor and equipment to defense projects (Odo 2004:149).[195]

Casting their close relationship to the military in a favorable, patriotic light, the "Hawaiian Sugar Planters' Association, its member plantations, their agents, and officials and individuals connected or associated therewith" were not shy about revealing the depth of that collaboration in a report submitted to a congressional committee:

This record of cooperation is one of established policy extending over a period of many years, built upon close relationship with the armed forces, and mutual recognition of the needs and requirements of the military and the contributions that could and have been made by the plantations in the defense plans of Hawaii. This policy of cooperation was further engendered and developed through the close liaison always maintained between the sugar industry and the military authorities by Major General Briant H. Wells (Ret.), a former Deputy Chief of Staff, United States Army, who in 1934 was made Vice-President and Executive Secretary of the Hawaiian Sugar Planters' Association following his retirement from the Army on completion of his tour of duty as Commanding General, Hawaiian Department.[196]

The exhaustive report detailed how, both in preparation for and during the war, the plantations made land, equipment, and labor available to the military. Plantation managers and other "prominent" citizens also organized and led the provisional police force (a separate entity from the local police) and numerous other "comprehensive civilian defense committees" to help the military deal with Hawaii's civilian population.[197]

The pawns at the bottom, subject to and carrying out wartime plans into which they had no input, workers gained first-hand knowledge of the tight relationship between the military and the employers. In the area of labor, as discussed earlier, the military governor predictably assigned plantation officials to the posts of director of labor control and head of the labor advisory council to advise him. The undue influence of employers on the military governor resulted in general orders favorable to them.[198]

Not unlike the end of penal contract labor at the start of the century, the end of martial law ushered in a period of fervent labor activism. Class conflict, tightly covered and seething in the pressure cooker of martial law, boiled over. Weaker but still functioning, the ILWU took full advantage of the volatile conditions wrought by military rule. Having established a foothold before the war, the ILWU was positioned "in the right place at the right time, with the right forces, with the right program that moved in a situation where a social upheaval developed."[199] The political opportunity, which had opened up with the NLRB's enforcement of the Wagner Act but abruptly closed with the imposition of martial law, reopened and unleashed a social movement that had been gathering strength standing still. According to NLRB representative Wills, "When the [military] controls were lifted, workers flocked into the unions by the tens of thousands. It was phenomenal."[200] Or, as an ILWU organizer described, "It went like wildfire."[201]

Over the Hump

Reviewing the early days of the ILWU/CIO in Hawai'i, from the establishment of the HoLA and the HiLA to martial law, the longtime ILWU secretary-treasurer Louis Goldblatt observed, "The thing that struck me was that in no case had we really made it over the hump."[202] In one sense, of course, he was right. For example, if reliable figures were available, a graph of union membership during this time period would show a shaky line with a slight upward slope from 1935 to December 7, 1941 and a plateau, or a slight downward slope, thereafter to 1944. The point at which the ILWU/CIO actually made it over the proverbial hump would appear a little farther to the right on the graph, as a soaring slope would rise out of the plateau from 1944 to 1946; during that time, the ILWU organized virtually all of stevedoring, sugar, and pineapple, and in 1946, the union defeated the employers in a dramatic showdown in an industrywide, territorywide sugar strike and staked its claim to permanence.

In another sense, Goldblatt underrated what had transpired. There was more than one hump to get over, and the ILWU/CIO cleared some of the less acknowledged ones before the war. Before 1935, no union in sugar, pineapple, or stevedoring had been recognized by an employer as a legitimate representative of workers. No union had forced an employer to come to the bargaining table and negotiate in good faith, and no union had signed a contract with an employer. By the end of summer 1941, all three humps had been cleared in all three industries.

At this auspicious moment, the ILWU/CIO's future turned grim, as the military took over the islands later in 1941 and clamped down on labor. However, though battered and, on the island of Kaua'i, barely breathing, the movement did not die out, and the surviving pieces proved vital in getting the ILWU over the big hump to which Goldblatt referred. In other words, the slightly upward slope and the plateau made the soaring slope of the mid-1940s possible.

The subsequent story of the ILWU's big organizing campaign between 1944 and 1946 was, in essence, the union's prewar story, especially as it had developed on the island of Kaua'i, writ large and rapid. The longshore unions again provided the initial push for the "march inland" to the plantations. With the partial restoration of civilian rule in March 1943, which freed most workers from the grasp of military provost courts, the ILWU revived its longshore locals and prepared to resume its organizing activities (Beechert 1985:289). In October and November 1943, Local 1–36 in Hilo informed Local 1–37 in Honolulu that plantation workers on the island of Hawai'i were anxious to join the union. Beginning in December 1943, the two locals jointly sent organizers to the Big Island sugar plantations. Presumably the local least ravaged by the war, Local 1–37 took charge, earmarking $5,000 for the effort and sending a team of organizers from its ranks. With the workers practically "inviting the Union to come in and organize them," "the results of the [organizers'] work there [on the Big Island] were remarkable," even though the plantation managers were often hostile and meetings had to be carried out in secret. From the Big Island, the organizers moved on to the other islands, with similarly remarkable results.[203]

As before the war, the ILWU on the West Coast supported the renewed effort, and in a much more substantial way than before the war. In the late 1930s, the CIO had given the UCAPAWA's national office "a lot of money . . . to organize agricultural workers." Focused on the continent, however, the national office "wasn't too much interested in Hawaii."[204] While the International of the ILWU was much more involved and instrumental than its UCAPAWA counterpart before the war, its support for Hawaii's locals was nonetheless modest. The longshore unions continually asked the International in San Francisco to send them experienced organizers, but the typical response to such pleas resembled the one Local 1–35 received in 1938: "At this time our International is carrying a very heavy financial burden and we have recently sent two organizers to New Orleans. Due to the fact that work is slack in the Pacific Coast ports and per capita is not coming in as it should, we would be unable to take on any further expenses at this time."[205] Although it did not ignore Hawai'i before the war, the ILWU concentrated its organizing efforts on West Coast warehousemen and on longshoremen of New Orleans, the East Coast, and the Great Lakes. When Hawaii's longshoremen made similar requests for organizing help in late 1943 and early 1944, however, the International responded much more favorably, placing Hawai'i at the top of its agenda and dispatching experienced organizers there. The most important among them was a longtime labor organizer from Sacramento by the name of Frank Thompson, whose gruff efficiency has since become legendary.[206]

The NLRB facilitated the organizing drive, resuming its enforcement of the Wagner Act. Closed during the early part of the martial law period and rendered ineffective by it thereafter, the NLRB, with Arnold Wills still at the helm, became active once again. Probably based on Wills's prewar record, the ILWU predicted confidently in early 1944, "The NLRB will give *complete* cooperation."[207] The union's confidence was not misplaced. In the next two years, the NLRB provided critical and, as it would turn out, timely assistance; the NLRB ceased to be an ally with the passage of the antilabor, antileft Taft-Hartley Act in 1947.

One way the sugar industry fought the union and the NLRB was by withholding cooperation in conducting representation elections, claiming that the plantations as agricultural enterprises were exempt from the Wagner Act. The union and the HSPA therefore had to argue their respective cases in NLRB hearings held in Hilo, Honolulu, and Washington, D.C. On January 12, 1945, the NLRB ruled that the Wagner Act covered all sugar workers except those in cultivating and harvesting; between 50 and 60 percent were thus covered by the law, exceeding even the union's hopes. With similar rulings in the pineapple industry, NLRB representation elections occurred in rapid succession, and the ILWU won with an average of more than 90 percent of the votes (Beechert 1985:291–292; Zalburg 1979:119–120).[208] Investigating charges, holding hearings, and conducting elections, the NLRB kept up with the torrid pace of the ILWU's organizing drive. "Mr. Wills of the NLRB is another reason for our success," an ILWU unit officer in Lihu'e, Kaua'i, wrote in 1945. "He is very efficient in his elections."[209]

At the same time, the workers mobilized politically and, in the process, redefined the working class. While it realized that a sizable proportion of the plantation workforce did not have the protection of the Wagner Act, the ILWU in Hawai'i took in all workers, in spite of the International's strenuous directive to concentrate on "industrial" workers.[210] Although the local organizers made it clear that "the Union could not guarantee them anything as far as collective bargaining was concerned," agricultural laborers signed up in large numbers, demonstrating an intense desire to be a part of the movement. "At any meeting . . . there [was] always a bunch of the field workers present."[211]

Thompson, the organizer sent to Hawai'i, explained to the reluctant International why the local organizers were right to bring agricultural workers into the union at this time: "The main purpose of the signing of these [agricultural] workers is political. All of these Local Units down here have a PAC [Political Action Committee] campaign in full swing to get everyone registered to vote. The opportunity to put candidates into the Territorial Legislature favorable to Labor is much better than any place on the mainland."[212] The strategy paid off in the 1944 territorial elections. Of the nineteen candidates endorsed by the ILWU-PAC for the territorial House of Representatives, fifteen won their races; two of the newly elected representatives were ILWU members. Of the eight senatorial candidates endorsed by the ILWU-PAC, six won their races.[213]

For the 1944 elections, the ILWU-PAC did not have an elaborate political agenda: the key test for garnering a PAC endorsement was support for the Hawaii Employment Relations Act (HERA).[214] Dubbed the "Little Wagner Act," HERA had been drafted by Hall and submitted to the legislature in 1939 by Senator J. B. Fernandez, the Democrat who had been endorsed by the CIO-backed Kaua'i Progressive League. Six years later, the law was finally passed; it went into effect on July 1, 1945, extending the rights guaranteed by the Wagner Act to agricultural workers.

Insisting on their inclusion in the labor movement, agricultural workers pressed the local organizers and, in turn, the International to go against the state's existing definition of who a legitimate worker entitled to organize was. The movement was thereby able to get HERA passed and created for itself a wider political opportunity, affording agricultural workers the same rights as other workers and thus preventing potentially serious intra-industrial splits. In no time, the ILWU represented nearly all workers in sugar, pineapple, and longshoring, and by 1946, the union signed industrywide contracts in all three.[215]

5

The Making of Working-Class Interracialism

TTEMPTING TO EXCAVATE an "explicit" theory of working-class formation ostensibly buried in the "somewhat cryptic" preface and detailed narrative of E. P. Thompson's *The Making of the English Working Class*, William H. Sewell Jr. writes, "What does Thompson mean when he claims the English working class was 'made' by the early 1830s? . . . It had, in short, developed a class *discourse*. At the same time, it had developed a working-class *movement*. . . . The discourse and the movement were intimately linked: it was within the institutions of the working-class movement that militants developed and disseminated working-class discourse; and it was the notions contained in the working-class discourse that shaped and motivated the working-class movement" (1990:51, 69; emphases in original). Whereas the last chapter focused on the institutional emergence of Hawaii's working-class movement from the mid-1930s to the mid-1940s, this chapter explores the development of the movement's working-class discourse, specifically its quintessential and unprecedented interracialism. The chapter begins with a critique of the prevailing explanation for the making of the working-class interracialism that has cast a long shadow on the sociology and history of Hawai'i. Offering an alternative explanation, it then attempts to shed light on what has been hidden from view.

Deracialization Thesis Reconsidered

As the ILWU's education director would later attest, racial "conflicts and controversies . . . were at the roots of the thorniest problems" of the union into the 1940s:

> The Japanese . . . tended to under-rate the importance of other groups, dismissing the Portuguese as being generally "no-good" and not worth organizing, while the

Filipinos were recognized as necessary to successful organization, but too "ignorant" to be admitted to leadership. Portuguese workers shared the Japanese scorn of the Filipino, but regarded the rising Japanese leadership with alarm and indignation as a threat to their own generally superior status on the job and in the community. Filipinos shared the Japanese suspicion of the more favored Portuguese, but were resentful of the condescending attitude of both groups toward them, and positively outraged by the thought that they as the largest group of workers should not enjoy a proportionate leadership position. (Thompson 1951:36)

The predominant explanation for the workers' subsequent interracialism has been that their identity and politics became deracialized: a decreasing significance of race brought about by an increasing significance of class. The more liberally inclined, assimilationist studies tend to view the deracialization of the working class as a part of a more general deracialization of postwar Hawai'i and offer no specific explanation.[1] Studies grounded in Marxism interpret it as the workers' belated realization of economic interests they had unknowingly shared all along.[2] In other words, "true" class consciousness eventually triumphed over "false" racial consciousness, since "consciousness does not depend on subjective factors, but on objective factors" (Beechert 1983:169).

This Marxist explanation certainly has much to recommend it. The workers did become class-conscious, and their newly constructed common interests were, in part, economic: they fought for higher wages and better working and living conditions. Furthermore, an unintended effect of wartime military rule on the postwar success of the ILWU came about, to a significant degree, through the relative economic deprivation and intensified regulation of labor.

The workers' interracialism, however, did not derive solely and directly from economic conditions and demands. Though important, they did not constitute the proverbial glue that bound the workers interracially against the employers. After all, Japanese and Filipino workers had pursued, on several occasions, similar material interests without forging durable interracial alliances. One of the enduring lessons of the 1920 strike, for instance, may be that interracial coalitions based purely on shared material ends are extremely frangible. Using the example of the 1946 sugar strike, the first major clash between the Big Five and the ILWU, a longtime ILWU officer explained, "The length of the '46 strike cannot be explained simply on these [economic] terms. . . . There are a lot of sociological issues involved. In other words, to try to understand these strikes in their simple economic terms, the way you would most strikes that take place these days, would be an error, I think."[3]

One such sociological issue was the obdurate opposition mounted by the employers against labor—including mass evictions, shootings, and deaths—that pushed the workers to draw a clear line of conflict between themselves and their employers. But the question of race remains. Rather than with solidarity, the workers had continually expressed their distinction from and resentment of the haole elite in racially refracted ways. Thus, even if the deracialization thesis were correct, existing explanations would prove to be inadequate to the task: they do not convincingly account for what they presume to be the workers' abrupt ideological conversion from "race" to "class."

To account for this conversion, studies appear to rely on an implicit self-evidence of interracialism.[4] The normative desirability of interracialism may indeed seem obvious in retrospect, but this is just a sign of the distance of today's world from that of mid-century Hawai'i.[5] In other words, self-evidence itself requires an explanation. The most persuasive studies argue that the ILWU, its leadership in particular, acted as the principal catalyst in the workers' conversion: "the potential of class consciousness required the arrival of an organization ... which brought to Hawaii the notion of the class *for itself*" (Beechert 1983:169; emphasis in original). The leftist leadership of the ILWU actuated working-class consciousness by "constantly presenting a class analysis in vivid terms" (Geschwender 1981:200).

Without doubt, the movement's discourse did offer workers a powerful analysis of class, and the long, bitter history of employer opposition had done much to prepare the workers to receive and act on it. But the question of race remains. The ILWU did not enter an ideological vacuum in which it could straightforwardly offer a compelling class ideology. Rather, the ILWU entered an ideological field in which workers had long been perceiving their interests in racially divergent and conflicting terms. Existing scholarship does not suf-ficiently recognize this reality, assuming that the workers' new "class" ideology wholly replaced their old "racial" ones. But, as Marshall Sahlins cautions, "things must preserve some identity though their changes, or else the world is a madhouse" (1985:153; see also Sewell 1990, 1992b).

So it was, I contend, with Hawaii's workers: despite the employers' opinions to the contrary, the world did not turn into a madhouse. A viable working-class ideology in Hawai'i had to deal with existing racial divisions; it could not simply erase or ignore them. From the beginning, the ILWU/CIO move-ment's class ideology rearticulated race, leading to several significant innova-tions. However, before the war, these efforts were limited by anti-Filipino and especially anti-Japanese racisms. World War II marked a key turning point, as anti-Japanese racism, structured in the nationalist language of Americanism, became widely discredited, and Japanese workers rejoined the labor movement in large numbers. In the mid-1940s, the movement built on its prewar advances and constructed a compelling interracial working-class ideology that proved to be a rearticulation—rather than a disarticulation—of race.

Prewar Possibilities and Limitations

The mid-1930s were not the first time that Hawaii's workers were exposed to ideas of class that, if not revolutionary, did conceive the interests of employers and workers to be in distinct conflict. In the unionization drive leading up to the 1920 sugar strike, members of the Federation of Japanese Labor (FJL) undoubtedly heard Noboru Tsutsumi, the union's charismatic secretary, espouse his sometimes pointed critique of "capitalists."[6] For two decades after the demise of the 1920 strike, *Yōen Jihō*, the Marxist-oriented paper on Kaua'i, kept radicalism among the Japanese from being completely extinguished (Beechert 1985:212; Chapin 1996:136).[7] In 1921, George Wright, who would later assist Manlapit in organizing Filipino workers, provoked fear with a manifesto that suggested, to the planters and the government, the radical influences of the Industrial Workers of the World (Beechert 1985:213).[8]

To the average worker, however, these early radical voices were marginal murmurs. Faced with intense anti-Japanese racism, the mainstream of the FJL, let alone the Filipino Labor Union, did not share Tsutsumi's views, and his subsequent call to build "a big, powerful and non-racial Labor organization" coincided with the expeditious exodus of the Japanese from the labor movement (Tsutsumi 1922:17). In contrast to the much larger *Nippu Jiji* and *Hawaii Hōchi*, *Yōen Jihō* provided an independent, leftist alternative for its Japanese readership, but the paper was not tied to an active working-class movement. And, while it may have riled employers and the government, Wright's manifesto did little to stir workers, quickly dashing his hope of "one big union."

This state of affairs changed in the mid-1930s when the ILWU/CIO movement started to take hold.[9] From its beginning, leftist ideas of class were not only tied to but central to the movement, as a group of maritime workers, radicals of one stripe or another who had taken part in the class conflict being played out in bloody battles on the West Coast, provided the initial driving force. As the islands' first CIO director recalled, "You had a sprinkling of practically every left-wing attitude among the people that came off the ships that were trying to organize labor here [in Hawai'i]. You had anarchists of those days; you had the old Wobblies of the Wobbly movement; you had Socialists, and you had Communists and Trotskyites."[10] This initial group knitted an expanding network of committed union activists drawn from the rank and file, many of whom also became radicals of one stripe or another. In the "sprinkling," Communists were the most numerous and influential (Holmes 1994).[11]

That leftist militants led the ILWU/CIO in Hawai'i is indisputable. But the current scholarship tends to draw a hasty conclusion from this fact, combining it with the union's eventual multiracial membership to form the empirical basis for the unchallenged claim that "class" *replaced* "race" in the minds and hearts of workers. However, studies have not closely examined the workers' actual discourse and practice to verify, or dispute, this claim, which assumes that the workers' class consciousness can be inferred from the political leanings of their top leaders and that this consciousness was necessarily deracialized. Examining the discourse of organizers and workers to define, persuade, and motivate themselves provides a much more complex picture of race and class than this standard interpretation affords.

Advanced by Communists and other leftists, working-class discourse in prewar Hawai'i had as a central organizing principle the construction of the workers' interests as being in conflict with those of their employers. Like their West Coast counterparts, the leaders proved to be far from doctrinaire ideologues, sharing instead a general but resolute antipathy toward capital.[12] At a typical meeting of sugar workers on the island of Kaua'i, the hotbed of prewar ILWU/CIO organizing, the president of the Port Allen longshoremen exclaimed, "We are not being treated right. The laborers make the money for the big bosses. In Hawaii [a new] generation is coming up, and we don't want to be tenant farmers like the south no more and have our children get $1.00 one day." In clear, understandable terms, the speech related a vaguely socialist notion of exploitation, pointing out that the workers were generating the wealth but not being "treated right." Also resonant with the workers, the $1.00 reference highlighted the sugar industry's infamous minimum wage.[13] "Condemn[ing]" the local plantation manager "Mr. Burns and his $5,000 monthly salary," a worker at the plantation similarly remarked to the racially mixed crowd: "He gets all—we do the work."[14] A third speaker extended this line of argument to talk about the concentration and organization of employers throughout Hawai'i: "Look up the records and see what big bosses you have. . . . [At] the next meeting, I will prove to you that 17 bosses run this Hawaii islands. Your bosses are organized so they can swear at you and work you and keep you living in shacks. So organize and get your better conditions."[15]

Already discernible, the movement's definition of the working class was not only oppositional but capacious. "The entir[e] laboring class must be organized," stated Grover Johnson, the lawyer defending the indicted Filipino leaders of Vibora Luviminda.[16] In the context of racial divisions of the 1930s, this expansive understanding of the working class, without regard to distinctions of craft or skill, had unavoidable racial implications: it meant organizing interracially—"regardless of race, color, or creed"—a notion that may sound rather commonplace today but was quite discordant with contemporary, and earlier, practices.[17] At a racially mixed gathering of 400 to 500 workers in Hanapēpē on the island of Kaua'i, an organizer implored the workers to build "a united front of all labor, Filipino, Japanese and Portuguese so that 'they' could get their rights from the capitalist."[18] At the same meeting, Johnson entreated the workers with a speech emphasizing the critical importance of interracialism in resisting the employers: "It is possible. We are all equal before the law. We are protected by the Constitution of the United States of America. The races here can organize themselves and can stand together as one in brotherly love. . . . At present, the big five is dealing with only one[,] Filipino laborer[s,] and if it is the case the only one is weak."[19] Critiquing Americanism—perhaps having happened upon that regnant discourse of race and nation—Johnson concluded, "The higher ups calls [sic] it Americanism when they can squeeze the laboring class to servitude."[20]

In practical terms, organizing such a "united front," a term transposed from the Communists' antisectarian stance against fascism, called for racially integrated unions. Unlike the Japanese and Filipino unions involved in the 1920 strike or even some CIO unions—but not the ILWU—in the Deep South, the renewed labor movement in Hawai'i would not be a coalition of racially segregated unions or locals (Nelson 1992). To effect this integration, a critical practice of the movement was, as seen in the last chapter, the holding of interracial meetings in multiple languages. Anticipating employer attempts to exacerbate already existing racial rifts, Hawaii's CIO director reasoned in a 1937 report, "Only one thing can counteract this move and that is the CIO with a program of publicity and education in the language of the workers affected, using workers of different nationalities who live right in Hawaii."[21] The multilingual teams of organizers no doubt also had the adventitious effect of creating then rare public displays of racial integration.[22] Furthermore, printed documents began to appear in multiple languages. For example, one notice announced in English, Ilocano, and Japanese a mass meeting in Lihu'e with "Filipino, Japanese, and Haole speakers" to "organize all workers into one big union, regardless of color or creed, citizen or non-citizen, male or female."[23]

Another early means of articulating an oppositional concept of capitalist class relations with race was to blame the employers not only for exploiting the workers but also for producing the racial divisions that existed among them through "divide and rule"—an expected move for the leftist leaders. At a HoLA meeting, a visiting organizer from the West Coast "spoke on the need of solidarity & United Front and how people here in Hawaii are coerced and exploited. How race, creed and color are pitied [sic] against each other by the men who are holding enormous wealth."[24] The Filipino head of the UCAPAWA unit at the Lihu'e plantation sounded a similar refrain at a meeting held on the steps of the county courthouse on the island of Kaua'i. To about 150 "enthusiastic" sugar workers, who were "enjoying the 'pokes'" directed at management, the officer exclaimed, "You know the plantations want organizations for nationalities—we don't."[25]

The movement's discourse also spoke to the racially hierarchical order that perpetually placed Filipinos, the largest segment of the workforce, at the bottom. For example, one of the main complaints of the lowly regarded Filipino workers had long been that they always received the worst housing on the plantations.[26] Addressing this persistent problem, an organizer rhetorically asked at a meeting, "You Filipinos living in the plantations, are you satisfied packed like sardines four, five and six men in a single room, just like pigs in a pig pen? . . . Join the union and you'll get better housing conditions and more money."[27]

The ILWU/CIO movement also offered the larger promise of racial equality to Filipino workers. At a meeting of 250 workers, the vast majority of whom were Filipino, an organizer stressed, "We want you in the CIO where all brothers are alike . . . Japanese, Filipinos, Portuguese, haoles and all are the same."[28] Organizers highlighted the fact that the CIO, unlike the AFL, welcomed all workers "regardless of whether citizens or not."[29] Revealing his motive for belonging to the ILWU, a Filipino longshoreman from Ahukini explained how the port captain treated the workers: "He just treat them like animals. If get little bit mistake he say, 'You monkey, jackass.'"[30] Having faced racial marginalization by not only the employers but also other workers, Filipinos were clearly concerned about their status within the ILWU/CIO movement. For example, at one HoLA meeting, "there was a question of doubt in the minds of some of the Filipino members whether they [would] be accorded the same privilege as their fellow members." The emphatic answer of "yes" undoubtedly solidified the Filipino workers' loyalty to the union and the movement, given that the response would not have been as obvious or affirmative anywhere else.[31]

A final way in which the prewar discourse of class incorporated race was by contrasting the fledgling interracial movement to the various unsuccessful, racially exclusive movements of the past. Though the union activists probably did not think in these deliberate terms, their reaching back to the past inextricably linked the current struggle to past struggles in the minds of workers who may have experienced or, more likely, heard about them, while at the same time distinguishing the current effort from the inadequacies of the past. Speaking in Japanese to a racially mixed crowd of 300, organizer George Goto reminded the audience,

> You have in your memory till to-day I'm sure the bitter fight in the strike[s] of 1909 and 1920. The reason the fight was bitter is because you were fighting alone, Japanese alone. The Filipinos also had a hard fight. Why? Simply because you didn't have an organization such as a union putting all races in one. We must all get together regardless of race, color, or creed in order to get better living condition by bargaining collectively. The American Factors and A & B declared big dividends even at the time of the depression. Why don't the capitalists be a little more considerate and divide some of the money among the laboring class. We will never get it if we just sit and wait. We must ask for it, not individually but collectively.[32]

In this speech, Goto adroitly tied together the bitter struggles of the past hampered by racial exclusiveness, the interracial imperative of the current struggle, the fundamental difference between the Big Five employers and the "laboring class," and the workers' need to act collectively. Delivering a similar message to Filipino workers, an organizer exhorted, "I call upon you brothers to avenge the Hanapepe affair when 17 of your brothers were shot in the back. This must not die and you can remember you got nothing out of the 1924 strike because you were doing it alone. It's different now with all joining the CIO."[33] Reiterating the same message to a racially mixed crowd, Ben Shear, a radical sailor, reasoned, "Strikes in the past have failed because the Japanese did it alone in 1920 and the Filipinos did it alone in 1924. . . . we must break down this race hatred and if you keep fighting among yourselves, what have you got? . . . Wake up workers [and] make one big union."[34]

As discussed in the last chapter, the ILWU/CIO movement before the war made real but slow progress, and much of the slowness had to do with the employers' continued resistance, albeit tempered by the intervention of the federal government. But the prewar pace also had to do with ideological constraints on the workers' capacity to cohere interracially. One prewar constraint concerned Filipino workers. Overall, they did not find the transition from their past organizing efforts, most recently through Vibora Luviminda, to the new movement problematic. After all, the change was eased by the ILWU/CIO's assistance before and during the 1937 Maui strike, the shift of key Vibora Luviminda leaders to the ILWU/CIO, and the ILWU/CIO's procurement of Johnson's legal services to defend Vibora Luviminda leaders, all of which made favorable impressions. Furthermore, except in the case of Port Allen, there is little evidence in employer or union documents to suggest unwillingness on the part of Filipino workers to join the ILWU/CIO after the demise of Vibora Luviminda.

In the port of Ahukini, however, there was evidence that *other* workers were reluctant at times to join the ILWU/CIO alongside Filipinos. In the late 1930s, Filipinos constituted a clear majority of the longshore workforce in Ahukini.[35] Sometime in mid-1937, ILWU/CIO organizers formed a longshore union there; it signed a contract in October that recognized it as the sole collective bargaining agency.[36] The union attracted Filipino workers, who tended to be hired, per the usual racial ordering of the day, as "casuals" rather than "regulars" and were paid significantly less as a result.[37] Filipino longshoremen joined the CIO union precisely because they felt it could address their always being relegated to the bottom. As ILWU/CIO organizer Calixto Piano observed firsthand, Filipino workers in Ahukini felt that "they were forced to do hard jobs; they [supervisors] call them monkeys and jackasses. . . . they think if they get organization and if they stick together they can get better conditions and they can get better wages."[38]

With time, it became clear why non-Filipino longshoremen in Ahukini did not join. Later in 1937, a group led by four longshoremen sought a charter from the AFL-affiliated HWWA. Juxtaposing themselves in opposition to the "Filipinos" who had joined the CIO, they wrote, "We who did not join the CIO feel that this Company has always been fair to us and has always met our reasonable demands, desire to form a Union . . . but [one] not believing in the radical principals [sic] of the Cio [sic]."[39] Those who joined the AFL union consciously defined themselves in opposition to the CIO union, which they viewed as "Filipino" as well as "radical," although not all who joined it were Filipinos.[40] And, the AFL unionists' characterizations of Filipino workers were familiar, revolving around the widely held assumptions that Filipinos were uncivilized, inferior, and noncitizen. According to one Japanese member of the AFL union, those belonging to the "Filipino" union were violent and "dumb."[41] A haole member was the most explicit in differentiating the AFL and the CIO in racist terms: "all those connected with the CIO are practically bums, all uncivilized monkeys." Referring to the "casual" status of the Filipino longshoremen, he continued, "Us fellows down there in the AFL we have a little bit of education—read, write and understand English. Do you think that we want a bunch of dumb-bells or canefield workers—not even citizens, not able to read and write—to be our bargaining agent down there, who work only when the steamer is in?"[42]

Although anti-Filipino racism certainly constrained interracialism in Ahukini, the evidence is not clear on how typical this phenomenon was. We do not know of other companies that the ILWU/CIO tried to organize but could not because non-Filipino workers were unwilling to join a union with Filipino members. What does become clear over time, however, is that interracial unity between Filipino and non-Filipino workers would be tested into the 1940s and 1950s.

The constraining effect of anti-Japanese racism on prewar interracialism, on the other hand, was clearly widespread. Unlike Filipino workers, Japanese workers had been inactive in the labor movement since the 1920 sugar strike. But no working-class movement could have hoped to succeed as a multi-industrial, interracial movement without the Japanese, whose share of the labor force trailed only the Filipinos'.[43] Anti-Japanese racism, articulated in the nationalist language of Americanism, had driven Japanese workers out of the labor movement, and there was little evidence, even toward the end of the 1930s, that they could be pulled back in on a large scale.

Continuing to face racial doubts of their national loyalty, most Japanese workers, many of whom were hired in the 1930s when the sugar industry urged nisei "New Americans" back to the plantations, did not see militant labor activism as a desirable or viable option. In the late 1930s, when labor activism was on the rise on multiple fronts, the Big Five-related employers, concerned about the possibility of Japanese workers' becoming involved once again, tried to gauge their thoughts and activities. The employers became acutely alarmed in 1937 when class relations seemed particularly volatile.[44]

To the employers' relief, however, there appeared to be little inclination on the part of Japanese workers to join this surge of activism. Through its surveillance of various Japanese newspapers and inquiries with those it presumed to be the key figures in the Japanese community, the HSPA concluded to its satisfaction that Japanese workers still had scant interest in the labor movement: "Except for the mild editorial which appeared in Nippu Jiji, no interest is shown by the Japanese in the movement of mainland labor union agents.... Inquiries show that Japanese as a whole have no interest, and do not care what malihini [newcomer] haoles [from the West Coast] are doing to strengthen their own labor union."[45] Although the employers' assessments should be considered with skepticism, there is indeed little evidence to gainsay their conclusion in this case; for example, Japanese newspapers of the period, with notable exceptions like *Yōen Jihō*, revealed an understandable preoccupation with the hegemonic politics of Americanization in its various manifestations and little support for renewed labor activism, particularly the ILWU/CIO movement with its specter of anti-American radicalism.[46] For the vast majority of Japanese workers, the potent combination of anti-Japanese racism and absence from the labor movement continued to obtain for the remainder of the 1930s.

Breaking this interwar pattern proved to be difficult for the ILWU/CIO, even in areas where it had a fairly large and active presence. The Honolulu waterfront exhibited the stiffest resistance to organizing efforts. Although much of it was due to the employers' escalated antiunion activities, there was also a major reason less directly involving them: the ILWU found the Japanese longshoremen, who comprised the largest segment of workers on the docks at the time, to be particularly hard to organize. In mid-1937, the Honolulu longshore local reported, "About two thirds of the Longshoremens [*sic*] are Japanese and in order that we can have the complete solidarity in this we must have them in this organization which we have tried but we couldn't have them to come to an un[der]standing of our move."[47] In early 1940, the local was still having a hard time recruiting Japanese workers. Its president, Jack Kawano, diagnosed, "The major problem of our union at this time is to recruit more workers from the Japanese group." The union "represent[ed] a very small portion of the workers among the Japanese group . . . and a successful campaign among this group is something that [has been] very difficult for our union up to now." Reflecting the omnipresent doubts of Japanese loyalty to the United States, the union had a hard time disabusing the Japanese longshoremen, a majority of whom were noncitizen issei at the time, of their fears of deportation.[48]

The longshore union in Port Allen faced the opposite problem for the same reason. As discussed in the last chapter, the PAWWA, the direct predecessor to ILWU Local 1–35, came into being with an April 1937 strike in which 95 percent of the port's longshoremen participated. However, immediately after its foundation, the union split into two factions, one Japanese and one non-Japanese.

The Japanese, who made up 56 percent of the port's workforce, remained in the PAWWA, and the others left and formed a company-favored AFL union that soon dissolved. As PAWWA members found out, the only basis for the racial splitting of their union was a familiar one: as in the 1920 strike, Japanese workers were accused of being anti-American and loyal to Japan and of commandeering the union. Attesting to its depth, the racial split in Port Allen was never bridged before the war, despite repeated attempts. Up to the attack on Pearl Harbor, this ILWU "Local consisted of practically all Japanese. The Portuguese and Filipino employees working at the port were not members of the Union."[49]

Collapse of Anti-Japanese Americanism

The ideology of Americanism posed a formidable obstacle to working-class interracialism in interwar Hawai'i. Following the 1920 strike, unrelenting attacks on Japanese loyalty to the United States pushed Japanese workers away from class conflict. During the Depression, the discourse of Americanism also drove a deeper wedge between Japanese and Filipino workers, as the nisei's reactive insistence on their Americanness led them to define themselves in contradistinction to the Filipino "alien race."

Because it overlooks the significance of interwar Americanism in effecting both the Japanese workers' absence from the labor movement and the racial divisions among workers, existing scholarship also overlooks the significance of World War II in facilitating both the Japanese workers' mass return to the labor movement and the movement's interracialism. In the course of the war, Americanism as anti-Japanese racism imploded, as its persistent questioning of Japanese loyalty could not be reconciled with the "loyal" actions of the Japanese, especially their bodily sacrifice on the battlefields. Consequently, this contradiction created an ideological or "cultural opportunity" (McAdam 1994).

The hegemonic ideology of Americanism affected practically every aspect of Japanese life in prewar Hawai'i. Buddhism, Japanese-language schools and newspapers, dual citizenship, and racial bloc voting, among myriad other issues, variously became the foci of scrutiny in the public's unceasing effort to uncover Japanese anti-Americanism. How the Japanese responded or whether there was evidence for the suspicions was beside the point: there simply were no viable ways for the Japanese to escape the ubiquitous questioning of their loyalty (Okihiro 1991:ch. 7).[50] The best they could hope for was expressed by the head of Castle & Cooke when he concluded that although the nisei "show[ed] every indication of being loyal American citizens . . . it will take time to clearly prove this."[51] In other words, outward indications (e.g., renouncing dual citizenship, not voting as a bloc, not organizing unions), however "American," could not exonerate the Japanese from charges of anti-Americanism, because what they were ultimately guilty of was not *acting* Japanese but *being* Japanese.

At the core of the prewar discourse of Americanism was the combination of two notions gripping the imagination of haole and, secondarily, other non-Japanese: Japan's rapid ascent as an imperialist power and a biologistic conception of race that inherently linked Hawaii's Japanese to Japan. In a speech not out of line with the prevailing ideas of the day, Admiral Yates Stirling Jr. exposed this core to a conference audience of nisei: "Gentlemen, when I questioned your loyalty to your new country, AMERICA, I did so because of [Japan's] marvelous heritage of accomplishment, for if I were of your race, I would be most proud of the meteoric rise of the Empire of the Rising Sun and be very loath to forget that my ancestors were a part of it."[52]

Thus explaining the nisei's difficult task of proving their loyalty, Stirling did suggest one criterion that he would find convincing: "Men and women willing to die in [the nation's] defense."[53] He was not alone. Throughout the 1930s, both those who doubted the loyalty of the Japanese and those Japanese who asserted their loyalty posed the same scenario as the ultimate test: What would Hawaii's Japanese do in the event of a war with Japan?[54] In 1929, three years before Stirling's speech, a nisei at the same conference had stated to his fellow delegates, "We must realize that we American citizens of Japanese descent are wholly on trial. . . . I know that if there should be a war between America and Japan, I should defend America."[55]

As the tension between the United States and Japan heightened, both doubts and assurances of Japanese loyalty in the event of a war were heard with accelerated frequency and urgency. Ambivalently expressing both doubt and assurance, a Portuguese lawyer told a gathering of 300 Republicans, "God forbid, but if our citizens of Japanese ancestry are made to face the 'gunpowder test,' I am sure that they will meet it as they have done in any other test."[56] Less charitably, a prominent haole stated matter-of-factly a year later,

> As American citizens of Japanese ancestry your political behavior will be more closely watched and more harshly judged than that of other American citizens. This may seem unfair but should be accepted as inevitable and normal. Since Japan is pursuing an aggressive foreign policy endangering our rights and interests in the Pacific, many are wondering which nation commands your sympathy and allegiance. You belong to the generation that must prove that your American citizenship is not a mere accident of birth on American soil.[57]

In a speech titled "Stop Fifth Columnists In Their Tracks," a representative of the army similarly warned Hawaii's Japanese, "We must join in wholeheartedly in all defense efforts; half-way measures cannot be permitted and will be misinterpreted."[58]

In the face of such admonitions, Hawaii's Japanese increasingly felt compelled to respond unequivocally and univocally (Stephan 1984:39–40). In June 1941, the *Honolulu Star-Bulletin* reported on one of the many public displays of patriotism to be held that year in the Japanese community: "Pledges to defend America and the American way of life against all internal and external forces 'even at the sacrifices of our lives' were given by leading Americans of Japanese ancestry and heartily supported by 1,500 others at a patriotic rally at McKinley high school auditorium Friday evening. In the presence of government, army and navy and business leaders, representatives of nearly all Japanese-American organizations on Oahu, and others, reaffirmed their 'unreserved loyalty to the United States.'"[59] Trying to convey a sense of unanimity among the Japanese, regardless of generation or citizenship status, *Hawaii Hōchi* editorialized, "Alien Japanese parents are proud to have their sons chosen to serve in the army of the United States because they also love this country where they have made their home and reared their children."[60] Even Buddhist priests, who were portrayed in the mainstream media as the epitome of Japanese anti-Americanism, attempted to assure the public that Hawaii's Japanese were loyal to the United States: "Speaking at the opening of the 12th territorial Buddhists' convention yesterday at Wahiawa, Bishop Gikyo Kuchiba of the Hompa Hongwanji Mission called the delegates to prove their readiness and loyalty to the Stars and Stripes through the Buddhist faith. . . . He went on to say that now is the time for the young people to prove themselves worthy even at the sacrifice of life for this country as American citizens of Japanese ancestry of Buddhist religion."[61]

It was in this ideological context that Japan's bombs fell on December 7, 1941. Leading up to the outbreak of war, both the Japanese and their doubters had constructed, in effect, a potential for a major contradiction in the discourse of Americanism: a war between the United States and Japan would "reveal," once and for all, the "true" loyalty of Hawaii's Japanese. Anti-Japanese racism predictably reached a new fevered pitch in wartime. Rumors of subversive fifth-column activities spread like cane fire (Allen 1950:ch. 3; Kotani 1985:75–76; Lind 1943:11–13).[62] Selective internment soon followed. From 1942 to 1945, 1,466 Japanese were interned in concentration camps in Hawai'i, and 1,875 Japanese were interned in concentration camps in the continental United States (Okihiro 1991:267).[63] Only the prospect of a major disruption to Hawaii's economy and defense work and the logistical impracticality of transporting and detaining the islands' nearly 160,000 Japanese spared them the fate of mass internment met by their counterparts in the metropole.[64]

The Japanese—primarily but not only the issei—were subject to numerous governmental restrictions in addition to those imposed on the rest of the population under martial law. "Alien Japanese" were restricted from possessing items like shortwave radios, cameras, and weapons; from changing jobs and residences without permission; and from writing, printing, or publishing attacks against the U.S. government. Radio broadcasts in Japanese and publication of Japanese newspapers were suspended.[65] Assembly of more than ten aliens was prohibited, and Japanese-language schools, Buddhist temples, and Shinto shrines were closed. Both citizen and noncitizen Japanese could no longer practice the trade of fishing, and they were barred from certain jobs in defense work and on the waterfront (Lind 1943:18–23; Okihiro 1991:226–232).[66]

Not confined to official acts of the government, discrimination against the Japanese was extensively and openly practiced during the war in all areas of life. A national magazine article—with "Japs" in its headline—noted the widespread antipathy toward the Japanese in Hawai'i: "They took a lot of punishment. They were openly hated and booed in the streets."[67] The military's announcement that "there must not be indiscriminate displacement" of Japanese workers did not keep Hawaii's private employers from adopting and even advertising discriminatory hiring policies (Lind 1943).[68]

Both despite and because of the heightened suspicion and widespread de jure and de facto discrimination, the Japanese community, on the whole, sought to demonstrate its "loyalty" even more assertively than it had in the interwar years. "As in the campaigns of the 1920s and 1930s," Gary Okihiro (1991:229) writes, it was "the Japanese [who] led in the wartime Americanization effort." By any standard, the Japanese matched and surpassed all others, disproportionately buying large quantities of war bonds and stamps and donating their time and labor in any voluntary war activity from which they were not prohibited (e.g., Kotani 1985:ch. 6; Rademaker and Lane 1951:ch. 4). There were also Japanese-led campaigns, both organized and not, to eradicate traces of Japanese culture. In the early days of the war, according to two nisei observers, "rumors circulated that any objects which were 'Japanesy' were incriminating and that many Issei were being interned because of possession of them. . . . almost every Japanese family had a thorough housecleaning, and all objects which were kept for sentimental reasons were pulled out of trunks and destroyed" (as quoted in Okihiro 1991:229). Changes in hairstyle, dress, and everyday rituals followed. The most organized and vigorous effort was the "Speak American Campaign" led by the Emergency Service Committee, a nisei voluntary group operating under the aegis of the military government (Okihiro 1991:229–237).

The public's hostility toward the Japanese probably would have been worse, had the Japanese not taken the preceding actions "voluntarily." However, the actions were not sufficient to stanch the flow of distrust. Anti-Japanese discourse of Americanism proliferated, as evidenced in the mainstream papers. Initially, they focused on possible fifth-column activities. With no credible evidence of such, the papers then turned to concerns very much like the ones from before the war, attacking virtually anything Japanese and championing Americanization efforts.[69] For example, the *Honolulu Star-Bulletin* called for the permanent abolition of Shintoism, foreign-language schools and papers, and Japanese social clubs. Lauding the "Speak American" campaign, the *Honolulu Advertiser* editorialized repeatedly against the use of Japanese, and even "pidgin," by both the issei and the nisei (Tamashiro 1972).[70]

Still framed in the nationalist language of Americanism, prewar racial dynamics in relation to the Japanese intensified in wartime but did not fundamentally change—until 1943. In January of that year, Lt. General Delos C. Emmons, the military governor and commanding general, issued the following "call to Americans of Japanese ancestry":

[The] role [of Americans of Japanese descent] has not been an easy one. Open to distrust because of their racial origin, and discriminated against in certain fields of the defense effort, they nevertheless have borne their burdens without complaint and have added materially to the strength of the Hawaiian area....

In view of these facts, and by War Department authority, I have been designated to offer the Americans of Japanese ancestry an additional opportunity to serve their country. This opportunity is in the form of voluntary combat service in the armed forces. I have been directed to induct 1,500 of them as volunteers into the Army of the United States....

The manner of response and the record these men will establish as fighting soldiers will be one of the best answers to those who question the loyalty of American citizens of Japanese ancestry in Hawaii.[71]

The "gunpowder test," spoken of so frequently before the war, had finally arrived.

Attesting to the immense racist pressure exerted upon and felt by the Japanese, as well as the inextricably intertwined sense of patriotism, nisei volunteered in overwhelming numbers. Although the original call was for 1,500, a total of 9,507 volunteered, which represented 4 out of 10 nisei men of military age. In the end, 2,600 were inducted to form, with 2,000 nisei volunteers from the metropole, the 442nd Regimental Combat Team.[72] At the time of this call for volunteers, another segregated nisei unit, the 100th Infantry Battalion (Separate), was already training on the continent; it had been formed from the approximately 1,400 nisei soldiers who had been serving in integrated units in Hawai'i before the outbreak of war. In September 1943, the 100th landed in North Africa. The battalion later merged into the 442nd when the latter arrived in Italy in June 1944 (Kotani 1985:96–100; Rademaker and Lane 1951:ch. 3). Lawrence Fuchs (1961:306) summarizes, "Between them, the 442nd and the 100th furnished 60 percent of Hawaii's fighting forces and 80 percent of the casualties." They suffered a casualty rate of more than 3 times the average for the entire army (Daws 1968:351; see also Odo 2004:234).

1 A rare photograph of all the presidents of the "Big Five" agencies, 1956. Left to right:
R. G. Bell, Alexander & Baldwin; A. G. Budge, Castle & Cooke; Alan Davis, C. Brewer &
Company; G. W. Sumner, American Factors; and J. E. Russell, Theo. H. Davies & Company.

2 Labor Day in Lihu'e, 1940.

March 30, 1942

MEMORANDUM to: All Employees

In accordance with Department regulations, all employees are directed not to hold conversation with unauthorized persons regarding work projects or labor conditions including hours of work and rates of pay, and particularly with Plantation laborers.

C. D. Baker
Capt., Corps of Engineers
Area Engineer

3 An attempt to silence discussion of pay differentials between defense workers and plantation workers "loaned" to the military during World War II.

Courtesy of the Anne Rand Research Library, ILWU, San Francisco.

4 First "AJA" volunteers for the armed forces in Hilo, March 18, 1943. HWRD Photograph 3847.

Courtesy of the University of Hawai'i Archives.

5 Executive board members of the Honolulu longshore union (ILWU Local 1-37) that initiated the organizing of plantation workers during World War II, 1944. Left to right: Benjamin Kahaawinui, Joseph "Blurr" Kealalio, Yoroku Fukuda, Frederick Kamahoahoa (secretary-treasurer), James Tanaka, unidentified, Jack Osakoda, and John Elias, Jr.

Courtesy of the Anne Rand Research Library, ILWU, San Francisco.

6 ILWU Political Action Committee Convention in Hilo, February 1946.

Courtesy of the ILWU Local 142 Archives.

7 Unionists from Hawaiʻi at a leadership training program in San Francisco, 1946. Left to right: Elias Domingo, Yasuki Arakaki, Thomas Yagi, Hideo "Major" Okada, Constantine Samson, Harry Bridges (ILWU International president), Leocadio Baldovi, Harry Kamoku, Yoshikazu Morimoto, Dominador Agayan, and Webb Tokeo Ideue.

Courtesy of the Anne Rand Research Library, ILWU, San Francisco.

8 Meeting of sugar workers in ʻŌlaʻa in preparation for the big strike, 1946. Frank Thompson at the microphone. Seated, left to right: Yasuki Arakaki, Kenji "Sleepy" Omuro, Saburo Fujisaki, David Thompson, and unidentified.

Courtesy of the ILWU Local 142 Archives.

9 A march of striking sugar workers and supporters on the Big Island, 1946.

Courtesy of the ILWU Local 142 Archives.

10 "Sugar Unity Conference" in Hilo, January 1948. Ichiro Izuka at the lectern. Seated on the dais, left to right: Constantine Samson, Antonio Rania, Yoshikazu Morimoto, and Louis Goldblatt.

Courtesy of the ILWU Local 142 Archives.

11 A picket line of striking longshoremen, 1949.

Courtesy of the ILWU Local 142 Archives.

12 ILWU Territorial Conference concerning further consolidation of the union in Hawaiʻi, January 1950.

Courtesy of the ILWU Local 142 Archives.

13 An address by Pedro de la Cruz to striking pineapple workers on Lanaʻi, 1951.

Courtesy of the Anne Rand Research Library, ILWU, San Francisco.

14 An ILWU protest against the Senate Internal Security Subcommittee hearings held by Senator James O. Eastland (D-Mississippi) in Honolulu, 1956.

Courtesy of the Anne Rand Research Library, ILWU, San Francisco.

The impact of the nisei's seemingly unhesitating response to the call for volunteers and of the soldiers' subsequent fighting and casualties on the anti-Japanese discourse of Americanism was almost immediate. Teaching in Hawai'i at the time, sociologist John Rademaker recalled, "No one could read the daily or weekly papers of Hawaii without being struck repeatedly right between the eyes by the casualty lists published every few days. . . . Repeatedly these lists included fifty to a hundred Japanese American names, a few Portuguese, Puerto Rican, and Filipino names, and one or two Euro-American (Caucasian or *haole*) names. To the ordinary newspaper reader, it was all too painfully clear who was paying the price of death and serious wounds" (Rademaker and Lane 1951:255). As reports of the nisei soldiers' exploits and casualties increased, there was a marked decrease in editorial comments questioning Japanese loyalty, which seems to have been matched by a parallel decline in anti-Japanese sentiment overall (Tamashiro 1972:59).[73]

By the war's end, Hawaii's Japanese had largely laid to rest the racially rooted, hegemonic prewar doubts of their "Americanism." In addition to news of their efforts and sacrifices, the fact that "sabotage and fifth-column activity was [*sic*] never engaged in at any time prior, during, or subsequent to the attack on Pearl Harbor" circulated widely through periodic announcements during and after the war.[74] Americanism as anti-Japanese racism suddenly became nearly unspeakable, even nonsensical.[75] As in a Kuhnian (1962) scientific revolution, the "normal" prewar racism against the Japanese, which had been so indifferent to contrary evidence, could not assimilate the "anomaly" of Japanese conduct during the war. Racial discrimination against the Japanese did not disappear, but it could no longer be exercised as flagrantly or be draped in the American flag (Nomura 1987). That wartime "patriotism" had this profound impact on anti-Japanese racism—but historically has not in relation to racisms against other people of color in the United States—offers further evidence for qualitatively different racisms.

For the Japanese, "the war gave birth to a battle-scarred generation confident in their claim to America," as Okihiro (1991:269) notes. One of many such claims was made by Japanese workers who returned to the labor movement in large numbers beginning in late 1943. As Americanism had served as a barrier between Japanese and Filipino workers in the 1930s, its collapse as anti-Japanese racism made the prospect of working-class interracialism more likely—there was no longer a need for Japanese workers to insist on their "Americanness" in distinction to Filipino workers. Conversely, other workers, like the public in general, could no longer view Japanese workers askance, as they had, for example, in Port Allen.

Without the decline of Americanism as anti-Japanese racism, postwar working-class formation in Hawai'i would most likely have turned out quite differently. Given the interwar history of Japanese workers, whether and how completely they, especially the thousands of unorganized in agriculture, would have joined the labor movement would be moot. Even if they had joined en masse, how would they have reacted to the postwar anticommunist attacks on the ILWU, also cloaked in the language of Americanism? If the 1920 strike, when Americanism combined anti-Japanese racism with antiradicalism, was any indication, history did not lend much confidence to postwar working-class interracialism. Furthermore, how would Japanese workers have reacted to the postwar anti-"alien" attacks on Filipino workers, if their own claim to "America" were still being impugned? If the 1930s, when Japanese workers participated in racially marginalizing Filipinos, were any indication, history again did not lend much confidence to postwar working-class interracialism.

Remaking History

Because the ILWU had established a foothold in organizing before the war, it was positioned "in the right place at the right time, with the right forces" at the end of martial law to mobilize the thousands of discontented workers.[76] Likewise, the movement drew on and extended its prewar innovations in constructing an ideology that would unite the workers interracially against the employers. As before the war, the movement defined the interests of the workers and those of their employers in conflictual terms. A discourse of class that starkly pitted workers against employers firmly took hold. The oppressive conditions for labor under martial law, especially for the much maligned but later vindicated Japanese, had sharpened the class cleavage, predisposing workers to a leftist ideology and movement that would confront their powerful employers aggressively. Statements differentiating the employers and the workers in oppositional terms, like the following example, became commonplace: "Of course, it is nothing new for Hawaii's top employers to fight unionization of their workers tooth and nail. They have always done so."[77] The ILWU in Hawai'i also committed itself to organizing sugar and pineapple, as well as longshoring, thereby reflecting the industrial setup in the islands. Across industries, workers increasingly constructed their antagonist to be not only their immediate employers but the "Big Five" that owned and controlled those employers.[78] Union newspaper articles detailing which companies those agencies controlled and how profits were "drained off directly to the Big Five" appeared frequently, and the term "Big Five" gained ubiquitous and opprobrious currency.[79]

More or less simultaneously, suggesting an affinity, the movement's discourse also incorporated and aligned the workers' racial antipathy toward the haole elite that had long been racially refracted and not expressed in uniformly conflictual terms. In a tone of epiphanous recognition, an internal ILWU report in early 1944, assessing the "organizing possibilities in Hawaii," observed that "the biggest source of irritation [among the workers] is the 'race' bars to promotion": "Top jobs are held 99 per cent by what Hitler would call Pure Aryan." The report noted that Hawaiian and Portuguese workers had been treated by the employers as "second-class citizens"; Japanese and Filipino workers had been treated as "third-class" and "definitely 'fourth-class'" citizens, respectively. The report concluded emphatically, "THE PRIMARY FACTOR IN THE NATIONAL QUESTION IS THE FACT THAT THE HAOLES (WHITES) OWN THE PLANTATIONS AND HAVE THE GOOD JOBS."[80] It followed that "one of the popular slogans and demands" of the movement would be "for an end to discrimination" (Thompson 1951:40). Or, as the ILWU regional director for Hawai'i stated in 1946, "Whether it is before the law, on the job, within the union, in the community, nation or world, the program of the ILWU can be summed up in two simple words: END DISCRIMINATION."[81] The movement thus came to provide, as one union officer put it, "new avenues for the sharp and open expression of anti-haole sentiment," and it "channelized that sentiment" (Thompson 1951:40). It should be noted that "discrimination," a term denoting, before the war, the unfair treatment of union members, assumed an additional, and promptly primary, racial meaning.[82]

A common class and racial foe, however, did not necessarily mean that Portuguese, Japanese, Filipino, and other workers would form a coherent collective, given their racially divided history. The most ready explanation for this situation was the notion of "divide and rule." Given the leftward lean of the movement, the reappearance of this idea, introduced before the war, was hardly a surprise. Viewing the world, including race, through the lens of class, prewar activists had invoked "divide and rule," the quintessentially leftist explanation, to make sense of the racial divisions among workers. But, abstractly and mechanically applied to Hawai'i, as seen earlier, it had been more of a left knee-jerk reaction than a fully articulated idea.

With repeated usage over time, however, this interpretive schema evolved to be much more than perfunctory, leftist rhetoric, becoming grounded in and contoured to the particularities of race and class in Hawai'i. Combined with another prewar innovation—that of contrasting the present against the past—"divide and rule" became indispensable to the construction of working-class interracialism. Reinterpreting the past through the schema, the workers conceived an interracial, working-class "narrative identity," selectively appropriating their divergent and conflicting racial histories to create a common interracial identity (Somers 1994).[83]

Before the war, the ILWU/CIO organizers had urged the workers to look to the past and realize that racially exclusive movements did not work. In the kinetic post–martial law years, this search continued, mining more details about previous labor struggles. In addition to the accumulation of knowledge—most likely culled from various sources, including workers' memories, newspapers, and government documents—examining the past naturally led to the question of *why* the workers had not formed interracial movements.

Surfacing in various embryonic forms before then, the "divide and rule" notion as a mnemonic schema to answer this question was well developed by 1946.[84] This construction of an interracial, working-class "narrative identity" can be seen clearly in 2 of the union's publications from 1946. In February, the ILWU in Hawai'i sent a group of 10 leaders to San Francisco to attend a 6-week "leadership training program," which included 2 weeks at the left-wing California Labor School; all grassroots officers elected at the local and unit levels, the 10 were "selected to secure the broadest island representation—territorial, industrial, and racial."[85] At the end of the program in April, the participants drafted a summary report, a "manual" on various aspects of union building and administration. It included a section on race with an interpretive history of Hawaii's workers. Five months later, in September, the ILWU published a 45-page pamphlet called *Raising Cane*, another interpretive history of labor that elaborated on the ideas contained in the earlier publication. Both publications—a manual distributed to ILWU locals and units and a pamphlet that came out at the start of the 1946 sugar strike—received wide circulation and readership.[86]

The main theme of the two pieces was that "the employers were quick to see that the workers could be kept weak and divided by race prejudice, and they have always done their best to keep prejudice alive in the islands."[87] According to the narrative, employers espoused racism against the various nonhaole groups to justify the recruitment of new nonhaole groups. Once on the plantations, "under the planters' divide and rule policy, no two national groups had the same working conditions" or wages (Weingarten 1946:19), as the employers "attempted to buy off the races which have been here longest."[88] The employers also set up segregated plantation camps to keep the workers divided. These practices "create[d] resentment of the favored races among the members of the races who [were] discriminated against in promotion, housing etc."[89] By keeping "the workers divided along racial lines, [the employers] could prevent union organizing and break any strikes that might occur."[90] And, in the strikes of 1909, 1920, 1924, and 1937, the employers used strikebreakers of different racial groups and otherwise "took advantage of the split[s] in labor's ranks" (Weingarten 1946:30). The turning point in this history was the advent of the ILWU/CIO movement: "The new organizers did not accept the planters' theory that a worker of one nation was better than the worker of another. All men, they held, are equal. . . . The planters resisted doggedly" (Weingarten 1946:35).

The employers were the unequivocal antagonists in this narrative; they were haole of missionary background who "had taken the land" from Native Hawaiians and later owned the plantations and the "Big Five" (Weingarten 1946:8). They were the antagonists not only because they exploited workers economically but also because they practiced racism. Written a year after the end of World War II, both writings made analogies to Nazi German racism to drive home this point. The pamphlet was also peppered with choice quotes of the employers' racist remarks through the years. For example, one that would be quoted repeatedly within the ILWU movement as well as in numerous academic studies was made by R. A. Cooke in 1930 as the president of the HSPA: "I can see little difference between the importation of foreign laborers and the importation of jute bags from India" (as quoted in Weingarten 1946:31).

As the protagonists of the story, Native Hawaiian, Chinese, Portuguese, Japanese, Puerto Rican, Filipino, and other workers had all been subjected to the employers' racist "divide and rule" practices. The narrative thereby highlighted the parallels in the histories of the various nonhaole groups, enabling them to "see" that the racisms to which they had been subject all had the same source, the employers: "The workers had learned the evil of 'divide and rule.'" Now belonging to the same, unified ILWU movement that held that "all men . . . are equal," all workers could fight for racial equality against the employers, who believed that the worker of one racial origin was "better than the worker of another" (Weingarten 1946:33, 35).

As the narrative wove together the fate of all nonhaole workers into a single story, a crucial effect was that each worker could identify with the *entire* history of labor in Hawai'i rather than a particular strand of it.[91] So the employers' draconian antiunion measures throughout history (e.g., the evictions that led to the flu deaths during the 1920 strike, the Hanapēpē Massacre of 1924) were made a part of all the workers' collective memory rather than just the Japanese or the Filipinos', especially since the employers carried this pattern of resistance into the interracial ILWU era (e.g., the Hilo Massacre). In other words, this reinterpretation of the past rendered the employers' unrelenting hostility and racism meaningful for *all* nonhaole workers' collective sense of class.

As important as what was remembered was what was forgotten.[92] First, the positioning of workers in the racial hierarchy did not strictly follow the pattern of placing the latest arrivals at the bottom, as asserted in the narrative (e.g., Portuguese, Puerto Ricans). Second, however much the employers had wanted to pit the various racial groups of workers against one another, which they explicitly stated on numerous occasions, they mostly had not been able to, due to immigration restrictions and recruitment costs (Beechert 1985). Third, the historical evidence is unclear on whether residential segregation on the plantations was carried out by the employers intentionally to divide and rule and/or whether it reflected the timing of migration and the preferences of the workers themselves.[93] Finally and most importantly, the workers' prewar participation in the production of racial divisions was predictably underplayed.

The foregoing amnesias point to a critical feature of the narrative: it was not empirically complete or accurate. An efficacious ideology need not be good sociology or history. Through the ironically unifying notion of "divide and rule," the narrative reimagined the past in an effort to imagine a new political community: the ILWU embodied the workers' interracial historical destiny that had too long been thwarted by the employers' racist opposition. Contrary to the pervasive deracialized view of interracialism in sociology, it was neither the intent nor the effect of this reimagination to replace the workers' racial consciousness with class consciousness but to render them coincident and mutually reinforcing.[94]

Not limited to the discursive realm, interracialism guided and justified the movement's other practices. The prewar practice of holding interracial meetings in multiple languages continued. Much more extensively than before the war, the union printed its materials, including the union newspaper, bulletins, election ballots, and contracts, in multiple languages. Later, concern for full interracial participation led the union to broadcast its radio programs in Japanese and Ilocano, as well as in English.[95]

The most important innovation put in place during the organizing drive of 1944–1946 was the race-conscious election of leaders, what we would now refer to as "affirmative action" (Takaki 1989; cf. Korstad and Lichtenstein 1988). The connection between this race-conscious practice and the concurrent elaboration of an interracial ideology can be seen in the justification for it: determining that "the employers had done a very thorough job of dividing the people," the ILWU's International instructed Frank Thompson, the organizer sent to Hawai'i in 1944, to "in effect, if necessary, force integration."[96] The union wanted racial equality in fact, not only in principle, and it did not want a re-creation of the racial hierarchy evident in the larger society. The practice decreased the likelihood of one racial group monopolizing the leadership in spite of democratic procedures, as had been the case in prewar Port Allen with disastrous effects. The policy does not appear to have involved any set percentages or quotas. No doubt, Thompson was conscious and conscientious of race; for example, in his report on the newly elected officers in Port Allen, he wrote, "The President is a Portuguese, the Secretary-Treasurer is a Filipino, and the Vice President is an American born Japanese."[97] But the results of elections Thompson conducted in 1944 and early 1945 did not reveal strictly proportionate representation.[98]

Early in the post–martial law organizing drive, from 1944 to mid-1945, most ILWU locals and units do not seem to have resisted the racial integration of leadership, if Thompson's not reporting much resistance is a fair indication. His mode of intervention seems to have been to convince the workers of the necessity of racial integration prior to the nomination process.[99] As they recognized its importance in building an interracial movement, there were some early signs that a political culture of proto-affirmative action was forming. For example, at a 1944 conference of all ILWU locals on the Big Island, the delegates held an election for the Hawaii ILWU Council. It turned out that no Filipino had been elected to an office, at which point a "Brother Paaluhi expressed his desire to withdraw from his office as 2nd Vice President to give the Filipino Brothers representation." The motion carried. Two Filipino delegates were then nominated, and "Leoncio Velasco was elected to replace Brother Edward Paaluhi as 2nd Vice President."[100]

The relative ease with which race-conscious elections were adopted changed in mid-1945. Because the Big Five "maintained the fiction" that each plantation was an independent company, early NLRB elections had been conducted on a company-by-company basis, creating a large number of ILWU locals and units.[101] So, after the union won its initial elections, it initiated a program of consolidation to streamline its administration, trying to reduce the number of locals to one per industry for each island. Because the union had initially concentrated on organizing "industrial" workers covered by the Wagner Act, field laborers on the plantations were not organized into officially recognized ILWU units until HERA went into effect in July 1945. And, because Filipino workers—the largest in number but "the low men on the totem pole"[102]—tended to be in unskilled field positions, they took part disproportionately in this second wave of organizing. Other workers, mostly Japanese and Portuguese, had taken part disproportionately in the initial wave. Hence, they, particularly the more numerous Japanese, tended to be highly represented in leadership positions at many locals.[103]

As an ever growing number of field laborers, disproportionately Filipino, joined the ILWU and as the number of locals decreased through consolidation, the current leadership of existing locals, disproportionately Japanese, felt threatened. On the island of Hawai'i, the problem was especially acute because the number of locals had been large.[104] In fall 1945, the jockeying for leadership brought latent racial tensions into the open. At some of the locals on the Big Island, the established Japanese leadership seemed to be resisting, or intentionally not putting much effort into, organizing Filipino field laborers. According to Thompson, these leaders expressed to him, as their rationale, that "many Filipinos are either going back to their own country, or, that they are too dumb or too tight to pay dues."[105]

Beginning in mid-1945, the International became increasingly concerned over the rising racial tensions and the insufficient representation of non-Japanese, particularly Filipinos, in prominent leadership positions. Thus, when three ILWU leaders from Hawai'i went to San Francisco in October 1945 to discuss the organizing drive, they and two of the International officers conferred at length on the subject. Agreeing that racial integration of the leadership was of utmost importance to the union's interracial unity and future, the five produced a strongly but carefully worded policy memorandum to be put into practice in Hawai'i:

One of the principle [sic] tasks before the ILWU in Hawaii, is the development of well-rounded representative local leadership. . . . The Japanese by and large are the most developed group in terms of educational advantages, longest participation in union membership, and general all-round training. Consequently, they have automatically assumed principle [*sic*] leadership of the labor movement, particularly in the locals and Councils. By no means has this been a deliberate attempt by the Japanese to take over control. . . . The importance of racial unity in the Islands makes it imperative that steps be taken to put Filipinos, Hawaiians, Portuguese and others into prominent positions, even though in some cases they might not be as qualified or as capable as the Japanese. . . . At all times, though, we have to be *completely conscious* of the need for developing racial unity. . . . It is our opinion that the more developed and advanced labor people in Hawaii will recognize this is sound, because the fight for racial unity is far from over. . . .

. . . where necessary we have to compel Filipinos, Hawaiians and others to take leadership, even though they [may be] somewhat unwilling at the present time. . . .

Nothing will be accomplished if anyone outruns the field—we will make progress as we collectively build the union movement and advance together.[106]

When Thompson tried to put the policy into effect on the Big Island, it initially escalated the racial conflict. In December 1945, the Big Island's sugar locals and units held a joint meeting at which "the matter of consolidation was taken up." Two locals and two units decided that they could not agree to consolidation at that time.[107] The locals and units that did agree with the plan then voted in the new local's officers: a Portuguese, a Japanese, a Filipino, and a part-Hawaiian. The local from the Olaa Sugar Company, one of the two locals that voted not to consolidate, later wrote a vociferous letter of complaint to the International, objecting to, among other things, Thompson's handling of the nomination process. Questioning "how democratically the I.L.W.U . . . is run," the letter asserted that "qualification [should be] given greater consideration rather than solely along racial lines."[108]

Although the complaint was argued primarily on procedural grounds, not without merit, the larger, underlying problem on the island was racial divisions, especially between Japanese and Filipino workers, exacerbated by consolidation and the influx of Filipino field workers into the union. Some of the Japanese leaders, voted into their offices during the early part of the organizing drive, were indeed not actively organizing Filipino field workers in their jurisdictions, apparently at times because of racist assumptions. Conversely, Filipino field workers complained of not being able to participate in running those locals. Meanwhile, some of the Portuguese leaders, representing a significant but small constituency, seemed to be leveraging the Japanese-Filipino split to secure their positions, at times alluding to the lingering racist imagery of the "domineering" Japanese.[109] The problem was that, as Thompson emphasized in frustration, "*the different racial groups particularly on this Big Island do not trust one another.* . . . All racial groups on this Big Island in particular are continually basting one another."[110]

Though a significant problem, the preceding racial conflict in the sugar industry on the island of Hawai'i was not representative of the entire territory; while not always smooth, organizing in other places did not arouse racial conflicts of this magnitude. Even on the Big Island, the interracial tide turned in early 1946. Not by accident, Yasuki Arakaki, president of the local at 'Ōla'a and the most vocal and pivotal figure among resistant Japanese leaders, was selected as one of the ten union officers to attend the ILWU's "leadership training program" in San Francisco. Through his participation, Arakaki became one of the authors of the "training manual." Apparently transformed by this experience, he was later described as having "shown particular interest in the necessity of establishing racial unity in order to extend and strengthen union organization."[111]

Evincing this change in outlook, upon his return to Hawai'i, Arakaki published a lengthy column in the union newspaper titled, "'Divide and Conquer'— That's Bosses['] Race Line."[112] It had a narrative structure similar to the one discussed earlier and also included the infamous quote by R. A. Cooke. The interracial ideology Arakaki articulated in the column also manifested itself in a change in his practice as a leader: as much as he and others may have dragged their feet in organizing Filipino field laborers and consolidating before his West Coast trip, Arakaki put forth a similar effort in the opposite direction upon his return to the Big Island. In his first two months back, he set out to expedite the consolidation of the island's sugar locals by meeting with each of the sugar units, to organize the unorganized field workers at 'Ōla'a, and to "activat[e] new Filipino laborers to be leaders in this movement."[113] Regarding the latter two activities, he wrote,

> Our members doubled since I left [San Francisco] and beginning last week we are holding sectional meetings of the newly organized agricultural workers. At each meeting we are initiating the members in and letting them swear membership oaths in three languages. . . . In order to strengthen . . . we are now making every effort in search of potential leaders from the different racial groups so they will be able to hold their own. . . . I found out if [Filipino leaders] are given recognition . . . they will work harder and put in lot more of their time in union activities.[114]

By the summer of 1946, the ILWU's organizing drive was all but complete, and the union had obtained industrywide contracts in sugar, pineapple, and stevedoring. With the most racially riven locals on the Big Island finally having turned the corner, the ILWU had emerged as an interracial, working-class organization.[115]

Inflection Event: 1946 Sugar Strike

Immediately, the ILWU's nascent working-class interracialism was put to a test. On September 1, 1946, the ILWU commenced an industrywide, territorywide strike of the sugar industry that lasted for 79 days. The union's primary demands were an 18 ½¢ per hour wage increase (to a minimum of 65¢ per hour), a union shop, a seniority clause, a no-discrimination clause, and, to sever paternalistic ties to the plantations, the conversion of so-called perquisites into wages. Fully aware that it still had a long way to go in organizing field workers and consolidating its locals, the union had signed a nominal contract in 1945, setting its sights on 1946 to force significant modifications.[116] As the August 31, 1946 expiration of the contract approached, "there was no doubt [on either side that] a strike was coming." Although the specific demands were important, the strike was foremost a premeditated test of strength for both the employers and the workers: the employers wanted to assess how strong the union was and render it ineffectual, and the workers had been chafing to challenge the Big Five (Zalburg 1979:139).[117] On August 1, over 99 percent of the sugar workers voted to strike.[118]

But, well before, the ILWU's interracial solidarity had faced a pretest with important implications for the union and the strike. In May 1945, the sugar and pineapple industries, experiencing deep drops in production due to wartime labor shortages, sought to "import" labor from the Philippines. Through a provision of the Tydings-McDuffie Act, the two industries applied for 6,000 and 3,100 workers, respectively.[119] They were subsequently approved for 6,000 workers total, 4,000 for sugar and 2,000 for pineapple.[120] Due to an initial labor shortage in the Philippines, the migration of the eventual 6,000 workers and 1,361 accompanying family members did not begin until January 1946 and did not end until just 3 months before the strike.[121]

Reminiscent of the late 1920s and early 1930s, the public on the whole opposed the labor migration plan. Some of the opposition stemmed from a concern that Filipino migrants, having suffered under Japanese occupation in the Philippines, would be hostile toward the local Japanese population. Some also stemmed from anti–Big Five sentiments. But much of the opposition was directed at Filipino workers themselves, who were characterized as "ignorant," sexually threatening, "barbarous," and violent. An unpublished study conducted by sociologist Andrew Lind and his students at the University of Hawai'i found such objections across various non-Filipino groups.[122]

It was within this context that the ILWU took its contrary position consonant with its emergent interracialism, even though the union itself was not wholly free of anti-Filipino racism (San Buenaventura 1996). When the sugar and pineapple industries first proposed their plan, the ILWU, with rank-and-file support, offered a conditional endorsement. Concerned about the impact of Filipino recruits on the union's inchoate interracialism, the ILWU demanded, as one of its conditions, that the recruited laborers be informed, prior to their arrival, that "local residents of Japanese ancestry [were] just as bitterly against [Japanese] imperialism as they themselves." Most important, the union stipulated that the "immigrants must be afforded *full and equal opportunity with present employees* under like wage rates and working conditions."[123] Given the extremely unequal treatment of Filipinos in the 1930s, including mass repatriation, which had the support of non-Filipino workers, the ILWU's insistence on the equality of Filipino migrant workers signaled a seldom recognized turning point in relations among Hawaii's workers. By contrast, in its opposition to the recruitment plan, the AFL drew a firm, hierarchical distinction between "our own citizen workers" and "labor from foreign lands" and insisted, if the plan were enacted, that the migrant laborers be repatriated "when citizen labor is again available."[124]

Having given the conditional endorsement when the war in the Pacific was still in progress, the ILWU withdrew it when the war ended, anticipating a decline in employment opportunities and the return of veterans. At the same time, the union articulated to members and the public that its withdrawal of approval did not signal a withdrawal of its insistence on racial equality: "We oppose the importation of any labor, be it Filipino, Mexican, or Haole (Caucasian) at this time."[125]

When the sugar and pineapple industries proceeded nonetheless with their labor recruitment plans, the ILWU's now vocal opposition did not bleed into an opposition to the migrant laborers themselves. Instead, an interracial ILWU committee, led by Filipino members, protested the "deplorable" conditions on the transport ships that had led to the death of one recruit and arranged to have each ILWU unit assist in the migrant workers' "social and civic adjustments as well as settlement of grievances with their employers."[126] Moreover, with the cooperation of the Marine Cooks and Stewards Union (CIO), many of the migrant laborers were signed up with the ILWU on their way to Hawai'i.[127] With the union accepting them as equals, "the newly imported Filipino workers [were] signed up with no trouble anywhere."[128]

The arrival of 4,000 sugar workers from the Philippines just months before the strike brought an unpredicted benefit for the ILWU. Probably because the sugar industry had aggressively pursued the renewed recruitment of Filipino workers against the union's and the public's wishes, it did not *overtly* appeal to the type of naked anti-Filipino racism that would later characterize the 1949 longshore strike. Following the employers' lead, the arch-conservative *Honolulu Advertiser*, which the workers considered to be the Big Five's mouthpiece, strongly opposed the strike but refrained from open race-baiting. And, just a year removed from the end of the war, with nisei veterans still returning home, even intimating anti-Japanese racism would have been risky for the employers and the newspapers.

The workers, however, did not take much comfort in, or even anticipate, the relatively calm racial climate of the strike. As interracialism among workers had never survived a strike and as no strike had ever been won in the sugar industry, the workers knew that they were entering an uncharted territory and did not take their interracial solidarity for granted. Furthermore, although the newly arrived workers from the Philippines had been signed up, they had no savings to draw on, rendering them vulnerable in a long, drawn-out strike.

In preparation, the union built a strike machinery with strategy committees at the territorial, island, local, and unit levels.[129] At the unit level, the strike strategy committee oversaw a long list of committees (e.g., picketing, publicity, transportation, morale, fishing, gardening, cooking), leaving little to chance. Impressed with the tight organization, a longtime ILWU officer from a West Coast longshore local declared a week into the work stoppage, "The sugar strike is one of the best planned I have ever seen. This strike can't lose" (as quoted in Zalburg 1979:143).

As during the organizing drive, "all major racial groups [were] represented in strike leadership."[130] The roll calls of the strike strategy committees at each level listed a thorough, if not always a proportionate, mixture of Japanese, Filipino, and Portuguese names, with a sprinkling of others.[131] More than during the organizing drive, the impetus to carry out proto-affirmative action appears to have come from below as well as from above. A low-level officer from an Oʻahu plantation explained to the territorial committee that "although [Waialua was] the last plantation to be organized, it [was] now one of the strongest . . . because they have been careful to include leader[s] *from each racial group* on all union committees." Echoing a common refrain, he continued, "This prevents the bosses from dividing us among ourselves."[132] Firmly routinized by then, the union held meetings and distributed information in Japanese and Ilocano as well as in English.

Sown in the course of the organizing drive, the movement's interracial discourse took root during the strike, as the strikers applied and extended rearticulations of race and class. The union continued to define the workers' adversaries as not only the sugar plantations or even the HSPA, but the "Big Five." For example, when the president of the Hawaiian Pineapple Company (Hapco) went on the radio to assail the ILWU, the union took out prominent advertisements with the headline, THE BIG FIVE DECLARES WAR! If not for Hapco's connection to Castle & Cooke, one of the Big Five, why else would this pineapple company, with which the union "has always had amicable relationship," attack the union's strike in the sugar industry?[133]

The workers also constructed the strike, like their movement as a whole, as a fight for racial equality. Although the employers insisted during negotiations that "no discrimination was practiced in the sugar industry," nonhaole workers on the plantations, and on the docks, had a common, intuitive sense of how high each racial group could go in the plantation hierarchy.[134] Above the low supervisory levels, they knew that the plantations usually hired from without rather than promoting from within, choosing haole either already employed by the Big Five elsewhere in the islands or from the metropole.[135] Underscoring the ILWU's stand against racial discrimination, an editorial in the union paper pointed out to the workers,

> An excellent illustration of the discrimination which exists is provided by the men who form the negotiating committees of the sugar companies and of the union. The International Longshoremen's and Warehousemen's Union committee includes representatives of almost every racial group, recognizing in this healthy fashion the equality of races and the ability of everyone regardless of his race. The HSPA (or "sugar industry") is represented by haoles only.
>
> Racial discrimination is not something to be overlooked and hushed up. It is something which needs badly to be eliminated from Hawaii. . . .
>
> The files of many business and sugar firms attest to the fact that there is discrimination, wage differentials, in promotion ceilings and rates, in hiring and firing policies, in work conditions, housing, and in other respects.[136]

Aside from the wage demand, the "no discrimination" and "seniority" clauses, aimed at eliminating discrimination based on "race, creed, or color," were what captured the strikers' imagination. As their picket signs read, the workers were STRIKING FOR END OF RACIAL DISCRIMINATION, EQUALITY OF OPPORTUNITY FOR ALL, and SENIORITY RIGHTS as well as FIGHTING FOR INDUSTRIAL DEMOCRACY and AGAINST BIG FIVE DICTATORSHIP.[137]

As a linchpin of the interracial ideology, the "divide and rule" narrative assumed central importance in the union's effort to build and sustain solidarity. Published in the first month of the strike, the pamphlet *Raising Cane* was "recommended reading during the strike period."[138] Both to incite and to inform, union leaflets and advertisements likewise continually referred to the Big Five's long history of antiunionism and racism and the resultant racial divisions among workers, positing the present struggle as one to establish a different racial and class future. In this strike, unlike in the past, "on the islands of Maui, Hawaii, Kauai, and Oahu, the 33 plantations which comprise the industry are picketed for the first time in history by Japanese, Filipino, Chinese, Portuguese and Hawaiian workers united in one union for one purpose."[139]

Recounting, in pointed language, the Big Five's history of using violence and racism to divide workers and break strikes, a leaflet titled "THE RECORD" argued, "The union-smashing drive of the Big Five is not a surprise to the striking sugar workers for they remember the history of labor relations here in the islands."[140] Another lengthy handout also recalled the agencies' history of "divide and rule," due to which, until the ILWU, the workers had been "divided among themselves." Reminding readers of the employers' mindset, a choice quote of a former HSPA secretary at a congressional hearing read, "The Territory of

Hawaii is now and is going to be American . . . the white race, the white people are going to dominate." In the handout's narrative, the ILWU marked the definitive break with this racist past: "first and foremost of ILWU preparations for this strike as well as for future struggles was the building of racial unity on the islands." The recent recruitment of workers from the Philippines represented only the latest example of the Big Five's unceasing effort to divide the workers racially. Unlike in the past, however, the employers' "divide and rule" tactic was foiled: "the Territorial ILWU went into action and organized them into the union."[141]

As it took hold in the course of the strike, this narrative could be evoked with shorthand references to the past. For example, at a meeting of the Filipino community on O'ahu attended by many ILWU members, a Filipino businessman "suggested that the Filipinos should have their own Filipino union." To defeat this suggestion, Antonio Rania, an ILWU representative at the meeting, only had to ask the gathered workers, "What happened in 1924? What happened in 1920?"[142]

One of the greatest worries during the strike concerned the newly recruited Filipino workers. Although the employers did not openly disparage them racially, they decided nevertheless to concentrate on splitting the newcomers from the union, figuring that, with families to support in the Philippines and no savings, they would "break ranks."[143] Before and throughout the strike, the employers implemented a sustained propaganda campaign aimed specifically at Filipino workers, urging them, in Ilocano, to accept management's offer. The employers broadcast radio programs, distributed literature, and hired antiunion Filipino speakers to visit the plantations.[144] A month and a half into the strike, a plantation manager was reported to have said confidently, "The Filipinos are ready to crack anytime now."[145]

Having anticipated that the new Filipino workers would be targeted, the strikers had also planned in advance. In mid-August, the territorial strike strategy committee convened three days of intensive meetings with Filipino union leaders to have more of them intimately involved with the execution of the strike.[146] Throughout it, the union stayed vigilant in attempting to meet the needs of not only the new arrivals but also other Filipino strikers, since they tended to be the lowest-paid:

> Because of our Filipino brothers are either new arrivals or have been employed at the lowest wage rates, few have substantial cash reserves with which to meet the strike. It is imperative, therefore, that responsible officials in each local and unit contact during the next few days each worker of Philippine nationality and determine his relief needs if any. These needs must be met at once.
>
> A number of small committees should be recognized at each unit, with an inter-racial composition, to make these contacts and determine the needs before Monday.[147]

At the same time, the union counteracted the employers' propaganda campaign. It led a boycott of the *Filipino News*, a weekly paper through which the employers had been disseminating appeals to Filipino workers.[148] Filipino leaders at the local and unit levels were expected to hold regular meetings to discuss the "vicious campaign of the industry to undermine [the union's] present solidarity on *racial* lines."[149] The union also sent one of its most effective Filipino speakers, Telesforo Manipon, on a tour around the islands to hold meetings with workers, which were attended with apparent enthusiasm.[150] In the end, both the "new" and the "old" Filipino workers stuck solidly with the union. As Ricardo Labez, the union's assistant regional director in charge of Filipino affairs, wrote, "[Filipino workers] are not the 'dumb animals' they have been called by some. They are intelligent. They are alert. They know the meaning of 'divide and rule'. . . . It's a far cry from 1924 when only the Filipino workers struck."[151]

By the end of the strike, all workers knew the "meaning of 'divide and rule'": on November 18, 1946, the strike officially ended with the workers claiming a clear victory. Their effective picketing had prevented supervisors and any would-be strikebreakers from irrigating the parching fields, undermining the resolve of some of the employers. The union won its wage demand. It did not get the union shop but did make other gains in union security. It also obtained the "no discrimination" and "seniority" clauses, enforceable through the grievance machinery, and the conversion of so-called perquisites into wages.[152]

For both employers and workers, the particulars of the settlement, however important, did not adequately capture the strike's lasting impact. A participant in the negotiations on the employers' side conceded, "the strike was a remarkable union victory, nevertheless. It frightened the employers, and it created a general awe of union power, on the part of the workers, employers and the public. For the first time in Hawaiian history the employers had been soundly and definitely thwarted" (Brooks 1952:160). For the workers—not only those in sugar but also those in longshoring and pineapple who aided the strikers morally, financially, and organizationally—the strike demonstrated the viability of the ILWU and firmly established it as an interracial working-class movement. On the night of the settlement, the union declared its strike victory over the radio, affirming its interracialism:

It is the first time in the history of Hawaii that a strike of sugar workers on the plantations of Hawaii has ever been won. The first time in the history that a strike of sugar workers has been conducted where there has been no split a[l]ong racial lines. The first time in the history of Hawaii when the leadership of that strike on the plantations, in the camps, in the islands, and on a territory wide bas[is] has been completely representative of all racial and national groups that make up plantation workers. Never at a single moment in this strike has there been any indication of a split among these workers. This is particularly significant when we realize that among the workers on strike were some six thousand new Filipino brothers . . . who had no money, no reserves. . . . And they are gains not only in economic conditions, they are gains in terms of establishing for the first time the principles of promotion, seniority, no discrimination, equal treatment.[153]

That "history" should be evoked repeatedly to describe the workers' interracialism was fitting, since the workers had come to define themselves in decidedly historic terms.

The success of the 1946 strike convinced the workers that they were right to organize interracially, unlike in their divided past, and that they were changing the course of history, in effect fulfilling the historic mandate of their narrative identity: it was, in short, a self-defining moment. As the ILWU's chief negotiator appraised the effect of the strike on Hawaii's workers, "whatever doubts or reservations any groups might have had about the program of [racial] integration . . . I'm convinced disappeared entirely with the 1946 strike."[154] While the union would face more tests of its interracialism from both within and without, and racial divisions would never disappear altogether, the subsequent history of the ILWU has borne out this assessment.[155] In other words, Hawaii's interracial working class had been made.

Durable Interracialism

In his discussion of the English and French working classes, Sewell writes that once they had been "achieved," their ideologies were "remarkably durable" (1990:71). So it was with Hawaii's working class. Cast during the prewar and post–martial law organizing drives and forged in the fire of the 1946 strike, Hawaii's working-class interracialism endured for years to come. Its continuing vitality could be seen in three episodes that followed the 1946 strike: the so-called "Ignacio revolt" in late 1947 and early 1948, the 1949 longshore strike, and the 1951 Lana'i pineapple strike. They demonstrated a persistent structuring of the workers' class ideology by race, contravening the prevailing assumption that Hawaii's working-class formation was a deracializing process and giving further proof that it was a transformation of race, a rearticulation of meanings and practices.

From 1947, an anticommunist movement, with the ILWU as its primary target, engulfed Hawai'i for the next seven years. Although there had been a modicum of red-baiting during the 1946 strike, it did not gain much traction until 1947, when the territorial governor Ingram Stainback took the lead, asking all citizens to join the fight to "unearth [Communist] activities that are going on in this Territory" (as quoted in Holmes 1994:45).[156] By February 1948, he had specifically identified the ILWU as being "completely dominated by the Communists" (as quoted in Holmes 1994:50).

The first serious anticommunist attack on the union, however, came from Ichiro Izuka, the longtime ILWU longshore leader from Port Allen, Kaua'i. In November 1947, Izuka, with the help of several unidentified co-authors, published a 25¢ pamphlet called *The Truth about Communism in Hawaii.*[157] The disaffected former Communist identified 47 alleged party members, many of them ILWU leaders, and charged that the party "controlled" the ILWU and the PAC. Widely distributed, the pamphlet added fuel to the anticommunist fire.[158]

A month later, the union was subject to an even more threatening attack. At a December 14 meeting of the Hawai'i island division of sugar units, Amos Ignacio, the division vice president, resigned from his position and announced that he was taking his home unit in Pepe'ekeo out of the ILWU. Citing the Izuka pamphlet, he stated that he planned to form a sugar union dedicated to Americanism and anticommunism.[159] Three days later, when the newly formed Union of Hawaiian Workers (UHW) put out a pamphlet in English, Japanese, and Ilocano, it listed eight ILWU sugar units as seceding and urged others to follow suit.[160] Suggesting the stubborn residues of the Portuguese racial disidentification with nonhaole, a disproportionate number of the defecting leaders, including Ignacio, were Portuguese.[161] According to some within the ILWU at the time, their decision to secede was at least partly motivated by their feeling that the Japanese had taken over the top leadership.[162]

Given the support Ignacio appeared to have at the December 14 meeting and the public's growing anticommunism, there was genuine concern within the union that it could be torn apart, especially on the Big Island. Rather than downplaying the divisive issue, the union's leadership decided to discuss it out in the open with the rank and file. On January 3–5, 1948, the ILWU held a "Sugar Unity Conference" in Hilo and invited both Izuka and Ignacio to present their case to the elected delegates; only Izuka showed up. He failed to win over the delegates, and if Ignacio had had any rank-and-file support—there were at least a few units on the proverbial fence at the beginning of the conference—he lost it.[163] To underscore, for its membership and the public at large, its unambiguous unity, commitment to democracy, and lack of support for Ignacio's anticommunist move, the union held a territorywide referendum on whether the members wanted to stay with the ILWU. The workers voted 98 percent to stay.[164] In the end, not a single sugar unit, including Pepe'ekeo, was lost.[165]

Among other things, the conference revealed the extent to which the workers' class identity and politics rested on race. The discourse at the meeting gave evidence of their newfound mastery or "knowledge" of interracialism, if knowledge "by definition means the ability to transpose" (Sewell 1992:18). Ingrained in the political culture of the workers, the logic of interracialism had become transposable to analogical situations—in this case, to red-baiting. Throughout the unity conference, a recurrent theme and the most convincing arguments against the anticommunist assault on the ILWU dealt with race, drawing a conceptual parallel between the racist "divide and rule" the workers had overcome and the anticommunist "divide and rule" they now faced. For example, the sugar workers' local president Antonio Rania "emphasized the progressive changes wrought in the social and racial picture in the plantations as compared to the days when racial groups defeated their own ends by displaying racial antipathy and discrimination. . . . He urged the delegates to . . . ask themselves whether they should allow any outside forces to destroy the security for which they have fought so earnestly."[166] In a discussion of the American Legion's strident anticommunist campaign against the ILWU, secretary-treasurer Louis Goldblatt pointed out to an approving audience, "American Legion is noted for the race-baiting of the worst type. They have race-baited the Japanese; they have race-baited the Filipinos, the Chinese and every other oriental group. . . . Remember these words, delegates. Turn over a red-baiter and you will find a race-baiter. Turn over a race-baiter and you will find a red-baiter."[167]

Izuka's pamphlet and the Ignacio revolt constituted only the first of many anticommunist attacks on the ILWU, which would include its expulsion from the CIO in 1950.[168] However, the workers' unequivocal response in this initial instance kept the union "in good stead" in the ensuing years.[169] While it did become politically more isolated from the public and within the Democratic Party as a result of the ferocious anticommunist movement, red-baiting never seriously jeopardized the internal solidarity of the ILWU again, and the union's radical leaders, both in Hawai'i and on the West Coast, received unstinting support from Hawaii's rank and file. The articulation of resistance to anticommunism and to racism also continued, as the last photograph included in this book illustrates.

A year later, in early 1949, the ILWU opened the longshore contract on the wage issue. Since 1945, the gap between the wages of longshoremen in Hawai'i and on the West Coast had widened from 10¢ to 42¢ per hour. Since both groups often worked the same ships for the same employers, Hawaii's longshoremen sought to narrow the gap, demanding a 32¢ increase. During negotiations, the union was willing to settle for as little as a 16¢ increase, but the employers would not go higher than 15¢ (Zalburg 1979:243–244).[170] Thus began a 177-day (6-month) strike on May 1, 1949, one of the longest maritime strikes in U.S. history. In the end, the workers won a 21¢ increase, 14¢ immediately and an additional 7¢ to be added in early 1950.

"The strike," in the words of one writer, "tore at the fabric of the community, stirred up passion and hysteria, set people against people" (Zalburg 1979:241). Mostly, it set the ILWU against everyone else. Even taking Hawaii's geography into account, the ideological furor stirred up was startling, given that only the seemingly straightforward, narrowly economic issue of wages was in dispute. Three days into the strike, the *Honolulu Advertiser* began running regular "Dear Joe" editorials on its front page, accusing the ILWU of executing Joseph Stalin's orders to take over Hawai'i. Though absurd in retrospect, numerous civic groups jumped zealously on the anticommunist bandwagon (Zalburg 1979:chs. 42–43). Again absurd in retrospect, when the union called for binding arbitration to settle the strike, an established practice on the West Coast, the employers equated arbitration with socialism.[171] As noted, this ongoing anticommunist campaign isolated the ILWU politically but had little effect on the solidarity of its workers.

Another line of attack on the union during the strike was anti-Filipino racism.[172] When the mainstream papers and the public discovered that a majority of the approximately 2,000 strikers were Filipino, there was a deluge of editorials and letters to the editor calling for their deportation and a law disallowing "aliens" from employment as stevedores.[173] Filipino longshoremen were portrayed as uneducated and therefore undeserving of high wages; as duped by their leaders; and, above all, as "aliens" not entitled to equal rights. Of course, the fact that the right of naturalization was not extended to Filipinos until 1946 was not mentioned. For example, a typical *Honolulu Advertiser* editorial read,

ILWU leaders are heedless of the welfare of the rank and file. Proof of this is the fact the ILWU leaders have jockeyed many hundreds of alien stevedores into a position where deportation to the Philippines would be a logical next step. Swift action [through] a special session of the Legislature also could remove aliens from the ranks of stevedores. . . . When 1,500 or so aliens return to their homeland seeking jobs they will view Honolulu employment as a rosy dream which was shattered by their own foolishness in accepting ILWU leadership.

So far as such deportation plans are concerned, the sooner action is taken the better.[174]

A special session of the territorial legislature did seriously consider, if not deportation, a bill to limit employment in stevedoring to citizens.

Upon learning that the legislature and the territorial governor were contemplating antialien legislation in relation to stevedoring employment, the executive officers of ILWU locals in all industries, not just longshoring, issued an angry press release, appealing especially to nonhaole legislators and citizens:

Only the most shameless, selfish, and bigoted men could ask that our Territorial Legislature deprive of their American rights those aliens who built Hawaii by their blood, sweat and tears.

It is shocking that men born of alien parents brought to these islands by our basic industries, and denied by archaic and unjust laws the privilege of U.S. citizenship, could stoop to such ugly and revolting schemes. . . .

We call upon all honorable citizens of these islands, particularly the sons and daughters of those immigrants who built Hawaii, to raise their voices in protest against those who would deny aliens equal protection under the law.[175]

This response highlighted what had been apparent from the mid-1930s: the movement's interracialism implied a redefinition of nation. The ILWU did not fundamentally question American jurisdiction over Hawai'i—and would go on to endorse statehood, not independence, as the means to eliminate "colonial" inequalities. But it did posit a subversive understanding of who legitimately belonged to the "American" nation, oxymoronically conflating the categories "alien" and "American"; "blood, sweat and tears"—not legal citizenship—entitled "aliens" to "*their* American rights" (emphasis added; see also photograph 11). Three days later, the entire membership of the longshore local unanimously passed a resolution that warned, "In case any legislation is adopted which would bar noncitizens from employment in the stevedoring industry, the strike will go on. . . . Discrimination against our Filipino workers will not be tolerated."[176] No such legislation was passed. As it had been four years earlier, the ILWU was one of the only organizations in the islands that insisted on Filipino equality.

The strikers' fight against racism, however, was not just against those targeting Filipinos to "drive a wedge between . . . the membership on the basis of their racial extraction."[177] The longshoremen constructed the strike as a whole as a fight against racial discrimination. They conceptualized the wage differential between Hawai'i and the West Coast as "discrimination against [the] islands['] workers." They did not see why, if not for racism, "the stevedoring companies in Hawaii who are in many respects the same employer group which recently negotiated a three-year peace pact on the west coast, will not give local workers equal consideration."[178] That the longshoremen on the West Coast were mostly "haole" was not lost on Hawaii's longshoremen. Asked what the 1949 strike was about, George Dantsuka, a nisei Honolulu longshoreman at the time, recalled without hesitation, "Well, first thing, discrimination, because we're getting, I believe, [it] was 32 cents less than the mainland workers." He said that he and his fellow strikers "figured the reason they [the employers] didn't give it to us [was] because the color of our skin."[179] Using Hawaiian Creole English, or "pidgin," to highlight the strikers' interracial identity as nonhaole and their fight for racial equality—thereby politicizing and elevating a devalued language— a union leaflet read, "How cum no more haole kine kanes stevedore job work? . . . Wassamatta, they scare for brake back dis kine hard job? Wassamatta, maybe haoles think us kine color hanahana man not so good like haoles? Wassamatta dis place no allasame USA? Wassamatta you like us work more hard for more cheap pay than any stevedore mainland side? Wassamatta you only like dis wun democracy for haoles? Wassamatta, you and boss kine noospepa alla time speak me stupid, me alien, me unAmerican?"[180]

Similar issues were also at stake in the 1951 Lana'i pineapple strike. Four years prior, in 1947, the ILWU's pineapple workers had lost an industrywide strike in just five days. Several factors accounted for the setback. Pineapple workers were not as well organized as their counterparts in sugar and longshoring. The relative absence of acrimony between employers and workers through the years had made the workers generally less receptive to ideas of class conflict (see chapter 2). Although the harsh conditions and strained employer-worker relations under martial law did much to change this disposition, consequent discontent was uneven, concentrated among plantation workers, who had been particularly shackled and exploited under martial law; on the whole, the large numbers of cannery workers had not experienced the same level of restrictions. This unevenness in the workers' disposition was then reinforced by the ILWU's decision at the outset of its post–martial law organizing campaign to concentrate on the larger sugar industry before the pineapple industry.[181] The union also made a tactical error in calling the strike during the peak harvest season, calculating that the pineapple companies would be more vulnerable. Instead, the union only made itself more vulnerable due to another long-standing feature of the industry: large numbers of irregular and seasonal workers. Neither category had been tightly organized (Matsumoto 1974:14).[182] Finally, as noted in chapter 2, the pineapple employers, from the 1930s onward, had become more cohesive and organized.

Recognizing the ILWU's weaknesses in the pineapple industry, the employers bargained aggressively in early 1947, almost daring the union to call the strike. With unorganized intermittent and seasonal workers crossing picket lines, particularly at the Honolulu canneries, the union capitulated and signed a contract on the employers' terms. In the aftermath of the strike, the union survived but was noticeably demoralized. While it redoubled its efforts in pineapple and started to recover, the employers held their upper hand for the remainder of the 1940s.[183]

In fall 1950, the industry tried to further weaken the ILWU in pineapple by unilaterally calling off industrywide negotiations and forcing the union to deal with the employers on a unit-by-unit basis. But the attempt to split the union backfired. While all other ILWU units signed their now individual, but still similar, contracts, pineapple workers on the island of Lana'i rejected the offer from Hapco and decided to strike.[184]

Starting on February 27, 1951, the approximately 800 workers at the world's largest pineapple plantation went on strike for 201 days with financial support from the rest of the ILWU.[185] None of the problems that had plagued the union in the 1947 industrywide strike afflicted the Lana'i unit in 1951. The workers, mostly Filipinos with a sizable minority of Japanese, had been solid during the earlier strike and had remained solid under the charismatic unit leadership of Pedro de la Cruz. Hapco did not operate a cannery on the island, and since the strike began in late February, well before harvest, seasonal workers were not an issue.[186]

Among the strikers' demands was a 12¢ per hour wage hike rather than the 8¢ that all of the other ILWU pineapple units had already accepted. But the wage was a secondary issue; almost 2 months after it had rejected the 8¢ offer, the Lanaʻi unit did not even have a specific figure in mind, only stating that it would be "substantially in excess of the 8¢."[187] The workers wanted the company to "pay" more than they wanted the pay increase. Taking advantage of the union's defeat in the 1947 strike, Hapco had been increasingly high-handed in its dealings with workers. Moreover, the strikers felt that the company's arrogance was inseparably linked to its racist practices.

As in the longshore strike, Lanai's strikers, both Filipino and Japanese, fought anti-Filipino racism. In 1949, Hapco had laid off 500 workers.[188] As during the Depression, the brunt was borne by Filipinos, specifically workers who had been recruited from the Philippines in 1946. As their initial three-year contracts expired, they were flown off the island on a few days' notice and shipped back to the Philippines. Hapco ignored the union's objection that seniority should govern layoffs.[189] According to the embittered workers, "Regardless of seniority . . . they were shipped home—discarded just like a pair of worn out shoes."[190]

The other major grievance concerned promotions. As one striker wrote straightforwardly, "Job promotion has been a difficult step to achieve by some of our brothers because of discrimination."[191] By "discrimination," the strikers meant both the favoritism shown to company "stooges" and racial discrimination, particularly in favor of haole; the latter is captured vividly in a cartoon that appeared in a strike bulletin (see figure 5.1). To effectively counter discrimination in layoffs and promotions, the workers sought strongly worded and enforceable seniority clauses. Hapco resisted the union's demands, having instituted a "Merit Rating System" in 1947 to execute layoffs and promotions, which the workers abhorred and, conjuring the image of past employer abuse, referred to as the "whip" used by "pencil-pushing-artists."[192]

In any plantation community, the haole management lived in the nicest homes, separated from the workers. However, seldom was segregation more conspicuous than on Lanaʻi. The haole managers lived on what the workers referred to as "Snob Hill" or "Haole Hill," with paved roads and brick houses, and the workers lived down below in what they described as "shacks." This racialized class segregation, combined with the company's discriminatory practices, made Lanaʻi a receptive home for the ILWU's racialized interracialism. An essay by a striker titled "Another Mason & Dixon Line?" read:

> What really makes [the manager and the supervisors] far better than we are, that they should live in such better conditions than we are? Is it because they are Superior, or is it because of the color of their skin[?] . . .

FIGURE 5.1 "Sorry, Already Taken!!!"

Source: ILWU Local 152, Unit 7, Strike Bulletin No. 28, April 2, 1951, file Lanai Strike 1951/Publicity/Union/ Strike Bulletins, ILWUH.

And as for us, oh we're of no worry to them; we're just plain Joe Japanese, Joe Filipino, and Joe's of many other nationality. The only time we are of a worry to them is when we don't break our backs to bring out a good out-put of profit. . . .

Why?, because of DISCRIMINATION!, and nothing else. Discrimination isn't a sort of desease [*sic*], it's a STINKING SET-UP made up by some Big Wheel, that our ways of living isn't good enough to be mixed-up with their Hill side territory. Despite the fact that our work is heavier and just as honest as the jobs they are undertaking.

We intend to change this situation . . . and if we can't do it before our time comes, then our children will take over the battle.[193]

By the end of the strike, the workers had taken a significant step toward "chang[ing] this situation," which they viewed as inextricably structured by both race and class. For example, note how easily the preceding essay weaves back and forth between themes of racial discrimination and class exploitation, between "color of . . . skin" and "break[ing] . . . backs" for "good out-put of profit." Faced with the possibility of losing not only the 1951 crop but also the following year's, Hapco finally gave in to the strikers' demands. The workers gained their coveted seniority clauses and a 15¢ wage increase, 3¢ higher than their original demand. Moreover, the strike scared the other pineapple companies into reestablishing industrywide bargaining, giving all pineapple workers the same benefits as the Lana'i unit.

6

Conclusion

N 1934, in the middle of the Depression, a keen observer of working-class politics in Hawaiʻi noted, "The Filipinos can see clearly enough how they are discriminated against in favor of the Latin [Portuguese] and Oriental [Japanese] workers." A public school teacher at the time who would later, during the McCarthy era, be tried under the Smith Act as one of the "Hawaiʻi Seven," John Reinecke was one of the few non-Filipinos to find objectionable, or even notice, the widespread racism against Filipino workers in the 1930s. He recognized that the "hostility to the Filipinos" came not only from the haole employers but also from fellow Japanese and Portuguese workers. Surmising that Filipino workers "probably [would] be willing to cooperate in any effort to better the lot of all workers if no racial distinctions are made," Reinecke also concluded that it would require the "greatest pressure" on the other workers to turn them away from "the present trend against alien labor."[1]

Fifteen years later, in the final month of the 1949 longshore strike, after the settlement had been negotiated but before it was ratified, the president of the consolidated ILWU sugar local spoke at a meeting of Kauai's dock workers. Congratulating the longshoremen on their "victory of the century," Antonio Rania stated that his "greatest thrill in modern unionism in Hawaii [was] to see all the Japanese, Filipinos, Portuguese and all other nationalities working together in one union and calling each other brothers and sisters." Unlike in the not-too-distant past, when "the workers had been treated like slaves in Hawaii," they were now, through their unity, "able to tell their bosses what [they] think about them." Rania likened the workers to "mochi, Japanese rice cookies": "The more pounding they take, the more they stick together."[2]

Almost everything about the 1949 union meeting on the island of Kaua'i would have been inconceivable to almost everyone, including Reinecke, in 1934: that the longshoremen would be organized at all, let alone into a union covering every port in Hawai'i; that the same union would embrace sugar and pineapple workers; that the union would be interracial; that a Filipino would be the president of the local covering the entire sugar industry, elected by Japanese and Portuguese as well as Filipino workers; that a Filipino leader would be congratulating the longshoremen on their interracial solidarity during a strike marked by vehement anti-Filipino racism; and that the leader could starkly differentiate all the workers from the "bosses" and be understood and applauded. Even Rania's choice of imagery signaled a profound change: a Filipino leader using a Japanese culinary simile to describe the workers' interracialism.

The central research problem of this book has been to explain how Hawaii's interracial working class, evident at the 1949 union meeting, emerged from its prewar absence, when race had divided workers seemingly intractably and indefinitely.

Discussion of Findings

Some employers claim that at heart, they are after the wellbeing of the "working class," attempting to eulogize the benefits to be gained by the laborers but on the other hand, hiding what they expect in return for their purported aims. . . . Nope, the employers' and laborers' interest[s] are as far apart as the North Pole from the South Pole.[3]

How did Hawaii's workers come to define themselves as a class in polar opposition to their employers? Confirming previous studies, I have found that employers' rigid refusal to extend economic rights to workers played a formative role. A decisive moment in the workers' development of a collective identity as a class was when they rendered, through the construction of a revisionist narrative, the hostility with which employers had confronted all past unionization efforts meaningful for themselves across race. But why had Hawaii's employers rigidly refused to recognize, negotiate, or compromise with any unions? How were they able to repress labor movements so inflexibly, conceding no voice to workers in decisions affecting their working and much of their nonworking lives until the late 1930s, and then only grudgingly and minimally?

The employers' capacity to fight, rather than partly accede to and accommodate, unionization rested on their own ability to organize themselves as a class. A necessary factor in their organization in the sugar industry was a prior concentration of capital, as a handful of sugar agencies, later to be known as the "Big Five," wrested away ownership and management of the plantations. The industrial cooperation among the Big Five was, in turn, strengthened via their ownership and management by a small number of interconnected haole families of missionary origin. The families maintained their firm hold on the agencies through intermarriages, interlocking directorates, and family trust companies. The HSPA was at once the cardinal manifestation and the primary mechanism of the industry's cooperation. Although the impetus for this cooperation before U.S. annexation had not been labor conflict, the sugar industry learned to transpose its schemas and resources to effectively, and at times brutally, resist workers' organizing efforts.

In the early decades of the twentieth century, the Big Five leveraged their predominant position in the territory's largest industry, sugar, to assume similar positions in a number of other industries including, most importantly, stevedoring and pineapple. Not surprisingly, the Big Five's combative opposition to organized labor in the sugar industry found its way to the others, though unevenly. That pineapple workers, employed in the industry with the shortest history of overt class conflict, turned out to be the weakest link within the ILWU suggests the importance of employer opposition in fomenting working-class mobilization.

Undoubtedly, the employers' obdurate opposition was an important factor in the making of Hawaii's working-class movement. However, that opposition was not perceived as being against *all* workers until the 1940s. Prewar workers did not yet interpret their interests to be common or their histories to be analogous. At the heart of divisions among them were the qualitatively different racisms they encountered, which constrained and enabled their divergent politics. Racisms faced and negotiated by migrant laborers from Portugal, Japan, and the Philippines and their descendants differed along two dimensions: presumed superiority/inferiority and presumed suitability/unsuitability for civic inclusion.

The Portuguese were constructed, initially by haole but eventually by all non-Portuguese, as a "race" related but distinctly inferior to haole. Being of European origin, Portuguese migrant workers were never considered or treated as "cheap labor." They were consistently given better jobs and paid higher wages than migrant laborers from Asia. Also, being of European origin, they were always deemed desirable as "citizens" and "permanent settlers." However, unique among Europeans, their persistent presence as plantation labor—initially under penally sanctioned indentures—signified the Portuguese as racially inferior, if related, to haole. Though privileged over the Japanese and the Filipinos, they were excluded from top managerial and professional positions. Aware that they were more fully accepted as "white" in the metropole, Hawaii's Portuguese sought acceptance as haole. They refrained from participating in movements against their haole employers and drew a rigid racial boundary between themselves and other nonhaole.

The Japanese were constructed, initially by haole but eventually by all non-Japanese, as an anti-American "race." The planters recruited Japanese labor to replace Chinese "coolies." Although considered to be a source of "cheap labor" like the Chinese, the Japanese were also considered to be quite unlike them. Projecting the potential hostility of an increasingly powerful Japanese state onto the Japanese in Hawai'i, the haole elite understood them as racially loyal to their nation of origin and carrying out its imperialist cause from within. The projection imagined the Japanese as racially superior to other nonhaole—including the Portuguese, who were nonetheless favored as a "race" *related to* haole. But, more than any others, the Japanese were presumed to be unassimilable—in fact, antithetical to "America." In the wake of the bitterly waged 1920 strike, during and after which their loyalty came under severe suspicion and attack, Japanese workers withdrew from the labor movement for over two decades.

Filipinos were constructed, initially by haole but eventually by all non-Filipinos, as an unequivocally inferior "race." If the Japanese imperial state, rival to Western powers, indicated the advanced and alarmingly advancing racial character of the Japanese, U.S. colonization of the Philippines indicated the backward racial character of Filipinos. Like the Japanese, Filipinos were presumed to be unassimilable. But their presumed inferiority and colonized status made their unassimilability less threatening: Filipinos were tacitly un-American, not anti-American. More than any others, Filipinos were the epitome of "cheap labor," relegated to the most physically taxing, least skilled, and lowest paid jobs and the worst living conditions. That they should occupy the bottom of the racial order was simply taken for granted. During the Depression, Filipino workers were laid off and repatriated to the Philippines, while "citizen" workers were being newly hired and promoted. As Reinecke observed, non-Filipino workers sanctioned and participated in this marginalization. From their socially isolated position, many Filipinos carried on the labor movement on their own in the 1920s and much of the 1930s.

Against this dominant prewar pattern of racial divisions, the second half of the 1930s witnessed the slow but crucial genesis of an interracial working-class movement through the CIO, laying the groundwork for the movement's dramatic growth in the mid-1940s. Hawaii's workers, whose struggles had been almost completely closed to developments in the metropole, emerged from isolation. Between 1935 and 1937, a core group of sailors returned or relocated to Honolulu and Hilo as longshoremen, radicalized by their involvement in the contagious movement of maritime workers on the West Coast and determined to spread the movement in Hawai'i. Beginning with the longshoremen in those ports, an ever denser network of committed organizers and workers stretched throughout the islands, reaching dock workers on Kaua'i, Filipino workers on Maui and Moloka'i, and then plantation workers on Kaua'i. Institutionally tied to unions on the continent, most notably the leftist ILWU, Hawaii's organizers and workers gained access to vital resources, though quite limited before the war, including financial support and organizational know-how.

At the same time, the metropolitan state intervened actively, foremost via the Wagner Act, and pried open a political opportunity for the renewed working-class movement, curtailing the employers' heretofore unrestrained opposition. The 1935 passage of the law initially had little effect on class relations in Hawai'i, as employers baldly defied it. However, the eventual arrival of the National Labor Relations Board in 1937, at the behest of the longshore unions in Hawai'i and on the West Coast, prompted immediate changes on the docks of Honolulu, Hilo, and Port Allen and on the plantations of Maui. Though their initial material gains in wages and conditions were marginal, the workers, through their militancy and the backing of a cooperative NLRB, established that the employers would no longer wield unmitigated, unilateral control over them.

The imposition of martial law in the wake of the Pearl Harbor attack abruptly closed off the political opportunity that had only recently begun to open. The military government froze plantation workers to their employers at their pre-war wages, compelled workers to work, limited physical movement, and over-rode contracts; all these measures were enforced by military provost courts unsympathetic to labor. Moreover, the restrictions were implemented with inordinate input from the Big Five; their close relationship with the military, formed in the decades before the war, persisted under martial law, as officers of the Big Five-related firms aided and participated in the military government as planners, advisers, and executors. Accordingly, while martial law effectively placed a lid on union activities, workers grew restive with seething resentment against the employers, especially on the plantations, where wartime restrictions were particularly oppressive.

When military control of labor relaxed and a political opportunity reopened, the ILWU, though weakened under military rule, was in place to organize the thousands of discontented workers. Within just two years, the union almost completely organized the workers in longshoring, sugar, and pineapple, repro-ducing, faster and on a much bigger scale, the pattern set during its prewar organizing drive: longshoremen's initiative to unionize sugar and pineapple workers, augmented support from the West Coast, resumed cooperation of the NLRB, and simultaneous political mobilization of the workers.

Besides the retreat of martial law and the restoration of civilian rule, the end of World War II expanded opportunity in another sense. Americanism as anti-Japanese racism crumbled under the weight of irreconcilable evidence of Japanese "loyalty," including a conspicuous absence of subversive activities and disproportionate sacrifices at home and on the battlefields. One effect of this crumbling was to make possible the mass reentry of Japanese workers into the labor movement. The demise of Americanism as anti-Japanese racism also made an interracial working-class movement more plausible. There was no longer a compelling reason for nisei workers to insist reactively on their Americanness, which had impelled their racial marginalization of Filipino workers before the war. Moreover, other workers, like the public at large, could no longer doubt, at least not openly, the national loyalty of the Japanese.

Toward the end of the war, conditions were ripe for the emergence of a mass working-class movement; given the impending passage of the Taft-Hartley Act and the frenzied postwar anticommunism that would turn the state and the public against the movement, the alignment of forces turned out to be as short-lived as it was propitious. With the backing of the NLRB, the collapse of Americanism as anti-Japanese racism, and, in 1945, the passing of the Little Wagner Act, workers had unprecedented opportunity. With the full attention of the West Coast ILWU and of the surviving locals in Hawai'i, they had unprecedented organizational resources at their disposal. Rankled by the anti-labor conditions of martial law, the workers were also as restless as they had been in a long time.

While these conditions made the prospect of a working-class movement more likely, they cannot account for its durable interracial form and substance. The predominant explanation for the unexampled emergence and persistence of interracial unity among the workers has been that a leftist ideology of class, propagated by the ILWU's radical leaders and organizers, broke down the long-standing racial walls among workers, making them realize that class mattered and race did not. Against this dominant narrative, I argued contrarily that a leftist class ideology was not straightforwardly adopted by Hawaii's workers. Instead, it served as the initial pivot for a transformation, a rearticulation, of race and class.

In the late 1930s, the movement's leftist discourse of class incorporated race in a predictable, but consequential, fashion, leading to a couple of significant innovations before World War II. One was the tentative introduction of the "divide and rule" notion to explain racial divisions, and another was the invocation of past labor struggles in Hawai'i to highlight, by contrast, the need to organize interracially. Growing moderately in size, the prewar movement experienced both intermittent successes, like the official recognition of several locals, and setbacks, like the racial rifts in Port Allen and Ahukini. With the relaxation of martial law, the pace of the movement's growth quickened. Having lived through the repressive conditions of military rule, the workers took more readily to the view of class that defined the interests of the workers and the Big Five, which had enjoyed a mutually beneficial relationship with the military government, as being in utter conflict. This development may have also spurred, and been spurred by, the recognition and alignment of the workers' racial antipathy toward their haole employers, which had been racially differentiated and not expressed in uniformly conflictual terms.

Sharing a common class and racial antagonist, however, did not necessarily mean that Portuguese, Japanese, and Filipino workers would see themselves as a coherent collective, given their history of racial divisions. But, projecting the leftist notion of "divide and rule" onto the past, the workers reimagined this history, constructing a narrative that "remembered" the employers' racist divide-and-rule practices and "forgot" the workers' participation in the construction of racial divisions. Working-class interracialism, through the ILWU, therefore embodied their historical mandate and destiny.

In the late 1930s and 1940s, this evolving discourse structured and justified the movement's other practices that were likewise racialized, including the use of multiple languages, attention to the material needs of the generally worst-off Filipinos, and, perhaps most critically, race-conscious election of the leadership. Firmly established by the conclusion of the 1946 sugar strike, Hawaii's working-class interracialism could then be transposed to novel analogical situations both similar, like the 1949 longshore and the 1951 Lana'i pineapple strikes, and dissimilar, like the anticommunist "Ignacio revolt."

In retrospect, the idea of the mostly nonhaole workers' coming together in opposition to the haole employers may seem obvious, probably in no small part due to the existence in the last half century of a notion of Third World and "people of color" coalitions.[4] But this retrospective obviousness quickly dissipates when one stops looking *back* and takes the vantage points of the 1930s, when racial divisions among nonhaole workers seemed just as obvious and inevitable, and of the 1940s and early 1950s, when interracialism among nonhaole was still not obvious outside the ILWU. Furthermore, it is instructive to note how fragile, infrequent, and fraught "people of color" coalitions can be.

Implications for Interracialism

The consensus in the study of Hawaii's working class has been that interracialism required deracialization: that the workers ostensibly threw away, or at least put down, the "false" ideological baggage of race they had long been carrying and pursued their "true," common class interests unencumbered. However, this study has found that the formation of Hawaii's interracial working-class movement was not a disarticulation but a rearticulation of race and class. The workers reworked and aligned their previously disarrayed racial and class interests to imagine a new interracial political community.

Marshall Sahlins (1985:143) refers to *transformation* as "a pragmatic redefinition of the categories that alters the relationship between them." Hawaii's working-class interracialism was a pragmatic redefinition of class and race that altered the relationship between the two categories: it redefined class as dichotomous and antagonistic between workers and employers, while it redefined race as historically and relationally more akin and analogous, though not identical, among nonhaole and more uniformly at odds between them and haole.

The consequent alteration of the relationship between class and race was not that race subsided in significance but that it no longer "cut at right angles to class" (Saxton 1971:1).

There is little reason to suppose that Hawaii's working class is singular with respect to its racialized interracialism. Given the continuing focus of U.S. sociology on blacks and whites, some may object that Hawaii's polyracial population is exceptional. But even a cursory glance at the recent census figures should disabuse us of any lingering illusion that the U.S. metropole still warrants a biracial lens, if it ever did (e.g., Almaguer 1994; Foley 1997; Tchen 1999). Beyond the United States, a biracial approach is even less tenable. Furthermore, if the historical relationship between blacks and whites in the United States has been *more* thoroughly racialized than others, as some may contend, it would seem to argue even more strongly against a deracialized approach to studying interracialism.

A broad implication for the study of interracialisms, not only working-class or progressive ones, is that we should not presume a priori the disappearance or the receding significance of race: the tight theoretical linkage between interracialism and deracialization, which flattens and disfigures the analysis of the former, needs to be severed.[5] In other words, interracialism should be conceptualized as an affirmative transformation of race that, discursively and practically, deals with and rearticulates extant racial divisions. A corollary implication is that the widespread calls during the past two decades to study the mutual constitution of race and class (and other categories) should not be confined to cases of racial divisions and conflicts but be extended to those of interracialism. Such an analytical move would reveal, I argue, a previously unnoticed, wide range of interracialisms to be examined and would open up the concept to comparisons and further theorizing. Interracialisms should be thought of as constituting, in the theoretical idiom of Omi and Winant (1994), a broad category of "racial projects" that, through a collective cumulation of studies, may lead to a number of "historically conditional theor[ies]" (Paige 1999:784).

If there is a wide range of interracialisms, as I suggest, how do we account for their differing "successes"? That is, how do we explain their variable durability, or "depth" (Sewell 1992:22)? Working-class interracialisms, for example, can range from fragile coalitions, like the 1920 strike in Hawai'i, to lasting elisions of extant racial boundaries, like the making of U.S. working-class whiteness (Barrett and Roediger 1997; Roediger 1991), the continuum along which Hawaii's working-class interracialism of the 1940s and 1950s would fall somewhere in the middle. I propose and discuss four factors related to the durability of interracialisms.

One factor may be *sufficient ideological openness* to the rearticulation of race toward interracialism. Put another way, although the requisite openness may prove empirically to be quite minimal in some cases, ideological fundamentalism would be ill-disposed to durable interracialism. For example, had the early activists insisted on doctrinaire adherence to any of their various leftist class-based ideologies, Hawaii's working-class interracialism would likely have suffered, less able to rearticulate race with class. At the other end of the political spectrum, an inflexibly impervious racism of "Anglo-Saxon" or "Nordic" supremacy would surely have failed to enlist large numbers of the "Celtic," "Slavic," and "Mediterranean" "races" in the formation of broader white supremacist projects of the nineteenth and twentieth centuries.

A second factor may be *inflection-event outcomes*. The depth of interracialisms is, I submit, path-dependent and nonlinear in its development. Facing contrary forces, interracialisms likely encounter inflection events in which their viability is tested. Contingent upon the outcomes, such tests can reinforce, naturalize, reshape, destabilize, or even destroy the interracial political communities being formed. For example, the 1946 strike, the first major clash between the Big Five and the newly organized ILWU, still stands as the most critical moment in the entrenchment of Hawaii's working-class interracialism. By contrast, the workers' defeat in the 1920 strike sealed the dismal fate of the fledgling interracialism between Japanese and Filipino workers.

The third proposed factor is *resources*. Although the dimensions of "depth" and "power," as Sewell (1992) points out, are not intrinsically linked, I would conjecture that they are correlated in the case of interracialisms. Whether an interracialism takes root would be partly dependent on resources marshaled for and against it and on resources to be gained and lost as a consequence. One reason for the success of working-class interracialism in post–martial law Hawai'i, for example, was the ILWU's increased commitment of resources. Likewise, as this and other studies reveal, the state, with laws and other considerable resources at its disposal, may figure prominently in many, if not necessarily all, interracialisms.[6]

Closely related to the previous point is the last factor I propose: *state recognition*. Besides controlling material resources, the state can decisively shape interracialisms conceptually. As Bourdieu (1994:1) argues, "one of the major powers of the state is to produce and impose ... categories of thought that we spontaneously apply to all things of the social world."[7] State sanction of an interracial identity as an official category is not necessary for interracialism, as Hawaii's working-class interracialism attests, but it may be necessary for the most "successful" ones, as the history of whiteness suggests (e.g., Barrett and Roediger 1997:186–191). If the most taken-for-granted interracialisms are self-negating—erasing racial lines behind them as they go, by forgetting that there were such lines, and thereby implicitly denying that they are interracialisms—such deep naturalization may require state recognition and, as a corollary, may favor conservative and moderate interracialisms.

For the study of Hawai'i, reinterpreting working-class interracialism as an affirmative transformation, rather than a necessary negation, of race resolves a couple of previously unposed and unanswerable questions. Why have prewar working-class racial divisions been so poorly, but similarly, remembered? Not only scholarly writings but also oral histories of workers and the ILWU's official histories attest to a particular amnesia: they attribute the prewar divisions wholly to the employers' racist divide-and-rule practices, disremembering, for example, the significant part played by the workers.[8] Only when we consider that "divide and rule" as a mnemonic schema assumed central importance in the making of working-class interracialism, that its very success would profoundly shape how the workers' pre-interracial past would be remembered henceforth becomes comprehensible.

If the making of the interracial working-class movement was but a part of a more general postwar trend toward interracialism in Hawai'i, as is often supposed, why was that trend first and foremost a working-class phenomenon? For example, the workers of the ILWU were virtually the only ones to fight against, or even find problematic, the heightened anti-Filipino racism occasioned by the sugar and pineapple industries' recruitment of 6,000 workers from the Philippines in 1945 and 1946 and by the 1949 longshore strike. Only when we consider that the workers' interracialism derived from a leftist discourse of class, which had little resonance and appeal outside of the working class, that the workers would be at the forefront in the racial democratization of Hawai'i becomes comprehensible.

Finally, Hawaii's working-class interracialism also holds an important implication for progressive interracial politics of antiracism. In the decades following the civil rights movement, conservatives effectively appropriated the movement's early ideology of "color-blindness" and integration, or deracialized interracialism, as both the means and the goal of their racial politics. Conservatives oppose race-conscious movements and programs (i.e., affirmative action) on the grounds that they are not "color-blind" and therefore racist. The liberals' and the left's response, particularly among whites, is often one of deep ambivalence, unable to reconcile fully their defense of race-conscious movements and programs and their own longing for a raceless society or working class. I propose that we conceptualize interracial antiracist politics as engaging in progressive transformations that "see" race, rather than in absolute, and utopian, breaks with it onto "color-blindness." Hawaii's working-class interracialism shows that constructing such a politics is difficult—demanding openness yet organization, creativity yet conviction, passion yet persistence. But it also suggests some of the promises and possibilities.

Notes

1. Introduction

1. *San Francisco Chronicle*, October 26, 1998, p. A1, November 5, 1998, p. A2; *Honolulu Star-Bulletin*, December 3, 1996, November 4, 1998; Kristen (1999).
2. "How Political Education Improved Hawaii's Labor Laws," April 1970, ILWUH; Cooper and Daws (1990:5); Coffman (1973:ch. 8).
3. http://www.washingtonpost.com/wp-dyn/politics/elections/2004/; http://en.wikipedia.org/wiki/U.S._Democratic_Party_Presidential_Primary,_2004. Kucinich received 16 percent in Maine, 17 percent in Minnesota, and 17 percent in Oregon.
4. While "foreigner" is the literal translation, the Hawaiian term, *haole*, is the racial category for non-Iberian people of European descent.
5. In the United States, the last of the indentured servants from Europe had completed their contracts by the end of the 1830s (Steinfeld 2001).
6. As the president of the ILWU's longshore local in Hawai'i wrote in a 1948 letter, "As the result of the [union members'] participation in politics, ... we have been able to revive the Democratic Party, make it more progressive, and now it is beginning to look like the people's party, and not the shadow of the reactionary Republican Party" (Jack Kawano to J. R. Robertson, June 3, 1948, file HI/Correspondence, Reports, etc./Local 136/1937–43, box 5, ILWUSF).
7. Jack Hall, "How Hawaii Has Dealt with Minorities," speech before the Western Jurisdictional Conference of the United Methodist Church, Honolulu, July 25, 1968, p. 4, file 9, box 1, SZ. David E. Thompson (1966:29), the longtime education director of Hawaii's ILWU, wrote similarly, "Union political action paid off too in state social and labor legislation which ranks with the nation's best. Last year, Hawaii scored a first with a negative income tax law which, instead of taking from taxpayers in the lowest brackets, makes payments to them." For a detailed list of major

labor and other legislation that the ILWU claims to have been instrumental in getting passed in Hawai'i, see Jack Hall, "The Unionization of Agricultural Labor and the Effect of Unionization on State Labor Laws," remarks prepared for ANCA 72nd Annual Convention, Honolulu, January 22, 1969, file 9, box 1, SZ.

8. By *political community*, I mean simply a social collectivity enmeshed and engaged in relations of power.

9. The obverse of Omi and Winant's (1986:64) definition of racialization, *deracialization* refers to the retraction or negation of racial meaning from a previously racially classified relationship, practice, or group.

10. Of course, I allude here to Anderson's (1991:6) celebrated definition of *nation* as an "imagined political community."

11. Though not discussed here, there is a long and varied tradition of non-Marxist sociology of race premised on interest-based conflicts (e.g., Blumer 1958; Blalock 1967; van den Berghe 1967; Wilson 1973; Olzak 1992; Bonilla-Silva 1997).

12. See Boswell and Brown (1995), Brueggemann (1994), Brown and Brueggemann (1997), and Brueggemann and Boswell (1998).

13. For an in-depth discussion of these two approaches, see chapter 5.

14. See also Bourdieu (1977, 1990b), Calhoun (1983), Giddens (1984), Sahlins (1981, 1994), and Sewell (1992). As Ferdinand de Saussure puts it, "What predominates in all change is the persistence of the old substance; disregard for the past is only relative" (1959:74; as cited in Sahlins 1985:153).

15. For examples, see Calhoun (1982), Griffin and Korstad (1995), Kelley (1990), Roediger (1991), Sewell (1980), Steinberg (1991), and Thompson (1963).

16. The passage quoted by Hall is from Gramsci (1971:331). In the original, Gramsci placed quotation marks around the word "critical."

17. Matt Meehan to Goldblatt and Robertson, April 21, 1944, file HI/Correspondence, Reports, etc./1944, box 5, ILWUSF.

18. The insufficiency of ILWU's leftist leadership and the importance of local context can also be seen in the unevenness of interracialism at various ILWU locals in the metropole (Nelson 1992, 1993, 1998, 2001; Quam-Wickham 1992).

2. Origins of Capital's Contentious Response to Labor

1. As Keith McClelland (1990:5) argues, "resistance and repression from above" also play a crucial, if largely unacknowledged, role in E. P. Thompson's account of English working-class formation.

2. "Report of E. J. Eagen on the Hawaiian Islands," p. 4602, in USHR (1940). The report was originally drafted in 1937, when E. J. Eagen, regional director of the National Labor Relations Board in Seattle, investigated Hawaii's labor situation, but was not made public until the 1940 congressional hearings.

   In 1937, there were obviously "truer" examples of fascism to be found in the world.

3. In 1933, the total value of sugar (and molasses) exported, all of it to the metropole, was $65,696,136, and the total value of all exports, including sugar, was $94,317,696. Of the latter, exports to "foreign countries" amounted to only $675,809 (*Hawaiian Annual* 1935:26–27).

4. While the treaty was an economic boon for Hawaii's sugar producers, the primary motive for the United States was not economic. The United States was not lacking for ready suppliers of sugar; aside from domestic producers, those in the Caribbean, Latin America, and the Philippines were eager to obtain greater access to the vast U.S. market (Beechert 1985). Rather, spurred in part by Hawai'i sugar planters' exaggerated reports, the United States sought to forestall other imperial powers—initially Britain—from establishing a predominant economic presence in Hawai'i, widely believed to be the first step toward eventual political incorporation (H. M. Whitney, "The Hawaiian Reciprocity Treaty," *Planters' Monthly* 1 [November 1882]: 188–196, 236–248, HC; "The Political Value of the Hawaiian Reciprocity Treaty to the United States," *Planters' Monthly* 5 [June 1886]: 59–63, HC; U.S. Senate 1894:67; Robinson 1904:123–124, 132–140; Stevens 1945:126–128; Tate 1968; Taylor 1935:15–16). Of course, there is obvious irony in this justification. In preventing other states from infringing on Hawaiian sovereignty, the United States—though initially ambivalent about its own imperialist ambitions—followed the precise path it discouraged others from taking.

5. Both figures are reported in 1910–1914 dollars.

6. See appendices B and D in Robinson (1904:197–200, 203–204) for the full text of the Reciprocity Treaty of 1875 and its 1887 renewal.

7. "The American Sugar Bounty," *Planters' Monthly* 12 (March 1893): 128–130, HC; Robinson (1904); Tate (1968).

8. "The Annexation of Hawaii," *Planters' Monthly* 17 (January 1898): 9, HC.

9. Within the U.S. colonial scheme, Hawai'i as an "incorporated territory" was legally distinct from its "nonincorporated" counterparts, e.g., Puerto Rico, the Philippines. While territories of both types were denied representation in the federal government, the rights of citizens of nonincorporated areas under the U.S. Constitution were further limited in two ways. First, the Supreme Court ruled that citizens of nonincorporated territories were not guaranteed "remedial rights": "the right to citizenship, to suffrage, and to the peculiar methods of procedure which are peculiar to Anglo-Saxon jurisprudence." Second, passages in the U.S. Constitution referring specifically to the "United States" applied to incorporated territories but not to nonincorporated ones. For example, of particular interest to Hawaii's planters, the Court ruled that the provision in Article I of the Constitution that "all duties, imposts, and excises shall be uniform throughout the United States" applied to incorporated territories, e.g., Hawai'i (*Downes v. Bidwell*, 182 United States 244, as cited in Littler 1929:40–41).

10. For the reaction of Hawaii's sugar industry to the 1934 law, see John Waterhouse, presidential address, *Proceedings of the Fifty-fourth Annual Meeting of the Hawaiian Sugar Planters' Association*, December 3, 1934, HC; R. A. Cooke, presidential address, *Proceedings of the Fifty-fifth Annual Meeting of the Hawaiian Sugar Planters' Association*, December 9–12, 1935, HC.

11. There were 59 plantations in 1900 and 47 in 1930 (*Hawaiian Annual* 1900:49–50; 1930:132–133).

12. Again, the figure is reported in 1910–1914 dollars.

13. This figure includes 48,072 full-time male and 1,552 full-time female workers, the remainder being either minors and/or part-time workers.

14. For the industry's acknowledgment of this fact, see John Waterhouse, presidential address, *Proceedings of the Forty-eighth Annual Meeting of the Hawaiian Sugar Planters' Association*, December 3–6, 1928, p. 14, HC.

15. In a "free" sugar market, new plantations would enter the industry if there were profits to be made, and existing plantations would leave the industry if there were losses. Hence, in the long term, the market would theoretically home in on an equilibrium at which costs of production equal revenues, i.e., no profit.

16. In 1877, the total value of sugar and molasses shipped to the United States was $2,131,982, of which $986,475 was due to tariff protection. The respective figures for 1900 were $13,919,410 and $9,757,633. In 1930, they were $56,563,847 and $36,978,520. Taylor (1935:170–171) calculated these values by multiplying total annual production by the effective duty.

17. *Hawaiian Annual* (1940:42–43). Almost all of the plantations had become incorporated during the 1880s and 1890s (*Planters' Monthly* 8 [October 1889]: 440, HC; Lind 1938b:181). Two of the companies cultivated and harvested sugar cane but did not own their own mills, and one of them was only a milling company.

18. For example, the Hawaiian Commercial and Sugar Company, the most productive plantation, harvested and milled 73,386 tons of sugar in 1939, merely 7.6 percent of the total output of 968,392 tons; the combined output of the top 5 plantations, each of which produced over 50,000 tons, amounted to only 32.4 percent of the total output (calculated from *Hawaiian Annual* 1940:38–39). If there had been perfect uniformity among them, each of the 38 plantations would have accounted for 2.63 percent of the total production.

19. The degree of plantation ownership by agencies varied widely; the agencies tended to grab larger shares of the more profitable plantations. Regardless, even as significant minority stockholders, they had predominant influence over plantations with otherwise diffuse ownership. By the 1930s, as Taylor (1935:68) concludes, "Either by ownership, by part-ownership, or by contracts which confer the benefits of ownership without risks, or by monopolization of essential services, the agencies dominate[d] and control[led] the entire system of sugar production."

20. Calculated from *Planters' Monthly* 17 (December 1898): 533–535, HC.

21. Calculated from *Hawaiian Annual* (1910:194–197). Starting out as partnerships, the Big Five agencies were incorporated in the 1890s; Alexander & Baldwin, incorporated in 1900, was the sole exception (Smith 1942).

22. As shown in table 2.1, Theo. H. Davies & Company's interests in sugar were considerably smaller than those of the other Big Five agencies. Its comparatively smaller size is also apparent in the other two industries discussed later, maritime and pineapple.

    In 1946, Theo. H. Davies & Company had $15.1 million in assets. By comparison, Alexander & Baldwin, American Factors, C. Brewer & Company, and Castle & Cooke owned $39.0 million, $44.5 million, $34.0 million, and $30.3 million in assets, respectively (Hawaiian Economic Foundation, "A Study of Ownership of Corporations in Hawaii," 1948, pp. 20–34, file Companies/HI/Big Five, ILWUSF).

    Despite its relatively diminutive size, Theo. H. Davies & Company is included as one of the Big Five in this study for three reasons. First, the company was significantly larger than the non–Big Five sugar agencies and hence wielded considerably more influence. Second, as discussed later in this chapter, it came to develop close business and social ties with the other Big Five agencies as they invested in the company. Third, it came to be perceived as one of the "Big Five" by Hawai'i's workers and other residents. Especially among workers, that term gained a rhetorical resonance that overflowed its debatable numerical aptness.

23. The literal translation of the Hawaiian term, *kama'āina*, is "child of the land." It usually refers to a native-born resident of Hawai'i.

24. Gerritt P. Judd, a missionary doctor, served as the land commissioner and an adviser to the king (Taylor 1935:10). For the history of dispossession of Hawaiian land, see Kelly (1980).

25. Joseph B. Atherton is a prominent example. When he arrived in Hawai'i from Boston, he was hired by Samuel N. Castle for a position at a Castle & Cooke general store. Later, he married Juliette M. Cooke, one of Amos S. Cooke's daughters. Upon the deaths of the founders of Castle & Cooke, Atherton was elected the firm's president (Day 1984:6).

26. Dying family members stipulated that whereas their children would technically own the stocks and receive dividends from them, voting rights and management of the stocks would remain with family trust companies, under which the stocks were registered (Taylor 1935:84).

27. "A Forty Thousand Tons Sugar Estate," *Planters' Monthly* 17 (October 1898): 440–441, HC; Adler (1966:80–85); Dean (1950:64–68); MacLennan (1979:160–161); Sullivan (1926:165, 170–171); Taylor, Welty, and Eyre (1976:133); Worden (1981:33).

28. H. Hackfeld & Company to "Patrons," August 20, 1918, and Allen W. T. Bottomley to "Gentlemen," August 20, 1918, KSC10/3, HSPAP. American Factors bought H. Hackfeld & Company for $7.5 million. In a suit filed by Hackfeld investors after the war, they placed the value of the company at $17.5 million (Taylor 1935:66, 86; *Walker's Manual* 1930:351–352).

29. As discussed later, Matson was substantially owned and controlled by four of the Big Five agencies. C. Brewer & Company had a long, close business relationship with Welch & Company and would eventually own it.

30. By 1945, however, the other agencies had divested from Theo. H. Davies & Company. Before doing so, Castle & Cooke, the largest shareholder, acquired the company's most valuable plantation assets in the Kohala district of the Big Island (MacLennan 1979:163–164).

31. See figures 2.1 and 2.2 and table 2.4. Given its comparatively smaller size, the company's ability not to conform was circumscribed, even if it had been so inclined.

32. For another elaborate chart and examples of direct and indirect interlocks among the Big Five, see USDJ (1932:185, exhibit no. 6) and Taylor (1935:194–202).

33. Arnold L. Wills, "History of Labor Relations in Hawaii," speeches before the Social-Economic Committee of the Hawaii Education Association, November 15 and December 20, 1945, p. 4, HC.

34. For a thorough history of the penalties and protections, see Beechert (1985:ch. 3).

35. The image of a manager or a *luna* (straw boss) on horseback striking or threatening workers with a "black snake whip" would linger in the minds of Hawaii's workers for generations, long after the whippings had stopped. See, for example, Lind (1938b:225–226).

36. F. M. Swanzy, B. Bolte, and P. C. Jones, "Report of Labor Committee," *Planters' Monthly* 14 (December 1895): 545, HC. Hawaii's sugar plantations employed 18,965 men, 1,193 women, and 326 children in 1895.

37. Premeditated, organized actions were hard to accomplish, even among day laborers. Limited to themselves, they could not even realistically hope to organize all workers of the same racial group. Furthermore, the dual existence of penal contract labor and day labor presented a mismatch in workers' grievances and capacities for resistance: those with the most pressing grievances against the employers were not day laborers but contract laborers, who were more constrained in their capacity to organize.

38. For specific examples, see Takaki (1983:127–152). On the limiting effects of penal contract labor on the range of worker resistance, see Munro (1993:23–25, 32) and Beechert (1993).

39. Arnold L. Wills, "History of Labor Relations in Hawaii," speeches before the Social-Economic Committee of the Hawaii Education Association, November 15 and December 20, 1945, p. 5, HC.

40. See also "Labor Disturbances in Hawaii, 1890–1925: A Summary," compiled by John E. Reinecke, July 1966, file Trade Unions/HI/Pamphlets, etc., ILWUSF.

41. Letter from Castle & Cooke, Bishop & Co., H. Hackfeld & Co., C. Brewer & Co., Theo. H. Davies & Co., G. W. Macfarlane & Co., W. G. Irwin & Co., F. A. Schaefer & Co., and E. P. Adams, February 18, 1882, as reprinted in "A Reminiscence. Origin of the Hawaiian Sugar Planters' Association," *Planters' Monthly* 16 (December 1897): 597–598, HC; Allen W. T. Bottomley, presidential address, *Proceedings of the Fiftieth Annual Meeting of the Hawaiian Sugar Planters' Association*, November 17–21, 1930, pp. 8–9, HC; Agee (1934:72–73).

42. Ibid.

43. *Planters' Monthly* 5 (September 1886): 138–141, 180, HC; *Planters' Monthly* 11 (November 1892): 487, HC.

44. For example, in 1890, 32.6 percent of plantations had different agencies representing them than in 1880; this calculation is based on the 43 plantations with same names in 1880 and 1890 (*Hawaiian Annual* 1880:68–69, 1890:104–105). The figure underestimates the percentage switching agencies, as it does not account for those plantations that switched and then switched back between the two time points.

45. "Plantation Agencies," *Planters' Monthly* 3 (May 1884): 410, HC.

46. This refinery had an agreement with the other, much smaller American Refinery whereby the latter was allowed to retain a share of the West Coast market by refining sugar only from the Philippines.

47. "The Treaty, the Advertiser, Mr. Spreckels and 'Discrimination,'" *Planters' Monthly* 4 (February 1886): 308–311, HC; "The American Sugar Trust," *Planters' Monthly* 11 (April 1892): 146–147, HC; Adler (1966:23–25); Dean (1950:34–40); MacLennan (1979:154–156). In the late 1880s, Hawaii's agencies took over American Refinery but soon found themselves forced to sell out to the gigantic Sugar Trust (American Sugar Refining Company). A costly price war ensued between the Sugar Trust and Spreckels. In the end, the Sugar Trust gained a controlling interest in Spreckels's refinery in Philadelphia and a half interest in his California Sugar Refinery. Renamed Western Sugar Refinery, the latter had Spreckels as its president. See Dean (1950) for a detailed account of the convoluted struggle.

48. *Planters' Monthly* 14 (December 1895): 537, HC.

49. Initially a response to the low sugar prices resulting from the McKinley Tariff Act and technical problems like soil exhaustion and pests, the experiment station exemplified the major transformations the industry was undergoing: concentration of capital in the sugar agencies, shift of production control from the plantations to the agencies, rationalization of production, and increased cooperation of the industry.

> *There is not an aspect of sugar production, from the first plowing of the ground to the preparation of raw sugar for the refinery, that has escaped [the experiment station's] attention. . . . With the assistance of science the work of agricultural and mill improvement has been carried on, by, and through this body. It has come to command a position as the central deciding authority for the determination of production policies and practices. This development has been coterminous with the progressive, financial domination of the plantations by the agencies, and with the increased curtailment of the power and prestige of the plantation manager. The joint control of the agencies of the sugar companies and the HSPA, of which the experiment station is a part, has made it mandatory upon the plantation manager that he adopt the latest and most effective devices without delay. The element of time lag between research and application has been reduced to a minimum. (Taylor 1935:42)*

50. M. S. Grinbaum & Co., C. Bolte, W. G. Irwin & Co., C. Brewer & Co., H. Hackfeld & Co., F. A. Schaefer & Co., Castle & Cooke, and Theo. H. Davies & Co. to the president of PLSC, *Planters' Monthly* 13 (February 1894): 64, HC.

51. "The Sugar Trade," *Planters' Monthly* 17 (March 1898): 109–114, HC; Dean (1933:17–21; 1950: 72–73, 91–94, 134–140); Emmet (1928:1–10); Sullivan (1926:164); Taylor, Welty, and Eyre (1976:144); *Walker's Mannual* (1930:394–395). For the most comprehensive account, see Dean (1950). In a 1921 restructuring, the company's name was changed to California and Hawaiian Sugar Refining Corporation, Ltd.

52. *Proceedings of the Fifty-first Annual Meeting of the Hawaiian Sugar Planters' Association*, December 7–10, 1931, p. 6, HC.

53. The association also had "individual" members, people who had direct interests in sugar plantations or mills (Agee 1934:80); most were officers at either an agency or a plantation. Entitled to one vote each, individual members participated in the annual meetings, but their ability to challenge the agency-controlled votes—even if they wished to—was negligible.

54. The only significant difference between the two tables is that three plantations appearing in table 2.1—producing a combined 1.28 percent of Hawaii's sugar output—did not belong to the HSPA and consequently do not appear in table 2.3.

55. *Proceedings of the Forty-sixth Annual Meeting of the Hawaiian Sugar Planters' Association*, November 15–18, 1926, p. 7, HC.

56. "By-laws of the Hawaiian Sugar Planters' Association," *Planters' Monthly* 14 (December 1895): 537–539, HC.

57. *Proceedings of the Forty-sixth Annual Meeting of the Hawaiian Sugar Planters' Association*, November 15–18, 1926, pp. 7–9, HC.

58. "Of the original founders of our Association only two, namely, Mr. G. N. Wilcox and Col. J. H. Soper, are still with us, though it is remarkable and a splendid record

for the industry that so many of the names appearing in the original organization are perpetuated in our Association today through the active participation in it by the succeeding generations of Cookes, Baldwins, Alexanders, Castles, Athertons, Hinds and Wilcoxes" (Allen W. T. Bottomley, presidential address, *Proceedings of the Fiftieth Annual Meeting of the Hawaiian Sugar Planters' Association*, November 17–21, 1930, p. 10, HC). Aside from the four families already discussed at length, the Athertons formed an important branch of the Cooke family, and the Hinds and the Wilcoxes were two kama'āina families of second-tier wealth and prominence.

59. Even a cursory examination of table 2.3 reveals that the three small agencies, with a combined 3.53 percent of the total votes, could not have voted a single trustee into office on their own.

60. In 1928, John Waterhouse, the president of the HSPA, spoke to the membership about the industry's solidarity: "Our industry, while highly centralized, is highly cooperative—the strong have not taken advantage of the weak, nor have the weak combined against the strong." Though factually correct about the highly centralized and cooperative character of the industry, the interpretation given to the facts by the head of the powerful Alexander & Baldwin rings more ironic than ingenuous. The industry became cooperative *because* it became centralized, and the weak combining against the strong had become all but impossible by 1928 (John Waterhouse, presidential address, *Proceedings of the Forty-eighth Annual Meeting of the Hawaiian Sugar Planters' Association*, December 3–6, 1928, p. 6, HC).

61. "Labor Disturbances in Hawaii, 1890–1925," p. 6.

62. "Address of President C. M. Cooke," *Planters' Monthly* 19 (November 1900): 501, HC.

63. "Labor Disturbances in Hawaii, 1890–1925," p. 6.

64. "Report of Committee on Labor," *Planters' Monthly* 19 (November 1900): 515, HC.

65. Ibid.

66. "Address of President C. M. Cooke," *Planters' Monthly* 19 (November 1900): 501, HC; Takaki (1983:83). The 1894 effort enjoyed "the assistance of the Japanese consular officials and inspectors" (H. P. Baldwin, C. Bolte, and F. M. Swanzy, "Report of Labor Committee," *Planters' Monthly* 13 [November 1894]: 499; F. M. Swanzy, C. Bolte, and P. C. Jones, "Report of Labor Committee," *Planters' Monthly* 14 [December 1895]: 547, HC). Beechert (1985:133) writes that the purpose of the 1894 system was to keep day laborers on the plantations.

67. Beechert (1985:133–139); Takaki (1983:83–87); "Report of Committee on Labor," *Planters' Monthly* 19 (November 1900): 514–517, HC.

68. "Labor Disturbances in Hawaii, 1890–1925," pp. 8–13; USBL (1902, 1903, 1906, 1912); Beechert (1985:ch. 8).

69. "Labor Disturbances in Hawaii, 1890–1925," pp. 6–12; USBL (1902:112–115, 254–257; 1906:493–501).

70. Ray Stannard Baker, "Wonderful Hawaii: A World Experimental Station," *The American Magazine* (November 1911): 28, as cited in Kent (1983:83). Two decades later, James H. Shoemaker of the U.S. Department of Labor expressed a similar sentiment, though in a tone more charitable to the employers: "Thus, although management has done much for labor in Hawai'i, it has also used every influence at its command to restrict labor organization" (USBLS 1940:198).

In 1944, the HSPA president stated, "Our industry has repeatedly been called paternalistic. The paternal attributes are care and protection of those who are weaker and less mature. When one considers the characteristics of the immigrant workers who in years past have made up so large a proportion of our plantation labor force, it appears that the term paternalistic is not one to be ashamed of. Let us accept it as true" (J. P. Cooke, "Report of President," *Proceedings of the Sixty-fourth Annual Meeting of the Hawaiian Sugar Planters' Association*, December 4, 1944, HC). Six year later, still unable to comprehend the workers' active opposition to employer paternalism, Arthur L. Dean, an Alexander & Baldwin executive, wrote: "Just why a father's care should be regarded as reprehensible has not been explained" (1950:205).

71. Negoro was unable to practice his profession due to his lack of citizenship. Under the Naturalization Act of 1790, naturalized citizenship was limited to "free white persons."

72. Fred K. Makino to W. O. Smith including Exhibits A–K, January 1909, as reprinted in USBL (1911:65–75).

73. Okihiro (1991:50) assigns slightly different dates for the strikes, seemingly using the same original source material. The "Fourth Report" (USBL 1911) did not, however, provide a start date for the strike at Waialua, for which I used the date from Okihiro (1991:50).

74. At one point, some plantations on the island of Hawai'i, and their agencies, considered the possibility and merits of talking with the island's union, since it was not on strike (Francis M. Swanzy to Geo. McCubbin, May 17, 1909, [T. H. Davies & Co.] to Geo. McCubbin, June 22, 1909, LSC47/1, HSPAP; F. A. Schaefer to August Ahrens, June 21, 1909, HSC47/5A, HSPAP). In the end, the HSPA decided that the Big Island plantations should adhere to the same policy of not negotiating with the union as their O'ahu counterparts (F. A. Schaefer to August Ahrens, June 28, 1909, and copy of resolution passed by the HSPA, June 28, 1909, HSC47/5A, HSPAP).

75. See Beechert (1985:172) for the May 10 resolution; slightly different wording of it is found in J. W. Waldron, F. A. Schaefer & Co., to August Ahrens, Pacific Sugar Mill, May 14, 1909, HSC47/5A, HSPAP. For a copy of the May 17 resolution, see LSC47/1, HSPAPP.

76. J. W. Waldron to August Ahrens, May 14, 1909, HSC47/5A, HSPAP. See also Pacific Sugar Mill to F. A. Schaefer & Company, January 14, 1909, HSC47/7, HSPAP; manager, Hawaiian Agricultural Company, to C. Brewer & Company, May 24, 1909, KAU9/1A, HSPAP; F. M. Swanzy to Geo. McCubbin, June 2, 1909, LSC47/1, HSPAP.

77. There is disagreement over the date of this announcement. Beechert (1985:172) cites the *Pacific Commercial Advertiser*, May 26, 1909, as his source for the May 22 date. USBL (1911:86) gives May 27 as the date.

78. F. M. Swanzy to Geo. McCubbin, June 2, 1909, LSC47/1, HSPAP.

79. F. M. Swanzy to Geo. McCubbin, May 17, 1909, LSC47/1, HSPAP; USBL (1911:87).

80. The editor of the *Hawaii Shimpō*, Sometaro Shiba, had ostensibly been given a $1,500 loan by an HSPA official to purchase his paper in 1908 and had been paid $100 monthly by the planters thereafter for carrying out these tasks. In February 1909, Shiba also recruited the *Hawaii Nichi Nichi*, another Japanese newspaper,

to the planters' side; in exchange for similar services, the *Hawaii Nichi Nichi* was also paid $100 per month by the planters (Okihiro 1991:52; see also Beechert 1985; Takaki 1983).

81. "Statement of Planters' Association," November 29, 1909, as reprinted in USBL (1911:89–90).

82. In terms of violence, "except in relation to strike breakers and nonsympathizers of their own nationality, the Japanese strikers were perfectly law-abiding in the sense of refraining from violence and destruction of property" (USBL 1911:62).

83. Letter from 92 signatories to E. K. Bull, May 12, 1909, as reprinted in USBL (1911:79–82).

84. Between 1914 and 1920, consumer purchasing power in Hawai'i dwindled by half (Reinecke 1979:93).

85. As noted earlier, the Organic Act of 1900 abolished *penal* contract labor. Here, the term "contract worker" refers to a worker who, as part of a work gang, contractually agrees to cultivate cane on a section of land and is paid on a piece-rate basis.

86. By contrast, there had been 27,989 Japanese sugar workers in 1909, comprising 67.0 percent of the sugar labor force (*Hawaiian Annual* 1912:29).

87. From 1913 to 1918, the wholesale sugar prices in New York rose steadily from 3.506¢ per pound to 6.447¢ per pound. In the next two years, the price rose more sharply, to 7.724¢ in 1919 and 12.326¢ in 1920, the latter of which was an all-time high. As anticipated by the workers, prices fell back down close to pre–World War I levels; the average price for the five-year period beginning in 1921 was 5.343¢ (Taylor 1935:168).

88. E. Faxon Bishop to James Webster, January 20 and 24, 1920, HCP1/11, HSPAP; A. W. T. Bottomley to A. W. Collins, January 22, 1920, PMC1/6, HSPAP; Beechert (1985:202).

89. The FJL publicly announced a territorywide strike as a bluff, but its plan all along was only for the O'ahu members to strike. See ibid.

90. A. W. T. Bottomley to A. W. Collins, January 30, 1920, PMC1/6, HSPAP.

91. The most notable and baffling case of possible espionage involved Manlapit. In a nebulous series of events, the HSPA may have tried to decollate the FLU by bribing him into antagonizing the Japanese strikers by calling off the strike for Filipinos. On February 9, Manlapit suddenly and publicly mimicked the prevailing view of the sugar industry and the larger community that the "real object of the Japanese in declaring a strike is to cripple the industries of the Territory of Hawaii in the hope that they may be taken over by an unscrupulous alien race" (as quoted in Reinecke 1979:107). Demonstrating that the FLU was not merely a charismatic movement, less than a third of Filipino workers were at work on February 10. Defied by the rank and file, Manlapit rejoined them on February 14, declaring the strike to be once again in effect. Manlapit blamed the directors of the FLU for having forced him to make the anti-Japanese statement and fired them as he assumed sole leadership of the union (Reinecke 1979:107). Adding to the confusion, Manlapit also charged that Frank Thompson, an HSPA attorney, had offered a bribe of $25,000 on January 26 to have him call off the strike. Thompson countered that Manlapit had offered to call off the strike in exchange for $50,000. Either way, the transaction presumably did not take place, although

Manlapit did actually call off the strike 14 days later. Further adding to the intrigue, an HSPA spy took credit for convincing Manlapit to call off the strike (Beechert 1985:203).

92. E. A. R. Ross to James Webster, 31 December 1920, HCP1/11, HSPAP; American Factors to Olaa Sugar Company, January 11, 1921, PSC12/10, HSPAP; Reinecke (1979:117).

93. Although never breaking ranks, the head of the agency quoted above, who had been pleased with the industry's hard-line stance, had some misgivings toward the end (Allen W. T. Bottomley to A. W. Collins, June 1, 1920, PMC2/40, HSPAP).

94. See the reports in the file Conditions on Oahu Plantations 1920, EB. From the beginning, Filipinos on Oʻahu were not as completely successful as the Japanese in inducing their compatriots to strike ("Strike Memoranda," February 3, 4, and 5, 1920, HCP1/11, HSPAP).

95. John Waterhouse, presidential address, *Proceedings of the Fortieth Annual Meeting of the Hawaiian Sugar Planters' Association*, November 29–30, 1920, p. 8, HC.

96. Wm. Searby to American Factors, September 2, 1920, PMC1/7, HSPAP; E. Faxon Bishop to James Webster, October 23, 1920, HCP1/11, HSPAP. For an example of the industry's desire not to appear to be reacting to the strike, see R. D. Mead to C. F. Eckart, August 10, 1920, and C. F. Eckart to R. D. Mead, August 23, 1920, PSC25/15, HSPAP.

97. Pablo Manlapit, *Filipinos Fight for Justice: Case of the Filipino Laborers in the Big Strike of 1924* (Honolulu: Kumalae Publishing, [1924] 1933), file Trade Unions/HI/Pamphlets, etc., ILWUSF.

98. There were 19,475 Filipino sugar workers by 1924, comprising 49.2 percent of the sugar labor force. Overall, there were 39,599 sugar workers, 12,781 or 32.3 percent of whom were Japanese (*Hawaiian Annual* 1925:12).

99. Into the 1930s, the industry also justified its wages by comparing them to farm wages in the metropole, neglecting to point out the substantially higher cost of living in Hawaiʻi: "there is nothing to be ashamed of, even in our lowest wage of $1.00 per day" (J. K. Butler to all plantations, November 24, 1933, and J. K. Butler to plantation managers and agencies of the HSPA, January 29, 1934, KAU22/4, HSPAP).

100. Much that is known about the 1924 strike from the strikers' point of view is through Pablo Manlapit's *Filipinos Fight for Justice*. It contains various reprints of original documents as well as his personal recollection of the event. As he was the main leader of the movement, Manlapit's relatively short memoir is "probably [an] idealized account" (Reinecke 1996:12).

101. "Petition to Hawaiian Sugar Planters' Association" from signatories to President and Board of Directors of HSPA [sent on April 10, 1923], as reprinted in Manlapit (1933:35–36); see also "Manifesto of the High Wages Movement" from Pablo Manlapit and George W. Wright to the public, January 2, 1924, pp. 1–2, MQ.

102. "Manifesto of the High Wages Movement" from Pablo Manlapit and George W. Wright to the public, January 2, 1924, p. 2, MQ.

103. Ibid., pp. 3–5.

104. "Strike Proclamation" by the Executive Committee of the HWM, March 14, 1924, as reprinted in Manlapit (1933:62–64).

105. The flip side of the Filipino workers' predicament was that they were more willing to engage in strikes, since "eviction and uprooting in a strike was no big thing in their lives" (Reinecke 1996:3)—or, not as big a thing as for other workers. For an example of Filipino peripateticism and the plantations' effort to limit it, see R. D. Moler to F. A. Alexander, January 19, 1923, and F. A. Alexander to R. D. Moler, January 24, 1923, LPC8/1, HSPAP.

106. Although tenants in Hawai'i had a right to ten days' prior notice, the HSPA received a favorable ruling from the territorial attorney general permitting immediate evictions; plantation housing was construed as being a part of the workers' wages and hence outside the purview of laws pertaining to owner-tenant relations.

107. J. K. Butler to plantation managers on Hawaii and Maui, June 6, 1924, MKC1/8, HSPAP; Manlapit (1933:66–67); Reinecke (1996:40–45).

108. *Hawaii Laws of 1919*, chap. 186, secs. 1–5, as cited in Beechert (1985:214). Of the laws discussed here, the criminal syndicalism law was the only one dealing with a felony.

109. *Hawaii Laws of 1921*, chap. 216, sec. 1, as cited in Beechert (1985:215).

110. *Hawaii Laws of 1923*, chap. 189, secs. 1–3, as cited in Beechert (1985:215).

111. See chapter 3 for a more in-depth analysis.

112. Indicative of the authorities' blitzkrieg strategy, they even tried—but failed—to convict four Filipinos, who had merely spoken at a rally, on a felony charge of criminal syndicalism; this case was the only instance in Hawai'i history in which the 1919 law would be invoked (Reinecke 1996:60).

113. J. K. Butler to plantation managers on Hawaii and Maui, June 6, 1924, MKC1/8, HSPAP; partly quoted in Beechert (1985:220–221). See also J. K. Butler to plantation managers, April 23, 1924, MKC1/8, HSPAP.

114. One investigation of the strike by the industry found that its uncompromising stance had exacerbated the conflict and induced more workers to join in than would have otherwise (H. Otley Beyer, "Talk to Directors of the HSPA," August 19, 1925, LSC57/2, HSPAP).

115. Beechert (1985:192–195, 244–247); Hawaiian Sugar Planters' Association, "Confidential Extracts from Industrial Survey of 1926," 1926, PE. For the full survey, see file Beyer Reports, EB.

116. A. G. Budge to B. H. Wells, May 14, 1937, reprinted in B. H. Wells to all plantation managers, June 10, 1937, PE.

117. In 1933, only 5.92 percent of all cultivated land in Hawai'i was devoted to crops other than sugar or pineapple (Coulter 1933:53, as cited in Taylor 1935:117).

118. In 1906, the number of steamships entering Honolulu Harbor exceeded the number of sailing ships for the first time, after which the trend continued toward the latter's inevitable obsolescence.

119. "Breakdown of Hawaiian Holdings in Matson," October 7, 1949, file Companies/HI/Big Five, ILWUSF; Worden (1981:40). By statehood in 1959, the four Big Five agencies' share of Matson stock increased to 73.58 percent (calculated from Mund and Hung 1961:53–58). In 1969, Matson became a wholly owned subsidiary of Alexander & Baldwin (Rho 1990:47).

120. In 1926, Matson had already added the once formidable but then struggling Oceanic Steamship Company to its list of acquisitions (Worden 1981:58–59).

121. Hawaii Education Association, Social Affairs Committee, "The Inter-Island Strike, May 26 to September 27, 1938," *Annual Report of the Social-Economic Plans Committee*, 1939, file HI/Correspondence, Reports, etc./Local 137/1937–45, box 5, ILWUSF; Thomas (1983:168–169).

122. In 1943, Matson and Inter-Island severed their ties, fearing "the governmental attitude against interlocking relations between carriers" (Stanley C. Kennedy, Inter-Island president, as quoted in Thomas 1983:184).

123. As with its noninvolvement in Matson, Theo. H. Davies & Company was the only Big Five agency not to have a direct presence in stevedoring.

124. NLRB, Twentieth Region, Intermediate Report, "In the Matter of Honolulu Long-shoremen's Association and Castle and Cooke, Ltd. and Honolulu Stevedores, Ltd.," Case No. XX-C-55, August 14, 1937, George O. Pratt, Trial Examiner, pp. 3–4, box 70, NA. Hereafter referred to as "Pratt Report."

125. Moreover, McCabe, Hamilton & Renny was a much smaller operation than Honolulu Stevedores. In 1937, the former employed 300 workers, whereas the latter employed 800 (ibid., p. 7).

126. As the ILWU secretary-treasurer figured out in the early 1940s, "longshoring in Hawaii played a slightly different role in Hawaii than it did on the mainland. In other words, it was more like a captive fleet, in the sense that Matson ... was owned by various agencies" (Goldblatt interview [with Beechert], p. 3).

127. See also "Labor Disturbances in Hawaii, 1890–1925."

128. Ibid., p. 15. See also Reinecke (1979:180) and Beechert (1985:159).

129. Given that Matson was the largest shipper on the West Coast as well as in Hawai'i (Kimeldorf 1988:58; Nelson 1988:122), the historical parallels in the two locales were intimately related.

130. "Pratt Report," pp. 10–13; emphasis added. For the 1936 payroll at Castle & Cooke, see Matson Terminal and Castle & Cooke, Wharf and Terminal Department, "Total Earnings of Stevedores for Year, 1936," box 240, NA. For an account from the Honolulu Longshoremen's Association's point of view, which is consonant with the NLRB findings, see Alexander Chang to Harry Bridges, January 21, 1937, folder HI/Correspondence, Reports, etc./1937–43, box 5, ILWUSF.

   Longshore employment on the outer islands was even more "casual" than in Honolulu, which, as the primary port for the territory, enjoyed a constant flow of cargo traffic. See letters from Randolph Sevier to C. Brewer & Company, Kahului Railroad Company, Hawaii Railway Company, Kauai Terminal, Ltd., Honokaa Sugar Company, Pioneer Mill Company, Kaeleku Sugar Company, Lihue Planta-tion Company, and Hutchinson Sugar Company, August 23, 1937 and July 16, 1938, LPC9/6, HSPAP. For a first-hand account of the shape-up on the Hilo waterfront, see Nakano interview (by Conybeare), pp. 2–3, and Nakano interview (by Zalburg), pp. 5–6.

131. "Labor Disturbances in Hawaii, 1890–1925," pp. 14–17.

132. Each case contained two dozen cans.

133. For an example of the pineapple industry's drawing of labor from the sugar industry and the friction it could cause, see D. Fraser to Leslie W. Wishard, July 1, 1936, LSC39/9, HSPAP; Chauncey Wightman to A. T. Spalding, October 5, 1944, PSC42/4, HSPAP.

134. This basic difference in the two crops allowed both industries to expand, at least in terms of land usage, without infringing on eachother (USBLS 1916:42; Morgan 1917:38).

135. W. A. Baldwin, "A Brief History and Commentary on the Pineapple Industry of Maui, Hawaii," 1938, p. 13, 2/2/7c, HPCDC.

136. For example, see "The World's Supply of Sugar," *Planters' Monthly* 17 (January 1898): 47–48, HC.

137. W. A. Baldwin, "A Brief History and Commentary on the Pineapple Industry of Maui, Hawaii," 1938, p. 6.

138. Like the other pineapple producers, Hapco faced a dismal prospect when the worldwide Depression dried up the pineapple market. Since the growing season for pineapples was two years, the companies could not adjust their plantings in time to anticipate the dramatic decrease in demand. In fact, their combined pack increased from 9.2 million cases in 1929 to over 12.6 million and 12.7 million cases in 1930 and 1931, respectively (*Hawaiian Annual* 1933:38). As a result, the industry as a whole had a 61 percent carryover of inventory in 1931 from the previous year's pack (Chapman 1933:12). Hapco suffered $3,875,000 in losses in 1931 and apparently needed $5 million to stay afloat (Joesting 1972:292). While the other two top-three pineapple companies relied on their parent corporations to cover their losses, Hapco had to turn elsewhere (MacDonald 1944:36–37).

    At this time of need, James Dole first made a decisive move to cut his costs. For a long time, he had been unhappy with Matson's monopoly in shipping, rightly feeling that his company was being overcharged (Worden 1981:70–71). So, in June 1931, he fatefully decided to take the lower bid of the Isthmian Steamship Company, drawing the ire of the Big Five (Fuchs 1961:241–242). Perhaps not surprisingly in retrospect but certainly to Dole's surprise then, banks in San Francisco and Honolulu suddenly refused to extend the loans he desperately needed; Lawrence Fuchs (1961:242) writes that the officers of Matson and Castle & Cooke—agent and principal stockholder of Matson as well as a minority shareholder of Hapco—used their considerable influence with the banks to effect this turn of fate, a conclusion no one disputes. In 1932, Castle & Cooke and a plantation it controlled, Waialua Agricultural Company, stepped in to provide the funds to bail Hapco out, through which they increased their ownership of Hapco to 56 percent. In the process, Castle & Cooke promptly ousted Dole from Hapco's presidency and installed in his stead one of its own, Atherton Richards, whose uncle Frank C. Atherton was the head of Castle & Cooke (MacDonald 1944:110–111; White 1957:25; Worden 1981:70–71). Taylor, Welty, and Eyre (1976:169–171) reported Castle & Cooke and Waialua as obtaining 58 percent ownership of Hapco.

139. A large minority remained in the hands of two corporations based in the metropole, which continued to be a source of division. As the secretary of the HSPA would lament in 1944, "While the pineapple producers have an association with the word 'cooperative' appearing in the name, the word is used in a very restrictive sense and there is cooperation only to the extent that one of the members deems necessary" (Chauncey B. Wightman to A. T. Spalding, October 5, 1944, PSC42/4, HSPAP).

140. The quota agreement expired in 1942. Worries concerning the Sherman Anti-Trust Act played a major part in its discontinuation (Dean 1950:196; MacDonald 1944:113–114). Dean (1950) dated the end of PPCA's operations as 1943.
141. "Pratt Report," p. 42.

3. Race and Labor in Prewar Hawai'i

1. For example, see Takaki (1983).
2. Even when invoked, pan-Asian categories, like "Oriental," usually referred to those of East Asian origin and excluded Filipinos (e.g., Okamura 1994:161; Chang 1996:140). For explicit examples from prewar Hawai'i, see Form 111, August 1930, LPC17/7, HSPAP; J. K. Butler to all plantations, March 23, 1933, KAU22/4, HSPAP.
3. For discussions of panethnicity, see Espiritu (1992) and Lopez and Espiritu (1990).
4. A similar case could be made for Hakkas and *bendi* among the Chinese (Lydon 1975; McKeown 2001).
5. A partial exception was the durable, hierarchical division between *Naichi*, those from the main islands of Japan, and *Uchinanchu*, Okinawans. In relation to Japanese participation in the labor movement, anecdotal evidence suggests that Okinawans were particularly active (ESOHP and UOAH 1981; Kaneshiro 1999).
6. For one among many examples, see Takaki (1990).
7. For a fuller discussion, see Jung (1999). Even before the 1910s, the sugar planters' express desire for a racially mixed workforce had continually been frustrated by recruitment costs and immigration restrictions (Beechert 1985).
8. For a concise, lucid discussion of race and Marxism, see chapter 1 of Roediger (1991).
9. For examples, see Almaguer (1994); Anthias and Yuval-Davis (1992); Gilroy (1991); Hall (1980); Hall et al. (1978); Omi and Winant (1986, 1994); San Juan (1992); Winant (1994).
10. Omi and Winant identify four major variants of the "nation-based paradigm": pan-Africanism, cultural nationalism, Marxism-Leninism on the "national question," and internal colonialism.
11. Given that they do not themselves proffer an alternative politics of race—although they seem partial to such a project—Omi and Winant's criticism of nation-based theories as inefficacious political ideologies rings somewhat hollow. Subjecting previous "paradigms" of racial thought to criticism on two registers—as sociological theories explaining racial phenomena and as political ideologies—Omi and Winant's own theory, as an aspiring paradigm shifter, may reasonably be expected to provide convincing alternatives on both counts. Thus, their silence on outlining a new politics of race consonant with their racial formation theory, which operates only on the register of sociological explanation, seems conspicuous. However, it cannot be readily attributed to mere oversight or neglect. I argue that it is immanent to their theory, which is foremost about "decenter[ing]" the category of race (1986:68), severing its essentialist ties to ostensibly more fundamental categories (e.g., class, nation) and seeing it as open to historical change and analysis. But,

decentering race, which makes racial formation theory compelling and useful as a sociological theory of race, works at cross purposes with constructing a new politics of race. As Dirks, Eley, and Ortner write, "politics consists of the effort to domesticate the infinitude of identity. It is the attempt to hegemonize identity, to order it into a strong programmatic statement. If identity is decentered, politics is about the attempt to create a center" (1994:32).

Not unique to Omi and Winant's work, the complex and slippery relationship between homologous sociological theories and political ideologies reappears, in a different form, later in this study (see chapters 5 and 6).

12. In the second edition of their book, Omi and Winant (1994:55) add that race is "a concept which signifies and symbolizes social conflicts and interests by referring to different types of human bodies."

13. The ten features are "boundaries," "indivisibility," "sovereignty," "an 'ascending' notion of legitimacy," "popular participation in collective affairs," "direct membership," "culture," "temporal depth," "common descent or racial characteristics," and "special historical or even sacred relations to a certain territory" (Calhoun 1997:4–5).

14. What Rogers Brubaker writes of nationalist discourses and practices also goes for racial and class ones: "nationalism is a way of seeing the world, a way of *identifying interests*, or more precisely, a way of specifying interest-bearing units, of *identifying the relevant units in terms of which interests are conceived*.... Thus it inherently links identity and interest—by *identifying how we are to calculate our interests*" (1998:291–292; emphases in original).

15. Goldberg (1993) applies his apt phrase to race and nation but not to class.

16. Race not only naturalizes history but also often invokes natural history. For example, with the popularization of findings in archaeology, evidence animating discussions of the racial identity of "Eve" is no longer restricted to the scriptures.

17. The phrase "modern ways of peoplehood" is paraphrased from the title of Lie (2004).

18. In contrast, although nationalist discourses and practices can be about inequalities, they need not be; when they are, they tend to be articulated with race.

19. Ancheta (1998) and Kim (2000) differentiate antiblack and anti-Asian racisms in similar terms.

20. See Reinecke (1996:144) for similar data on the ratio of "foremen" to "laborers" in 1920.

21. The advantages of looking at this plantation are that, among the plantations whose records have been archived, its records are the most complete and that, compared to the less complete records of other plantations and of the sugar industry as a whole, the data are quite representative. Cf. *Hawaiian Annual* 1920–1940; Hawaiian Sugar Planters' Association, "Labor Report of All Islands," June 1944, PSC40/7, HSPAP; various Forms 54 and Forms 111 in KSC23/28, LPC17/7, LPC42/4, and LSC22C/5, HSPAP; payroll records in HSC36/7, LPC5/6, LPC5/9, LPC11/4, LPC11/6, and LPC36/2, HSPAP; Lind (1938b:324); USBLS (1931:3; 1940:63).

22. The "skilled" category includes supervisory positions, including top management. It excludes semiskilled positions and, from at least 1935 but possibly in 1929 as well, any skilled positions not paid on a monthly salary basis. In 1941, the category

became even more elite, as only those with a monthly salary of $100 or more were included.

In 1920, jobs paying more than $68 per month were "skilled," and those paying between $30 and $68 per month were "semi-skilled" (J. K. Butler to all agents and plantations, December 29, 1920, PSC22/7, HSPAP).

23. Trends apparent in table 3.2 will become clearer in later parts of this chapter and book. As discussed later in this chapter, the number of Japanese workers in the sugar industry increased during the 1930s in response to the Depression and the move to "Americanize" the sugar industry with "citizen" workers; it dipped between 1938 and 1941 with the aforementioned categorical redefinition of "skilled." During the same period, the number of Filipino workers decreased, as the Depression and the Americanization movement conspired to push them out of the industry and territory. As discussed in later chapters, the war years continued the trends of increasing numbers of Japanese workers and decreasing numbers of Filipino workers. However, the causal forces at work were quite different. Under martial law, Japanese workers, long suspected of disloyalty to "America," were severely restricted in the types of employment in which they could engage; however, plantation work remained open to them, leading to their increasing numbers. Like others, many Filipinos sought higher-paying jobs in the defense industry before and after the start of the war, leading to their shrinking numbers on the plantations.

24. In 1929, 90 of the 114 women and 257 of the 344 minors were Japanese. All 126 women in 1935 and 146 of 158 women in 1938 were Japanese. The other figures for women and minors in table 3.2 were not broken down by racial category.

25. Payroll records for 1934 in PSCPV.45, HSPAP.

26. Ibid. For Japanese men, there was one additional job that paid the median salary in 1934. Listed as "expt station," the worker probably held a research-related position at the plantation's agricultural experiment station. Based on his age (29) and salary ($65/month)—2 other Japanese men with the same title were slightly younger and earned less—I would venture that he worked under the supervision of the haole "agriculturalist," who, though only 4 years older, made $275 per month in 1934.

27. Payroll records for 1926 and 1942 in PSCPV.45, HSPAP.

28. For base wage rates by gender adopted in late 1920, see E. F. Bishop to James Webster, October 23, 1920, HCP1/11, HSPAP. The base wage rate for unskilled men was $30–$33 for 26 days worked in a month, depending on the locale of the plantation, while it was $22.50 for unskilled women.

29. HSPA, "Census of Employees and Families on Sugar Plantations," June 30, 1930, PSC34/2, HSPAP. Of the 13,685, 3,932 were men, and 2,915 were women, while the remaining 6,838 were children. Of the 30,624, 30,570 were men, while only 46 were women and 8 were children; the children were presumably living with single parents.

30. Ibid.

31. Randolph Sevier to C. Brewer & Company, Kahului Railroad Company, Hawaii Railway Company, Kauai Terminal, Ltd., Honokaa Sugar Company, Pioneer Mill Company, Kaeleku Sugar Company, Lihue Plantation Company, and Hutchinson Sugar Company, August 23 1937, LPC9/6, HSPAP. The memorandum listed

724 Japanese, 629 Filipinos, 518 Hawaiians, 32 Portuguese, 16 Puerto Ricans, 14 Chinese, and 148 "Others." (One of the firms provided a range, rather than a specific number, for each category. I used the midpoints of the ranges to calculate these sums.)

This memo provides the most complete data available for the entire industry. However, it does not include the smaller 2 of the 3 stevedoring firms in Honolulu. Therefore, it undercounted the total number by probably around 400. The racial breakdown of the workforce at these 2 firms is unknown. (On September 29, 1937, 316 longshoremen voted in an NLRB election at McCabe, Hamilton & Renny. On March 31, 1938, 77 cast votes in an NLRB election at Inter-Island Steam Navigation Company [Hawaii Education Association, Social Affairs Committee, "The Inter-Island Strike, May 26 to September 27, 1938," *Annual Report of the Social-Economic Plans Committee*, 1939, pp. 105–107, file HI/Correspondence, Reports, etc./Local 137/1937–45, box 5, ILWUSF].)

32.   Including only longshoremen in Honolulu and Hilo, this study's sample was 35.4 percent Japanese, 33.8 Hawaiian, 13.6 percent "Caucasian," 10.3 percent Filipino, and 6.9 percent "others" (USBLS 1940:171). Given the large and fluctuating number of casual workers employed in the industry during the 1920s and 1930s, any study's sample would have been suspect.

33.   This study's sample of 3 plantations (of the 8 in Hawai'i) included 4,123 men and 298 women (USBLS 1940:94–95). Its sample of 4 canneries included 5,547 men and 5,073 women; the numbers were, however, more skewed among just the year-round "regular" workers—808 men to 431 women (USBLS 1940:102, 111).

34.   The mean earnings for men and women were, respectively, $16.30 and $8.50 per month in the canneries (USWB 1940:8–9) and $58.62 and $30.44 per month on the plantations (USBLS 1940:94–95).

35.   Filipinos actually earned slightly more than the Japanese—33.3¢ to 33.0¢ per hour. The remaining 14.3 percent of the male labor force on the plantations was distributed fairly evenly across 5 different racial categories.

36.   The raw numbers of men in the sample were 233 Japanese, 189 Filipinos, 86 Chinese, 70 "Caucasians," 45 Hawaiians, 8 Koreans, and 177 "all others." Whether, and how many, Portuguese were included in the "Caucasian" (or possibly "all others") category was unspecified.

37.   The relative absence of racial disparities in pay among intermittent and seasonal workers—all or nearly all unskilled—is further evidence that the disparities among these regular workers were due to differential placement in skilled jobs (USBLS 1940:111).

38.   See also "Facts concerning the Hawaiian or Sandwich Islands," *Planters' Monthly* 13 (March 1894): 106, HC; Beechert (1985:34–41); Fuchs (1961:ch. 2); Love (2004: ch. 3); Thurston (n.d.:31–32).

39.   Somewhat counterintuitively, the haole elite favored Hawaiians for government posts and the very few Hawaiians on the plantations for supervisory positions in the first half of the twentieth century. Hawaiians, whose franchise had been limited by property requirements before annexation, held a majority of the electorate to 1922 and a plurality to 1938. Haole fought off the challenge from the anti-haole Home Rule Party at the turn of the century by building a patronage system

through the Republican Party (Fuchs 1961:156–162; Lind 1980:102). This patronage no doubt dovetailed with and gave sustenance to the haole notion that Hawaiians were "their natives" to be reformed and assimilated.

40. Even today, note the ambiguous positioning of Filipinos in the debate over Asians and colonialism in Hawai'i. For example, see the special issue of *Amerasia Journal* 26 (2), "Whose Vision? Asian Settler Colonialism in Hawai'i," edited by Candace Fujikane and Jonathan Okamura.

41. In reaction to the anti-Chinese movement there, around 8,000 Chinese from California arrived in Hawai'i during the late 1870s and 1880s (Kuykendall and Day 1948:156).

42. See also *Hawaiian Gazette*, January 19, 1870, as quoted in Conroy ([1949] 1973:17).

43. See also "Contract Laborers in Hawaii," *Planters' Monthly* 15 (April 1896): 156, HC; "Hawaiian Reciprocity and Contract Labor," *Planters' Monthly* 16 (January 1897): 7–10, HC; "Hawaiian Labor System and Annexation," *Planters' Monthly* 17 (February 1898): 59–61, HC.

44. Letter from Castle & Cooke, Bishop & Co., H. Hackfeld & Co., C. Brewer & Co., Theo. H. Davies & Co., G. W. Macfarlane & Co., W. G. Irwin & Co., F. A. Schaefer & Co., and E. P. Adams, February 18, 1882, as reprinted in "A Reminiscence. Origin of the Hawaiian Sugar Planters' Association," *Planters' Monthly* 16 (December 1897): 597–598, HC; Beechert (1985:80–83).

45. Samuel T. Alexander, G. N. Wilcox, William O. Smith, and A. Unna, "Report of the Committee on Labor," *Planters' Monthly* 2 (November 1883): 245–247, HC.

46. *Hawaiian Gazette*, October 13, 1869, as quoted in Kuykendall (1953:190); R. G. Davies, an influential "part-Hawaiian lawyer," as quoted in Merry (2000:133).

47. "Chinese Immigration," *Planters' Monthly* 2 (May 1883): 25, HC. See also "The Chinese Population," *Planters' Monthly* 2 (June 1883): 49–50, HC; "The Disproportion of Sexes," *Planters' Monthly* 2 (September 1883): 122–124, HC; Samuel T. Alexander, G. N. Wilcox, William O. Smith, and A. Unna, "Report of the Committee on Labor," *Planters' Monthly* 2 (November 1883): 245–247, HC. From 1878, the British government in Hong Kong prevented ships from boarding passengers under contract, allowing Chinese laborers to evade indentures (Beechert 1985:64; McKeown 2001:34).

48. "Hawaii as an American Territory," *Planters' Monthly* 17 (September 1898): 394–395, HC; J. B. Atherton and C. Bolte, "Memorial Presented to the United States Commissioners by Hawaiian Sugar Planters' Association September 8, 1898," *Planters' Monthly* 17 (November 1898): 497–507, HC.

    The U.S. Congress, in a 1790 law, limited naturalization to "free white persons" and, in a 1870 law, expanded it to "aliens of African nativity and to persons of African descent." For the legal history of whiteness and U.S. naturalization, including the naturalization acts of 1790 and 1870, see Haney-López (1996).

    The planters also pleaded for excepting Hawai'i from restrictive U.S. immigration laws.

49. The planters had advocated this type of policy for Chinese labor since at least the early 1880s and would advocate it, albeit unsuccessfully, after annexation (USBL 1903).

50. From 1879 to 1898, there were 48,816 Chinese arrivals and 26,741 Chinese departures recorded. Due to multiple departures and arrivals, neither number represents separate individuals. Of the estimated total of 50–56,000 arrivals between 1852 and 1898, the number of separate individuals has been estimated at 30–40,000 (Kuykendall 1967:152–153; see also Char 1975:305; Glick 1980:12).

51. "The Louisiana Planters and the Treaty," *Planters' Monthly* 4 (February 1886): 305, HC. See also "Contract Laborers in Hawaii," *Planters' Monthly* 15 (April 1896): 156, HC; "Hawaiian Reciprocity and Contract Labor," *Planters' Monthly* 16 (January 1897): 7–10, HC; "Hawaiian Labor System and Annexation," *Planters' Monthly* 17 (February 1898): 59–61, HC; Beechert (1985:80–84, 91); Kuykendall (1967:ch. 15).

52. C. Bolte, J. F. Hackfeld, and E. D. Tenney, "Report of the Labor Committee," *Planters' Monthly* 15 (November 1896): 486–487, HC; "Annual Meeting of the HSPA," *Planters' Monthly* 18 (December 1899): 529–540, HC; W. O. Smith, secretary's report, *Proceedings of the Twenty-ninth Annual Meeting of the Hawaiian Sugar Planters' Association*, November 15–18, 1909, pp. 7–9, HC.

53. Nordyke (1977:table 10) places the number of Portuguese arrivals before 1905 at 14,670. The figure based on Schmitt (1977:97–98, 100) is 11,073 for the same period.

54. Samuel T. Alexander, G. N. Wilcox, William O. Smith, and A. Unna, "Report of the Committee on Labor," *Planters' Monthly* 2 (November 1883): 245, HC. Emphases in original.

55. S. M. Damon, presidential address, *Proceedings of the Twenty-ninth Annual Meeting of the Hawaiian Sugar Planters' Association*, November 15–18, 1909, p. 3, HC. See also manager, Pacific Sugar Mill, to F. A. Schaefer & Co., January 14, 1909, HSC47/7, HSPAP.

56. For the timing of migration to Hawai'i, see Nordyke (1977:table 12) and Schmitt (1977:97).

57. "The Disproportion of Sexes," *Planters' Monthly* 2 (September 1883): 123, HC. See also Samuel T. Alexander, G. N. Wilcox, William O. Smith, and A. Unna, "Report of the Committee on Labor," *Planters' Monthly* 2 (November 1883): 245–247, HC; "Homesteads for Immigrants," *Planters' Monthly* 3 (February 1885): 644–645, HC; A. H. Smith, "Report of Committee on Labor," *Planters' Monthly* 4 (January 1886): 259–264, HC; "Annual Meeting of the HSPA," *Planters' Monthly* 18 (December 1899): 529–540, HC; "Governor Frear's Report," *Planters' Monthly* 28 (January 1909): 8–9, HC; F. H. Newell, Director of the United States Reclamation Service, "Hawaii, Its Natural Resources and Opportunities for Home Making," *Planters' Monthly* 28 (March 1909): 93–109, HC; W. Pfotenhauer, presidential address, *Proceedings of the Thirtieth Annual Meeting of the Hawaiian Sugar Planters' Association*, November 14–17, 1910, pp. 2–6, HC; A. W. T. Bottomley to J. Watt, December 13, 1910, PSC25/13, HSPAP; USBL (1903); Kuykendall (1953).

    The many letter contributions by plantation managers to J. F. Freitas's ([1930] 1992) *Portuguese-Hawaiian Memories* are also pertinent. That the letters for this celebratory volume would be laudatory is neither surprising nor interesting. What is notable is that they repeatedly sound the themes of labor, citizenship, and permanent settlement in praising the Portuguese.

58. "The Last and Future Portuguese Immigration," *Planters' Monthly* 28 (December 1909): 492, HC.

59. "Contract Laborers in Hawaii," *Planters' Monthly* 15 (April 1896): 156, HC.

60. Ibid.; "Report of the Committee on Labor," *Planters' Monthly* 1 (November 1882): 196–198, HC; "The Disproportion of Sexes," *Planters' Monthly* 2 (September 1883): 122–124, HC; Samuel T. Alexander, G. N. Wilcox, William O. Smith, and A. Unna, "Report of the Committee on Labor," *Planters' Monthly* 2 (November 1883): 245–247, HC; A. H. Smith, "Report of Committee on Labor," *Planters' Monthly* 4 (January 1886): 259–264, HC.

61. "Portuguese Immigrant Laborers—Bureau of Immigration," *Planters' Monthly* 6 (November 1887): 498, HC. See also Coman (1903:29–30); Felix and Senecal (1978:28–29).

62. "Chinese Immigration," *Planters' Monthly* 2 (May 1883): 25–26, HC; "The Chinese Population," *Planters' Monthly* 2 (June 1883): 49–50, HC; "The Disproportion of Sexes," *Planters' Monthly* 2 (September 1883): 122–124, HC; Samuel T. Alexander, G. N. Wilcox, William O. Smith, and A. Unna, "Report of the Committee on Labor," *Planters' Monthly* 2 (November 1883): 245–247, HC; "Are the Planters Responsible for the Preponderance of Male Chinese," *Planters' Monthly* 4 (July 1885): 90–91, HC.

    At one point, the planters suggested, as a remedy, the possibility of the government "importing negro women from the West Indies and Jamaica in particular, where there is a superabundance of females of excellent physique who speak English and are accustomed to all kinds of hard work" (R. A. Macfie, Jr., "Report of Committee on Labor," *Planters' Monthly* 8 [November 1889]: 507, HC).

63. Before annexation, the planters paid for the passage of male laborers, and the government paid for the passage of their wives and children.

64. A. H. Smith, "Report of Committee on Labor," *Planters' Monthly* 4 (January 1886): 262, HC. Coman (1903:35) placed the "cost of importation" in 1886 for Portuguese, Chinese, and Japanese laborers at $112.00, $76.83, and $65.85, respectively.

65. "Comparative Statement of Portuguese Immigration, June 14, 1884 to December 31, 1886" and "Comparative Statement of Japanese Immigration—1885 and 1886," *Planters' Monthly* 6 (November 1887): 498, HC.

66. "Governor Frear's Report," *Planters' Monthly* 28 (January 1909): 9, HC. See also "The Last and Future Portuguese Immigration," *Planters' Monthly* 28 (December 1909): 491–493, HC.

67. G. H. Fairchild, "A Practical Illustration of the Contract Labor System in Hawaii," *Planters' Monthly* 15 (April 1896): 157–160, HC. For the period between 1888 and 1890, the monthly wages for Portuguese, Chinese, and Japanese laborers under contract were $19.53, $17.61, and $15.58, respectively. For day laborers, the respective numbers were $22.25, $17.47, and $18.84 (Coman 1903:23).

68. Samuel T. Alexander, G. N. Wilcox, William O. Smith, and A. Unna, "Report of the Committee on Labor," *Planters' Monthly* 2 (November 1883): 246, HC. Emphasis in original.

69. Ibid., pp. 245–246. See also "Portuguese Immigration," *Planters' Monthly* 13 (May 1894): 197–198, HC.

70. "Labor Conditions of Hawaii (From the Annual Report of the Governor of the Territory of Hawaii for 1904)," *Planters' Monthly* 24 (May 1905): 229, HC.

71. W. Pfotenhauer, presidential address, *Proceedings of the Thirtieth Annual Meeting of the Hawaiian Sugar Planters' Association*, November 14–17, 1910, p. 4, HC.

For a few of many examples linking the Portuguese to penal labor contracts, the specter of enslavement, and non-European laborers, see "Contract Laborer in Hawaii," *Planters' Monthly* 15 (April 1896): 156–160, HC; "Hawaiian Reciprocity and Contract Labor," *Planters' Monthly* 16 (January 1897): 7–10, HC; "Hawaiian Labor System and Annexation," *Planters' Monthly* 17 (February 1898): 59–61, HC.

72. H. P. Baldwin, C. Bolte, and F. M. Swanzy, "Report of Labor Committee," *Planters' Monthly* 13 (November 1894): 497–499, HC. Similarly, expressing disappointment with recently recruited Russian laborers, the HSPA president, in 1910, found solace in the prospect of further migration of Portuguese laborers, "by far the most desirable element" (W. Pfotenhauer, presidential address, *Proceedings of the Thirtieth Annual Meeting of the Hawaiian Sugar Planters' Association*, November 14–17, 1910, p. 4, HC).

73. G. H. Fairchild, "A Practical Illustration of the Contract Labor System in Hawaii," *Planters' Monthly* 15 (April 1896): 157, HC.

74. According to Eric T. L. Love (2004), many in the United States objected to the annexation of a land populated mostly by "nonwhites," grouping the racially equivocal Portuguese with "nonwhites." Addressing this objection, Thurston insisted on Portuguese Europeanness to inflate the size of Hawaii's "white" population. Together, both positions had the effect of marking the Portuguese as distinct from and less than the racially unequivocal haole.

75. A. W. T. Bottomley to J. Watt, December 13, 1910, PSC25/13, HSPAP; "Governor Frear's Report," *Planters' Monthly* 28 (January 1909): 9, HC.

76. For examples, see territorial vital statistics as reprinted in *Hawaiian Annual* 1910–1940; Hawaiian Sugar Planters' Association, annual census reports of sugar plantations, 1928–1935, KSC19/29, HSPAP; tables 3.2 and 3.3. Regarding the centrality of the state in imposing and naturalizing social categories, see Bourdieu (1994) and Jung and Almaguer (2004).

77. Haole rated the Chinese higher and the Puerto Ricans lower (except in relation to tact) than the Portuguese. The Portuguese and the Hawaiians were each rated higher than the other on four of the eight scales.

   Largely an inversion, the "tact" ratings were the most out of line with the others. Only the presumed superiority of the unrated haole likely kept this measure from being modified or discarded.

   Other parts of the same study, based not on haole raters but on psychometric testing, found a similar ranking of racial groups.

78. For examples, see files HSC36/7, LPC5/6, LPC5/9, LPC11/4, LPC11/6, LPC36/2, and PSCPV.45, HSPAP.

79. For examples of the enduring image of the belligerent Portuguese luna with his whip, see Kotani (1985:13–14) and the feature film *Picture Bride*.

80. Letter to the editor, *Honolulu Advertiser*, March 5, 1937, file 1/1/48, RASRLC.

81. Interestingly, the implications of the fact that many of Estep's (1941b) own measures of "assimilation" with haole (e.g., levels of education, welfare use, crime) placed the Chinese and the Japanese ahead of the Portuguese went unexplored.

82. *Honolulu Advertiser*, October 29, 1940, file 1/4/53, RASRLC. See also *Honolulu Advertiser*, January 16, 1929, March 5, 1937; *Honolulu Star-Bulletin*, April 5, 1947, April 11, 1947; Kimura (1955).

83. Martin interview (by author).

84. Even when the Portuguese had been more active in labor politics at the turn of the century, when their racial distinction from haole had not been fully settled, their efforts, like those of haole workers, were directed at the Chinese and Japanese workers as much as the haole employers (G. H. Fairchild, "A Practical Illustration of the Contract Labor System in Hawaii," *Planters' Monthly* 15 [April 1896]: 157–160, HC; Beechert 1985:146–147; Kuykendall 1967:172–175; USBL 1902).

85. *Pacific Commercial Advertiser*, n.d., as quoted in Baker (1912:330).

86. Consistently, some Portuguese also joined haole in the overthrow of the Hawaiian monarchy, forming a part of the Honolulu Rifles (Kuykendall 1967:351–352).

87. Holmberg interview, p. 96. See also Goldblatt interview (by Ward), pp. 405–406; Kotani (1985:13–14).

88. As an agency executive prescribed to a plantation manager in 1910, "I think our policy should be to substitute white men or Portuguese for Japanese in skilled positions, even at the expense of a certain amount of efficiency or a certain extra cost. This is good policy Politically as well as Economically" (A. W. T. Bottomley to J. Watt, December 13, 1910, PSC25/13, HSPAP). See also Takaki (1983:76).

89. Conroy ([1949] 1973:38) reported that 149 began the trip but one man died on the way; citing a doctor who accompanied the migrants, Conroy also wrote that there were 6 women and 1 child among the 148. Kuykendall (1953:183) counted 6 women and 2 children, although the source of this information is unclear.

90. For the political-economic changes in Japan that led to the displacement and emigration of farmers, see Azuma (2005:27–28).

91. Between 1905 and 1916, there were 62,647 Japanese arrivals, compared to 30,119 and 28,068 departures to Japan and the U.S. West Coast, respectively (Beechert 1985:132). See also Kotani (1985:24).

92. "Hawaiian Labor System and Annexation," *Planters' Monthly* 17 (February 1898): 60, HC.

93. "Report of Committee on Labor," *Planters' Monthly* 19 (November 1900): 517, HC.

94. *Pacific Commercial Advertiser*, August 8, 1868, as cited in Beechert (1985:76); *Pacific Commercial Advertiser*, July 26, 1904, as cited in Okihiro (1991:34). Anti-imperialists in the United States referred to Hawaii's Japanese, as well as the Portuguese, as "coolies" more liberally (Love 2004).

95. HSPA resolution, November 18, 1904, as quoted in Takaki (1983:76).

96. Minutes of Bureau of Immigration, March 19, 1868, as quoted in Kuykendall (1953:183). See also enclosure in Kapena to Gibson, November 14, 1882, as quoted in Kuykendall (1967:159–160).

97. "Précis of an interview between Their Excellencies Inouye Kaoru, His Imperial Japanese Majesty's Minister for Foreign Affairs, and John M. Kapena, His Hawaiian Majesty's Envoy Extraordinary and Minister Plenipotentiary, held at the Foreign Office, Tokio, November 24th, 1882," enclosure in Webb to Iaukea, December 15, 1883, as quoted in Kuykendall (1967:160).

98. The king also made another unsuccessful proposal: the marriage of his five-year-old niece to a fifteen-year-old Japanese prince. Though unsuccessful, the two proposals, among others, made favorable impressions.

99. "Treaty of Friendship and Commerce between the Kingdom of Hawaii and the Empire of Japan," August 19, 1871, as reprinted in Okahata and PCUJSH (1971:285–286).

100. "Hawaii and Japan," *Planters' Monthly* 16 (April 1897): 158–162, HC; Conroy ([1949] 1973:192).

101. "Hawaii and Japan," p. 161.

102. See also Bailey (1931) and Hobson (1897).

103. The relative weights were: six for planning capacity, three for self-determination, two for inhibition of impulse, two for resolution, two for self control, two for tact, two for dependability, and one for stability of interest (Porteus and Babcock 1926:108–109).

104. A part of Porteus and Babcock (1926) appeared earlier as one among many reports that comprised an external study of the industry commissioned by the HSPA in the aftermath of the 1924 strike. For the identities of the haole survey respondents, see Stanley Porteus, "Report on Filipino Labor," 1925, p. 7, files Porteus Report/HSPA Industrial Survey, EB. As this report listed twenty-seven names, two of the respondents were apparently dropped from the results discussed in Porteus and Babcock (1926).

105. For the haole elite of the late nineteenth and early twentieth centuries, ideals of manhood blended what Bederman (1995) refers to as civilized, self-restrained *manliness* and primitive, virile *masculinity*.

106. The Japanese term *issei* refers to first-generation migrants from Japan. The term *nisei* refers to their children.

107. *Proceedings of the Annual Conference of New Americans*, 1932, pp. 7–8, HC. See also Stirling (1939) for an elaboration of his views of the Japanese as well as of Filipinos, whom he had fought in the Philippine-American War.

108. For the best example, see Merry (2000:131–144).

109. Indicative of the link between colonization and presumption of inferiority, all the U.S. colonial subjects included in the Porteus and Babcock (1926:109) study—Hawaiians, Puerto Ricans, and Filipinos, in descending order—rated the lowest on the composite scale of haole ratings.

110. For examples of the distinctions haole made among Filipinos from different regions, see H. Otley Beyer, "Talk to Directors of the HSPA," August 19, 1925, LSC57/2, HSPAP; Fern interview, p. 511; Porteus and Babcock (1926:ch. 6); C. J. Welch, as quoted in *New York Commercial*, August 23, [1925?], file 1924 Strike/1925, EB.

111. A. W. T. Bottomely to John Watt, September 26, 1910, PSC25/13, HSPAP. See also J.K. Butler, as quoted in *Honolulu Times*, August 8, 1924, in Reinecke (1996:3); C. J. Welch, as quoted in *New York Commercial*, August 23, [1925?], file 1924 Strike/1925, EB.

112. See, for example, interviews with Cabico, de la Cruz, and Gueco; Anderson (1984:12–14); Ariyoshi (2000:14–15); Jung (2004); Masuoka (1931); Reinecke (1979:36); Sharma (1984a:601). One fact that most commentators, sympathetic and unsympathetic alike, fail to note about the persistent association of Filipinos and knives, particularly cane knives, is that Filipino workers, holding the most physically taxing and lowest paid positions on the plantations, were predominantly the ones in the field actually cutting and handling cane.

113. Kramer (1998:93); Roediger (1994:117–118); de la Cruz interview, p. 141; Gueco interview, pp. 172–173.

114. S. M. Damon, presidential address, *Proceedings of the Twenty-ninth Annual Meeting of the Hawaiian Sugar Planters' Association*, November 15–18, 1909, p. 4, HC. Note how this statement was prefigured by Commissioner William Howard Taft's statement on the role of the United States in the Philippines: "[Preparing] a whole people for self-government, and that problem includes not only the teaching of that people how to read, write, and figure in arithmetic, but also to teach them how to labor" (as quoted in Jacobson 2000:246).

115. S. M. Damon, presidential address, p. 4.

116. Manager, Hawaiian Agricultural Company, to C. Brewer & Co., August 4, 1909, KAU9/1A, HSPAP.

117. "The Last and Future Portuguese Immigration," *Planters' Monthly* 28 (December 1909): 492, HC. U.S. colonial subjects like the Filipinos, Puerto Rican laborers were also mentioned as being "poor material for good citizenship."

118. Baysa interview; Corpuz interview; de la Cruz interview. Many Filipinos feigned illiteracy and poor backgrounds in order to be picked by the HSPA in the Philippines, for example, lying about their schooling, pretending not to understand English-speaking interviewers, and roughing up their hands.

119. *Pacific Commercial Advertiser*, February 2, 1920.

120. *Pacific Commercial Advertiser*, March 6, 1920.

121. *Honolulu Star-Bulletin*, February 13, 1920.

122. *Honolulu Star-Bulletin*, March 27, 1920.

123. For example, Takaki writes that the planters "deliberately stressed the racial issue in order to shroud the economic issue" (1983:172).

124. [A. W. Collins] to A. W. T. Bottomley, February 18, 1920, PMC1/6, HSPAP.

125. George M. Brooke to O. W. [A. W.] Collins, May 7, 1920, PMC2/40, HSPAP. See also H. R. Preston to A. W. Collins, September 3, 1920, October 12, 1920, and March 25, 1921, PMC1/7, HSPAP; A. W. Collins to H. R. Preston, September 17, 1920, October 18, 1920, and May 9, 1921, PMC1/7, HSPAP; testimony of Peyton Harrison, "Official Report of the Proceedings before the NLRB, Case No. XX-C-55 and XX-R-80," April 28, 1937, pp. 2242–2244, box 238, NA. For the most comprehensive account of the military vis-à-vis Hawaii's Japanese, see Okihiro (1991).

126. *Pacific Commercial Advertiser*, January 27, 1920.

127. *Hawaii Shimpō*, March 8, 1924, as cited in Reinecke (1996:36). See also memo by Rev. Okumura enclosed in G. P. Wilcox to Lihue Plantation Company, March 10, 1924, LPC5/6, HSPAP.

128. Executive Committee of the HWM, "Strike Proclamation," March 14, 1924, as reprinted in Manlapit (1933:62–64).

129. Anonymous and Oroc interview, p. 779.

130. Beechert (1985:220); Theo. H. Davies to John T. Moir, June 26, 1924, H. A. Walker to John T. Moir, June 27, 1924, and J. K. Butler to plantation managers on Hawaii, August 5, 1924, MKC1/8, HSPAP.

131. As discussed earlier, the Republican patronage system channeled Hawaiians into government positions. Consequently, a disproportionate number of the police, both regular and special, were Hawaiians.

132. Bulletin to plantation managers of Kauai, Maui, and Hawaii, April 17, 1924, as cited in Beechert (1985:220).
133. Faye interview, pp. 470–473. Lindsay Faye was manager of a Kaua'i sugar plantation in 1924 and arrived at the scene of the violence shortly after it had begun.
134. See Jung (2004) for a fuller analysis of the Hanapēpē Massacre.
135. A "short-term" contract specified piecework rates for a gang of workers to complete certain tasks like cutting, wedding, irrigation, etc. Under a "long-term" contract, a gang of workers, provided with equipment and supplies from the plantation, was responsible for the cultivation of cane on a given section of land, from planting to harvest, and received payment based on the yield. By 1938, HSPA determined that short-term contractors accounted for 36.8 percent of the work done in the sugar industry, while long-term contractors accounted for 12.7 percent. The remaining 50.5 percent was performed by workers under per diem rates (USBLS 1940:38).
136. J. K. Butler to HSPA trustees and all plantation managers, May 11, 1928, PSC33/15, HSPAP. For Filipino overrepresentation in plantation employment, see Lind (1938:325).
137. Indicative of the shift were the two Americanization efforts organized by Takie and Umetaro Okumura, who worked with the sugar industry. A reaction to the 1920 strike, the "Educational Campaign," lasting from January 1921 to December 1929, was directed at the issei, while the Conferences of New Americans, held annually from 1927 to 1941, targeted the nisei (Okihiro 1991). The Okumuras were sponsored by various haole elite; Eiichi Shibusawa, a business leader in Japan; and the Japanese state (Monobe 2004).
138. In 1924, Japan changed its laws so that the default status of children born to Japanese subjects in Hawai'i was noncitizen. Parents or guardians had to register with the consulate within 14 days of birth for their children to *become* Japanese citizens (Odo 2004:94); between 1924 and 1933, around 40 percent of nisei newborns were registered by their parents (Stephan 1984:24).
139. "Where 1.0 reflects equilibrium with regard to 'ethnic occupancy,' the proportion of Japanese Americans in English Standard schools in 1925 was 0.03; for part-Hawaiians, 1.53; for Portuguese, 0.91; for haoles, a whopping 53.49" (Odo 2004:63; see also Tamura 1994).
140. J. K. Butler to John T. Moir, January 14, 1922, MKC1/8, HSPAP.
141. John Hind, presidential address, *Proceedings of the Forty-fifth Annual Meeting of the Hawaiian Sugar Planters' Association*, November 16–20, 1925, p. 9, HC. An industrial survey conducted by the sugar industry in 1926 similarly concluded that the industry should rely less on a constant flow of migrant Filipino labor and more on "attracting native-born workers" (Hawaiian Sugar Planters' Association, "Confidential Extracts from Industrial Survey of 1926," 1927, p. 1, PE).
142. R. A. Cooke, presidential address, *Proceedings of the Forty-ninth Annual Meeting of the Hawaiian Sugar Planters' Association*, December 2–4, 1929, p. 7, HC. See also *Honolulu Star-Bulletin*, November 27, 1928, file 1/3/21, RASRLC.
143. For examples, see Takie and Umetaro Okumra, "Educational Campaign among Japanese for the Year 1936," LSC41/1, HSPAP; "Work among the Plantation Japanese, Report for the Year 1937," PSC42/3, HSPAP; Takumi Akama to C. E. S. Burns, July 28, 1938, LPC15/13, HSPAP; Umetaro Okumura to William Cushnie, June 1, 1940,

KAU21/6, HSPAP. Takie Okumura apparently coined the term "New Americans" (Monobe 2004:76). Monobe (2004) argues that Takie Okumura promoted Americanization and farming among the nisei for reasons compatible with, but not identical to, those of the haole elite.

144. Like Monobe (2004) in relation to Hawai'i, Azuma (2005) argues that many issei on the West Coast saw Americanization—if conceived as fostering autonomy through, for example, independent farming—as compatible with good Japanese citizenship.

145. *Proceedings of the Annual Conference of New Americans*, 1927–1941, HC. See also Nomura (1989), Okihiro (1991), and Tamura (1994).

146. For examples of explicit cooperation, see Mrs. Oma L. Duncan, principal, Olaa School, to W. L. S. Williams, May 5, 1938, PSC44/25, HSPAP; manager, Lihue Plantation Company, to American Factors, August 17, 1939, LPC11/6, HSPAP.

147. Vaughan MacCaughey, as quoted in "Educational Needs of Hawaii," *Christian Science Monitor* (September 5, 1919), PSC22/6, HSPAP. For in-depth discussions of nisei education during the interwar period, see Okihiro (1991:ch. 7) and Tamura (1994:ch. 6).

148. For examples, see *Hawaii Hōchi*, August 7, 1928, August 9, 1928, August 16, 1928. See also *Honolulu Advertiser*, August 7, 1928; Dr. Harry I. Kuriasaki, letter to the editor, *Hawaii Hōchi*, August 13, 1928; *Nippu Jiji*, September 6, 1928; Adams and Kai (1928); Monobe (2004:115–116); Nomura (1987).

149. For examples, see *Nippu Jiji*, September 18, 1931, November 16, 1933, file 1/2/85, RASRLC; *Hawaii Hōchi*, December 8, 1930, November 22, 1933; *Honolulu Star-Bulletin*, March 14, 1933, file 1/3/30, RASRLC. See also Monobe (2004:171–173); Tamura (1994:142–143).

150. J. K. Butler [to all agencies], April 29, 1933, HSC25/6, HSPAP. See also J. K. Butler to agencies, May 2, 1933, HSC25/6, HSPAP; J. K. Butler to all plantations, May 29, 1933, KAU22/4, HSPAP. Leaving school, of course, did not necessarily mean graduating.

151. B. H. Wells to plantation managers, September 1, 1937, PSC38/21, HSPAP; USBLS (1940:79). Beechert (1985:253) cited a slightly smaller gain, from 15.9 percent in 1930 to 31.4 percent in 1936.

152. See also USBLS (1940:35). Among Japanese workers at the Olaa Sugar Company, citizens overtook noncitizens as of June 1939 (Form 54, June 1939, PSC40/7, HSPAP).

153. The HSPA became obsessed with growing and keeping track of its "citizen" labor force. For two samples, see documents in files HSC25/6 and KAU22/4, HSPAP.

154. J. K. Butler to all plantations, September 29, 1930, LSC22C/5, HSPAP.

155. HSPA, "Census of Employees and Families on Sugar Plantations," December 31, 1928, KSC19/29, HSPAP; HSPA, "Census of Employees and Families on Sugar Plantations," June 30, 1929, PSC34/1, HSPAP; HSPA, "Census of Employees and Families on Sugar Plantations," June 30, 1930, PSC34/2, HSPAP.

156. HSPA, "Census of Hawaiian Sugar Plantations," June 30, 1931, KSC19/29, HSPAP.

157. For examples, see tables 3.2 and 3.3; Olaa Sugar Company, "Bonus Paid to Plantation Employees from November 1st, 1937 to October 31st, 1938," PSC33/11, HSPAP; Kekaha Sugar Company, "Employment by Job Classification," as of September 30,

1933, KSC23/28, HSPAP. The Olaa Sugar Company form listed "Anglo-Saxon" as a "Nationality," and the Kekaha Sugar Company form listed "Citizens," "Filipinos," and "Aliens" as three mutually exclusive and exhaustive categories; not particular to these plantations, these two generic forms just happened to have been filled out by the two plantations.

158. For an example of the public pressure felt by the HSPA to deal with unemployment, particularly in relation to "local citizens and second generation youths," see J. K. Butler to all plantations, June 18, 1932, KAU22/4, HSPAP.

159. W. van H. Duker to W. F. Robertson, February 24, 1933, LSC22C/5, HSPAP; J. K. Butler to W. P. Naquin, August 12, 1932, HSC25/5, HSPAP.

160. J. K. Butler, "Remarks before the Territorial Senate," April 13, 1933, HSC25/6, HSPAP. Butler stated that more than 2,000 of the 7,421 Filipinos sent back between February 1932 and April 1933 were indigents.

161. Allen W. T. Bottomley, presidential address, *Proceedings of the Fiftieth Annual Meeting of the Hawaiian Sugar Planters' Association*, November 17–21, 1930, HC. See also J. K. Butler, "Plantation Employment through Hawaiian Sugar Planters' Association, Employment Office, Honolulu," December 26, 1930, and J. T. Phillips to all plantations, January 12, 1931, HSC25/4, HSPAP; J. K. Butler to all plantations, February 28, 1933, KAU22/4, HSPAP; W. van H. Duker to W. F. Robertson, March 1, 1933, LSC22C/5, HSPAP; J. K. Butler to all plantations, May 29, 1933, KAU22/4, HSPAP.

162. W. P. Naquin to HSPA, July 15, 1932, HSC25/5, HSPAP.

163. J. K. Butler to all agencies, June 27, 1933, LPC11/1, HSPAP.

164. J. K. Butler to W. P. Naquin, August 12, 1932, HSC25/5, HSPAP . See also J. K. Butler to all managers and agencies, January 6, 1932, HSC25/5, HSPAP.

165. R. A. Cooke to Ray M. Allen, March 8, 1934, file C. Brewer, EB. How many Filipinos were repatriated under this new policy is unknown.

166. HSPA, "Summary of Replies to Questionnaire Sent Out to Plantations … ," [March 1933], KAU22/4, HSPAP.

167. Of the 2,101 citizens hired in 1932, 1,233 were Japanese and 321 were Portuguese (HSPA, "Citizen Employees on Plantations Who were Newly Employed during the Year 1932," KAU22/4, HSPAP). See also HSPA, "Summary of Citizen Employees, by Islands, as of June, 1931 and December, 1932," KAU22/4, HSPAP.

168. J. K. Butler to all plantation managers, August 17, 1932, HSC25/5, HSPAP. The industry was conscious of the Filipino–Japanese substitution taking place through its policy of employing "citizens." For example, a letter circulated throughout the industry in 1933 noted the increase in the number of Japanese workers and the decrease in the number of Filipino workers, making no mention of any other racial groups (J. K. Butler to plantation managers, all agencies and trustees, HSPA, September 13, 1933, KAU22/4, HSPAP).

169. HSPA Committee on Industrial Relations to the president, trustees and members of the HSPA, reprinted in *Honolulu Advertiser*, November 22, 1933.

170. J. K. Butler to all plantation managers, March 23, 1933, HSC25/6, HSPAP. See also Frank C. Atherton, presidential address, *Proceedings of the Fifty-first Annual Meeting of the Hawaiian Sugar Planters' Association*, December 7–10, 1931, HC; E. W. Greene, "Plantation Jobs for Local Young Men," October 11, 1932, HSC25/5, HSPAP;

HSPA, "Summary of Replies to Questionnaire Sent Out to Plantations ... ," [March 1933], KAU22/4, HSPAP; HSPA Industrial Relations Committee, "Summary of Replies to Question Series IV ... ," March 20, 1933, KAU22/4, HSPAP.

171. W. P. Naquin to HSPA, July 15, 1932, HSC25/5, HSPAP.

172. *Hawaii Hōchi*, August 2, 1929.

173. For example, when war broke out between Japan and China in 1937, Hawaii's Japanese bought 3 million yen of war bonds and contributed 1.2 million yen to the National Defense and Soldier's Relief Fund; the latter figure outpaced per capita contributions in Japan (Stephan 1984:33). See also *Honolulu Star-Bulletin*, January 11 and 30, 1939, file 1/4/35a, RASRLC.

174. *Hawaii Hōchi*, November 19, 1930.

175. Before the Tydings-McDuffie Act, Filipinos were virtually the only first-generation migrants from Asia legally *not* classified as "aliens."

176. *Nippu Jiji*, June 22, 1937, as translated by the HSPA, KSC29/9, HSPAP. See also *Hawaii Hōchi*, May 20, 1936, LSC39/9, HSPAP.

177. *Hawaii Hōchi*, February 7, 1930. See also *Hawaii Hōchi*, September 1, 1929, file 1/3/21, RASRLC; November 19, 1930, December 8, 1930, file 1/2/85, RASRLC.

   Hawaii Hōchi and *Nippu Jiji* were, by far, the largest Japanese newspapers, each reporting a circulation of over 10,000 (Sakamaki 1928:11). Of the two, *Nippu Jiji* took a more accommodationist stance toward the haole planters than its rival. The paper's less vitriolic attitude toward Filipino workers can be more accurately read as stemming from its favorable assessment of management than from a favorable assessment of Filipinos. From at least the mid-1920s, the HSPA regarded *Nippu Jiji* as "the best of the Japanese papers in Honolulu" (J. K. Butler to plantation managers on Hawaii and Maui, July 11, 1924, MKC1/8, HSPAP).

178. *Hawaii Hōchi*, June 23, 1933.

179. *Yōen Jihō*, June 1, 1937, as translated by the HSPA, KSC29/9, HSPAP; see also June 22 and July 6, 1937. A number of Japanese individuals also surreptitiously aided the 1937 Filipino strike financially (Hall interview, p. 7).

180. *Maui Shinbun*, June 11, 1937, as translated by the HSPA, KSC29/9, HSPAP.

181. *Maui Record*, June 8, 1937 and June 18, 1937, as translated by the HSPA, KSC29/9, HSPAP.

182. At least in the 1920s, but I suspect later as well, many planters believed that Filipinos were incapable of operating machines (Beechert 1989:136).

183. *Proceedings of the Annual Conference of New Americans*, 1937, pp. 66–67, HC. Less restrained expressions can be found in Masuoka (1931). See also Office of the Assistant Chief of Staff for Military Intelligence, Headquarters Hawaiian Department, "A Survey of the Filipinos in the Territory of Hawaii" (revision of a 1926 survey), September 1929, p. 45, EB; Lind (1938a); Monobe (2004:126); Ozaki (1940).

184. *New Freedom*, October 25, 1930, file 1/2/85, RASRLC; see also *New Freedom*, November 30, 1928, file 1/3/21, RASRLC.

185. As seen previously, one of these strikes prompted *Hawaii Hōchi* to call for deportation.

186. J. K. Butler to all agencies, June 27, 1933, LPC11/1, HSPAP.

187. Ibid.

188. Ibid.

189. J. K. Butler to plantations on Oahu, July 1, 1932, and J. K. Butler to plantation managers on Hawaii, July 13, 1932, HSC25/5, HSPAP.

190. According to the HSPA, there was a union in between the Filipino Labor Union and Vibora Luviminda, which went by the name of Hawaii Labor Association (J. K. Butler to all plantations, August 14, 1933, HSC25/6, HSPAP).

191. Office of the Assistant Chief of Staff for Military Intelligence, "A Survey of the Filipinos in the Territory of Hawaii," p. 39.

192. Pablo Manlapit to the President of the United States, March 28, 1934, MQ.

193. E. A. Taok to the Territorial Legislature, reprinted in *News-Tribune*, November 6, 1933.

194. E. A. Taok to Manuel Quezon, May 21, 1935, MQ. See also *News-Tribune*, November 6, 1933; J. K. Butler to all plantation managers, February 2, 1934, HSC25/7, HSPAP; Pablo Manlapit to Manuel Quezon, January 6, 1934, MQ; Pablo Manlapit to the President of the United States, March 28, 1934, MQ; *Honolulu Star-Bulletin*, April 14, 1934, file 1/2/85, RASRLC; E. A. Taok to Manuel Quezon, August 13, 1935, MQ.

195. L. W. Wishard to Theo. H. Davies & Company, November 1, 1937, LSC69/17, HSPAP.

196. Quintin Paredes to Manuel L. Quezon, n.d., as quoted in B. H. Wells to plantation managers, February 13, 1937, PSC38/26, HSPAP.

197. J. K. Butler to all plantations on Oahu, December 9, 1933, HSC25/7, HSPAP; J. K. Butler to all plantations, December 14, 1933, KAU22/4, HSPAP.

198. Espionage report of a Vibora Luviminda meeting held in Ahukini, April 8, 1938, LSC69/17, HSPAP. See also Claveria interview, p. 2; Damaso interview, p. 1.

199. L. W. Wishard to Theo. H. Davies & Company, November 1, 1937, LSC69/17, HSPAP. See also B. H. Wells to American Factors, Ltd., September 20, 1937, KSC27/21, HSPAP.

4. Shifting Terrains of the New Deal and World War II

1. Edward Berman, "Report on Hawaiian Labor Movement," August 30, 1937, p. 1, file HI/Correspondence, Reports, etc./1937–43, box 5, ILWUSF.

2. Ernest Burlem, Mrs. Marion Kelly, and Arthur A. Rutledge, "Memorandum on Military Control of Hawaiian Labor," March 27, 1944, p. 5, 38.08(1), HWRD.

3. For examples, see Daws (1968), Fuchs (1961), Geschwender (1981, 1982), Geschwender and Levine (1983, 1986), Joesting (1972), Kuykendall and Day (1948), Larrowe (1972), Levine and Geschwender (1981), Wills (1954), and Zalburg (1979). Anthony (1955), Beechert (1985), and USBLS (1948) are exceptions.

4. E. J. Eagen, NLRB, Honolulu, to NLRB, Washington, D.C., March 19, 1937, box 69, NA.

5. Hall interview, p. 1.

6. Ibid., pp. 1–3.

7. Kamoku interview, p. 1.

8. Ibid.

9. Paaluhi interview, p. 1.

10. Occupational transition from seaman to longshoreman was not unique to Hawai'i. As Kimeldorf (1988) points out, many West Coast longshoremen of the 1930s had been seamen earlier in their lives and became longshoremen as they grew older and settled down.

11. The SUP union hall was established in the aftermath of the 1934 strike. The influence of the AFL-affiliated SUP in Hawaii's labor movement soon declined with the AFL-CIO split, when Hawaii's longshoremen became affiliated, through the ILWU, with the newly formed CIO.

12. Weisbarth interview.

13. Jack Hall, Labor Day speech, Honolulu, September 5, 1955, p. 1, file 9, box 1, SZ.

14. For example, see espionage report from Andrew Gross to C. E. S. Burns, September 12, 1937, LPC17/12, HSPAP.

15. Between 1935 and 1937, the issuance of charters became arguably the topic of most intense concern for Hawaii's longshoremen, appearing in countless documents in the union archives in San Francisco and Honolulu. For an example of the Honolulu and Hilo longshore unions' persistence and insistence on receiving ILA charters, see 49 longshoremen of HoLA and HiLA and organizer William Craft to Joseph Ryan, ILA president, n.d., file HI/Correspondence, Reports, etc./1937–43, box 5, ILWUSF. (Although the copy of the letter I examined did not have a date, Beechert [1985:260, 366] cites it as January 21, 1937. What is clear is that HoLA had voted to draft the letter on December 30, 1936 [Minutes of Regular Meeting, December 30, 1936, file Honolulu Longshoremen's Association/Minutes/Membership/1936, ILWUH].) See also the minutes of union meetings for the years 1936 and 1937 in file Honolulu Longshoremen's Association/Minutes/Membership/1936 and file Honolulu Longshoremen's Association/Minutes/Membership/1937, ILWUH.

16. A letter from the Pacific Coast District to Harry Kealoha—which includes copies of the tortuous and contentious correspondence between the Pacific Coast District and the ILA's International—provides a glimpse into the internecine politics of granting the charters (Sub-committee of the District Executive Board of the Pacific District Coast District of the ILA to H. Keaolka [sic], March 5, 1937, file HI/Correspondence, Reports, etc./1937–43, box 5, ILWUSF). See also "Report of Organizer William Craft," *Proceedings of the Thirtieth Annual Convention of the Pacific Coast District No. 38, International Longshoremen's Association*, May 3–22, 1937, pp. 107–111, ILWUSF.

17. Minutes of Special Meeting, October 30, 1936, file Honolulu Longshoremen's Association/Minutes/Membership/1936, ILWUH.

18. Frederick K. Kamahoahoa to Harry Bridges, July 29, 1937, file HI/Correspondence, Reports, etc./Local 136/1937–43, box 5, ILWUSF.

19. "Report of Organizer William Craft," pp. 107–108.

20. Alexander Chang to Harry Bridges, January 21, 1937, file HI/Correspondence, Reports, etc./1937–43, box 5, ILWUSF.
    According to union documents, the intra-ILA feud between the Pacific Coast District and the International was the primary reason for the International's reluctance to grant charters to Hawaii's longshoremen. But most of Hawaii's longshoremen assumed that the primary reason was that the International did not want so many nonwhites in the union (Beechert 1985:260).

Hall (interview, pp. 6–7) tries to reassure that race, though probably a secondary factor, could not have been the *primary* factor by pointing out that the ILA had admitted Hawaii's nonwhite longshoremen earlier in the century.

Despite Hall's insistence, Hawaii's longshoremen had sound reasons to believe otherwise. First, what Hall did not recall was that the ILA had made a special exception for its locals in Hawai'i to allow Asian "aliens" into the union. Moreover, the newly admitted "alien" members continued to hold second-class status, as they had not been allowed to transfer their memberships to ILA locals on the continent as was permitted others (see chapter 2). Second, even in the 1930s, the Honolulu and Hilo Longshoremen's Associations would still have required a similar "dispensation clause" in their charters to become ILA locals (Brooks 1952:64). Third, mainstream newspapers, which were against unionization on the waterfront, argued in their editorials that the ILA was withholding the charters because there were too many "Orientals" (e.g., *Honolulu Star-Bulletin,* November 9, 1936). Fourth, the longshoremen's suspicion of racial discrimination was even more understandable in the context of AFL leadership. As an organizer in Hawai'i pointed out in 1937, "William Green [AFL president] two years ago publicly showed his antagonism toward Hawaii's workers when he made the following statement to the press: 'I am opposed to statehood for Hawaii because there are too many orientals there.' Thus, Green and the AFL leadership have in the past completely ignored the Hawaiian workers [*sic*]" (Edward Berman, "Report on Hawaiian Labor Movement," August 30, 1937, pp. 2–3, file HI/Correspondence, Reports, etc./1937–43, box 5, ILWUSF).

21. Frederick K. Kamahoahoa to Harry Bridges, July 29, 1937, file HI/Correspondence, Reports, etc./Local 136/1937–43, box 5, ILWUSF.

22. A passage of the Wagner Act as quoted in U.S. Department of Labor (1970).

23. NLRB, Twentieth Region, Intermediate Report, "In the Matter of Honolulu Longshoremen's Association and Castle and Cooke, Ltd. and Honolulu Stevedores, Ltd," Case No. XX-C-55, August 14, 1937, George O. Pratt, Trial Examiner, p. 43, box 70, NA. Hereafter referred to as "Pratt Report."

24. Ibid.; Beechert (1985:255).

25. Exhibit No. 62, IAH, "Certificate Accompanying Petition for Charter," September 23, 1935, box 238, NA.

26. Exhibit No. 61, "Members of Industrial Association of Hawaii," n.d., box 239, NA.

27. "Pratt Report"; Aller (1957:50–51); Beechert (1985:257).

28. "Pratt Report," pp. 14–15. See also Alexander Chang to Harry Bridges, January 21, 1937, file HI/Correspondence, Reports, etc./1937–43, box 5, ILWUSF; *Honolulu Advertiser*, April 21, 1937, file 1/1/53, RASRLC; "Report of E. J. Eagen on the Hawaiian Islands," pp. 4524–4539, 4598–4624 in USHR (1940), hereafter referred to as "Report of E. J. Eagen."

29. Minutes of Regular Meeting, August 29, 1936, file Honolulu Longshoremen's Association/Minutes/Membership/1936, ILWUH; "Pratt Report," p. 21. HoLA picked C. L. Taft and R. Bodie as its representatives.

30. NLRB charge, "In the matter of Castle & Cooke, Ltd. and Honolulu Longshoremen's Assn.," filed by Harry Kealoha, October 12, 1936, amended NLRB charge, filed by Ralph Rogers, December 12, 1936, and amended charge, filed by Edward Berman,

March 12, 1937, box 70, NA; Honolulu Longshoremen's Association to E. S. Neal, February 23, 1937, box 69, NA; Sub-committee of the District Executive Board of the Pacific District Coast District of the ILA to H. Keaolka [sic], March 5, 1937, p. 5, file HI/Correspondence, Reports, etc./1937–43, box 5, ILWUSF; Minutes of Regular Meeting, March 10, 1937, file Honolulu Longshoremen's Association/Minutes/ Membership/1937, ILWUH; B. M. Stern to E. J. Eagen, March 10, 1937, box 69, NA.

31. E. J. Eagen to NLRB, March 19, 1937, box 69, NA.

32. "Report of E. J. Eagen," pp. 4524, 4612.

33. "Pratt Report," pp. 3–4. Hereafter, for clarity, I refer to the defendant as Castle & Cooke, disregarding the various name changes.

34. Ibid., p. 2.

35. "Official Report of the Proceedings before the NLRB, Case No. XX-C-55 and XX-R-80," April 21 and 22, 1937, p. 1611, box 237, NA. Slightly different quotes of this testimony appeared in the Honolulu Star-Bulletin, April 22, 1937, as quoted in Beechert (1985:257) and the Honolulu Advertiser, April 23, 1937, file 1/1/53, RASRLC.

36. For example, the same nine justices had declared section 7a of the National Industrial Recovery Act to be unconstitutional. As Dubofsky (1994:145) argues, the most important intervening factors in the Supreme Court's turnaround were "the rise of the CIO, the growing assertiveness of militant workers, and the spread of industrial warfare."

37. Honolulu Star-Bulletin, April 12, 1937, as cited in "Honolulu Star-Bulletin Index to Entries on Hawaiian Labor, January 1935–August 1952," said to have been compiled by John E. Reinecke, n.d., ILWUSF.

38. "Pratt Report," pp. 44–45. For the company's agreement to accept the recommendations of the intermediate report and for the NLRB's termination of the case upon the company's compliance, see, respectively, Randolph Sevier to Alice M. Rosseter, September 10, 1937, and NLRB, 20th Region, "Cases Closed" report, January 1, 1938, box 69, NA.

39. "Pratt Report," p. 44.

40. The IAH vanished, quite literally, without a trace. Subpoenaed by the NLRB to produce all records of the IAH at the Castle & Cooke hearing, Judd submitted an account book with one page of figures for April 1937. All other records had disappeared, apparently with the IAH's secretary and treasurer, who had left for a new job in China just days before the start of the hearing (Exhibit No. 64, box 238, NA; testimony of Judd, "Official Report of the Proceedings before the NLRB, Case No. XX-C-55 and XX-R-80," April 21 and 22, 1937, box 237, NA). See also "Report of E. J. Eagen."

41. Honolulu Star-Bulletin, September 4, 1937, as cited in "Honolulu Star-Bulletin Index to Entries on Hawaiian Labor."

42. Edward Berman and Maxie Weisbarth to Harry Bridges, June 8, 1937, file HI/ Correspondence, Reports, etc./Local 136/1937–43, box 5, ILWUSF.

In February 1937, before Berman's trip to the West Coast as its "representative," HoLA had elected Berman as a "legal adviser" and an "honorary member" (Harry Kealoha to "whom it may concern," February 25, 1937, file HI/Correspondence, Reports, etc./1937–43, box 5, ILWUSF).

43. Because the sessions of the NLRB hearing were closely reported in the local newspapers and because the Supreme Court ruling coincided with the hearing, the

three developments—on the docks of Hilo and of Port Allen, and on Maui's sugar and pineapple plantations—began long before the NLRB trial examiner's official issuance of his ruling on August 14, 1937.

44. Jack Kawano to Harry Bridges, February 4, 1938, file HI/Correspondence, Reports, etc./Local 137/1937–43, box 5, ILWUSF. See also Honolulu Longshoremen's Association to E. S. Neal, February 23, 1937, box 69, NA.

45. Hall interview, p. 3.

46. Randolph Sevier to C. Brewer & Company, Kahului Railroad Company, Hawaii Railway Company, Kauai Terminal, Ltd., Honokaa Sugar Company, Pioneer Mill Company, Kaeleku Sugar Company, Lihue Plantation Company, and Hutchinson Sugar Company, August 23, 1937, LPC9/6, HSPAP; "Pratt Report," p. 9.

47. Delegate report of Jack Kawano, Conference of the Hawaiian Locals of the International Longshoremen's and Warehousemen's Union, May 16–17, 1940, p. 2, file Joint Conference, ILWUC.

48. The size of the ports may again account for this difference. Although the observation that shipping and stevedoring were less autonomous economic enterprises than subsidiary extensions of the sugar industry may have been true for every stevedoring operation in Hawai'i (see chapter 2), it was less true in Honolulu than in Hilo. As its operation in Honolulu dwarfed all other stevedoring firms in the islands, Castle & Cooke had more incentive than the other sugar agencies to view stevedoring as a revenue-producing enterprise and to thwart unionization. Likewise, McCabe, Hamilton & Renny had no choice but to view stevedoring as an autonomous economic enterprise, being the only stevedoring outfit not associated with a sugar agency.

49. Delegate report of Abraham Pohina, *Proceedings of the Thirtieth Annual Convention of the Pacific Coast District No. 38, International Longshoremen's Association,* May 3–22, 1937, pp. 81–82, ILWUSF.

50. E. J. Eagen to Hilo Longshoremen's Association, April 23, 1937, file Longshore Strike 1949/Hawaii Joint Action Committee/HT&T Lockout, ILWUH.

51. A. H. Armitage to E. J. Eagen, May 5, 1937, file Longshore Strike 1949/Hawaii Joint Action Committee/HT&T Lockout, ILWUH.

52. Delegate report of Abraham Pohina, p. 82.

53. "Report of E. J. Eagen," p. 4611.

54. Delegate report of Tsuruo Ogoshi, *Proceedings of the First Annual Convention of the International Longshoremen's and Warehousemen's Union,* April 4–17, 1938, pp. 177–178, ILWUSF.

55. Hall interview, p. 5.

56. Goto interview, p. 1; "Hall Diary" (a detailed self-authored account of his life given to his lawyers for their use during Hall's Smith Act trial of 1951–52), p. 3, file 7, box 1, SZ.

   "George Goto" was the pseudonym used by Noboru Furuya, presumably to shield his radical politics. The Japanese term *kibei* refers to nisei who received their education in Japan. Although he was still in Japan at the time, Goto recalled that reading about the 1924 Filipino sugar strike convinced him to enter labor organizing and get workers to unionize on an interracial, industrial basis (Goto interview, p. 2).

57. Goto interview, p. 3.

58. "Hall Diary," p. 3.

59. Ibid.; Izuka interview, p. 2; Izuka (1974:32–33). What is not clear in the three sources cited here or in other primary sources concerning the early days of PAWWA is the date on which the contract with the formal recognition was signed. The strikers seem to have returned to work on April 24, 1937 with at least an agreement on overtime. But whether they returned to work with a signed contract or returned with an informal agreement and later signed a contract remains indeterminate.

60. One of the original participants of the strike and union members also concludes that the NLRB's presence was the pivotal factor (Izuka 1974:32).

61. "Hall Diary," p. 3.

62. Edward Berman and Maxie Weisbarth to Harry Bridges, June 8, 1937, folder HI/Correspondence, Reports, etc./Local 136/1937–43, box 5, ILWUSF.

63. George Goto to Matt Meehan, July 10, 1937, file HI/Correspondence, Reports, etc./Local 136/1937–43, box 5, ILWUSF.

64. "Report of E. J. Eagen," pp. 4608–4609. As his sentence, Manlapit was sent back to the Philippines. Of the three original leaders, only Fagel continued his active involvement with the union.

65. For examples, see HSC25/7, HSPAP. Lending credence to the Big Five's "Big Brother" reputation, the reach and power of Hawaii's sugar interests often took on Orwellian overtones. In one case, the HSPA circulated a "confidential" letter concerning a Filipino insurance salesperson who had recently given a speech in a plantation community. According to the HSPA, he had spoken about how "Filipinos were neglected, down-trodden and mis-treated, ... [and] a lot of other such incendiary and false statements." After finding out that the speaker was in the process of switching employment from one insurance company to another—neither of which was directly tied to the Big Five, the HSPA, or the plantations—the HSPA "suggested" to both insurance companies that they did not need such a man on their payrolls. Both companies acted readily on the HSPA's "suggestion," agreeing that the man "would not be useful to them" (J. K. Butler to all plantation managers, February 2, 1934, HSC25/7, HSPAP).

66. Claveria interview, p. 2.

67. "Report of E. J. Eagen," p. 4609; Felipe (1970b:5). Some of the espionage reports can be found in file Labor/HI/History/1937 Maui Strike, ILWUH.

68. *Honolulu Star-Bulletin*, April 1, 1937, p. 7, as cited in "Honolulu Star-Bulletin Index to Entries on Hawaiian Labor"; Felipe (1970b:5).

69. Weisbarth interview, p. 4; Bill Bailey to Sanford Zalburg, November 4, 1974, file 30, box 3, SZ. Note that Weisbarth had dispatched Hall to Maui and, almost immediately upon his return to Honolulu, dispatched him to Port Allen, Kaua'i. Based on different sources, Edward Beechert identifies Berman, not Weisbarth, as the person who directed Fagel to Hall and Bailey (Beechert to author, August 17, 2005).

70. Affidavit of Richard F. Hyland, an HSPA staff member, [on or just before May 22, 1937], file Labor/HI/History/1937 Maui Strike, ILWUH; Bailey (1993:ch. 20); Felipe (1970b:6–7). The affidavit was not dated, but the *Honolulu Star-Bulletin* reported on May 22, 1937 that it had been received by the territorial attorney general Samuel B. Kemp.

71. *Honolulu Star-Bulletin*, April 24 and May 18, 1937, file 1/2/83, RASRLC; Zalburg (1979:22–23).

72. Later, when the strike spread to other Maui plantations, evictions were no longer confined to the leadership (R. Lonadaniba [approximate spelling of a signature] to Maxie Weisbarth, June 15, 1937, file Labor/HI/History/1937 Maui Strike, ILWUH).

73. On May 14, Fagel withdrew the charge he had filed, because he had mistakenly referred to HC&S as "Puunene Plantation Company" (Antonio A. Fagel to E. J. Eagen, May 14, 1937, reprinted in "Report of E. J. Eagen," p. 4616). The following day, Edward Berman filed a new, replacement charge against the HSPA and HC&S. Although the Wagner Act had explicitly excluded agricultural workers from its purview, the new charge indicated that some of the workers affected by the HSPA's and HC&S's unfair labor practices worked in the sugar mill, qualifying them as industrial workers (NLRB, Twentieth region, "In the Matter of Hawaiian Sugar Planters' Assn., and Hawaiian Commercial and Sugar Co., Ltd., and Edward Berman," May 15, 1937, box 159, NA). Although the exact line of demarcation between field and mill work was not yet determined, a vast majority of the strikers were likely outside NLRB's jurisdiction.

74. "Report of E. J. Eagen," p. 4609.

75. "Statement of Edward Berman," May 21, 1937, as reprinted in "Report of E. J. Eagen," pp. 4618–4619; Felipe (1970b:11–13).

76. Agreement, July 15, 1937, LPC7/10, HSPAP; Arnold Wills, "Explanatory note on agreement," November 27, 1940, file Labor/HI/History/1937 Maui Strike, ILWUH; Felipe (1970b:15–17). The three central Maui plantations were HC&S, Maui Agricultural Company, and Wailuku Sugar Company. The remaining two sugar plantations at which Filipino workers struck in sympathy were Pioneer Mill Company and Kaeleku Sugar Company.

77. Ibid.

78. B. H. Wells to C. E. S. Burns, July 27, 1937, p. 4, LPC7/10, HSPAP. A self-satisfied interpretation of the Vibora Luviminda strike, this letter contains the revised pay scale that was referred to but not included in the agreement.

79. Japanese newspapers across the political spectrum covered these strikes in more detail than the mainstream dailies. Apparently aware of the extensive coverage, the HSPA translated many of the articles and editorials, in part to assess the Japanese propensity to join a plantation labor movement. For the HSPA's translations of the articles and its opinions of them, see KSC29/9, HSPAP.

80. G. E. Schaefer to the manager, Honokaa Sugar Company, October 8, 1937, HSC20/6, HSPAP; "Labor Disturbances in Hawaii, 1890–1925: A Summary," compiled by John E. Reinecke, July 1966, file Trade Unions/HI/Pamphlets, etc., ILWUSF. Pineapple workers at Libby, McNeill, & Libby formed the United Pineapple Workers of Moloka'i, a branch of Vibora Luviminda, which went out on strike in 1937 and 1938 and affiliated with HoLA.

81. The HSPA calculated the total cost of the Vibora Luviminda strike to be $780,588.80 (G. E. Schaefer to Manager of Honokaa Sugar Company, December 13, 1937, HSC20/8, HSPAP). The cost of hiring strikebreakers alone during the 1909 strike amounted to $2 million (Beechert 1985:173). The total cost of the 1920 strike for the sugar industry was $11,483,358 (Beechert 1985:209). Due to

the indeterminate nature of the 1924 strike, its cost to the industry was also indeterminate but was likely much higher than that of the 1937 strike (Reinecke 1996:133–134).

82. *Honolulu Star-Bulletin*, May 19, 1937, file 1/2/83, RASRLC; Felipe (1970b).

83. G. E. Schaefer to the manager, Honokaa Sugar Company, August 11 and 23, 1937, HSC20/4, HSPAP; S. O. Halls to all the sugar agencies, December 13, 1937, HSC20/8, HSPAP; letters from G. E. Schaefer to the manager, Honokaa Sugar Company, December 13 and 16, 1937, HSC20/8, HSPAP.

Perhaps owing to the increasing involvement and scrutiny of the federal government, the HSPA decided in September 1937, two months after the strike settlement, to terminate the loss agreement (H. P. Faye to C. E. S. Burns, September 4, 1937, LPC11/4, HSPAP). In the face of new union efforts in the islands, one manager of a small plantation, and probably others, wondered what the implication of this policy shift might be for the future (W. P. Naquin to F. A. Schaefer & Co., December 21, 1937, HSC20/8, HSPAP).

84. *Honolulu Star-Bulletin*, May 19, 1937, file 1/2/83, RASRLC; Felipe (1970b).

85. "Report of E. J. Eagen," pp. 4609–4610. Although they would not find out about these specific statements for a few years, when the "Eagen Report" was made public, the Big Five employers were already quite aware that they did not have an ally in the NLRB (Felipe 1970b:13).

86. NLRB petition filed by the Maui Plantation and Mill Workers Industrial Union against the Hawaiian Commercial and Sugar Company, June 26, 1937, KSC27/22, HSPAP. The same petition filed against the Wailuku Sugar Company, also on June 26, 1937, can be found in LPC7/10, HSPAP. According to B. H. Wells to C. E. S. Burns, August 2, 1937 (LPC7/10, HSPAP), the same petition was also filed against Pioneer Mill Company and most probably against Kaeluku Sugar Company and Maui Agricultural Company.

87. B. H. Wells to all plantation mangers, August 25, 1937, KSC29/9, HSPAP; G. E. Schaefer to the manager, Honokaa Sugar Company, August 27, 1937, HSC20/4, HSPAP.

88. Edward Berman, "The Situation at Present in the Hawaiian Islands," October 4, 1937, p. 1, file HI/Correspondence, Reports, etc./1937–43, box 5, ILWUSF. Organizers in the field also relayed to the workers the opportunity offered by the Wagner Act and the NLRB. See United Cannery, Agricultural, Packing, and Allied Workers of America, "What Does the Wagner Act Mean to Cannery Workers?," n.d., LPC12/1, HSPAP; espionage reports from Jose Bulatao to Lindsay Faye and Hans Hansen, July 31 and August 11, 1937, KSC27/22, HSPAP; espionage reports from Andrew Gross to C. E. S. Burns, July 28 and 31, August 11 and 20, September 4 and 12, 1937, from Arthur Souza to C. E. S. Burns, September 19, 1937, and from A. Gross to McKeever, March 25, 1938, LPC17/12, HSPAP; remarks by Vicente Peralta, March 30, 1938, LPC17/12, HSPAP. (Though likely from Gross to Burns, the August 11 and 20, 1937 reports did not have the names of the addressee or the author.)

89. Frederick Kamahoahoa to Harry Bridges, December 19, 1940, file HI/Correspondence, Reports, etc./Local 137/1937–45, box 5, ILWUSF.

90. For an example of the HSPA's continuing antiunion stance, see Theo H. Davies & Co. to Waiakea Mill Co., Laupahoehoe Sugar Co., Kaiwiki Sugar Co., Ltd., and

Hamakua Mill Co., April 4, 1938, LSC62/6, HSPAP; H. A. Walker to C. E. S. Burns, April 4, 1938, LPC7/10, HSPAP.

91. *Voice of the ILWU*, January 17, 1964, p. 4.

92. Delegate report of Tsuruo Ogoshi, p. 178. See also Anders Larsen to NLRB, October 23, 1937, and Edward Berman to Harry Hopkins, December 31, 1937, box 184, NA.

93. Espionage report of a "Meeting of Union Agitators" in Lihue, September 4, 1937, LPC17/12, HSPAP. The rumor of "Lt. Comdr[s]" may have come from a testimony at the April 1937 NLRB hearing that, in turn, was based on rumors in Port Allen. A former officer in the U.S. Navy and employee of Alexander & Baldwin, Peyton Harrison testified that he did intelligence work for U.S. Army G-2 and the Office of Naval Intelligence, focusing on Hawaii's Japanese. In the early 1930s, he followed up on, and believed, a "certain Portuguese on Kauai, whose Americanism I have no reason whatever to doubt," that Japanese longshoremen in Port Allen were pro-Japan and anti-American. He testified that "a shipment of books [were] brought into these islands" at this time, a book "written by a Lieutenant-Commander in the Japanese Navy." He "found out around Port Allen and Hanapepe that a number of these books had found their way to Kauai and were in circulation among the younger Japanese." He added, "I was not, however, able to lay my finger on a copy on Kauai" (Testimony of Peyton Harrison, "Official Report of the Proceedings before the NLRB, Case No. XX-C-55 and XX-R-80," April 28, 1937, pp. 2242–2244, box 238, NA).

94. Espionage report of a PAWWA meeting held in Hanapēpē, August 20, 1937, LPC17/12, HSPAP.

95. Ibid.

96. Ibid.

97. Randolph Sevier to C. Brewer & Company, Kahului Railroad Company, Hawaii Railway Company, Kauai Terminal, Ltd., Honokaa Sugar Company, Pioneer Mill Company, Kaeleku Sugar Company, Lihue Plantation Company, and Hutchinson Sugar Company, August 23, 1937, LPC9/6, HSPAP. See also the list of employees at Kauai Terminal, June 23, 1937, KSC27/21, HSPAP.

98. Delegate report of Tsuruo Ogoshi, p. 178.

99. On the whole, however, the union did not care for the particular field examiner the NLRB sent, Anders Larsen, who "was so indifferent and apathetic that a hearing was never even held on the case" (ibid.). See also Anders Larsen to A. M. Rosseter, July 5, 1938, box 834, NA. Both NLRB records and employer reactions indicate that Larsen was indeed less aggressive than field examiners E. J. Eagen before him and Arnold Wills after him.

100. In October 1938, the AFL union received a charter separate from HWWA and became Kauai Terminal & Waterfront Workers Association, Local 21743, AFL (A. L. Wills to A. M. Rosseter, January 2, 1940, box 1487, NA).

101. A. L. Wills to A. M. Rosseter, January 4, 1940, box 1487, NA; Alice M. Rosseter, "Election Report" for Cases R-1590 and R-1591, March 13, 1940, box 1516, NA.

102. For examples of the employers' preference for the AFL over the ILWU/CIO, see J. W. Bertrand to C. E. S. Burns, January 13, 1938, LPC8/14, HSPAP; G. W. Sumner to C. E. S. Burns, August 29, 1938, LPC7/8, HSPAP. For details on the struggle

involving the ILWU, the AFL, the employers, and the NLRB, see folders LPC7/8, LPC7/10, LPC16/15A, LPC17/11, and LPC17/12, HSPAP. For descriptions of the 1940–41 strike in Ahukini and Port Allen, see delegate reports of Ichiro Izuka and of F. K. Kamahoahoa, *Proceedings of the Fourth Annual Convention of the International Longshoremen's and Warehousemen's Union*, April 7–14, 1941, pp. 208–213, ILWUSF; Beechert (1985:277–279); Izuka (1974:50–63); Zalburg (1979:48–52).

103. While this interport cooperation across racial lines was notable, it should also be kept in mind that interracialism failed to take hold at the respective ports until after World War II (see above and chapter 5).

104. Kawano interview, p. 5.

105. Jack Kawano to Harry Bridges, June 10, 1940, file HI/Correspondence, Reports, etc./Local 137/1937–45, box 5, ILWUSF.

106. A U.S. Department of Labor report (USBLS 1940:198) noted the widespread nature of this fear:

> Whether it is justified or not, there is a prevalent feeling among the majority of Hawaiian workers that a bad record with any important concern in the Territory makes it difficult to obtain employment in any other concern, and that to be associated with labor-union activities is certain to weaken their employment opportunities, if not destroy their economic future.

107. See also Kawano interview, p. 6. For the weekly fluctuations in union meeting attendance from 1935 to 1937, see files Honolulu Longshoremen's Association/Minutes/Membership/1935, Honolulu Longshoremen's Association/Minutes/Membership/1936, and Honolulu Longshoremen's Association/Minutes/Membership/1937, ILWUH.

108. Delegate report of Ed Berman, *Proceedings of the Second Annual Convention of the International Longshoremen's and Warehousemen's Union*, April 3–14, 1939, p. 224, ILWUSF.

109. "Pratt Report," p. 17.

110. Jack Kawano to Harry Bridges, February 4, 1938, file HI/Correspondence, Reports, etc./Local 137/1937–45, box 5, ILWUSF.

111. Delegate report of Solomon Niheu, *Proceedings of the First Annual Convention of the International Longshoremen's and Warehousemen's Union*, April 4–17, 1938, p. 180, ILWUSF. See also Hall interview, p. 3.

112. As quoted in Edward Berman, "The Situation at Present in the Hawaiian Islands," October 4, 1937, pp. 1–2, file HI/Correspondence, Reports, etc./1937–43, box 5, ILWUSF. See also Edward Berman to Henry Schmidt, December 14, 1937, box 184, NA.

   HWWA was widely suspected of being directly supported by the companies and of being chartered by the ILA president, Joseph Ryan. For examples, see the two Berman documents above; Levi Kealoha to Local 38–12, July 11, 1937, file HI/Correspondence, Reports, etc./Local 136/1937–43, box 5, ILWUSF; Edward Berman, "The Situation at Present in the Hawaiian Islands," October 4, 1937, pp. 1–2, file HI/Correspondence, Reports, etc./1937–43, box 5, ILWUSF. For similar dynamics on the continent, see Dubofsky (1994), Gross (1981), Tomlins (1985), and Zieger (1995).

113. Hawaii Education Association, Social Affairs Committee, "The Inter-Island Strike, May 26 to September 27, 1938," *Annual Report of the Social-Economic Plans Committee*, 1939, pp. 105–108, file HI/Correspondence, Reports, etc./Local 137/1937–45, box 5, ILWUSF.

114. Jack Kawano to Harry Bridges, June 10, 1940, file HI/Correspondence, Reports, etc./Local 137/1937–45, box 5, ILWUSF; emphases in original. See also Jack Kawano to Harry Bridges, January 13, 1940, and Frederick Kamahoahoa to Harry Bridges, December 19, 1940, file HI/Correspondence, Reports, etc./Local 137/1937–45, box 5, ILWUSF.

115. Jack Kawano to Matt Meehan, September 18, 1940, file HI/Correspondence, Reports, etc./Local 137/1937–45, box 5, ILWUSF.

116. Delegate reports of Ichiro Izuka and of Frederick Kamahoahoa, p. 212.

117. Hawaii Education Association, "The Inter-Island Strike, May 26 to September 27, 1938," pp. 129–130.

118. Ibid., pp. 137–138; Beechert (1991:154); Puette (1988:15–18).

119. Henry K. Martin to Inter-Island as publicly read by Sheriff Martin and reported in *Hilo Tribune-Herald*, July 28, 1938, as cited in Puette (1988:19).

120. See also Nakano interview (by Zalburg), p. 6.

121. Hawaii Education Association, "The Inter-Island Strike, May 26 to September 27, 1938," p. 141; Nakano interview (by Zalburg), p. 7. Hospitalized for 17 months, Nakano was crippled for the rest of his life.

122. Delegate report of Isaac Kauwe, *Proceedings of the Third Annual Convention of the International Longshoremen's and Warehousemen's Union*, April 1–11, 1940, p. 189, ILWUSF. Through the years, the Hilo Massacre has gained a deep symbolic significance for the ILWU in Hawai'i. To the present day, ILWU members reverently remember and commemorate August 1 as "Bloody Monday," analogous to the West Coast longshoremen's remembrance and commemoration of "Bloody Thursday," which refers to a particularly violent episode during the 1934 maritime strike.

123. Delegate report of Harry Kamoku, Conference of the Hawaiian Locals of the International Longshoremen's and Warehousemen's Union, May 16–17, 1940, p. 1, file Joint Conference, ILWUC.

124. Frederick Kamahoahoa to Harry Bridges, December 19, 1940, file HI/ Correspondence, Reports, etc./Local 137/1937–45, box 5, ILWUSF.

125. There are numerous union documents that argue this point. For example, see "Resolution," copies sent from Local 1–37 to all locals in Hawai'i and to the International, December 16, 1938, file HI/Correspondence, Reports, etc./Local 137/1937–45, box 5, ILWUSF; *Longshoremen's Bulletin*, no. 18, January 19, 1941, file Local 136 Publicity Leaflets, ILWUH.

126. Arnold L. Wills, "History of Labor Relations in Hawaii," Speeches before the Social-Economic Committee of the Hawaii Education Association, November 15 and December 20, 1945, p. 12, HC.

127. The ILWU's intuition about the centrality of Honolulu and of Castle & Cooke, in particular, seems also to be borne out by employer documents. In the late 1930s, presumably in response to increased union activities, stevedoring firms of Hawai'i took steps toward industrial organization. They began to compare and seek to equalize wages and working conditions between ports and to confer with one another on those

matters. They also exchanged information on the state of unionizing at their respective ports. Not surprisingly, Castle & Cooke in Honolulu headed these efforts. See, for example, letters from Randolph Sevier, Castle & Cooke, to C. Brewer & Company, Kahului Railroad Company, Hawaii Railway Company, Kauai Terminal, Ltd., Honokaa Sugar Company, Pioneer Mill Company, Kaeleku Sugar Company, Lihue Plantation Company, and Hutchinson Sugar Company, July 18, 1937, LPC11/4, and August 23, 1937 and July 16, 1938, LPC9/6, HSPAP (carbon copies of the July 18, 1937 and July 16, 1938 letters were also sent to the companies' respective agencies); Randolph Sevier to Arthur Armitage, August 24, 1939, and Randolph Sevier to C. E. S. Burns, August 24, 1939, LPC7/8, HSPAP. See also H. P. Faye to Lihue Plantation Company, August 24, 1937 and September 3, 1937, LPC11/4, HSPAP.

128. Frederick Kamahoahoa to Harry Bridges, December 19, 1940, file HI/ Correspondence, Reports, etc./Local 137/1937–45, box 5, ILWUSF.

129. Bailey interview, pp. 2–3.

130. Hall interview, p. 7.

131. Ibid., pp. 7–8; Damaso interview, p. 2.

132. Claveria interview, p. 2; Hall interview, p. 7. For Vibora Luviminda's insistence on Filipino racial exclusivity, see chapter 3.

133. Eddie Wailehua to Harry Kealoha, June 18, 1937, file Labor/HI/History/1937 Maui Strike, ILWUH.

134. Maui Plantation and Mill Workers Industrial Union, "Constitution, By-laws, and Rules of Order," organized June 24, 1937, p. 1, KSC27/22, HSPAP.

135. Maui Plantation and Mill Workers Union Strike Defense Committee to Executive Board, Honolulu Longshoremen's Association, June 27, 1937, file Labor/HI/ History/1937 Maui Strike, ILWUH.

136. Damaso interview, p. 1; Claveria interview, p. 2. Moises Claveria was one of the four signatories of the letter.

137. Bob Gandall to Harry Kealoha, June 27, 1937, file Labor/HI/History/1937 Maui Strike, ILWUH.

   In a highly self-congratulatory letter, the HSPA secretary-treasurer claimed cryptically that "we [the HSPA] had driven a wedge between the Filipinos and haole [organizers from Honolulu] and the former rowed with the latter and threw them out plumb complete" (B. H. Wells to C. E. S. Burns, July 27, 1937, LPC7/10, HSPAP). This letter should not be taken at face value. First, the organizers from Honolulu were not all haole. Second, the rift between the two groups had been there from the beginning and should not be attributed, certainly not entirely, to the HSPA or the plantations. Third, Grover Johnson, the haole lawyer who was most directly responsible for the formation of MPMWIU, continued to represent and defend indicted Vibora Luviminda leaders, indicating that the HSPA overestimated the rift.

138. HSPA, espionage report of a "meeting at Waikapu, Maui," May 25, 1938, KSC29/10, HSPAP.

139. Hall interview, p. 8.

140. For example, see espionage reports from Andrew Gross to C. E. S. Burns, July 31 and September 12, 1937, LPC17/12, HSPAP, and from Jose Bulatao to Lindsay Faye and Hans W. Hansen, July 31, 1937, KSC27/22, HSPAP.

141. Bailey interview, p. 2; Hall interview, p. 7; Beechert (1985:228).

142. *Nippu Jiji*, June 23, 1937; Zalburg (1979:24).

   "An attorney who takes a case against the interests of the 'Big Five' soon learns that he cannot stay in business. Consequently very few of them are willing to jeopardize their business" ("Report of E. J. Eagen," p. 4601). Helping out with organizing on Kaua'i, Johnson, as well as other CIO-oriented organizers, often appealed to Filipino workers by making the connection between his role in defending Filipino strikers on Maui and the need for Filipino workers to join an interracial union. For examples, see espionage reports from Jose Bulatao to Lindsay Faye and Hans Hansen, July 31 and August 11, 1937, KSC27/22, HSPAP; espionage report from Andrew Gross to C. E. S. Burns, July 31, 1937, LPC17/12, HSPAP. (A. Gross was Lihue Plantation Company's "welfare worker" [Lihue Plantation Company, "Statement of Earnings, Skilled and Semi-skilled Employees," 1934, LPC36/2, HSPAP].)

143. In fact, Calixto (Carl) Damaso, one of the signatories of the agreement Vibora Luviminda signed with the Maui sugar plantations, later became president of the ILWU for all of Hawai'i.

144. Jack Hall, Speech before the Social Action Committee of Congregational Churches, Honolulu, June 25,1960, as excerpted by Zalburg, file 9, box 1, SZ.

145. See letters and espionage reports in files KSC29/10, LPC7/10, and LSC69/17, HSPAP, and in file Carl Damaso Speeches/Hamakua 1937, EB. Especially useful are the following: L. W. Wishard to T. H. Davies & Company, November 1, 1937, LSC69/17, HSPAP; an exchange of eight letters among B. H. Wells, C. E. S. Burns, and S. L. Austin, September 17 to 27, 1937, LPC7/10, HSPAP.

146. L. W. Wishard to T. H. Davies & Company, December 18, 1937, LSC69/17, HSPAP. For other reports on the union's activities on the Big Island, see L. W. Wishard to T. H. Davies & Co., October 30, 1937, LSC69/17, HSPAP; W. P. Naquin to F. A. Schaefer & Co., December 21, 1937, HSC20/8, HSPAP. For reports on Kaua'i, see L. A. Faye to American Factors, June 22, 1938, KSC29/10, HSPAP; B. H. Wells to C. E. S. Burns, September 17, 20, 21, and 22, 1937, C. E. S. Burns to B. H. Wells, September 18 and 21, 1937, B. H. Wells to S. L. Austin, September 22, 1937, and S. L. Austin to B. H. Wells, September 27, 1937, LPC7/10, HSPAP; "Vivora Luviminda," September 23, 1937, LPC17/12, HSPAP.

147. Jack Hall, Speech before the Social Action Committee of Congregational Churches.

148. Delegate reports of John Brun and of Matsuki Arashiro, Conference of the Hawaiian Locals of the International Longshoremen's and Warehousemen's Union, May 16–17, 1940, pp. 6–7, file Joint Conference, ILWUC.

149. For the ILWU, the phrase "march inland" has resonance beyond Hawai'i. It also captures the 1934–38 West Coast longshoremen's "march inland" to organize warehouse workers (Schwartz 1978).

150. Goto interview, p. 1.

151. Espionage report from Jose Bulatao to Lindsay Faye and Hans Hansen, July 31 and August 11, 1937, KSC27/22, HSPAP.

152. *Hawaii Hōchi*, September 30, 1937, as reproduced by the HSPA, KSC27/22, HSPAP.

153. Hall interview, p. 8; see also "Hall Diary," p. 6, file 7, box 1, SZ.

154. Hall interview, p. 9.

155. For examples, see espionage reports in files KSC27/21, KSC27/22, and LPC17/12, HSPAP.

156. Hall interview, p. 10.

157. Delegate report of Edward Miyake, *Proceedings of the Third Annual Convention of the International Longshoremen's and Warehousemen's Union*, April 1–11, 1940, p. 188, ILWUSF.

158. For examples, see "Eagen Report"; *Voice of the ILWU*, January 17, 1964, p. 4; Jack Hall, Speech before the Social Action Committee of Congregational Churches; Goldblatt interview (by Beechert), p. 27; Reinecke (1993:22).

In this regard, I discovered a letter sent by the manager of The Lihue Plantation Company on Kaua'i to the head of the Castle & Cooke agency in Honolulu that included a cross-tabulation of Kaua'i voters according to race, gender, registration status, and votes cast. Given that Lihue was an American Factors plantation, the letter seems to suggest a ready exchange of such data across agencies and plantations. C. E. S. Burns to Frank Atherton, October 23, 1937, LPC6/3, HSPAP.

159. Delegate report of Edward Miyake, p. 188.

160. Arashiro interview, p. 1.

161. NLRB charge of unfair labor practices against Lihue Plantation Company filed by UCAPAWA Local 76, March 30, 1938, LPC7/10, HSPAP. More generally, see files KSC27/21, KSC27/22, KSC29/25, LPC7/8, LPC7/10, LPC16/15A, LPC17/11, and LPC17/12, HSPAP; Arnold L. Wills, "History of Labor Relations in Hawaii," p. 12; Zalburg (1979:72–75).

162. Arthur Smith to Caleb E. S. Burns, July 15, 1938, LPC16/15A, HSPAP.

163. A. L. Wills to J. T. McTernan, June 6, 1939, box 799, NA; Matsumoto (1958:60).

164. NLRB, Twentieth Region, "Certification of Counting and Tabulation of Ballots," October 24, 1940, box 1540, NA; Brooks (1952:83). The next day, workers at Kekaha Sugar Company, also on the island of Kaua'i, voted against being represented by UCAPAWA by a margin of 136 to 60 (NLRB, Twentieth Region, "Certification of Counting and Tabulation of Ballots," October 25, 1940, KSC29/25, HSPAP).

165. Minutes of the Senate Committee of the Whole, September 17, 1941, as quoted in Anthony (1955:4).

166. J. B. Pointdexter, "Proclamation of the Governor of Hawaii," December 7, 1941, as reprinted in Anthony (1955:127). As Okihiro (1991:199–201) finds, the army was Janus-faced about its war plans. On behalf of the army, Short was publicly advocating the passage of the Hawaii Defense Act, while the army continued to plan for martial law, a plan that harkened back to 1923.

167. Walter C. Short, "Proclamation of the Military Governor of Hawaii," December 7, 1941, as reprinted in Anthony (1955:127–128).

168. Office of the Military Governor, General Order 38, December 20, 1941, as reprinted in Anthony (1955:141).

169. Contract terms for procuring labor and supplies from employers, January 1, 1942, Colonel Theodore Wyman Jr., U.S. District Engineer, mimeographed, 38.08(1), HWRD; emphasis added.

170. Ibid.; Van Zwalenburg (1961:30–33).

171. "The War Record of Civilian and Industrial Hawaii," produced by the HSPA for the Joint Congressional Committee to Investigate the Pearl Harbor Attack, December 1, 1945, p. 24, 1.03(4), HWRD.

172. Ernest Burlem, Mrs. Marion Kelly, and Arthur A. Rutledge, "Memorandum on Military Control of Hawaiian Labor," March 27, 1944, p. 2, 38.08(1), HWRD; Fuchs (1961:354); Van Zwalenburg (1961:32). The "gentlemen's agreement" does not appear to have been ironclad. For example, in September 1942, supervisors of the Oahu Sugar Company continued to complain about losing workers to the defense industry. See report from K. B. Tester to Hans L'Orange, [September] 1942; report from William Wolters to Hans L'Orange, September 15, 1942; report from J. C. Osler to Hans L'Orange, August 31, 1942; report from C. J. Fleener to Hans L'Orange, [September] 1942, 1.03, HWRD.

173. Office of the Military Governor, General Order 56, January 26, 1942, as reprinted in Anthony (1955:141–142).

174. Ibid.

175. Clifford O'Brien to Harry Bridges, January 28, 1942, file HI/Correspondence, Reports, etc./Local 137/1937–45, box 5, ILWUSF.

176. Office of the Military Governor, General Order 91, March 31, 1942, as reprinted in Anthony (1955:155–156); emphasis added.

177. Garner Anthony to Ingram M. Stainback, December 1, 1942, as reprinted in Anthony (1955:191–199).

178. See also C. E. S. Burns to R. M. Allen, June 9, 1942, LPC6/3, HSPAP.

179. See Ingram M. Stainback, "Proclamation of the Governor of Hawaii," February 8, 1943, and Delos C. Emmons, "Proclamation of Military Governor of Hawaii," February 8, 1943, as reprinted in Anthony (1955:129–132).

180. Clifford O'Brien to Harry Bridges, January 28, 1942, file HI/Correspondence, Reports, etc./Local 137/1937–45, box 5, ILWUSF.

181. Ernest Burlem, Mrs. Marion Kelly and Arthur A. Rutledge, "Memorandum on Military Control of Hawaiian Labor," p. 5; Izuka (1974:64–75). On the island of Kaua'i, Lieutenant Colonel Eugene Fitzgerald, the Kaua'i military commander, gave a three-member Office of Civilian Defense wide latitude in dealing with labor. Notably, all three members were sugar plantation managers on the island (ibid.). An ILWU organizer reported on the conditions he found in the aftermath of martial law:

> On Dec. 7th, the day of Pearl Harbor, the Island of Kauai was placed under martial law and all meetings of any kind were banned.... Izuka [president of Local 1–35] tried everyway possible to carry on the affairs of the Local by himself. In April [1942] some four months after Pearl Harbor, Izuka was placed under arrest, and was put in jail at the county seat of Lihue for a period of some five months. This was the finishing touch as far as the Local was concerned. Nobody paid dues or met after that so the Local was put out of existence. Local 1–35 also had a Unit 2 of its organization at the Port of Ahukini some 21 miles from Port Allen. This Unit was also put out of business. (Frank Thompson to Louis Goldblatt, July 31, 1944, file HI/Correspondence and Reports/Frank Thompson/1944, box 6, ILWUSF)

182. Goldblatt interview (by Beechert), p. 11.

183. Robertson interview (by Zalburg), p. 20.

184. Hall interview, p. 11.

185. As is well known, an unusual source of heightened nationalism during World War II in Communist-led unions was their leaders, who pledged no strikes and

encouraged maximum production from the rank and file. With a predominantly leftist leadership, both on the West Coast and in Hawai'i, the ILWU was no exception. For example, on December 8, 1941, the day after the Pearl Harbor attack, ILWU president Harry Bridges telegraphed Honolulu:

You are instructed to immediately see that all ILWU members and resources are marshaled to aid national government in combating Japanese forces in every way especially in that our Hawaiian longshore unions accept share of burden in seeing that ships and cargoes are moved with full dispatch and each ILWU member be alert against any attempted sabotage and to fully cooperate with government forces against nations [sic] enemies. (Harry Bridges to Clifford O'Brien, December 8, 1941, file HI/Correspondence, Reports, etc./1937–43, box 5, ILWUSF)

But Bridges was preaching to the choir. The hypernationalism and extreme sensitivity to subversive activities, as well as martial law, prevailing in wartime Hawai'i made such admonishments from San Francisco largely immaterial and redundant.

Nonetheless, it is noteworthy that the ILWU was quieter than the AFL, whose representatives criticized and called for the end of the military's control of labor (Ernest Burlem, Mrs. Marion Kelly, and Arthur A. Rutledge, "Memorandum on Military Control of Hawaiian Labor," p. 5).

186. Letter from [illegible signature], transportation department, to [W. L. S. Williams], July 6, 1942, PSC42/3, HSPAP. See also W. A. Baddaky to W. L. S. Williams, January 18, 1943, PSC42/4, HSPAP.

187. Report from C. J. Fleener to Hans L'Orange, [September] 1942, 1.03, HWRD. See also report from K. B. Tester to Hans L'Orange, [September] 1942; report from William Wolters to Hans L'Orange, September 15, 1942; and report from J. C. Osler to Hans L'Orange, August 31, 1942, 1.03, HWRD. According to a December 2, 1948 letter from Hans L'Orange, the manager of Oahu Sugar Company, to the plantation's department heads (1.03, HWRD), the HSPA in 1942 had requested all of its member plantations to "prepare a factual history relative to their participation in the war." For his part, L'Orange gathered the foregoing reports produced by his department heads to prepare his factual history.

188. John T. Moir, 3rd, to W. L. S. Williams, July 14, 1942, PSC42/3, HSPAP.

189. For examples of the workers' increasingly open expressions toward the end of martial law, see Anastacio Rarungol, et al. to Gilbert Hay, January 18, 1944, and Olaa Filipino Labor League to manager, March 28, 1944, PSC42/4, HSPAP.

190. Bert Nakano, an ILWU organizer on the island of Hawai'i, as quoted in an espionage report from G. Moir [unclear signature] to W. L. S. Williams, February 19, 1944, PSC42/4, HSPAP. See also Hall interview, p. 11.

191. Memorandum by Captain C. D. Baker, Area Engineer, Corps of Engineers, March 30, 1942, as quoted in Ernest Burlem, Mrs. Marion Kelly, and Arthur A. Rutledge, "Memorandum on Military Control of Hawaiian Labor," p. 16.

192. Nakamoto interview, p. 1. See also Arakaki and Omuro interview, pp. 3–5; Beechert (1985:287). Hall similarly recalled, "The employers were even loaning sugar workers to defense contractors and getting back 60¢ or 70¢ an hour and then paying the workers the regular plantation wages of 20¢ an hour or 19¢ or less" (*Voice of Labor*, January 17, 1964, p. 4).

193. Report from J. C. Osler to Hans L'Orange, August 31, 1942, 1.03, HWRD.

194. For details of this long history, see Okihiro (1991). See also "Pratt Report" and "Report of E. J. Eagen."

195. The Honolulu Chamber of Commerce actually sent a telegraph, on December 27, 1942, to a number of federal and territorial government officials, including President Roosevelt, opposing the restoration of civilian rule (Anthony 1955:28–29).

196. "The War Record of Civilian and Industrial Hawaii," produced by the HSPA for the Joint Congressional Committee to Investigate the Pearl Harbor Attack, December 1, 1945, p. 2, 1.03(4), HWRD. See also R. A. Vitousek to B. H. Wells, January 23, 1941, PSC42/3, HSPAP, and for a more personalized example of the close ties between the sugar industry and the military, see C. E. S. Burns to Major General E. A. Anderson, September 8, 1942, LPC6/3, HSPAP; Lt. J.M. Noel to Mr. & Mrs. Burns, July 28, 1944, LPC15/13, HSPAP.

197. "The War Record of Civilian and Industrial Hawaii," pp. 2–3; Ernest Burlem, Mrs. Marion Kelley, and Arthur A. Rutledge, "Memorandum on Military Control of Hawaiian Labor," p. 8.

198. Another notable appointment was that of Lorrin P. Thurston, president and general manager of the *Honolulu Advertiser*, as the public relations advisor to the military governor (Anthony 1955:38).

199. McElrath interview, p. 20.

200. Arnold L. Wills, "History of Labor Relations in Hawaii," p. 13.

201. Kealalio interview, p. 2.

202. Goldblatt interview (by Beechert), p. 2.

203. Among many documents available at the ILWU archives in San Francisco, see Louis Goldblatt to Bert Nakano, December 8, 1943, and Bert Nakano to Louis Goldblatt, February 3, 1944, file HI/Correspondence, Reports, etc./Local 136/1937–43, box 5, ILWUSF; Jack Kawano to Harry Bridges, January 28, 1944, and Jack Kawano to Louis Goldblatt, February 25, 1944, file HI/Correspondence, Reports, etc./Local 137/1937–43, box 5, ILWUSF; Jack Kawano to Louis Goldblatt, April 20, 1944, file HI/Correspondence, Reports, etc./1944, box 5, ILWUSF. The quotes were from the January 28, 1944 letter from Kawano to Bridges and the April 20, 1944 letter from Kawano to Goldblatt. I first heard about the secret union meetings from Abba Ramos, a retired ILWU officer, who, as a boy growing up on the Big Island, had acted as a lookout (Ramos interview [1996]).

204. Hall interview, p. 8. See also Goto interview; Zalburg (1979:28).

205. Matt Meehan to Edward Berman, January 3, 1938, file HI/Correspondence, Reports, etc./1937–43, box 5, ILWUSF. See also Berman interview, pp. 8–10; Bridges interview, p. 1; Robertson interview (by Zalburg), p. 21; Zalburg (1979:18); delegate report of Edward Berman, *Proceedings of the Second Annual Convention of the International Longshoremen's and Warehousemen's Union*, April 3–14, 1939, pp. 223–224, ILWUSF.

206. Thompson was also known for his detailed biweekly reports to San Francisco, through which one can chart the rapid progress of the ILWU's organizing campaign between 1944 and 1946. See files HI/Correspondence and Reports/Frank Thompson/1944, HI/Correspondence and Reports/Frank Thompson/1945, and HI/Correspondence and Reports/Frank Thompson/1946, box 6, ILWUSF.

207. "Notes on Organizing Possibilities in Hawaii," February 1944, file HI/Correspondence, Reports, etc./1944, box 5, ILWUSF; emphasis in original. This report was attached to a copy of a letter from ILWU secretary-treasurer Louis Goldblatt to Matt Meehan, in which Goldblatt seems to indicate that the report was written by someone at one of the ILWU locals in Hawai'i; Matt Meehan would shortly leave for Hawai'i to become the territory's regional director.

208. NLRB, "Decision and Direction of Elections," January 12, 1945, PSC29/8, HSPAP; Beechert (1985:291–292); Zalburg (1979:119–120). For copies of the NLRB election results, see 38.08(1), HWRD. For a summary table of the election results, see Hawaii Employers Council Research Department, "Unionization of Non-agricultural Sugar Workers in Hawaii," October 1949, PSC44/15, HSPAP; *The Dispatcher, Hawaiian Edition*, June 19, 1945, p. 2, 38.08 (The Dispatcher), HWRD.

209. Takumi Akama to Harry Bridges, June 10, 1945, file HI/Correspondence, Reports, etc./Local 136/1937–43, box 5, ILWUSF. See also Arakaki and Omuro interivew, pp. 12–13; Goldblatt interview (by Beechert), p. 23.

210. Hearing about the local organizers' signing up agricultural workers, the ILWU secretary-treasurer wrote the following admonition to Hawai'i from San Francisco, "*We [the International officers] are not interested in organizing agricultural workers at this time.* . . . we are thoroughly and absolutely convinced that any move to organize field workers at this time will lead to wholesale disaster. . . . The officials . . . are unanimously convinced that moves to organize agricultural workers must be stopped at once" (Louis Goldblatt to Jack Hall, August 18, 1944, file HI/Correspondence and Reports/1944, box 5, ILWUSF; emphasis in original). See also Louis Goldblatt to Frank Thompson, August 18, 1944, file HI/Correspondence and Reports/Frank Thompson/1944, box 6, ILWUSF.

211. Frank Thompson to Louis Goldblatt, September 2, 1944, file HI/Correspondence and Reports/1944, box 5, ILWUSF.

212. Ibid. See also meeting minutes, July 18 and 19, 1944, file Local 136 Territorial Longshore Conference, ILWUH.

213. Frank Thompson to Louis Goldblatt, September 30, 1944, file HI/Correspondence and Reports/Frank Thompson/1944, box 6, ILWUSF. For a rundown of the individual endorsements, see Jack Hall to Louis Goldblatt, October 23, 1944, file HI/Correspondence and Reports/1944, box 5, ILWUSF.

214. Goldblatt interview (by Ward), pp. 344–345.

215. There were three companies in the sugar industry whose workers were not represented by the ILWU. Against a jurisdictional agreement with the ILWU, the AFL had organized the Waiakea Mill Company on the Big Island in late 1943; both the company and the AFL unit there folded in 1948. In addition, two small plantations on Kaua'i—Gay & Robinson and Waimea Sugar Mill Company—stayed nonunion (Beechert 1985:290, 292).

5. The Making of Working-Class Interracialism

1. For examples, see Brooks (1952), Daws (1968), Larrowe (1972), Lind (1980), Wills (1954), and Zalburg (1979).

2. For examples, see Beechert (1984, 1985), Geschwender (1981, 1982), Geschwender and Levine (1983, 1986), Kent (1983), MacLennan (1979), Levine and Geschwender (1981) and Sharma (1984a). Takaki (1983, 1990) asserts a similar argument. However, unlike the others, he places the making of Hawaii's interracial working class much earlier, dating its birth to the dual union sugar strike of 1920.

3. Goldblatt interview (by Beechert), pp. 116–117.

4. Most Marxist studies seem to reason: of course, the workers (eventually) recognized their "real" class interests. (There is also a liberal version: of course, all "races" are equal, and thus race should never have divided the workers.)

5. This sentence borrows from Sewell's (1980:213) analysis of working-class formation in nineteenth-century France: "In retrospect, the idea of fraternal association of all trades seems obvious, but this is just a sign of the distance of today's world from that of the 1830s."

6. For example, Tsutsumi (1922:5) wrote, "First of all the capitalists must be made to recognize the personality of the laborers.... We strive to build a community which is fair and just and which respects the personality of individuals, who have been disgusted with a community tyrannized over by the capitalists."

7. The Kaua'i paper was begun by a group of Japanese workers who had been a part of the FJL movement. Its circulation was about one tenth of those of *Nippu Jiji* and *Hawaii Hōchi* and was all but confined to Kaua'i (Sakamaki 1928). As he told Edward Beechert later, Jack Kimoto, the head of the Community Party in Hawai'i, burned all files and back issues of *Yōen Jihō* the day after the Pearl Harbor attack (Beechert to author, August 17, 2005).

8. An excerpt from the manifesto read: "We believe that the conditions of modern industry in this territory make it necessary to readjust the craft and trade union movement and build up an industrial form of organization that will unite in one body all the wage workers in Hawaii, without discrimination as to race, sex, creed, craft or color.... We believe that labor is entitled to a voice in the management of industry and has a right to determine the conditions under which it shall function, to that end that it shall receive the full value of what it produces" ("Manifesto to the Workers of Hawaii," printed in *Honolulu Star-Bulletin*, November 23, 1921, as cited in Beechert [1985:213]). As Beechert (1985) points out, Wright consistently denied any ties to the Wobblies.

9. In this section of the chapter, I use "ILWU/CIO movement" as a shorthand label for the movement that began with the maritime workers in Hilo and Honolulu and spread to other ports and to sugar and pineapple plantations. The label is not always technically accurate, since neither the ILWU nor the CIO existed in the islands until late 1937, two years after the movement had begun.

10. Berman interview, p. 3. The Wobbly influence can be glimpsed in the intermittent references to the "one big union." For examples, see espionage report of a "Meeting of Union Agitators" in Lihue, September 4, 1937; Hawaiian Islands Federation of Labor, "Mass Meeting!!" notice, n.d. [1937]; espionage reports from Andrew Gross to C. E. S. Burns, September 12, 1937, from Arthur Souza to C. E. S. Burns, September 19, 1937, from A. Gross to McKeever, March 25, 1938, LPC17/12, HSPAP.

11. Not accidentally, the beginning of the ILWU/CIO movement coincided with the beginning of the Communist Party in Hawai'i. Contrary to the popular image

of the Communists' taking control of the union by underhanded means, the leaders of the ILWU/CIO movement in Hawai'i usually became leaders, voted into positions through democratic elections, *before* they considered or were approached about joining the Communist Party (Holmes 1994; Melendy 2002).

12. First and foremost, the focus of the Communists and fellow travelers in the ILWU was on labor organizing (Beechert 1985:305–306). In an interview with historian Lawrence Fuchs, John Reinecke stated that the Communist Party in Hawai'i was single-mindedly focused "on the building of a labor movement in TH [Territory of Hawai'i]" and that the Communist Party in the metropole and elsewhere had little interest or influence there. It was this local, pragmatic approach that was key to the party's growth from the late 1930s to 1946. In fact, according to an FBI interview of Jack Kawano in 1950, a prominent unionist in longshore who resigned from the ILWU that year and would testify before the House Committee on Un-American Activities the following year, ILWU leaders began to leave the party in 1947 when nonlabor leadership of the party sought to "inject Party discipline and program into the day to day" operations of the union (Melendy 2002:47–48, 84–85).

    For a discussion of Communists and the ILWU on the West Coast, see Kimeldorf (1988).

13. Shimonishi as quoted in espionage report from Andrew Gross to C. E. S. Burns, September 12, 1937, LPC17/12, HSPAP. See also espionage report from Jose Bulatao to Lindsay Faye and Hans Hansen, July 31, 1937, KSC27/22, HSPAP; espionage report from Andrew Gross to C. E. S. Burns, July 31 and August 20, 1937, LPC17/12, HSPAP; espionage report from J. W. Bertrand to C. E. S. Burns, August 8, 1937, LPC17/12, HSPAP. During the 1924 strike, Manlapit similarly had told a crowd that "one dollar a day is not enough for my people" (espionage report of "speeches at Mooheau Park" to J. K. Butler, June 15, 1924, MKC1/8, HSPAP).

14. Reyes as quoted in Gross to Burns, September 12, 1937.

15. Ben Shear as quoted in ibid. See also espionage report from Andrew Gross to C. E. S. Burns, July 28, 1937, LPC17/12, HSPAP.

16. As quoted in espionage report from Jose Bulatao to Lindsay Faye and Hans Hansen, July 31, 1937, KSC27/22, HSPAP. See also Ben Shear's speech in the same report. This spy estimated the size of the crowd to be 300 people.

17. Espionage reports from Chas. Kaneyama to Lindsay Faye and Hans Hansen, July 31, 1937, KSC27/22, HSPAP and from Andrew Gross to C. E. S. Burns, July 31, 1937, LPC17/12, HSPAP. See also Honolulu Longshoremen's Association, "Constitution By-laws and Rules of Order," October 15, 1935, box 239, NA.

18. Shear as paraphrased in espionage report from Andrew Gross to C. E. S. Burns, July 31, 1937, LPC17/12, HSPAP. The report stated that 150 of those gathered were Filipino and the rest were Japanese and Portuguese. See also espionage report from Andrew Gross to C. E. S. Burns, September 4 and 12, 1937, LPC17/12, HSPAP; Harry Kamoku to Harry Bridges, October 11, 1938, file HI/Correspondence, Reports, etc./Local 136/1937–43, box 5, ILWUSF.

19. As quoted in espionage report from Jose Bulatao to Lindsay Faye and Hans Hansen, July 31, 1937, KSC27/22, HSPAP; Bulatao estimated the size of the crowd to be 300 people. For another espionage report of Johnson, see Andrew Gross to

C. E. S. Burns, July 31, 1937, LPC17/12, HSPAP. See also Ben Shear's remarks in the same report and in Andrew Gross to C. E. S. Burns, July 28, 1937, LPC17/12, HSPAP.

20. Bulatao to Faye and Hansen, July 31, 1937.

21. Edward Berman, "The Situation at Present in the Hawaiian Islands," October 4, 1937, p. 2, file HI/Correspondence, Reports, etc./1937–43, box 5, ILWUSF.

22. For examples, see espionage reports in LPC17/12, HSPAP. Although speakers of different racial groups led the meetings, they did not all receive equal coverage in the employers' espionage reports, on which much of this section is based. English speakers, disproportionately haole, tended to get more coverage, probably indicating the spies' linguistic limitations and/or the employers' heightened sensitivity to "haole outsiders." In one instance, the employer assumed that a haole organizer was the leader, aided by a Filipino, only to be contradicted by the Filipino (see interview with Calixto Piano, conducted by John E. Parks of Law Offices of Philip L. Rice for the Lihue Plantation Company, November 1, 1938, LPC17/12, HSPAP.)

23. Hawaiian Islands Federation of Labor, "Mass Meeting!!" notice, n.d. [1937], LPC17/12, HSPAP.

24. William Craft as paraphrased in the Minutes of Regular Meeting, January 13, 1937, file Honolulu Longshoremen's Association/Minutes/Membership/1937, ILWUH.

25. Robles as quoted in espionage report from Andrew Gross [to C. E. S. Burns], December 6, 1937, LPC17/12, HSPAP. See also Shear as quoted in espionage reports of a PAWWA meeting held in Hanapēpē, August 20, 1937, LPC17/12, HSPAP, and of a "Meeting of Union Agitators" in Lihue, September 4, 1937, LPC17/12, HSPAP; espionage report from Jose Bulatao to Lindsay Faye and Hans Hansen, August 11, 1937, KSC27/22, HSPAP.

Robles would be demoted from the mill to field work and then fired in February 1938. With NLRB intervention, he would be reinstated in November 1938 (interviews with Lorenzo Robles, conducted by John E. Parks of Law Offices of Philip L. Rice for the Lihue Plantation Company, November 1 and 4, 1938, LPC17/12, HSPAP).

26. For example, see Quintin Paredes to Manuel Quezon, as reproduced in "Confidential" memo from B. H. Wells to all HSPA plantation managers, February 13, 1937, p. 3, PSC38/26, HSPAP. In an otherwise obsequious report on the plantations, even Celestino Rodriguez, a senator of the Philippine legislature from Cebu, informed the HSPA that he had heard "complaints from Filipino laborers that the managers give preference to Japanese for better housing conditions" (Celestino Rodriguez to HSPA board of directors, August 13, 1921, PSC22/10, HSPAP).

27. Shear as quoted in espionage report from Chas. Kaneyama to Lindsay Faye and Hans Hansen, August 11, 1937, KSC27/22, HSPAP. See also Shear as quoted in espionage report from Andrew Gross to C. E. S. Burns, August 11, 1937, LPC17/12, HSPAP; espionage report from Jose Bulatao to Lindsay Faye and Hans Hansen, July 31, 1937, KSC27/22, HSPAP.

28. Shear as quoted in espionage report of a "Meeting of Union Agitators" in Lihue, September 4, 1937, LPC17/12, HSPAP. See also Revilla as quoted in espionage report from Andrew Gross [to C. E. S. Burns], December 6, 1937, LPC17/12, HSPAP.

29. Ben Shear quoted in *Maui Record*, June 4, 1937, as translated by the HSPA, KSC29/9, HSPAP; *Hawaii Hōchi*, September 30, 1937, as reproduced by the HSPA, KSC27/22, HSPAP.

30. Interview with Escolastico Relacion, conducted by John E. Parks of Law Offices of Philip L. Rice for the Lihue Plantation Company, October 26, 1938, LPC17/11, HSPAP. See also interview with Calixto Piano, conducted by John E. Parks of Law Offices of Philip L. Rice for the Lihue Plantation Company, November 1, 1938, LPC17/12, HSPAP; de la Cruz interview.

    "Monkey" was a racial slur often used against Filipinos. A. L. Rockwell, who was responsible for hiring some of the casual workers in Ahukini and clearly favored the AFL, referred to a Filipino affiliated with the CIO as a "nigger in the woodpile" (interview with Rockwell, conducted by John E. Parks of Law Offices of Philip L. Rice for the Lihue Plantation Company, October 26, 1938, LPC17/11, HSPAP).

31. Minutes of Special Meeting, January 31, 1937, file Honolulu Longshoremen's Association/Minutes/Membership/1937, ILWUH.

32. As quoted in espionage report from Chas. Kaneyama to Lindsay Faye and Hans Hansen, July 31, 1937, KSC27/22, HSPAP. See also Goto as quoted in espionage report of a "Meeting of Union Agitators" in Lihue, September 4, 1937, LPC17/12, HSPAP.

33. Berman as quoted in espionage report from Andrew Gross [to C. E. S. Burns], December 6, 1937, LPC17/12, HSPAP. See also Shear as quoted in espionage report from Chas. Kaneyama to Lindsay Faye and Hans Hansen, August 11, 1937, KSC27/22, HSPAP, and as quoted in espionage report from Arthur Souza to C. E. S. Burns, September 19, 1937, LPC17/12, HSPAP.

34. As quoted in espionage report from Andrew Gross to C. E. S. Burns, September 12, 1937, LPC17/12, HSPAP.

35. For example, in August 1937, 85 of the port's 130 longshoremen were Filipino; by contrast, there were 25 Japanese, 6 Native Hawaiians, and 14 "others" (Randolph Sevier to C. Brewer & Company, Kahului Railroad Company, Hawaii Railway Company, Kauai Terminal, Ltd., Honokaa Sugar Company, Pioneer Mill Company, Kaeleku Sugar Company, Lihue Plantation Company, and Hutchinson Sugar Company, August 23, 1937, LPC9/6, HSPAP).

36. "Agreement between the Ahukini Longshoremen's Industrial Association and the Lihue Plantation Co., Limited," October 22, 1937, box 197, NA. Ending a strike that began in Port Allen and spread to Ahukini, the contract was signed on the same date as the one signed in Port Allen. "Agreement by and between the Kauai Terminal, Limited ... and the International Longshoremen['s] and Warehousemen's Union, District #1, Local 35," October 22, 1937, box 184, NA.

37. For a list of workers who went out on a strike in September 1937, see C. E. S. Burns, "Review of Ahukini Labor Trouble," September 13, 1937, LPC17/12, HSPAP; possibly all 75 listed were Filipinos. For pay differentials among "regulars" and two classes of "casuals" for January to July 1938, see C. E. S. Burns to H. A. Walker, August 25, 1938, LPC7/10, HSPAP.

38. Interview with Calixto Piano, conducted by John E. Parks of Law Offices of Philip L. Rice for the Lihue Plantation Company, p. 3, November 1, 1938, LPC17/12, HSPAP. Prior to his arrival on Kaua'i, Piano had been active in the organization of Vibora Luviminda on Maui.

39. Copy of M. Morioka, T. Omoto, G. Baptist[e], B. Sandlin to John Wilson, November 28, 1937, LPC16/15A, HSPAP. Based on their last names, respectively, they were

presumably two Japanese, a Portuguese, and a haole; many documents list "Baptiste" as the correct spelling, e.g., "Memorandum of a telephone conversation from Mr. Arthur G. Smith to Philip L. Rice," September 23, 1938, LPC17/12, HSPAP.

40. Sixteen of the "regular" workers in November 1937 joined the CIO, while the others opted for the AFL. Of the sixteen, according to an employer report, the Japanese joined the CIO "at the instigation of the Port Allen C.I.O. Japanese" (J. W. Bertrand to C. E. S. Burns, January 13, 1938, LPC8/14, HSPAP).

41. Interview with Makoto Morioka, conducted by John E. Parks of Law Offices of Philip L. Rice for the Lihue Plantation Company, p. 3, October 26, 1938, LPC17/11, HSPAP. See also interview with Tetsuji Omoto, conducted by John E. Parks of Law Offices of Philip L. Rice for the Lihue Plantation Company, October 26, 1938, LPC17/11, HSPAP.

These interviews of the longshoremen in Ahukini were conducted by lawyers of the Lihue Plantation Company, which owned and operated the port of Ahukini. Faced with an investigation by NLRB field agent Arnold Wills, they conducted their own investigation of NLRB charges. Arthur G. Smith, "Memorandum of conference with Mr. A. L. Wills," September 21, 1938, LPC17/11, HSPAP; John Parks to Arthur Smith, November 1, 1938, LPC16/15A, HSPAP; on the start of the law firm's involvement, see "Review of Ahukini Labor Trouble," September 13, 1937, p. 5, LPC17/12, HSPAP.

42. Interview with Bruce Knight Sandlin, conducted by John E. Parks of Law Offices of Philip L. Rice for the Lihue Plantation Company, pp. 2, 12, October 26, 1938, LPC17/11, HSPAP. See also "Statement by Gilbert Baptiste" and "Statement by B. K. Sandlin," attached to John Parks to Arthur Smith, November 4, 1938, LPC17/12, HSPAP.

43. For example, in the sugar industry, Japanese workers comprised 28 percent of the workforce in 1938 (*Hawaiian Annual* 1939:23).

44. For the major changes that took place in 1937, see last chapter. For examples of the HSPA's effort to surveil the Japanese community, see KSC29/9, HSPAP.

45. Hawaiian Sugar Planters' Association, "Memo," [probably July 1937], KSC29/9, HSPAP. Based on the memo's concerns and on the other contents of this folder, I would estimate that this HSPA memo was drafted in early July 1937 and distributed to all sugar plantation managers. Among those interviewed by the HSPA were the editor of *Hawaii Hōchi* and those who had been active in the 1920 sugar strike.

As seen in the quote, the employers insisted and would go on insisting for decades that the ILWU/CIO movement was a *malihini* movement led by West Coast haole, even in the face of clear evidence to the contrary.

See also HSPA memo, "Work Among the Plantation Japanese," March 2, 1938, PSC42/3, HSPAP.

46. Hawaiian Sugar Planters' Association, "Memo."

47. Frederick K. Kamahoahoa to Harry Bridges, July 29, 1937, file HI/Correspondence, Reports, etc./Local 136/1937–51, box 5, ILWUSF.

48. Jack Kawano to Harry Bridges, January 13, 1940, file HI/Correspondence, Reports, etc./Local 137/1937–45, box 5, ILWUSF.

49. Frank Thompson to Louis Goldblatt, July 31, 1944, p. 2, file HI/Correspondence and Reports/Frank Thompson/1944, box 6, ILWUSF. See also Frank Thompson to

Louis Goldblatt, August 23, 1944, p. 2, file HI/Correspondence and Reports/Frank Thompson/1944, box 6, ILWUSF.

50. Lie (2004:189) makes a similar point: "Chasing predicates misses the cardinal importance of categorical essentialization and distinction that generate them in the first place. It is not because Jews were communists or capitalists that Hitler reviled them; Hitler hated them and therefore associated them with other things he disliked."

51. Frank C. Atherton, *Proceedings of the Annual Conference of New Americans*, 1932, pp. 7–8, HC. See also Major General Briant H. Wells's speech at the same conference. Upon his retirement from the army in 1934, Wells became the secretary of the HSPA.

52. Admiral Yates Stirling Jr., the Commandant of the Fourteenth Naval District, *Proceedings of the Annual Conference of New Americans*, 1932, pp. 7–8, HC. Many of the nisei delegates at the conference were not "gentlemen."

53. Ibid., p. 8.

54. Sociologist Andrew Lind wrote in 1943, "The difficult situation faced by the Japanese in Hawaii in the event of the war had been anticipated long before the actual catastrophe occurred. For years the Nisei in particular have been told that they were 'on the spot'" (Andrew W. Lind, *The Japanese in Hawaii Under War Conditions* [Honolulu: American Council, Institute for Pacific Relations, 1943], p. 29, 56.05[2], HWRD). See also Office of the Assistant Chief of Staff for Military Intelligence, Headquarters Hawaiian Department, "A Survey of the Japanese in the Territory of Hawaii" (revision of a 1926 survey), September 1929, p. 2, EB.

55. Walter Mihata, *Proceedings of the Annual Conference of New Americans*, 1929, p. 14, HC.

56. Oliver Soares as quoted in *Nippu Jiji*, August 22, 1940, file 1/4/34b, RASRLC.

57. Paul S. Bachman, *Proceedings of the Annual Conference of New Americans*, 1941, p. 33, HC.

58. Lt. Colonel Walter C. Phillips, *Proceedings of the Annual Conference of New Americans*, 1941, pp. 12–13, HC.

59. *Honolulu Star-Bulletin*, June 14, 1941, file 1/4/34b, RASRLC. See also Rademaker and Lane (1951:2) for description of a similar gathering of the Oahu Citizens Committee for Home Defense.

60. *Hawaii Hōchi*, December 19, 1940, file 1/2/64, RASRLC. See also Rademaker and Lane (1951:3, 9) for issei testimonials of loyalty, declaring their pride in having their children serve in the armed forces.

61. *Nippu Jiji*, August 22, 1941, file 1/4/34b, RASRLC.

62. The earliest rumors concerned the possible involvement of Hawaii's Japanese in the bombing of Pearl Harbor itself. Ironically, more Japanese civilians died in the attack than civilians of all the other racial groups combined (Lind 1943:14).

63. The two figures overlap; about two thirds of those initially interned in Hawai'i were later transferred to metropolitan concentration camps. The internees were mostly Shinto and Buddhist priests, language school teachers, newspaper publishers, other leaders of the Japanese community, and *kibei* (nisei who were educated in Japan).

64. As Assistant Secretary of War John McCloy explained, "The Japanese problem is very complex and all tied up with the labor situation.... mass evacuation from

Hawaii is impractical" (*Honolulu Star-Bulletin*, March 27, 1941, as quoted in Lind [1943:27]). As of June 1941, there were 159,534 Japanese residents in Hawai'i, representing 34.2 percent of the territory's population. And the Japanese represented over one third of those gainfully employed, including half of all in skilled crafts (Lind 1943:3, 27).

65. The two largest papers, *Hawaii Hōchi* and *Nippu Jiji* (renamed *Hawaii Times*), were later allowed to resume publishing, but only under the strictest military censorship.

66. For an example of discrimination in defense work, see U.S. Navy, "Confidential Memo," February 25, 1943, 56.05(3), HWRD. This confidential memo was a guideline used by "agents" to determine the loyalty of Japanese workers on naval projects. Not many issei passed the screening, and the screening of nisei was not much looser. Regarding nisei "whose background is strongly Japanese, *but who have demonstrated no positive pro-Japanese sentiments,*" the memo instructed the agents, "These individuals are classed as undesirable on any Naval project" (emphasis added). Another example is that those Japanese who were allowed to work in restricted areas had to wear a special badge that marked them as Japanese (Okihiro 1991:227). For a personal account of this practice, see Otanza interview, pp. 1–2.

67. George Horne, "Are the Japs Hopeless?," *The Saturday Evening Post*, September 9, 1944, p. 17, 56.05(2), HWRD.

68. The quote is of Lt. General Delos C. Emmons, the military governor, in Lind (1943:17).

69. For excerpts of official statements denying Japanese involvement in fifth-column activities, see Eileen O'Brien, "Making Democracy Work," *Paradise of the Pacific*, December 1943, p. 44, 56.05(2), HWRD; Lind (1943:11–12); Rademaker and Lane (1951:30–31).

70. Of the two major dailies, the *Honolulu Advertiser* was much more stridently and unambiguously anti-Japanese, which would result in extremely low circulation numbers among the Japanese after the war (Odo 2004).

71. Lt. General Delos C. Emmons, commanding general of Hawaiian department and military governor, "A Call to Americans of Japanese Ancestry," [January 1943], 56.05(2), HWRD.

72. Eileen O'Brien, "Making Democracy Work," p. 45; Daws (1968:351); Rademaker and Lane (1951:62).

73. For example, noticing a change from just a year before, a nisei observer remarked in September 1943, "When the call was made, four hundred young men [in the area] volunteered.... this volunteer movement has restored better race relations in Kona. Other races do not ridicule [the Japanese] any more" (Shiku Ogura, "Morale of the Japanese in Kona," September 1, 1943, 56.05[2], HWRD).

74. Congressional testimony of Robert Shivers, head of the FBI in Hawai'i, January 15, 1946, as quoted in Rademaker and Lane (1951:31).

75. One longtime resident observer of Hawaii's race relations wrote in 1946, "In 1941 [the Japanese community's] wholesale internment was freely predicted; in 1943 threat of permanent relegation to 'second class citizenship' and economic discrimination was still a matter of deep concern. By 1945 its splendid war record had won its acceptance even from those who still dislike it. The person who now talks

publicly about the 'Japanese menace' ... is regarded as a 'nut'" (John Reinecke, "Nisei in Hawaii's Trade Unions," *Pacific Citizen*, December 21, 1946, p. 27).

76. McElrath interview, p. 20.

77. *The Dispatcher*, October 17, 1944, p. 4.

78. The public release of two governmental documents in 1940, both of which critically assessed the high concentration of capital in the Big Five, seems to have been influential in this elaboration. The reports by the NLRB and by the U.S. Department of Labor gained widespread coverage in Hawai'i at the time (Beechert 1985:270–271). They also attracted the attention of ILWU leaders in Hawai'i and San Francisco, who, especially through the report of the Department of Labor, learned of the interlocking directorates among Hawaii's employers. This knowledge was one of the critical factors in the ILWU's decision to fully support the organization of Hawaii's agricultural industries. See "Report of E. J. Eagen on the Hawaiian Islands," pp. 4524–4539, 4598–4624 in USHR (1940); USBLS (1940); Goldblatt interview (by Ward), pp. 298–305, 344; Goldblatt interview (by Zalburg), p. 11; Hall interview; letter to the editor from Ah Quon McElrath, *Honolulu Star-Bulletin*, September 19, 1946; memo from ILWU research department to all locals and units, June 16, 1948, file HI/Correspondence, Reports, etc./Local 136/1937–43, box 5, ILWUSF.

79. *The Dispatcher*, February 20, 1945, p. 4. For earlier examples, see *The Dispatcher*, July 3, July 8, August 15, September 26, and October 17, 1944. See also Hal Hanna, "Big 5 Monopoly in Hawaii," pamphlet, 1945, file Companies/HI/Big Five, ILWUSF.

80. "Notes on Organizing Possibilities in Hawaii," February 1944, file HI/Correspondence, Reports, etc./1944, box 5, ILWUSF; emphasis in original. This report did not bear the name of its author. According to the attached letter, it was drafted by someone at one of the ILWU locals in Hawai'i and mailed to the union's International office in San Francisco. It was later given, as a primer, to at least one organizer who was being sent from the West Coast to Hawai'i. The phrase "national question" may indicate the author's leftist political leanings.

Similarly, an espionage report on an organizing meeting of truck drivers at the Olaa Sugar Company related how one worker compared the fate of his retired father to that of other plantation employees "drawing their fat salaries ... because they are haoles" (R. K. Conant to W. L. S. Williams, April 19, 1944, PSC42/4, HSPAP).

81. Jack Hall's speech before the Territorial Filipino Forum for Inter-Racial Unity, as quoted in *The Dispatcher*, June 28, 1946, p. 17. Emphasis in original.

82. Cf. Hilo Longshoremen's Association, "Resolution," June 23, 1937, file HiLA Minutes & Resolutions 1936–1937, ILWUH.

83. I use the concept of "narrative identity" here because it fits and gives a name to the analysis I am presenting. Concerning Somers's broad claim that all "social life is *storied* and that narrative is an *ontological condition of social life*" (Somers 1994:613–614; emphases in original), I remain skeptically agnostic. In response to a similar article by Somers, Sewell (1992a:487) observes reasonably that much of what she "refer[s] to as narrative could as easily be spoken of as cultural idioms, ideologies, political programs, or moral beliefs," which may call for a narrower application of the "narrative" concept.

84. For examples, see Mat Meehan to Goldblatt and Robertson, April 21, 1944, file HI/ Correspondence, Reports, etc./1944, box 5, ILWUSF; *The Dispatcher*, September 12, 1944, February 9, 1945, and April 19, 1946; Dominador Agayan, Yasuki Arakaki, Leocadio Baldovi, Elias Domingo, Webb Tokeo Ideue, Harry Kamoku, Yoshikazu Morimoto, Hideo "Major" Okada, Constantin Samson, and Thomas Yagi, "Building the ILWU Road to Higher Wages and Better Living in Hawaii: A Report on the Training Program and a Study Manual for Hawaii's Unionists," April 1946, file HI/Local 142/Education Dept./General, ILWUSF; Victor Weingarten, *Raising Cane: A Brief History of Labor in Hawaii* (Honolulu: ILWU, September 1946), LC. See also Goldblatt interview (by Ward), p. 31; "Meehan Back with Report on Hawaii," *The Dispatcher*, June 16, 1944, in Foner and Rosenberg (1993:285–286).

85. *The Dispatcher*, April 19, 1946. An eleventh delegate, Frederick Kamahoahoa, apparently did not complete the program.

86. See regional office to all island strike strategy committees, October 8, 1946, file Sugar Strike 1946/Correspondence/Union/Circular Letters, ILWUH. Of the two, the training manual had a more restricted readership, intended for union officials and "not for general distribution" (minutes of "Meeting for Discussion of Recent Leadership Training Program Given by ILWU for Hawaiian Members," May 21, 1946, file 1946 Leadership Training Program in SF, ILWUH).

87. Dominador Agayan, Yasuki Arakaki, Leocadio Baldovi, Elias Domingo, Webb Tokeo Ideue, Harry Kamoku, Yoshikazu Morimoto, Hideo "Major" Okada, Constantin Samson, and Thomas Yagi, "Building the ILWU Road to Higher Wages and Better Living in Hawaii: A Report on the Training Program and a Study Manual for Hawaii's Unionists," April 1946, p. 59, file HI/Local 142/Education Dept./General, ILWUSF.

88. Ibid., p. 60.

89. Ibid., p. 60.

90. Ibid., p. 60.

91. In other words, all nonhaole workers could claim this collective history the way that most (white) Americans, regardless of their degree of separation from the *Mayflower*, claim the entire U.S. history as *their* history.

92. An International officer who helped organize Hawaii's workers in the 1940s, Bob Robertson reflected two decades later, "I think if I was asked one single item that made it possible to obtain the high degree of organization we have today, I would say it was based on the simple fact that the leaders of the various language and ethnic groups know the value of forgetting" (Robertson interview [by Beechert], p. 5).

93. Most scholars tend to argue the former; Beechert (1985:234–235) strongly asserts the latter. The evidence seems too scant to favor either side definitively. As far as the workers of the 1940s were concerned, the fact that there were "Portuguese," "Japanese," "Filipino," etc. "camps" likely provided the *prima facie* evidence to support the narrative's claim; the practice of racially naming plantation camps had been in place for so long that the workers, and others, probably did not know how it had started.

94. There were multiple layers of slippage and irony when academics later offered an explanation homologous to that of workers whom they studied: like the workers of the 1940s who interpreted their prewar past through the notion of "divide and

rule," giving an interracial coherence to a history rife with racial divisions, scholars of Hawaii's prewar workers adopted the notion of "divide and rule" as the foremost theory for explaining working-class racial divisions (Jung 1999). First, workers and social scientists studying them were accountable to different, though overlapping, standards of validity. The workers' ideology was valid to the degree that it defined, persuaded, and motivated them as a collective subject. That it was not always logically consistent or included amnesias and false memories was not necessarily a flaw, which was, of course, antithetical to social-scientific aims. Second, the deployments of the "divide and rule" notion as workers' ideology and as social-scientific explanation also entailed two quite different understandings of race and class. As workers' ideology, the divide-and-rule narrative provided a new way of articulating racialized concerns. The aim was not to assert the prior importance of class over race, an assertion that would have been, at best, academic and, at worst, self-defeating. Ironically, as social-scientific theory, the divide-and-rule explanation posited the analytical primacy of capitalists' class interests. Third, as ideology, the divide-and-rule narrative was an innovative product and medium of workers' agency. Ironically, as social-scientific theory, the divide-and-rule explanation minimized workers' agency, portraying them, in effect, as "dupes, even if virtuous ones" (Roediger 1991:9). The final irony was that by accepting the workers' historical interpretation as their own, latter-day social scientists may have been the ones duped, even if with virtuous intentions.

95. See Frank Thompson to Louis Goldblatt, January 8, 1945, and Frank Thompson to Louis Goldblatt, April 5, 1945, file HI/Correspondence and Reports/Frank Thompson/1945, box 6, ILWUSF; *The Dispatcher*, July 3, 1945; Goldblatt interview (by Ward), pp. 345–348.

96. Goldblatt interview (by Ward), pp. 319–320; Goldblatt interview (by Beechert), pp. 31–33.

97. Frank Thompson to Louis Goldblatt, September 2, 1944, file HI/Correspondence and Reports/Frank Thompson/1944, box 6, ILWUSF.

98. See the 31 letters from Frank Thompson to Morris Watson, February 27, 1945 to September 25, 1945, file HI/Correspondence and Reports/Frank Thompson/1945, box 6, ILWUSF.

99. Frank Thompson to Louis Goldblatt, December 14, 1944, file HI/Correspondence and Reports/Frank Thompson/1944, box 6, ILWUSF; Frank Thompson to Louis Goldblatt, January 8, 1945, file HI/Correspondence and Reports/Frank Thompson/1945, box 6, ILWUSF; Martin interview.

100. [Island of] Hawaii ILWU Conference Minutes, September 16–17, 1944, file HI/Correspondence, Reports, etc./1944, box 5, ILWUSF.

101. Quotation is from Goldblatt's interview (by Beechert), p. 36. In anticipation of labor strife after martial law, the sugar, pineapple, stevedoring, and other industries organized, in 1943, the Hawaii Employers Council (HEC), whose hired experts assisted them in dealing with unions. The idea to insist on company-by-company elections was apparently James Blaisdell's; with previous experience representing the warehouse industry against the ILWU on the West Coast, Blaisdell had been hired as HEC's president (Goldblatt interview [by Beechert]; Edward Beechert to author, February 11, 2005; Beechert 1985; Brooks 1951).

102. Goldblatt interview (by Beechert), p. 33. In June 1944, Filipinos made up 50.8 percent of the sugar workforce; Japanese and Portuguese made up 36.7 percent and 6.4 percent, respectively (Hawaiian Sugar Planters' Association, "Labor Report of All Islands," June 1944, PSC40/7, HSPAP).

103. I state "particularly Japanese" because the Portuguese, even as the third largest group of workers, were only around one sixth the size of the second largest group of workers, the Japanese. Furthermore, among "skilled" workers, the Portuguese tended to be in supervisory *luna* (foreman) positions, thereby disproportionately placed outside the bargaining unit.

104. The Big Island had the largest number of plantations, though they tended to be smaller in size.

105. Frank Thompson to Louis Goldblatt, September 24, 1945, file HI/Correspondence and Reports/Frank Thompson/1945, box 6, ILWUSF. See also Frank Thompson to Louis Goldblatt, October 1, 1945, file HI/Correspondence and Reports/Frank Thompson/1945, box 6, ILWUSF.

106. Louis Goldblatt, Jack Hall, Jack Kawano, K. K. Kam, and J. R. Robertson, "Memorandum on Conference on Hawaiian Problems," October 1945, file HI/Correspondence, Reports, etc./1944, box 5, ILWUSF. Emphasis added.

107. Zalburg (1979:124–125) suggests that another source of resistance to consolidation may have been some of the locals' and units' reluctance to pool their financial resources.

108. Saburo Fujisaki to J. R. Robertson, December 20, 1945, file HI/Correspondence, Reports, etc./1945–49, box 5, ILWUSF. See also Arakaki interview, pp. 24–25; Hall interview, p. 13; Kotani (1985:ch. 8); Odo (2004:260, 285). In January 1946, the local called for the International to remove Thompson. The International refused and firmly backed Thompson (Leoncio Velasco and Yukinori Fujioka to Harry Bridges, January 18, 1946, Harry Bridges to Frank Thompson, January 22, 1946, and Harry Bridges to Yasuki Arakaki, January 22, 1946, file Local 142 Consolidation: 1944-47, ILWUH).

109. Frank Thompson to Louis Goldblatt, December 28, 1945, file HI/Correspondence and Reports/Frank Thompson/1945, box 6, ILWUSF; letters from Frank Thompson to Louis Goldblatt, January 23, February 4, and May 13, 1946, file HI/Correspondence and Reports/Frank Thompson/1946, box 6, ILWUSF. Because Thompson was so centrally involved in this conflict, his statements should be read with circumspection; at times, in frustration, he revealed his own racial prejudices (see the December 28, 1945 letter; Zalburg 1979:126). See also Arakaki and D. Thompson interviews.

110. Frank Thompson to Louis Goldblatt, February 4, 1946, file HI/Correspondence and Reports/Frank Thompson/1946, box 6, ILWUSF. Emphasis in original.

111. *The Dispatcher*, April 19, 1946, p. 16.

112. Ibid.

113. Yasuki Arakaki to J. R. Robertson, June 26, 1946, file HI/Leadership Training School/1946, Box 6, ILWUSF.

114. Ibid.

115. For an example of lingering tensions on the Big Island that would contribute to the "Ignacio Revolt," discussed later, see Henry Johnson Jr. to all units of Local 142,

Jack Hall, and Frank E. Thompson, November 25, 1946, file Local 142 Consolidation: 1944-47, ILWUH.

116. ILWU Territorial Policy and Sugar Committee, "Statement to All Members of Sugar Locals and Units," January 27, 1945, PSC29/8, HSPAP. A copy of the 1945 agreement is in the same folder.

117. See also Steele interview, p. 2; F. Thompson interview, pp. 25–26.

118. *Honolulu Advertiser*, August 1, 1946. The vote tally was 15,406 in favor and 123 opposed; 22 votes were voided.

119. Application for Authorization to Import Filipino Citizens from the Philippine Islands, submitted by Chauncey B. Wightman, secretary of HSPA, May 21, 1945, and application for Authorization to Import Filipino Citizens from the Philippine Islands, submitted by E. C. Auchter, Vice President of the Pineapple Growers' Association of Hawaii, June 1, 1945, file Miscellaneous/Hawaii Sugar Planters' Association & Pineapple Growers Association of Hawaii/Filipino Labor Importation, IS.

Section 8(a)(1) of the Tydings-McDuffie Act of 1934, which had been included in the law through the HSPA's lobbying efforts, provided Hawaii's industries a loophole in the law's general ban on Filipino immigration. With the authorization of the U.S. Department of Interior and Hawaii's territorial governor, the provision allowed Hawaii's industries to recruit workers from the Philippines to Hawai'i (and only Hawai'i) until the Philippines' full independence from the United States, which took effect on July 4, 1946.

120. Memo from Chauncey B. Wightman to HSPA trustees, June 25, 1945, file Miscellaneous/Hawaii Sugar Planters' Association & Pineapple Growers Association of Hawaii/Filipino Labor Importation, IS.

121. Memo from Chauncey B. Wightman to HSPA trustees, June 29, 1945, file Miscellaneous/Hawaii Sugar Planters' Association & Pineapple Growers Association of Hawaii/Filipino Labor Importation, IS; Beechert (1985:299).

122. War Research Laboratory, University of Hawai'i, "What People in Hawaii Are Saying and Doing, Report No. 7," November 1, 1945, 24.01, HWRD.

123. Jack Hall to Governor Ingram M. Stainback, May 28, 1945, file Miscellaneous/Hawaii Sugar Planters' Association & Pineapple Growers Association of Hawaii/Filipino Labor Importation, IS; emphasis added. See also Joseph A. Kaholokua Jr. to Governor Ingram M. Stainback, June 6, 1945, file Miscellaneous/Hawaii Sugar Planters' Association & Pineapple Growers Association of Hawaii/Filipino Labor Importation, IS; *The Dispatcher*, June 19, 1945.

124. John A. Owens to Governor Ingram M. Stainback, May 29, 1945, file Miscellaneous/Hawaii Sugar Planters' Association & Pineapple Growers Association of Hawaii/Filipino Labor Importation, IS.

125. Robert McElrath, "Filipino Labor Importation," radio broadcast, November 9, 1946, 1.03, HWRD. See also Frank Thompson to Louis Goldblatt, October 1, 1946, file HI/Correspondence and Reports/Frank Thompson/1946, box 6, ILWUSF; *The Dispatcher*, December 3, 1945.

126. ILWU Second Territorial Conference minutes, January 31 to February 2, 1946, pp. 13–17, and "Report of Committee to Confer with Attorney General re: Filipino Labor Importation," February 8, 1946, 38.08, HWRD. See also Frank Thompson

to Louis Goldblatt, February 4, 1946, file HI/Correspondence and Reports/Frank Thompson/1946, box 6, ILWUSF; *The Dispatcher*, February 8, 1946.

127. Corpuz interview; Quitevis interview; F. Thompson interview, p. 18; Luis (1996); Zalburg (1979:134). One oft-told story has workers walking off the ships donning ILWU buttons.

128. Frank Thompson to Louis Goldblatt, May 28, 1946, file HI/Correspondence and Reports/Frank Thompson/1946, box 6, ILWUSF.

129. The territorial strike strategy committee had twenty-four members, eight from sugar units and the remaining from longshoring, pineapple, and miscellaneous units; while all delegates had "voice," only the sugar delegates had voting power to enact strike policies (Zalburg 1979:141).

130. *Allied Labor News*, September 20, 1946.

131. For examples, see files Sugar Strike 1946/Territorial Strike Strategy Committee Minutes, Sugar Strike 1946/Kauai Strike Strategy Committee Minutes, and Sugar Strike 1946/[Island of] Hawaii Strike Strategy Committee Minutes, ILWUH.

132. "Report on Second Day of Territorial Strike Committee Meeting with Filipino Leaders," August 20, 1946, file Sugar Strike 1946/Territorial Strike Strategy Committee Minutes, ILWUH. Emphasis in original.

133. ILWU advertisement, *Honolulu Star-Bulletin* and *Hilo Tribune Herald*, September 28 and 30, 1946, file Sugar Strike 1946/Publicity/Union/Advertisements and Throwaways, ILWUH.

134. Report to the Membership, ILWU sugar negotiating committee, August 28, 1946, file Sugar Strike 1946/Territorial Strike Strategy Committee/Reports to Membership, ILWUH. The union's negotiating committee responded to the employers' assertion that there was no discrimination by "giv[ing] dozens of examples of rank discrimination because of race."

135. Arakaki interview; Dantsuka interview; Goldblatt interview (by Ward); Martin interviews.

136. *The Dispatcher*, September 6, 1946, p. B. The editorial was written in response to an August 31, 1946 *Honolulu Advertiser* editorial denying the existence of racism in Hawai'i. See also letter to the editor from Ronald Toyofuku, *Honolulu Star-Bulletin*, September 2, 1946; Local 145–6, "ILWU–News," October 11, 1946, file 6, box 9, RASRCLF; John Reinecke, "Nisei in Hawaii's Trade Unions," *Pacific Citizen*, December 21, 1946.

137. Territorial strike strategy committee to all island strike strategy committees, October 8, 1946, file Sugar Strike 1946/Correspondence/Union/Circular Letters, ILWUH. For the employers' resistance to the principle of no discrimination, see Report to the Membership, ILWU sugar negotiating committee, August 28, 1946, file Sugar Strike 1946/Territorial Strike Strategy Committee/Reports to Membership, ILWUH; Goldblatt interview (by Beechert).

138. Regional office to all island strike strategy committees, October 8, 1946, file Sugar Strike 1946/Correspondence/Union/Circular Letters, ILWUH.

139. *The Dispatcher*, September 20, 1946, file Sugar Strike 1946/Publicity/Union/ Advertisements and Throw-aways, ILWUH.

140. "The Record," leaflet, territorial strike strategy committee, n.d., file Sugar Strike 1946/Publicity/Union, Leaflets/English, ILWUH.

141. *The Dispatcher*, September 20, 1946, file Sugar Strike 1946/Publicity/Union/ Advertisements and Throw-aways, ILWUH.

142. Territorial strike strategy committee to all island strike strategy committees, October 7, 1946, file Sugar Strike 1946/Correspondence/Union/Circular Letters, ILWUH.

143. Apparently, the union learned of the employers' intentions early on through a sympathetic maid of one of the employers (Zalburg 1979:146–147).

144. [Island of] Hawaii Strike Strategy Committee Minutes, August 29 and September 5, 1946, file Sugar Strike 1946/Hawaii Strike Strategy Committee Minutes, ILWUH; regional office to all sugar locals and units, October 2, 1946, file Sugar Strike 1946/ Correspondence/Union/Circular Letters, ILWUH; confidential negotiating committee minutes, October 14, 1946, file Sugar Strike 1946/Territorial Strike Strategy Committee Minutes, ILWUH.

145. Confidential negotiating committee minutes, October 12, 1946, file Sugar Strike 1946/Territorial Strike Strategy Committee Minutes, ILWUH.

146. Minutes of Special Sugar Strike Committee Meetings of Filipino Leaders, August 19 and 20, 1946, file Sugar Strike 1946/Territorial Strike Strategy Committee Minutes, ILWUH.

147. Territorial strike strategy committee to all island strike strategy committees, September 26, 1946, file Sugar Strike 1946/Correspondence/Union/Circular Letters, ILWUH. See also "Special Meeting of the Big Island ILWU Central Strike Committee," September 9, 1946, file Sugar Strike 1946/Hawaii Strike Strategy Committee Minutes, ILWUH; [Island of] Hawaii Strike Strategy Committee Minutes, September 25, 1946, file Sugar Strike 1946/Hawaii Strike Strategy Committee Minutes, ILWUH; confidential negotiating committee minutes, October 12, 1946, file Sugar Strike 1946/Territorial Strike Strategy Committee Minutes, ILWUH.

148. One of the first things the employers did at the beginning of the strike was to buy and distribute 25,000 copies of the *Filipino News*, a notoriously antiunion weekly ([Island of] Hawaii Strike Strategy Committee Minutes, September 5, 1946, file Sugar Strike 1946/Hawaii Strike Strategy Committee Minutes, ILWUH). During the war, the paper, published on Kaua'i, had colluded with the island's plantations and the military, surveilling Filipino workers and making sure they showed up for work. It had even urged the aggressive prosecution of those Filipinos not working the military-mandated twenty days per month as "vagrants" (Abe A. Albayalde, publisher, to C. E. S. Burns, June 25, 1942, HSPAP).

149. Regional office to all island strike strategy committees, October 8, 1946, file Sugar Strike 1946/Correspondence/Union/Circular Letters, ILWUH. Emphasis in original.

150. Confidential negotiating committee minutes, October 14, 1946, file Sugar Strike 1946/Territorial Strike Strategy Committee Minutes, ILWUH; [Island of] Hawaii Strike Strategy Committee Minutes, October 18, 21, and 23, 1946, file Sugar Strike 1946/Hawaii Strike Strategy Committee Minutes, ILWUH.

151. *The Dispatcher*, September 6, 1946, p. D. The "dumb animals" comment may refer to a remark made by one of the employers' negotiators. ILWU regional director Jack Hall relayed to the territorial strike strategy committee, "People on the other side of the bargaining table have told me that Filipinos are a bunch of animals and don't need good housing" (as quoted in Zalburg 1979:143).

Born in Hawai'i, Ricardo Labez had been a thorn in the side of the sugar industry, on behalf of Filipino workers, since at least the 1930s (C. E. S. Burns to H. B. Wells, August 17, 1936, LPC7/10, HSPAP).

152. The seniority clause was applicable up to the first level above the bargaining unit; thus, management could no longer unilaterally choose even some of its supervisors.

153. Louis Goldblatt, transcript of radio address, November 15, 1946, PSC29/10, HSPAP.

154. Goldblatt interview (by Beechert), p. 33.

155. For examples of continuing racial friction among the workers, see the reports in folder HI/Correspondence and Reports/David Thompson/1946–51, box 6, ILWUSF; D. Thompson interview.

156. For examples of red-baiting during the 1946 sugar strike, see *Honolulu Advertiser*, September 30 and October 13, 1946.

157. Ichiro Izuka, *The Truth about Communism in Hawaii* (Honolulu: n.p., November 15, 1947), HC. For a list of people who helped Izuka publish the pamphlet, see Zalburg (1979:207–208).

158. Izuka initially published 29,000 copies. Later, two people connected to Big Five firms financed the publication and distribution of an Ilocano edition (Zalburg 1979:208–209).

159. Minutes of the Hawaii Division Executive Board Meeting, ILWU Local 142, December 14, 1947, file ILWU Hawaii/History Files/Ignacio Revolt, ILWUH.

160. Union of Hawaiian Workers, pamphlet, December 17, 1947, file HI/History Files/ Ignacio Revolt, ILWUH.

161. However, Japanese, Filipinos, and Hawaiians were among the would-be defectors (ibid.).

162. Since Izuka's pamphlet contained the names of many of the union's top Japanese leaders, Ignacio supposedly decided to combine his antipathy toward them with his apparent antipathy toward communism. See report from Dave Thompson to Lou Goldblatt, J. R. Robertson, and Jack Hall, December 15, 1947, file HI/Correspondence and Reports/David Thompson/1946–51, box 6, ILWUSF; D. Thompson interview, p. 11; McElrath interview, p. 46. See also the statement of Frank Silva, a Portuguese ILWU member from Kaua'i, who stated that Ignacio had told him the defection was a move against Japanese leadership (minutes of the Sugar Unity Conference, January 4, 1948, p. 9, file HI/History Files/Unity Conference, ILWUH).

163. See file HI/Correspondence and Reports/David Thompson/1946–51, box 6, ILWUSF. Between Ignacio's resignation and the start of the conference, Ignacio's lack of rank-and-file support became apparent. However, nobody could be quite sure, and the loss of at least a couple of units seemed possible.

164. *Honolulu Star-Bulletin*, January 20, 1948, p. 6; the percentage was based on the voting on the islands of Hawai'i (5,908 vs. 122) and O'ahu (3,032 vs. 78). Incomplete tallies from Maui and Kaua'i showed similar results (Unity votes, Maui and Kauai Divisions, January 20, 1948, file HI/History Files/Unity Conference/Referendum, ILWUH).

165. In August 1948, UHW tried to wrest collective bargaining agency away from the ILWU in Laupahoehoe through an NLRB election. It lost the election by a margin of 28 to 164. Hawaii Employers Council Research Department, "Unionization of Non-agricultural Sugar Workers in Hawaii," October 1949, PSC44/15, HSPAP.

166. Minutes of the Sugar Unity Conference, January 3, 1948, p. 6, file HI/History Files/ Unity Conference, ILWUH.

167. Ibid., p. 18. Of all the arguments he presented at the conference, it is instructive that Goldblatt later remembered another race-based argument—drawing a parallel between the "yellow menace" and the "red menace"—as having been the most effective in convincing the workers (Goldblatt interview [by Beechert], pp. 45–47; Goldblatt interview [by Ward], pp. 469–470).

168. Other attacks included an intense anti-Communist campaign during the 1949 longshore strike, the 1950 arrival of the House Committee on Un-American Activities to investigate Communism in the islands, and the 1951–52 Smith Act trial and conviction of seven alleged Communists, including the ILWU's regional director.

169. Goldblatt interview (by Beechert), p. 49.

170. The last penny held a large symbolic value for the workers. Since the West Coast longshoremen had recently won a 15¢ gain, a 16¢ increase would have meant a narrowing of the gap.

171. See, for example, seven stevedoring companies, advertisement, "Why Is Arbitration So Important to the ILWU?" *Garden Island*, July 5, 1949.

172. A major omission in *all* historical writings on the 1949 strike that I am aware of is the anti-Filipino racism. This may be symptomatic of the prevailing view that conceives postwar class relations in deracialized terms.

173. Whether or not Filipinos constituted a majority of the strikers is uncertain. Whether or not they accounted for 75 percent of them is even more uncertain. The *Honolulu Advertiser* (July 17, 1949) appears to have derived this figure by extrapolating from police records of a mass arrest: "about three-fourths of the men who were arrested on Honolulu's waterfront recently on charges of massed interference with traffic are not American citizens." Within 3 days, the paper projected the fraction onto the entire longshoring workforce and editorialized about the "1,500 or so aliens" from the Philippines (July 20, 1949). Although the ILWU vigorously contested the anti-Filipino attacks, I have not come across evidence of its contesting the numbers.

According to a 1947 report by the U.S. Department of Labor, Filipinos comprised 48.5 percent of the longshoring labor force—not even a majority, though by far the largest of any group. They were followed by the Japanese (18.7%), "Hawaiians and part-Hawaiians" (17.5%), "Caucasians" (8.3%), and others (7.0%). Still, the percentage of Filipino longshoremen in 1949 could have been somewhat higher than the 1947 Department of Labor figure, if below 75 percent. The 1947 figure was based on only the 3 largest stevedoring firms in Honolulu and Hilo, and Filipinos tended to be a more rural population. The overall trend, from at least the late 1930s, has also been an increase in the proportion of Filipino longshoremen, which may have continued between 1947 and 1949; however, the greatest shift came during the war, which may have stalled or even reversed. Finally, the overall longshoring workforce had shrunk from 1947 to 1949, as the 1947 report estimated the number of workers at 2,500; the effect of this shrinkage on proportions, however, is not clear (USBLS 1948:130–133).

Of the Japanese longshoremen, 74 were noncitizens. Though they would have been affected by anti-"alien" legislation, the primary targets of the attacks were expressly Filipino "aliens" (ILWU, press release, July 18, 1949, file Longshore Strike 1949/Publicity/Union/Press Releases, ILWUH).

174. *Honolulu Advertiser*, July 20, 1949. See also *Honolulu Advertiser*, July 14, 15, 17, 23, and 30, 1949.

Although it published anti-Filipino letters to the editor, the *Honolulu Star-Bulletin* did not publish anti-Filipino editorials. When listing the names of strikers who were arrested for confrontations with strikebreakers, the two Honolulu papers adopted the practice of placing an asterisk next to the names of noncitizens (*Our Times*, August 5, 1949).

175. ILWU, press release, July 18, 1949, file Longshore Strike 1949/Publicity/Union/Press Releases, ILWUH.

176. Territorial strike strategy committee, strike bulletin-54, July 21, 1949, file Longshore Strike 1949/Publicity/Union/Strike Bulletins, ILWUH.

177. Territorial strike strategy committee, strike bulletin-48, July 13, 1949, file Longshore Strike 1949/Publicity/Union/Strike Bulletins, ILWUH.

178. ILWU, press release, March 21, 1949, file Longshore Strike 1949/Publicity/Union/Press Releases, ILWUH.

179. Dantsuka interview. His recollection was slightly off on the wage differential, which was 42¢; the union's demand was 32¢.

180. Territorial strike strategy committee, leaflet, June 15, 1949, file Longshore Strike 1949/Publicity/Union/Strike Bulletins, ILWUH. For a prewar social analysis of "pidgin," see Reinecke (1938).

181. "Notes on Organizing Possibilities in Hawaii," February 1944, file HI/Correspondence, Reports, etc./1944, box 5, ILWUSF; Frank Thompson to Louis Goldblatt, September 30, 1944, file HI/Correspondence and Reports/Frank Thompson/1944, box 6, ILWUSF.

182. The union leadership was apparently convinced that irregular and seasonal workers could be persuaded to join the strike (Zalburg 1979:177).

183. For examples, see T. Oshiro to J. R. Robertson, August 14, 1948, and Clara Yoshimura to Bob Robertson, September 7, 1948, file HI/Correspondence, Reports, etc./Local 152/1946–50, box 5, ILWUSF.

184. The workers rejected the agreement, 618 votes to 33. Pedro de la Cruz to Takeo Furuike, October 28, 1950, file Lanai Strike 1951/Correspondence, ILWUH.

185. File Lanai Strike 1951/Finances/Strike Contributions/Territorial Locals, ILWUH.

186. Kenji Omuro to J. R. Robertson, July 26, 1947, file HI/Correspondence, Reports, etc./Local 152/1946–50, box 5, ILWUSF. In 1948, the plantation employed 1,021 Filipinos, 393 Japanese, and 206 "others" (Tuttle 1959:24). In 1950, there were 1,910 male and 1,226 female residents on this company-owned island, of whom 1,430 males and 730 females were 14 years of age or older—the age at which one could be a part of the labor force. Filipinos were the largest group on the island with 1,083 males and 435 females. The respective numbers for the Japanese were 539 and 488 (U.S. Census 1953:52/22).

187. Pineapple Negotiations, December 14, 1951, file Lanai Strike 1951/Bargaining Sessions, ILWUH.

188. *ILWU Reporter*, May 2, 1951.

189. Takeo Furuike to C. C. Cadagan, April 19, 1949, and Takeo Furuike to Pedro de la Cruz, June 9, 1949, file Hapco/Lanai/Mass Layoffs/1949–50, ILWUH.
190. ILWU Local 152, Unit 7, Strike Bulletin No. 86, June 29, 1951, file Lanai Strike 1951/Publicity/Union/Strike Bulletins, ILWUH.
191. ILWU Local 152, Unit 7, Strike Bulletin No. 8, March 9, 1951, file Lanai Strike 1951/Publicity/Union/Strike Bulletins, ILWUH.
192. ILWU Local 152, Unit 7, Strike Bulletin No. 42, April 18, 1951, file Lanai Strike 1951/Publicity/Union/Strike Bulletins, ILWUH. For a dissimilar case of racial politics of seniority involving the ILWU, see Nelson (2001:ch. 3) and Quam-Wickham (1992).
193. ILWU Local 152, Unit 7, Strike Bulletin No. 69, May 19, 1951, file Lanai Strike 1951/Publicity/Union/Strike Bulletins, ILWUH.

6. Conclusion

1. John E. Reinecke, "What Must We Do?" as quoted in Holmes (1994:100). Reinecke wrote this never-published treatise—with a title alluding to Lenin's "What Is to be Done?"—as a private exercise, sharing it with only a few people. But the army somehow managed to obtain a copy and then passed it on, along with a long list of suspected Communists, to the territorial governor in 1947. Soon thereafter, Governor Stainback launched his anticommunist campaign by, inter alia, portraying the thirteen-year-old document as a revolutionary Communist plan. It should be noted that Reinecke had not been a Communist Party member, and no organized Communist Party had existed in Hawai'i, in 1934 (John Reinecke to Ingram M. Stainback, June 18, 1949, file Communism 1949–1951, IS; Reinecke 1993:22–24; Zalburg 1979:195–196).
2. Kauai strike strategy committee minutes, October 8, 1949, file Longshore Strike 1949/Kauai Strike Strategy Committee Minutes, ILWUH.
3. ILWU Local 152, Unit 7, Strike Bulletin No. 86, June 29, 1951, file Lanai Strike 1951/Publicity/Union/Strike Bulletins, ILWUH. Emphasis in original.
4. More generally, I submit there is an "obvious" quality to all social identities once they are achieved.
5. For example, the ever growing literature on the historical making of whiteness, which includes both working-class and nonworking-class varieties, can be read fruitfully as providing examples of interracialism that are neither deracialized nor progressive (e.g., Jacobson 1998; Roediger 1991).
6. For examples of other studies related to labor, see Boswell and Brown (1995), Brueggemann (1994), Brown and Brueggemann (1997), and Brueggemann and Boswell (1998), discussed in chapter 1.
7. See also Jung and Almaguer (2004).
8. For examples, see ILWU (1996, 1997) and any number of oral histories, some of which appear in the bibliography. For a contrasting case of racial politics of memory involving the ILWU, see Nelson (2001:ch. 3).

Bibliography

Archival Collections

EB   Edward Beechert Papers. Labor History Archive, Center for Labor Education and Research, University of Hawai'i, West O'ahu.

HC   Hawaiian Collection. Special Collections, University of Hawai'i, Mānoa.

HM   Hilo Massacre Files. Labor History Archive, Center for Labor Education and Research, University of Hawai'i, West O'ahu.

HPCDC   Archives of Hawaiian Pineapple Company/Dole Corporation. Special Collections, University of Hawai'i, Mānoa.

HSPAP   Hawaiian Sugar Planters' Association Plantation Archives. Special Collections, University of Hawai'i, Mānoa.

HWRD   Hawai'i War Records Depository. Special Collections, University of Hawai'i, Mānoa.

ILWUC   International Longshore and Warehouse Union Collection. Labor History Archive, Center for Labor Education and Research, University of Hawai'i, West O'ahu.

ILWUH   Records of the International Longshore and Warehouse Union. Priscilla Shishido Library, ILWU Local 142, Honolulu.

ILWUSF   Records of the International Longshore and Warehouse Union. Anne Rand Research Library, ILWU, San Francisco.

IS   Ingram Macklin Stainback Papers. State Archives of Hawai'i, Honolulu.

LC   Labadie Collection. Special Collections Library, University of Michigan, Ann Arbor.

MQ   Manuel Quezon Papers. Special Collections, University of Hawai'i, Mānoa.

NA   Records of the National Labor Relations Board (RG 25). National Archives and Records Administration, College Park, Maryland.

PE   Plantation Era Files. Labor History Archive, Center for Labor Education and Research, University of Hawai'i, West O'ahu.

RASRLC   Romanzo Adams Social Research Laboratory Clippings. Special Collec-
         tions, University of Hawaiʻi, Mānoa.
RASRLCF Romanzo Adams Social Research Laboratory Confidential Files. Special
         Collections, University of Hawaiʻi, Mānoa.
SZ   Sanford Zalburg Papers. Special Collections, University of Hawaiʻi, Mānoa.
WF   Wallace Rider Farrington Papers. State Archives of Hawaiʻi, Honolulu.

Periodicals

Allied Labor News
American Magazine
Dispatcher, Hawaiian Edition
Garden Island
Hawaii Hōchi
Hawaii Shimpō
Hawaiian Annual
Honolulu Advertiser
Honolulu Star-Bulletin
Honolulu Times
ILWU Reporter
Kazan
Labor Today
Maui Record
Maui Shinbun
New Freedom
New York Commercial
News-Tribune
Nippu Jiji
Our Times
Pacific Citizen
Pacific Commercial Advertiser
Paradise of the Pacific
Planters' Monthly
San Francisco Chronicle
Saturday Evening Post
Voice of the ILWU
Walker's Manual of Pacific Coast Securities
Yōen Jihō

Oral History Interviews

Anonymous and Gregario Oroc. Interviews by Ed Gerlock and Chad Taniguchi.
    October 31 and December 5, 1978. Transcript in *The 1924 Filipino Strike on Kauai*,
    vol. 2. Ethnic Studies Oral History Project, University of Hawaiʻi, Mānoa.

Arakaki, Yasuki. Interview by [Chris Conybeare]. April 23, 1996. Transcript. Center for Labor Education and Research for Rice & Roses program "1946: The Great Hawaii Sugar Strike," University of Hawai'i, West O'ahu.

Arakaki, Yasuki and Kenji Omuro. Interviews by Edward Beechert. April 20 and May 4, 1966. Transcript, Pacific Regional Oral History Program, EB.

Arashiro, Matsuki. Interview by Sanford Zalburg. January 26, 1976. Notes, File 28, Box 3, SZ.

Bailey, Bill. Interview by Sanford Zalburg. June 27, 1973. Transcript, File 28, Box 3, SZ.

Baysa, Faustino. Interview by Vivien Lee. June 1976. Transcript in *Waialua and Haleiwa: The People Tell Their Story*, vol. 3. Ethnic Studies Oral History Project, University of Hawai'i, Mānoa.

Berman, Edward. Interview by Sanford Zalburg. April 29, 1974. Transcript, File 18, Box 2, SZ.

Bridges, Harry. Interview by Sanford Zalburg. June 1, 1975. Transcript, File 22-A, Box 2, SZ.

Cabico, Emigdio. Interview by Pablo Lazo. June and July 1976. Transcript in *Waialua and Haleiwa: The People Tell Their Story*, vol. 3. Ethnic Studies Oral History Project, University of Hawai'i, Mānoa.

Claveria, Moses P. Interview by Sanford Zalburg. August 10, 1974. Notes, File 28, Box 3, SZ.

Corpuz, Jose. Interview by Gael Gouveia. June 1976. Transcript in *Waialua and Haleiwa: The People Tell Their Story*, vol. 3. Ethnic Studies Oral History Project, University of Hawai'i, Mānoa.

Damaso, Carl. Interview by Sanford Zalburg. August 4, 1975. Notes, File 28, Box 3, SZ.

Dantsuka, George. Interview by author. April 11, 1997. Tape recording.

de la Cruz, Justo. Interview by Perry Nakayama. June 1976. Transcript in *Waialua and Haleiwa: The People Tell Their Story*, vol. 3. Ethnic Studies Oral History Project, University of Hawai'i, Mānoa.

Faye, Lindsay Anton. Interview by Chad Taniguchi. December 9, 1978. Transcript in *The 1924 Filipino Strike on Kauai*, vol. 2. Ethnic Studies Oral History Project, University of Hawai'i, Mānoa.

Fern, Charles James. Interviews by Chad Taniguchi. December 14, 1978 and May 16, 1979. Transcript in *The 1924 Filipino Strike on Kauai*, vol. 2. Ethnic Studies Oral History Project, University of Hawai'i, Mānoa.

Goldblatt, Louis. Interview by Sanford Zalburg. September 17, 1975. Transcript, File 22-B, Box 2, SZ.

——. Interviews by Estolv Ethan Ward. 1978 and 1979. Transcript in *Working Class Leader in the ILWU, 1935–1977*. Regional Oral History Office, Bancroft Library, University of California, Berkeley.

——. Interviews by Edward Beechert. July 22 and October 31, 1979. Transcript, Pacific Regional Oral History Program, EB.

Goto, George (Furuya, Noboru). Interview by Sanford Zalburg. February 1, 1976. Notes, File 29, Box 3, SZ.

Gueco, Frank. Interview by Araceli Agoo. July 1976. Notes in *Waialua and Haleiwa: The People Tell Their Story*, vol. 3. Ethnic Studies Oral History Project, University of Hawai'i, Mānoa.

Hall, Jack. Interview by Edward Beechert. August 1, 1966. Transcript No. 10, Pacific Regional Oral History Program, University of Hawai'i.

Holmberg, Adam. Interview by Gael Gouveia. June 1976. Transcript in *Waialua and Haleiwa: The People Tell Their Story*, vol. 8. Ethnic Studies Oral History Project, University of Hawai'i, Mānoa.

Izuka, Ichiro. Interviews by Sanford Zalburg. Honolulu, August 14, 21, and 28, 1975. Transcript and notes, File 29, Box 3, SZ.

Kamoku, Isaac Kekaulike (Chicken). Interview by Sanford Zalburg. September 5, 1973. Notes, File 31-A, Box 3, SZ.

Kawano, Jack. Interview by Sanford Zalburg. September 4, 1974. Transcript, File 23, Box 2, SZ.

Kealalio, Joseph (Joe Blurr). Interview by Sanford Zalburg. February 25, 1975. Transcript, File 23, Box 2, SZ.

McElrath, Robert. Interview by Sanford Zalburg. March 28, 1975. Transcript, File 25, Box 2, SZ.

Martin, George. Interview by Harvey Schwartz. July 8, 1983. Tape recording, ILWU Oral History Project, ILWUSF.

———. Interview by author. April 10, 1997. Tape recording.

Nakamoto, Haruo (Dyna). Interview by Sanford Zalburg. January 27, 1976. Notes, File 30, Box 3, SZ.

Nakano, Bert. Interview by Chris Conybeare. n.d. Transcript, HM.

———. Interview by Sanford Zalburg. September 6, 1973. Transcript, File 24, Box 1, SZ.

Otanza, Tommy. Interview by Bruce Dunford and John Atkinson. March 15, 1967. Transcript No. 15, Pacific Regional Oral History Program, University of Hawai'i.

Paaluhi, Edwin. Interview by Sanford Zalburg. September 7, 1973. Notes, File 31A, Box 3, SZ.

Quitevis, Benny. Interview by author. April 11, 1997. Tape recording.

Ramos, Avelino (Abba). Interview by author. July 12, 1996. Notes.

———. Interview by author. April 10, 1997. Tape recording.

Robertson, James R. (Bob). Interview by Edward Beechert. June 6, 1967. Transcript, Pacific Regional Oral History Program, EB.

———. Interview by Sanford Zalburg. September 26, 1974. Transcript, File 26, Box 3, SZ.

Thompson, David E. Interview by Edward Beechert. July 20, 1966. Transcript, Pacific Regional Oral History Program, EB.

Thompson, Frank. Interview by Edward Beechert. January 29, 1967. Transcript No. 23, Pacific Regional Oral History Program, University of Hawai'i.

Weisbarth, Marcus K. (Maxie). Interview by Sanford Zalburg. September 1, 1975. Transcript, File 27, Box 3, SZ.

Published Government Documents

U.S. Department of Commerce, Bureau of the Census. 1953. *Census of Population: 1950, Volume II, Characteristics of the Population, Parts 51–54, Territories and Possessions.* Washington, DC: Government Printing Office.

U.S. Department of Commerce and Labor, Bureau of Labor (USBL). 1902. "Report of the Commissioner of Labor on Hawaii, 1901." 57th Congress, 1st Session, Serial Set 4231, Vol. 13, Senate Document No. 169. Washington, DC: Government Printing Office.

——. 1903. *Report of the Commissioner of Labor on Hawaii.* Bulletin No. 47. Washington, DC: Government Printing Office.

——. 1906. *Third Report of the Commissioner of Labor on Hawaii.* Bulletin No. 66. Washington, DC: Government Printing Office.

——. 1911. "Fourth Report of the Commissioner of Labor on Hawaii, 1910." 61st Congress, 3rd Session, Senate Document No. 866. Washington, DC: Government Printing Office.

U.S. Department of Justice (USDJ). 1932. "Law Enforcement in the Territory of Hawaii." 72nd Congress, 1st Session, Serial Set 9511, Vol. 78, Senate Document No. 78. Washington, DC: Government Printing Office.

U.S. Department of Labor (USDL). 1970. *A Brief History of the American Labor Movement.* Washington, DC: Government Printing Office.

——, Bureau of Labor Statistics (USBLS). 1916. "Fifth Report of the Commissioner of Labor Statistics on Labor Conditions in the Territory of Hawaii." 64th Congress, 1st Session, Serial Set 6952, Vol. 42, Senate Document No. 432. Washington, DC: Government Printing Office.

——, ——. 1931. *Labor Conditions in the Territory of Hawaii, 1929–1930.* Bulletin No. 534. Washington, DC: Government Printing Office.

——, ——. 1940. *Labor in the Territory of Hawaii, 1939.* Bulletin No. 687. Washington, DC: Government Printing Office.

——, ——. 1948. *The Economy of Hawaii in 1947.* Bulletin No. 926. Washington, DC: Government Printing Office.

——, Women's Bureau (USWB). 1930. *The Employment of Women in the Pineapple Canneries of Hawaii.* Bulletin No. 82. Washington, DC: Government Printing Office.

——, ——. 1940. *Earnings and Hours in Hawaii: Woman-Employing Industries.* Bulletin No. 177. Washington, DC: Government Printing Office.

——, Immigration and Naturalization Service (INS). 1935. "Enforcement of Immigration Laws in Relation to Insular Possessions and Territories." [2nd Series], Lecture No. 31, January 14, 1935. (http://uscis.gov/graphics/aboutus/history/LS31.htm)

U.S. House of Representatives (USHR). 1940. "Hearing before the Special Committee to Investigate the National Labor Relations Board." 76th Congress, 3rd Session, Vol. 22, May 2–3, 1940, pp. 4485–4685. Washington, DC: Government Printing Office.

——. 1941. "Report of the Special Committee to Investigate the National Labor Relations Board." 76th Congress, 3rd Session, Serial Set 10446, Vol. 7, House Report 3109. Washington, DC: Government Printing Office.

U.S. Senate. 1894. "Report from the Committee on Foreign Relations and Appendix in Relation to the Hawaiian Islands." 53rd Congress, 2nd Session, February 26, 1894, No. 227. Washington, DC: Government Printing Office.

Published Primary and Secondary Sources

Adams, Romanzo and Dan Kane-Zo Kai. 1928. *The Education of the Boys of Hawaii and Their Economic Outlook.* Honolulu: University of Hawai'i Research Publication.

Adler, Jacob. 1966. *Claus Spreckels: The Sugar King in Hawaii*. Honolulu: University of Hawai'i Press.

Agee, H. P. 1934. "A Brief History of the Hawaiian Sugar Planters' Association." *Hawaiian Annual* 1935:72–86.

Allen, Gwenfread. 1950. *Hawaii's War Years, 1941–1945*. Honolulu: University of Hawai'i Press.

Aller, Curtis. 1957. *Labor Relations in the Hawaiian Sugar Industry*. Berkeley: University of California, Institute of Industrial Relations.

Almaguer, Tomás. 1984. "Racial Domination and Class Conflict in Capitalist Agriculture: The Oxnard Sugar Beet Workers' Strike of 1903." *Labor History* 25:325–350.

——. 1994. *Racial Fault Lines: The Historical Origins of White Supremacy in California*. Berkeley: University of California Press.

Ancheta, Angelo N. 1998. *Race, Rights, and the Asian American Experience*. New Brunswick, NJ: Rutgers University Press.

Anderson, Benedict. 1991. *Imagined Communities: Reflections on the Origin and Spread of Nationalism*. New York: Verso.

Anderson, Robert N. with Richard Coller and Rebecca F. Pestano. 1984. *Filipinos in Rural Hawaii*. Honolulu: University of Hawai'i Press.

Anthias, Floya and Nira Yuval-Davis. 1992. *Racialized Boundaries: Race, Nation, Gender, Colour and Class and the Anti-racist Struggle*. New York: Routledge.

Anthony, J. Garner. 1955. *Hawaii Under Army Rule*. Stanford: Stanford University Press.

Arnesen, Eric. 1991. *Waterfront Workers of New Orleans: Race, Class, and Politics, 1863–1923*. New York: Oxford University Press.

——. 1998. "Up from Exclusion: Black and White Workers, Race, and the State of Labor History." *Reviews in American History* 26 (1): 146–174.

Azuma, Eiichiro. 2005. *Between Two Empires: Race, History, and Transnationalism in Japanese America*. New York: Oxford University Press.

Baganha, Maria Ioannis Benis. 1991. "The Social Mobility of Portuguese Immigrants in the United States at the Turn of the Nineteenth Century." *International Migration Review* 25 (2): 277–299.

Bailey, Bill. 1993. *The Kid from Hoboken: An Autobiography*. San Francisco: Circus Lithographic Prepress.

Bailey, Thomas A. 1931. "Japan's Protest against the Annexation of Hawaii." *Journal of Modern History* 3 (1): 46–61.

Baker, Ray Stannard. 1912. "Human Nature in Hawaii." *The American Magazine* 73:328–339.

Balch, J. A. 1942. *Shall the Japanese Be Allowed to Dominate Hawaii?* Honolulu: Privately published.

Baldwin, Arthur D. 1915. *A Memoir of Henry Perrine Baldwin, 1842 to 1911*. Cleveland: Privately published.

Balibar, Etienne. 1991. "Racism and Nationalism." In *Race, Nation, Class: Ambiguous Identities*, by Etienne Balibar and Immanuel Wallerstein, 37–67. New York: Verso.

Barrett, James R. and David Roediger. 1997. "Inbetween Peoples: Race, Nationality and the New Immigrant Working Class." In *American Exceptionalism?*, ed. Rick Halpern and Jonathan Morris, 181–220. New York: St. Martin's Press.

Beechert, Edward D. 1977. "Racial Divisions and Agricultural Labor Organizing in Hawaii." Unpublished paper, ILWU Papers, San Francisco.

——. 1982. "Racial Divisions and Agricultural Labor Organizing in Hawaii." In *American Labor in the Southwest: The First One Hundred Years*, ed. James Foster, 112–120. Tucson: University of Arizona Press.

——. 1984. "The Political Economy of Hawaii and Working Class Consciousness." *Social Process in Hawaii* 31:155–181.

——. 1985. *Working in Hawaii: A Labor History*. Honolulu: University of Hawaiʻi Press.

——. 1988. "Technology and the Plantation Labour Supply: The Case of Queensland, Hawaii, Louisiana and Cuba." In *The World Sugar Economy in War and Depression, 1914–40*, ed. Bill Albert and Adrian Graves, 131–141. New York: Routledge.

——. 1989. "Mechanization and the Plantation Labor Supply." In *One World, One Institution: The Plantation*, ed. Sue Eakin and John Tarver, 111–153. Baton Rouge: Louisiana State University Agricultural Center.

——. 1991. *Honolulu: Crossroads of the Pacific*. Columbia: University of South Carolina Press.

——. 1993. "Patterns of Resistance and the Social Relations of Production in Hawaii." In *Plantation Workers: Resistance and Accommodation*, ed. Brij V. Lal, Doug Munro, and Edward D. Beechert, 45–67. Honolulu: University of Hawaiʻi Press.

Bonacich, Edna. 1972. "A Theory of Ethnic Antagonism: The Split Labor Market." *American Sociological Review* 37:533–547.

——. 1984. "Asian Labor in the Development of California and Hawaii." In *Labor Migration Under Capitalism: Asian Workers in the United States Before World War II*, ed. Lucie Cheng and Edna Bonacich, 130–185. Berkeley: University of California Press.

——. 1992. "Reflections on Asian American Labor." *Amerasia Journal* 18 (1): xxi–xxvii.

Bonilla-Silva, Eduardo. 1997. "Rethinking Racism: Toward a Structural Interpretation." *American Sociological Review* 62:465–480.

Boswell, Terry E. 1986. "A Split Labor Market Analysis of Discrimination Against Chinese Immigrants, 1850–1882." *American Sociological Review* 51:352–371.

Boswell, Terry E. and Cliff Brown. 1995. "Strikebreaking or Solidarity in the General Steel Strike of 1919: A Split Labor Market, Game-Theoretic, and QCA Analysis." *American Journal of Sociology* 100 (6): 1479–1519.

Bourdieu, Pierre. 1977. *Outline of a Theory of Practice*. New York: Cambridge University Press.

——. 1984. *Distinction*. Cambridge, MA: Harvard University Press.

——. 1990a. *In Other Words: Essays Towards a Reflexive Sociology*. Stanford: Stanford University Press.

——. 1990b. *The Logic of Practice*. Stanford: Stanford University Press.

——. 1991. *Language and Symbolic Power*. Cambridge, MA: Harvard University Press.

——. 1994. "Rethinking the State: Genesis and Structure of the Bureaucratic Field." *Sociological Theory* 12 (1): 1–18.

Brooks, Philip. 1952. "Multiple-Industry Unionism in Hawaii." Ph.D. diss., Columbia University.

Brown, Cliff and John Brueggemann. 1997. "Mobilizing Interracial Solidarity: A Comparison of the 1919 and 1937 Steel Industry Labor Organizing Drives." *Mobilization* 2 (1): 47–70.

Brubaker, Rogers. 1998. "Myths and Misconceptions in the Study of Nationalism." In *The State of the Nation*, ed. John A. Hall, 272–306. New York: Cambridge University Press.

Brueggemann, John. 1994. "Realizing Solidarity: Comparative Historical Analyses of Inter-racial Labor Organizing in the Coal, Steel and Auto Industries, 1927–1941." Ph.D. diss., Emory University.

Brueggemann, John and Boswell, Terry. 1998. "Realizing Solidarity: Sources of Interracial Unionism During the Great Depression." *Work and Occupations* 25 (4): 436–482.

Burawoy, Michael. 1981. "The Capitalist State in South Africa: Marxist and Sociological Perspectives on Race and Class." *Political Power and Social Theory* 2:279–335.

Calhoun, Craig. 1982. *The Question of Class Struggle*. Chicago: University of Chicago Press.

——. 1983. "The Radicalism of Tradition: Community Strength or Venerable Disguise and Borrowed Language?" *American Journal of Sociology* 88:886–914.

——. 1997. *Nationalism*. Minneapolis: University of Minnesota Press.

Cariaga, Roman R. [1936] 1974. *The Filipinos in Hawaii: A Survey of Their Economic and Social Conditions*. San Francisco: R and E Research Associates.

Chang, Jeff. 1996. "Lessons of Tolerance: Americanism and the Filipino Affirmative Action Movement in Hawaiʻi." *Social Process in Hawaii* 37:112–146.

Chapin, Helen Geracimos. 1996. *Shaping History: The Role of Newspapers in Hawaiʻi.* Honolulu: University of Hawaiʻi Press.

Chapman, Royal N. 1933. *Cooperation in the Hawaiian Pineapple Business*. New York: American Council, Institute for Pacific Relations.

——. 1934. "The Hawaiian Pineapple Industry in Depression Years." *Hawaiian Annual* (1935):87–89.

Char, Tin-Yuke. 1975. *The Sandalwood Mountains: Readings and Stories of the Early Chinese in Hawaii*. Honolulu: University of Hawaiʻi Press.

Cheng, Lucie and Edna Bonacich, eds. 1984. *Labor Immigration Under Capitalism: Asian Workers in the United States Before World War II*. Berkeley: University of California Press.

Coffman, Tom. 1973. *Catch a Wave: A Case Study of Hawaii's New Politics*. Honolulu: University Press of Hawaiʻi.

Coman, Katharine. 1903. *The History of Contract Labor in the Hawaiian Islands*. New York: American Economic Association and Macmillan.

Conroy, Hilary. [1949] 1973. *The Japanese Expansion Into Hawaii, 1868–1898*. San Francisco: R and E Research Associates.

Cooper, George and Gavan Daws. 1985. *Land and Power in Hawaii: The Democratic Years*. Honolulu: University of Hawaiʻi Press.

Cordova, Fred. 1983. *Filipinos: Forgotten Asian Americans*. Seattle: Demonstration Project for Asian Americans.

Coulter, J. W. 1933. *Land Utilization in the Hawaiian Islands*. Honolulu: University of Hawaiʻi Research Publication, no. 8.

Dahl, Robert A. 1958. "A Critique of the Ruling Elite Model." *American Political Science Review* 52:463–469.

Daniels, Roger. 1988. *Asian America: Chinese and Japanese in the United States Since 1850*. Seattle: University of Washington Press.

Daws, Gavan. 1968. *Shoal of Time: A History of the Hawaiian Islands*. New York: MacMillan.

Day, A. Grove. 1984. *History Makers of Hawaii: A Biographical Dictionary*. Honolulu: Mutual Publishing.

Dean, Arthur L. 1933. *Cooperation in the Sugar Industry of Hawaii*. New York: American Council, Institute of Pacific Relations.

———. 1950. *Alexander & Baldwin, Ltd. and the Predecessor Partnerships*. Honolulu: Alexander & Baldwin, Ltd.

Dirks, Nicholas B., Geoff Eley, and Sherry B. Ortner. 1994. "Introduction." In *Culture/Power/History: A Reader in Contemporary Social Theory*, ed. Nicholas B. Dirks, Geoff Eley, and Sherry B. Ortner, 3–45. Princeton: Princeton University Press.

Dole, Richard and Elizabeth Dole Porteus. 1990. *The Story of James Dole*. ʻAiea, HI: Island Heritage Publishing.

Dubofsky, Melvyn. 1994. *The State and Labor in Modern America*. Chapel Hill: University of North Carolina Press.

Duus, Masayo Umezawa. 1999. *The Japanese Conspiracy: The Oahu Sugar Strike of 1920*. Berkeley: University of California Press.

Dye, Bob. 1997. *Merchant Prince of the Sandalwood Mountains: Afong and the Chinese in Hawaiʻi*. Honolulu: University of Hawaiʻi Press.

Eley, Geoff. 1996. "Is All the World a Text? From Social History to the History of Society Two Decades Later." In *The Historic Turn in the Human Sciences*, ed. Terrence J. McDonald, 193–243. Ann Arbor: University of Michigan Press.

Eliel, Paul. 1949. "Industrial Peace and Conflict: A Study of Two Pacific Coast Industries." *Industrial and Labor Relations Review* 2 (3): 477–501.

Emmet, Boris. 1928. *The California and Hawaiian Sugar Refining Corporation*. Stanford: Stanford University Press.

Espiritu, Yen Le. 1992. *Asian American Panethnicity*. Philadelphia: Temple University Press.

Estep, Gerald A. 1941a. "Portuguese Assimilation in Hawaii and California." *Sociology and Social Research* 26:61–69.

———. 1941b. "Social Placement of the Portuguese in Hawaii as Indicated by Factors in Assimilation." M.A. thesis, University of Southern California.

Ethnic Studies Oral History Project (ESOHP). 1979. *Women Workers in Hawaii's Pineapple Industry*, vol. 1. Honolulu: Ethnic Studies Program, University of Hawaiʻi at Mānoa.

Ethnic Studies Oral History Project and United Okinawan Association of Hawaii (UOAH). 1981. *Uchinanchu: A History of Okinawans in Hawaii*. Honolulu: ESOHP, University of Hawaiʻi.

Fantasia, Rick R. 1988. *Cultures of Solidarity: Consciousness, Action, and Contemporary American Workers*. Berkeley: University of California Press.

———. 1995. "From Class Consciousness to Culture, Action, and Social Organization." *Annual Review of Sociology* 21:269–287.

Felipe, Virgilio M. 1970a. "1938 Inter-Island Shipping Strike in Hawaii: A Lesson in Political Unionism." Unpublished paper, Hawaiian Collection, Special Collections, University of Hawaiʻi, Mānoa.

———. 1970b. "The Vibora Luviminda and the 1937 Puunene Plantation Strike." Unpublished paper, Hawaiian Collection, Special Collections, University of Hawaiʻi, Mānoa.

Felix, John Henry and Peter F. Senecal. 1978. *The Portuguese in Hawaii*. Honolulu: Privately published.

Foner, Philip S. and Daniel Rosenberg, eds. 1993. *Racism, Dissent, and Asian Americans from 1850 to the Present*. Westport, CT: Greenwood Press.

Francisco, Luviminda. 1987. "The Philippine-American War." In *The Philippines Reader: A History of Colonialism, Neocolonialism, Dictatorship, and Resistance*, ed. Daniel B. Schirmer and Stephen R. Shalom, 8–20. Boston: South End Press.

Freitas, J. F. [1930] 1992. *Portuguese-Hawaiian Memories*. Newark, CA: Communications Concepts.

Friday, Chris. 1994. "Asian American Labor and Historical Interpretation." *Labor History* 35 (4): 524–546.

Fuchs, Lawrence H. 1961. *Hawaii Pono: A Social History*. New York: Harcourt, Brace and World.

Geschwender, James A. 1981. "The Interplay Between Class and National Consciousness: Hawaii 1850–1950." *Research in the Sociology of Work* 1:171–204.

——. 1982. "The Hawaiian Transformation: Class, Submerged Nation, and National Minorities." In *Ascent and Decline in the World-System*, ed. Edward Friedman, 189–226. Beverly Hills, CA: Sage.

——. 1983. "The Capitalist World-System and the Making of the American Working Class." *Contemporary Sociology* 14 (4): 421–424.

——. 1987. "Race, Ethnicity, and Class." In *Recapturing Marxism: An Appraisal of Recent Trends in Sociological Theory*, ed. Rhonda Levine and Jerry Lembke, 136–160. New York: Praeger.

Geschwender, James A., Rita Carroll-Seguin, and Howard Brill. 1988. "The Portuguese and Haoles of Hawaii: Implications for the Origin of Ethnicity." *American Sociological Review* 53:515–527.

Geschwender, James A. and Rhonda F. Levine. 1983. "Rationalization of Sugar Production in Hawaii: A Dimension of Class Struggle." *Social Problems* 30 (3): 352–368.

——. 1986. "Class Struggle and Political Transformation in Hawaii, 1946–1960." *Research in Political Sociology* 2:243–268.

Giddens, Anthony. 1984. *The Constitution of Society: Outline of a Theory of Structuration*. Berkeley: University of California Press.

Gilroy, Paul. [1987] 1991. *'There Ain't No Black in the Union Jack': The Cultural Politics of Race and Nation*. Chicago: University of Chicago Press.

Gitlin, Todd. 1995. *Twilight of Our Common Dreams: Why America Is Wracked by Culture Wars*. New York: Metropolitan Books.

Glazer, Nathan. 1971. "Blacks and Ethnic Groups: The Difference, and the Political Difference It Makes." *Social Problems* 18:444–461.

Glenn, Evelyn Nakano. 2002. *Unequal Freedom: How Race and Gender Shaped American Citizenship and Labor*. Cambridge, MA: Harvard University Press.

Glick, Clarence E. 1980. *Sojourners and Settlers: Chinese Migrants in Hawaii*. Honolulu: Hawaii Chinese History Center and University of Hawai'i Press.

Go, Julian. 2004. "'Racism' and Colonialism: Meanings of Difference and Ruling Practices in America's Pacific Empire." *Qualitative Sociology* 27 (1): 35–58.

Goldberg, David Theo. 1993. *Racist Culture: Philosophy and the Politics of Meaning*. Cambridge, MA: Blackwell.

Bibliography 269

Goldfield, Michael. 1993a. "Race and the CIO: The Possibilities for Racial Egalitarianism During the 1930s and 1940s." *International Labor and Working-Class History* 44:1–32.

——. 1993b. "Race and the CIO: Reply to Critics." *International Labor and Working-Class History* 44:142–160.

Goodwin, Jeff and James M. Jasper. 1999. "Caught in a Winding, Snarling Vine: The Structural Bias of Political Process Theory." *Sociological Forum* 14 (1): 27–54.

Gramsci, Antonio. 1971. *Selections from the Prison Notebooks.* New York: International Publishers.

Griffin, Larry J. 1995. "How Is Sociology Informed by History?" *Social Forces* 73 (4): 1245–1254.

Griffin, Larry J. and Robert R. Korstad. 1995. "Class as Race and Gender: Making and Breaking a Labor Union in the Jim Crow South." *Social Science History* 19 (4): 425–454.

Griffin, Larry J., Michael E. Wallace, and Beth A. Rubin. 1986. "Capitalist Resistance to the Organization of Labor Before the New Deal: Why? How? Success?" *American Sociological Review* 51:147–167.

Gross, James A. 1981. *The Reshaping of the National Labor Relations Board: National Labor Policy in Transition, 1937–1947.* Albany: State University of New York Press.

Hall, Stuart. 1980. "Race, Articulation and Societies Structured in Dominance." In *Sociological Theories: Race and Colonialism,* ed. United Nations Educational, Scientific and Cultural Organization, 305–345. Paris: UNESCO.

——. 1986. "Gramsci's Relevance for the Study of Race and Ethnicity." *Journal of Communication Inquiry* 10 (2): 5–27.

Hall, Stuart, Chas Critcher, Tony Jefferson, John Clarke, and Brian Roberts. 1978. *Policing the Crisis: Mugging, the State, and Law and Order.* New York: Holmes & Meier.

Halpern, Rick. 1994. "Organized Labour, Black Workers and the Twentieth-Century South: The Emerging Revision." *Social History* 19 (3): 359–383.

Haney-López, Ian F. 1996. *White by Law: The Legal Construction of Race.* New York: New York University Press.

Harada, Tasuku. 1927. *The Social Status of the Japanese in Hawaii: Some of the Problems Confronting the Second Generation.* Honolulu: Institute of Pacific Relations.

Harris, Howell John. 2000. *Bloodless Victories: The Rise and Fall of the Open Shop in the Philadelphia Metal Trades, 1890–1940.* New York: Cambridge University Press.

Haydu, Jeffrey. 1989. "Trade Agreement vs. Open Shop: Employers' Choices before WWI." *Industrial Relations* 28 (2): 159–173.

——. 2002. "Business Citizenship at Work: Cultural Transposition and Class Formation in Cincinnati, 1870–1910." *American Journal of Sociology* 107 (6): 1424–1467.

Hill, Herbert. 1996. "The Problem of Race in American Labor History." *Reviews in American History* 24 (2): 189–208.

Hobsbawm, Eric. 1989. *The Age of Empire, 1875–1914.* New York: Vintage.

——. 1996. "Identity Politics and the Left." *New Left Review* 217:38–47.

Hobson, Thos. C. 1897. "Japan's 'Peaceful Invasion.'" *Hawaiian Annual* (1898):131–134.

Hodson, Randy. 1983. *Workers' Earnings and Corporate Economic Structure.* New York: Academic Press.

Hoganson, Kristin L. 1998. *Fighting for American Manhood: How Gender Politics Provoked the Spanish-American and Philippine-American Wars.* New Haven: Yale University Press.

Holmes, T. Michael. 1994. *The Specter of Communism in Hawaii*. Honolulu: University of Hawai'i Press.

Holt, James. 1977. "Trade Unionism in the British and U.S. Steel Industries, 1880–1914: A Comparative Study." *Labor History* 18 (1): 5–35.

Horne, George. 1944. "Are the Japs Hopeless?" *Saturday Evening Post* (September): 16–17, 75–76.

Ikeda, Kiyoshi. 1951. "Unionization and the Plantation." *Social Process in Hawaii* 15:14–25.

International Longshoremen's and Warehousemen's Union. 1996. *1946 Sugar Strike and the ILWU*. Honolulu: ILWU.

———. 1997. *The ILWU Story: Six Decades of Militant Unionism*. San Francisco: ILWU.

Iwata, Taro. 2003. "Race and Citizenship as American Geopolitics: Japanese and Native Hawaiians in Hawai'i, 1900–1941." Ph.D. diss., University of Oregon.

Izuka, Ichiro. 1974. "The Labor Movement in Hawaii (1934–1949)." Unpublished paper, University of Hawai'i.

Jacobson, Matthew Frye. 1998. *Whiteness of a Different Color*. Cambridge, MA: Harvard University Press.

———. 2000. *Barbarian Virtues: The United States Encounters Foreign Peoples at Home and Abroad, 1876–1917*. New York: Hill and Wang.

Jaynes, Gerald D. and Robin M. Williams. 1989. *A Common Destiny*. Washington, DC: National Academy Press.

Joesting, Edward. 1972. *Hawaii: An Uncommon History*. New York: Norton.

Jung, Moon-Ho. Forthcoming. *Coolies and Cane: Race, Labor, and Sugar Production in the Age of Emancipation*. Baltimore: Johns Hopkins University Press.

Jung, Moon-Kie. 1999. "No Whites, No Asians: Race, Marxism, and Hawaii's Preemergent Working Class." *Social Science History* 23 (3): 357–393.

———. 2002. "Different Racisms and the Differences They Make: Race and 'Asian Workers' of Prewar Hawai'i." *Critical Sociology* 28:77–100.

———. 2004. "Symbolic and Physical Violence: Legitimate State Coercion of Filipino Workers in Prewar Hawai'i." *American Studies* 45 (3): 107–137.

Jung, Moon-Kie and Tomás Almaguer. 2004. "The State and the Production of Racial Categories." In *Race and Ethnicity: Across Time, Space and Discipline*, ed. Rodney C. Coates, 55–72. Leiden, Netherlands: Brill.

Kaneshiro, Edith Mitsuko. 1999. "'Our Home Will Be the Five Continents': Okinawan Migration to Hawaii, California, and the Philippines, 1899–1941." Ph.D. diss., University of California, Berkeley.

Katznelson, Ira and Aristide R. Zolberg, eds. 1988. *Working-Class Formation: Nineteenth-Century Patterns in Western Europe and the United States*. Princeton: Princeton University Press.

Kelley, Robin D.G. 1990. *Hammer and Hoe: Alabama Communists During the Great Depression*. Chapel Hill: University of North Carolina Press.

Kelly, Marion. 1980. "Land Tenure in Hawaii." *Amerasia Journal* 7 (2): 57–73.

Kennedy, Michael and Naomi Galtz. 1996. "From Marxism to Postcommunism: Socialist Desires and East European Rejections." *Annual Review of Sociology* 22:437–458.

Kent, Noel J. 1983. *Hawaii: Islands Under the Influence*. New York: Monthly Review Press.

Kerkvliet, Melinda Tria. 2002. *Unbending Cane: Pablo Manlapit, a Filipino Labor Leader in Hawaiʻi*. Honolulu: Office of Multicultural Student Services, University of Hawaiʻi, Mānoa.

Kim, Claire Jean. 2000. *Bitter Fruit: The Politics of Black-Korean Conflict in New York City*. New Haven: Yale University Press.

Kimeldorf, Howard. 1988. *Reds or Rackets? The Making of Radical and Conservative Unions on the Waterfront*. Berkeley: University of California Press.

——. 1994. "Class, Not Strata: It's Not Just Where You Stand, But What You Stand For." In *From the Left Bank to the Mainstream: Historical Debates and Contemporary Research in Marxist Sociology*, ed. Patrick McGuire and Donald McQuarie, 13–28. New York: General Hall.

Kimura, Yukiko. 1955. "A Sociological Note on the Preservation of the Portuguese Folk Dance." *Social Process in Hawaii* 19:45–50.

Korstad, Robert. 1993. "The Possibilities for Racial Egalitarianism: Context Matters." *International Labor and Working-Class History* 44:41–44.

Korstad, Robert and Nelson Lichtenstein. 1988. "Opportunities Found and Lost: Labor, Radicals, and the Early Civil Rights Movement." *Journal of American History* 75 (3): 786–811.

Kotani, Roland. 1985. *The Japanese in Hawaii: A Century of Struggle*. Honolulu: Hawaii Hōchi.

Kramer, Paul A. 1998. "The Pragmatic Empire: U.S. Anthropology and Colonial Politics in the Occupied Philippines, 1898–1916." Ph.D. diss., Princeton University.

Kristen, Elizabeth. 1999. "The Struggle for Same-Sex Marriage Continues." *Berkeley Women's Law Journal* 14:104–115.

Kuhn, Thomas S. 1962. *The Structure of Scientific Revolutions*. Chicago: University of Chicago Press.

Kuykendall, Ralph S. 1953. *The Hawaiian Kingdom, 1854–1874: Twenty Critical Years*. Honolulu: University of Hawaiʻi Press.

——. 1967. *The Hawaiian Kingdom, 1874–1893: The Kalakaua Dynasty*. Honolulu: University of Hawaiʻi Press.

Kuykendall, Ralph S. and A. Grove Day. 1948. *Hawaii: A History*. Englewood Cliffs, NJ: Prentice-Hall.

Larrowe, Charles P. 1972. *Harry Bridges: The Rise and Fall of Radical Labor in the U.S.* Westport, CT: Lawrence Hill.

Letwin, Daniel. 1995. "Interracial Unionism, Gender, and 'Social Equality' in the Alabama Coalfields, 1878–1908." *Journal of Southern History* 61 (3): 519–554.

——. 1998. *The Challenge of Interracial Unionism*. Chapel Hill: University of North Carolina Press.

Levine, Rhonda F. and James A. Geschwender. 1981. "Class Struggle, State Policy, and the Rationalization of Production: The Organization of Agriculture in Hawaii." *Research in Social Movements, Conflict and Change* 4:123–150.

Levinson, Harold M. 1967. "Unionism, Concentration, and Wage Changes: Toward a Unified Theory." *Industrial and Labor Relations Review* 20 (2): 198–205.

Lichtenstein, Nelson. 1982. *Labor's War at Home: The CIO in World War II*. New York: Cambridge University Press.

Lie, John. 2004. *Modern Peoplehood*. Cambridge, MA: Harvard University Press.

Lind, Andrew. 1938a. "Attitudes Toward Interracial Marriage in Kona, Hawaii." *Social Process in Hawaii* 4:79–83.

———. 1938b. *An Island Community: Ecological Succession in Hawaii*. New York: Greenwood.

———. 1943. *The Japanese in Hawaii Under War Conditions*. Honolulu: Hawaii Group, American Council, Institute of Pacific Relations.

———. 1946. *Hawaii's Japanese: An Experiment in Democracy*. Princeton: Princeton University Press.

———. 1980. *Hawaii's People*. 4th ed. Honolulu: University Press of Hawai'i.

Lipset, Seymour Martin. 1983. "Radicalism or Reformism: The Source of Working-class Politics." *American Political Science Review* 77:1–18.

Littler, Robert M. C. 1929. *The Governance of Hawaii*. Stanford: Stanford University Press.

Liu, John M. 1984. "Race, Ethnicity, and the Sugar Plantation System: Asian Labor in Hawaii, 1850–1900." In *Labor Migration Under Capitalism: Asian Workers in the United States Before World War II*, ed. Lucie Cheng and Edna Bonacich, 186–210. Berkeley: University of California Press.

———. 1985. "Cultivating Cane: Asian Labor and the Hawaiian Sugar Plantation System with the Capitalist World Economy, 1835–1920." Ph.D. diss., University of California, Los Angeles.

Lubove, Seth. 1997. "The People's Republic of Hawaii." *Forbes* 159 (12): 66–70.

Luis, Anastacio. 1996. "The Last Mass Migration of Workers to Hawai'i." *The Hawaiian Journal of History* 30:195–210.

Lopez, David and Yen Le Espiritu. 1990. "Panethnicity in the United States: A Theoretical Framework." *Ethnic and Racial Studies* 13 (2): 198–224.

Love, Eric T. L. 2004. *Race Over Empire: Racism and U.S. Imperialism, 1865–1900*. Chapel Hill: University of North Carolina Press.

Lydon, Edward C. 1975. *The Anti-Chinese Movement in the Hawaiian Kingdom, 1852–1886*. San Francisco: R and E Research Associates.

McAdam, Doug. 1994. "Culture and Social Movements." In *New Social Movements: From Ideology to Identity*, ed. Enrique Laraña, Hank Johnston, and Joseph R. Gusfield, 36–57. Philadelphia: Temple University Press.

McAdam, Doug, John D. McCarthy, and Mayer N. Zald. 1996. "Introduction: Opportunities, Mobilizing Structures, and Framing Processes—Toward a Synthetic, Comparative Perspective on Social Movements." In *Comparative Perspectives on Social Movements: Political Opportunities, Mobilizing Structures, and Cultural Framings*, ed. Doug McAdam, John D. McCarthy, and Mayer N. Zald, 1–20. New York: Cambridge University Press.

McClelland, Keith. 1990. "Introduction." In *E. P. Thompson: Critical Perspectives*, ed. Harvey J. Kaye and Keith McClelland, 1–11. Cambridge, UK: Polity Press.

MacDonald, Alexander. 1944. *Revolt in Paradise: The Social Revolution in Hawaii After Pearl Harbor*. New York: Stephen Daye.

McDonald, Terrence J., ed. 1996. *The Historic Turn in the Human Sciences*. Ann Arbor: University of Michigan Press.

McElrath, Robert. 1946. "The ILWU." In *Labor and Management Relations in Hawaii, Part II*, ed. Harold S. Roberts, 17–23. Honolulu: Industrial Relations Center, University of Hawai'i.

McIvor, Arthur J. 1996. *Organised Capital: Employers' Associations and Industrial Relations in Northern England, 1880–1939*. New York: Cambridge University Press.

McKeown, Adam. 2001. *Chinese Migrant Networks and Cultural Change: Peru, Chicago, Hawaii, 1930–1936*. Chicago: University of Chicago Press.

MacLennan, Carol Ann. 1979. "Plantation Capitalism and Social Policy in Hawaii." Ph.D. diss., University of California, Berkeley.

Manlapit, Pablo. [1924] 1933. *Filipinos Fight for Justice: Case of the Filipino Laborers in the Big Strike of 1924*. Honolulu: Kumalae Publishing Company.

Marques, Auguste. 1908. "The Pineapple Industry in Hawaii." *Hawaiian Annual* (1909):58–82.

Massey, Douglas and Nancy Denton. 1993. *American Apartheid: Segregation and the Making of the Underclass*. Cambridge, MA: Harvard University Press.

Masuoka, Jitsuichi. 1931. "Race Attitudes of the Japanese People in Hawaii: A Study in Social Distance." M.A. thesis, University of Hawai'i.

Matsumoto, Joyce Ayako. 1958. "The 1947 Pineapple Strike." M.B.A. thesis, University of Hawai'i.

Melendy, H. Brett. 2002. *The Federal Government's Search for Communists in the Territory of Hawaii*. Lewiston, NY: Edwin Mellen Press.

Merry, Sally Engle. 2000. *Colonizing Hawai'i: The Cultural Power of Law*. Princeton: Princeton University Press.

Miles, Robert. 1982. *Racism and Migrant Labour*. London: Routledge.

Mitchell, Timothy. 1991. "The Limits of the State: Beyond Statist Approaches and Their Critics." *American Political Science Review* 85 (1): 77–96.

Mizruchi, Mark S. and Thomas Koenig. 1991. "Size, Concentration, and Corporate Networks: Determinants of Business Collective Action." *Social Science Quarterly* 72 (2): 299–313.

Mollett, J. A. 1961. *Capital in Hawaiian Sugar: Its Formation and Relation to Labor and Output, 1870–1957*. Agricultural Economics Bulletin 21. Honolulu: Hawaiian Agricultural Experiment Station.

Monobe, Hiromi. 2004. "Shaping an Ethnic Leadership: Takie Okumura and the 'Americanization' of the Nisei in Hawai'i, 1919–1945." Ph.D. diss., University of Hawai'i.

Morgan, J. P. 1917. "The Hawaiian Pineapple Industry." *Hawaiian Annual* (1918):36–46.

Morris, Aldon D. 1984. *The Origins of the Civil Rights Movement: Black Communities Organizing for Change*. New York: The Free Press.

Mund, Vernon A. and Fred C. Hung. 1961. *Interlocking Relationships in Hawaii and Public Regulation of Ocean Transportation*. Honolulu: Economic Research Center, University of Hawai'i.

Munro, Doug. 1993. "Patterns of Resistance and Accommodation." In *Plantation Workers: Resistance and Accommodation*, ed. Brij V. Lal, Doug Munro, and Edward D. Beechert, 1–43. Honolulu: University of Hawai'i Press.

Murphy, Thomas D. 1954. *Ambassadors in Arms*. Honolulu: University of Hawai'i Press.

Nelson, Bruce. 1988. *Workers on the Waterfront: Seamen, Longshoremen, and Unionism in the 1930s*. Urbana: University of Illinois Press.

——. 1992. "Class and Race in the Crescent City: The ILWU, from San Francisco to New Orleans." In *The CIO's Left-led Unions*, ed. Steve Rosswurm, 19–46. New Brunswick, NJ: Rutgers University Press.

——. 1993. "Organized Labor and the Struggle for Black Equality in Mobile during World War II." *Journal of American History* 80 (3): 952–988.

——. 1998. "The 'Lords of the Docks' Reconsidered: Race Relations among West Coast Longshoremen, 1933–1961." In *Waterfront Workers: New Perspectives on Race and Class*, ed. Calvin Winslow, 155–192. Urbana: University of Illinois Press.

——. 2001. *Divided We Stand: American Workers and the Struggle for Black Equality*. Princeton: Princeton University Press.

Niemonen, Jack. 1997. "The Race Relations Problematic in American Sociology." *The American Sociologist* 28 (1): 15–54.

Nomura, Gail M. 1989. "The Debate Over the Role of Nisei in Prewar Hawaii: The New Americans Conference, 1927–1941." *Journal of Ethnic Studies* 15 (1): 95–115.

Nordyke, Eleanor C. 1977. *The Peopling of Hawaii*. Honolulu: East-West Center.

O'Brien, Eileen. 1943. "Making Democracy Work." *Paradise of the Pacific* 55 (12): 42–45.

Odo, Franklin. 2004. *No Sword to Bury: Japanese Americans in Hawai'i During World War II*. Philadelphia: Temple University Press.

Odo, Franklin and Kazuko Sinoto. 1985. *A Pictorial History of the Japanese in Hawai'i, 1885–1924*. Honolulu: Bishop Museum Press.

Okahata, James H. and the Publication Committee, United Japanese Society of Hawaii (PCUJSH), eds. 1971. *A History of Japanese in Hawaii*. Honolulu: The United Japanese Society of Hawaii.

Okamura, Jonathan Y. 1994. "Why There Are No Asian Americans in Hawai'i: The Continuing Significance of Local Identity." *Social Process in Hawaii* 35:161–78.

Okihiro, Gary Y. 1988. "Migrant Labor and the 'Poverty' of Asian American Studies." *Amerasia Journal* 14 (1): 129–136.

——. 1991. *Cane Fires: The Anti-Japanese Movement in Hawaii, 1865–1945*. Philadelphia: Temple University Press.

Olzak, Susan. 1992. *The Dynamics of Ethnic Competition and Conflict*. Stanford: Stanford University Press.

Omi, Michael and Howard Winant. 1986. *Racial Formation in the United States: From the 1960s to the 1990s*. New York: Routledge.

——. 1994. *Racial Formation in the United States: From the 1960s to the 1990s*. 2nd ed. New York: Routledge.

Ortner, Sherry B. 1984. "Theory in Anthropology since the Sixties." *Comparative Studies in Society and History* 26 (1): 126–166.

Ozaki, Shigeo. 1940. "Student Attitudes on Interracial Marriage." *Social Process in Hawaii* 6:23–28.

Paige, Jeffery. 1999. "Conjuncture, Comparison, and Conditional Theory in Macrosocial Inquiry." *American Journal of Sociology* 105 (3): 781–800.

Palmer, Albert W. 1924. *The Human Side of Hawaii: Race Problems in the Mid-Pacific*. Boston: Pilgrim Press.

Park, Robert E. [1926] 1950. "Our Racial Frontier on the Pacific." In *Race and Culture*, by Robert E. Park, 138–151. Glencoe, IL: The Free Press.

Parkin, Frank. 1979. *Marxism and Class Theory: A Bourgeois Critique*. New York: Columbia University Press.

Platt, Sanford L. 1950. *Immigration and Emigration in the Hawaiian Sugar Industry*. Honolulu: [Hawaiian Sugar Planters' Association].

Porteus, S. D. and Marjorie E. Babcock. 1926. *Temperament and Race*. Boston: The Gorham Press.

Posadas, Barbara M. 1982. "The Hierarchy of Color and Psychological Adjustment in an Industrial Environment: Filipinos, The Pullman Company, and the Brotherhood of Sleeping Car Porters." *Labor History* 23:349–373.

Puette, William J. 1988. *The Hilo Massacre: Hawaii's Bloody Monday, August 1st, 1938*. Honolulu: Center for Labor Education and Research, University of Hawai'i.

Quam-Wickham, Nancy. 1992. "Who Controls the Hiring Hall? The Struggle for Job Control in the ILWU During World War II." In *The CIO's Left-led Unions*, ed. Steve Rosswurm, 47–67. New Brunswick, NJ: Rutgers University Press.

Rademaker, John A. and James T. Lane. 1951. *These Are Americans: The Japanese American in Hawaii in World War II*. Palo Alto, CA: Pacific Books.

Rafael, Vicente L. 2000. *White Love and Other Events in Filipino History*. Durham: Duke University Press.

Reinecke, John E. 1938. "'Pidgin English' in Hawaii: A Local Study in the Sociology of Language." *American Journal of Sociology* 43 (5): 778–89.

——. 1966. *Labor Unions of Hawaii: A Chronological Checklist*. Honolulu: Industrial Relations Center, University of Hawai'i.

——. 1979. *Feigned Necessity: Hawaii's Attempt to Obtain Chinese Contract Labor, 1921–23*. San Francisco: Chinese Materials Center.

——. 1993. *A Man Must Stand Up: The Autobiography of a Gentle Activist*. Honolulu: Biographical Research Center, University of Hawai'i Press.

——. 1996. *The Filipino Piecemeal Sugar Strike of 1924–1925*. Honolulu: Social Science Research Institute, University of Hawai'i.

Rho, Marguerite. 1990. *Alexander & Baldwin, Inc*. Honolulu: Alexander & Baldwin, Inc.

Robinson, Chalfant. 1904. *A History of Two Reciprocity Treaties*. New Haven, CT: Tuttle, Morehouse & Taylor Press.

Roediger, David R. 1991. *The Wages of Whiteness: Race and the Making of the American Working Class*. New York: Verso.

——. 1994. *Towards the Abolition of Whiteness: Essays on Race, Politics, and Working Class History*. New York: Verso.

Rowland, Donald. 1943. "Orientals and the Suffrage in Hawaii." *Pacific Historical Review* 12 (1): 11–21.

Russ, William Adam, Jr. 1991. *The Hawaiian Republic (1894–98): And Its Struggle to Win Annexation*. Selinsgrove, PA: Susquehanna University Press.

Russell, John E. 1933. "Sugar." *Hawaiian Annual* (1934):55–61.

Sahlins, Marshall. 1981. *Historical Metaphors and Mythical Realities*. Ann Arbor: University of Michigan Press.

——. 1985. *Islands of History*. Chicago: University of Chicago Press.

——. 1994. "Cosmologies of Capitalism: The Trans-Pacific Sector of 'The World System.'" In *Culture/Power/History: A Reader in Contemporary Social Theory*, ed. Nicholas B. Dirks, Geoff Eley, and Sherry B. Ortner, 412–455. Princeton: Princeton University Press.

Sakamaki, Shunzo. 1928. "A History of the Japanese Press in Hawaii." M.A. thesis, University of Hawai'i.

Salman, Michael. 2001. *The Embarrassment of Slavery: Controversies over Bondage and Nationalism in the American Colonial Philippines*. Berkeley: University of California Press.

San Buenaventura, Steffi. 1996. "Hawaii's '1946 *Sakada*.'" *Social Process in Hawaii* 37: 74–90.

San Juan, Epifanio, Jr. 1992. *Racial Formations/Critical Transformations: Articulations of Power in Ethnic and Racial Studies in the United States*. Atlantic Highlands, NJ: Humanities Press International.

Saussure, Ferdinand de. 1959. *Course in General Linguistics*. New York: McGraw-Hill.

Saxton, Alexander. 1971. *The Indispensable Enemy*. Berkeley: University of California Press.

Schirmer, Daniel B. and Stephen R. Shalom, eds. 1987. *The Philippines Reader: A History of Colonialism, Neocolonialism, Dictatorship, and Resistance*. Boston: South End Press.

Schmitt, Robert C. 1977. *Historical Statistics of Hawaii*. Honolulu: University of Hawai'i Press.

Schuman, Howard, Charlotte Steeh, Lawrence Bobo, and Maria Krysan. 1997. *Racial Attitudes in America*. Cambridge, MA: Harvard University Press.

Schwartz, Harvey. 1978. *The March Inland: Origins of the ILWU Warehouse Division, 1934–1938*. Los Angeles: Institute of Industrial Relations, University of California.

Sewell, William H., Jr. 1980. *Work and Revolution in France: The Language of Labor from the Old Regime to 1848*. New York: Cambridge University Press.

——. 1990. "Thompson's Theory of Working-Class Formation." In *E. P. Thompson: Critical Perspectives*, ed. Harvey J. Kaye and Keith McClelland, 50–77. Philadelphia: Temple University Press.

——. 1992a. "Introduction: Narratives and Social Identities." *Social Science History* 16 (3): 479–488.

——. 1992b. "A Theory of Structure: Duality, Agency, and Transformation." *American Journal of Sociology* 98 (1): 1–29.

——. 1993. "Toward a Post-materialist Rhetoric for Labor History." In *Rethinking Labor History: Essays on Discourse and Class Analysis*, ed. Lenard R. Berlanstein, 15–38. Urbana: University of Illinois Press.

Sharma, Miriam. 1984a. "Labor Migration and Class Formation among the Filipinos in Hawaii, 1906–1946." In *Labor Immigration Under Capitalism: Asian Workers in the United States Before World War II*, ed. Lucie Cheng and Edna Bonacich, 579–615. Berkeley: University of California Press.

——. 1984b. "The Philippines: A Case of Migration to Hawaii, 1906–1946." In *Labor Immigration Under Capitalism: Asian Workers in the United States Before World War II*, ed. Lucie Cheng and Edna Bonacich, 337–358. Berkeley: University of California Press.

Shimazu, Naoko. 1998. *Japan, Race and Equality: The Racial Equality Proposal of 1919.* New York: Routledge.

Shirley, Orville C. 1946. *Americans: The Story of the 442d Combat Team.* Washington, DC: Infantry Journal Press.

Smith, Jared G. 1942. *The Big 5: A Brief History of Hawaii's Largest Firms.* Honolulu: Advertiser Publishing.

Solomos, John. 1986. "Varieties of Marxist Conceptions of 'Race,' Class and the State: A Critical Analysis." In *Theories of Race and Ethnic Relations*, ed. John Rex and David Mason, 84–109. New York: Cambridge University Press.

Solomos, John and Les Back. 1994. "Conceptualising Racisms: Social Theory, Politics and Research." *Sociology* 28 (1): 143–161.

Somers, Margaret R. 1989. "Workers of the World, Compare!" *Contemporary Sociology* 18 (3): 325–329.

——. 1994. "The Narrative Constitution of Identity: A Relational and Network Approach." *Theory and Society* 23 (5): 605–649.

Stein, Judith. 1993. "The Ins and Outs of the CIO." *International Labor and Working-Class History* 44:53–63.

Steinberg, Marc. 1991. "Talkin' Class: Discourse, Ideology, and Their Roles in Class Conflict." In *Bringing Class Back In*, ed. Scott McNall, Rhonda Levine, and Rick Fantasia, 261–284. Boulder, CO: Westview Press.

Steinberg, Stephen. 1995. *Turning Back: The Retreat from Racial Justice in American Thought and Policy.* Boston: Beacon.

Steinfeld, Robert J. 2001. *Coercion, Contract, and Free Labor in the Nineteenth Century.* New York: Cambridge University Press.

Steinmetz, George. 1999. "Introduction: Culture and the State." In *State/Culture: State Formation after the Cultural Turn*, ed. George Steinmetz, 1–49. Ithaca: Cornell University Press.

Stephan, John J. 1984. *Hawaii Under the Rising Sun: Japan's Plans for Conquest After Pearl Harbor.* Honolulu: University of Hawai'i Press.

Stevens, Sylvester K. 1945. *American Expansion in Hawaii, 1842–1898.* New York: Russell and Russell.

Stevenson, Marshall F. 1993. "Beyond Theoretical Models: The Limited Possibilities of Racial Egalitarianism." *International Labor and Working-Class History* 44:45–52.

Stirling, Yates. 1939. *Sea Duty: The Memoirs of a Fighting Admiral.* New York: G. P. Putnam's Sons.

Sullivan, Josephine. 1926. *A History of C. Brewer & Company, Limited: One Hundred Years in the Hawaiian Islands.* Boston: Walton Advertising and Printing.

Takaki, Ronald. 1982. "'An Entering Wedge': The Origins of the Sugar Plantations and a Multiethnic Working Class in Hawaii." *Labor History* 23:32–46.

——. 1983. *Pau Hana: Plantation Life and Labor in Hawaii, 1835–1920.* Honolulu: University of Hawai'i Press.

——. 1989. *Strangers from a Different Shore: A History of Asian Americans.* Boston: Penguin.

——. 1990. "Ethnicity and Class in Hawaii: The Plantation Labor Experience, 1835–1920." In *Labor Divided: Race and Ethnicity in United States Labor Struggles, 1835–1960*, ed.

Robert Asher and Charles Stephenson, 35–47. Albany: State University of New York Press.

Tamashiro, John Gerald. 1972. "The Japanese in Hawaii and on the Mainland During World War II as Discussed in the Editorial Pages of the *Honolulu Advertiser* and the *Honolulu Star Bulletin*." M.A. thesis, University of Hawai'i.

Tamura, Eileen. 1994. *Americanization, Acculturation, and Ethnic Identity: The Nisei Generation in Hawaii*. Urbana: University of Illinois Press.

Tate, Merze. 1968. *Hawaii: Reciprocity or Annexation*. East Lansing: Michigan State University Press.

Taylor, William. 1935. "The Hawaiian Sugar Industry." Ph.D. diss., University of California, Berkeley.

Taylor, Frank J., Earl M. Welty, and David W. Eyre. 1976. *From Land and Sea: The Story of Castle & Cooke of Hawaii*. San Francisco: Chronicle Books.

Tchen, John Kuo Wei. 1999. *New York before Chinatown*. Baltimore: Johns Hopkins University Press.

Teodoro, Luis V., Jr., ed. 1981. *Out of This Struggle: The Filipinos in Hawaii*. Honolulu: University Press of Hawai'i.

Therborn, Göran. 1983. "Why Some Classes Are More Successful than Others." *New Left Review* 138:37–55.

Thomas, Mifflin. 1983. *Schooner from Windward: Two Centuries of Hawaiian Interisland Shipping*. Honolulu: University of Hawai'i Press.

Thompson, David E. 1951. "The ILWU as a Force for Interracial Unity in Hawaii." *Social Process in Hawaii* 15:32–43.

———. 1966. "Agricultural Workers Made It in Hawaii." *Labor Today* (November):24–32.

Thompson, Edward P. 1963. *The Making of the English Working Class*. London: Victor Gollancz.

———. 1978. *The Poverty of Theory and Other Essays*. New York: Monthly Review Press.

Thurston, Lorrin A. N.d. *Handbook on the Annexation of Hawaii*. St. Joseph, MI: A. B. Morse Company.

Tilly, Charles. 1978. *From Mobilization to Revolution*. Reading, MA: Addison-Wesley.

Tomasky, Michael. 1996. *Left for Dead: The Life, Death and Possible Resurrection of Progressive Politics in America*. New York: The Free Press.

Tomlins, Christopher L. 1985. *The State and the Unions: Labor Relations, Law, and the Organized Labor Movement in America, 1880–1960*. New York: Cambridge University Press.

Toyoma, Henry and Kiyoshi Ikeda. 1950. "The Okinawan-Naichi Relationship." *Social Process in Hawaii* 14:51–65.

Tsutsumi, Noboru [Takashi]. 1922. *History of Hawaii Laborers' Movement*. Trans. Umetaro Okumura. Honolulu: Hawaiian Sugar Planters' Association.

Tuttle, Harold Saxe. 1959. "Lanai—Lanai: A Culture Lost—a Culture Gained." *Social Process in Hawaii* 23:20–28.

van den Berghe, Pierre L. 1967. *Race and Racism*. New York: Wiley.

van Zwalenburg, Paul R. 1961. "Hawaiian Labor Unions Under Military Government." M.A. thesis, University of Hawai'i.

Wakukawa, Ernest K. 1938. *A History of the Japanese People in Hawaii*. Honolulu: The Toyo Shoin.

Wallerstein, Immanuel. 1991. "The Ideological Tensions of Capitalism: Universalism Versus Racism and Sexism" and "The Construction of Peoplehood: Racism, Nationalism, Ethnicity." In *Race, Nation, Class*, by Etienne Balibar and Immanuel Wallerstein, 29–36, 71–85. New York: Verso.

Waters, Mary C. and Tomás R. Jiménez. 2005. "Assesssing Immigrant Assimilation: New Empirical and Theoretical Challenges." *Annual Review of Sociology* 31:105–125.

Weinberg, Daniel Erwin. 1967. "The Movement to 'Americanize' the Japanese Community in Hawaii: An Analysis of One Hundred Percent Americanization Activity in the Territory of Hawaii as Expressed in the Caucasian Press, 1919–1923." M.A. thesis, University of Hawai'i.

Weingarten, Victor. 1946. *Raising Cane: A Brief History of Labor in Hawaii*. Honolulu: International Longshoremen's and Warehousemen's Union.

Weinstein, Michael G., Peter T. Manicas, and Joseph J. Leon. 1989. "The Portuguese and Haoles of Hawaii." *American Sociological Review* 54:305–308.

Welch, Richard E. 1979. *Response to Imperialism: The United States and the Philippine-American War, 1899–1902*. Chapel Hill: University of North Carolina Press.

Wellman, David. 1995. *The Union Makes Us Strong: Radical Unionism on the San Francisco Waterfront*. New York: Cambridge University Press.

Wentworth, Edna Clark. 1941. *Filipino Plantation Workers in Hawaii: A Study of Incomes, Expenditures and Living Standards of Filipino Families on an Hawaiian Sugar Plantation*. San Francisco: American Council, Institute of Pacific Relations.

White, Henry A. 1957. *James D. Dole: Industrial Pioneer of the Pacific*. Princeton: Princeton University Press for the Newcomen Society.

Wills, Arnold. 1954. *Labor-Management Relations in Hawaii*. Honolulu: Industrial Relations Center, University of Hawai'i.

Wilson, William J. 1973. *Power, Racism, and Privilege*. New York: Macmillan.

——. 1999. *The Bridge Over the Racial Divide: Rising Inequality and Coalition Politics*. New York: Russell Sage Foundation and Berkeley: University of California Press.

Winant, Howard. 1994. *Racial Conditions: Politics, Theory, Comparisons*. Minneapolis: University of Minnesota Press.

——. 2000. "Race and Race Theory." *Annual Review of Sociology* 26:169–85.

Wolpe, Harold. 1986. "Class Concepts, Class Struggle and Racism." In *Theories of Race and Ethnic Relations*, ed. John Rex and David Mason, 110–130. New York: Cambridge University Press.

Worden, William L. 1981. *Cargoes: Matson's First Century in the Pacific*. Honolulu: University Press of Hawai'i.

Yamamoto, George Y. 1976. *Origin of Buddhism in Hawaii* and *Brief Chronological Table of Japanese in Hawaii*. Honolulu: Young Buddhist Association of Honolulu.

Yen, Ching-Hwang. 1985. *Coolies and Mandarins*. Singapore: Singapore University Press.

Zalburg, Sanford. 1979. *A Spark Is Struck! Jack Hall and the ILWU in Hawaii*. Honolulu: University of Hawai'i Press.

Zieger, Robert H. 1995. *The CIO, 1935–1955*. Chapel Hill: University of North Carolina Press.

Index

Inferiority *(continued)*
and Filipinos, 84, 85, 86, 186; and Japanese, 81–82, 186; and Portuguese, 185; and racism, 61. *See also* Racism
Inflection event: concept of, 191; sugar strike of 1946 as an example of, 168–74
Inland Boatmen's Union (IBU), 126
Inter-Island Steam Navigation Company, 44, 45, 115–16, 124–27, 205*n*122
International Labor Defense, 129
International Longshoremen's and Warehousemen's Union (ILWU): and agricultural workers, 143, 239*n*210; and anticommunist movement, 174–77, 255*n*168; and Big Five, 160, 247*n*78; and charters, 118; and Democratic Party, 2, 176, 193*n*6; and democratization of Hawai'i, 2–3; dispute with AFL, 123–24; and employers' antiunionism, 153, 165; and Filipinos, 105, 150, 151, 168–69; and ideas of class, 7, 10; and interracialism, 7, 191; and interracial movement, 5, 8, 146, 161–67, 168, 173–76, 183–84; and Lana'i pineapple strike of 1951, 174, 179–82, 181(figure), 189; leftists in, 147, 240–41*n*11; and longshore strike of 1949, 174, 176–79, 183, 189, 192, 255*nn*170, 172, 255–56*n*173; and martial law, 137, 138, 139, 140, 141, 145, 160, 187, 236*n*181, 236–37*n*185; membership fluctuations in, 124–25, 141; organizing drive of, mid-1930s, 54, 108, 186; and Political Action Committee, 143; postwar growth of, 8, 107, 108, 141, 167, 187; progress made by, 141, 147, 151; and racial conflicts, 144–45, 146, 161–63, 165–67, 174; integration of leadership in, 164–65; and sugar strike of 1946, 145, 162, 168–74; and territory-wide agreement, 127–28, 232–33*n*127; and World War II, 107, 132
International Longshoremen's Association (ILA): and charters, 111, 112, 223*nn*15, 16, 223–24*n*20; organizing efforts of, 46, 109, 110. *See also* Pacific Coast District of the ILA

Interracialism: and antiracism, 192; concept of, 3; and deracialization, 3–6, 7, 9, 144–46, 164, 189, 190, 194*n*9; durability of, 190–92; implications for, 189–92; reconceptualization of, 3–7, 190–91; and sociology, 3–4, 6, 164
Interracial labor movement: and CIO, 128, 129, 130, 186; and demise of anti-Japanese Americanism, 154, 159–60, 187–88; and deracialization, 5, 6, 144–46; durability of, 174–82; and Filipinos, 130; formation of, 3, 94, 107, 184, 186; and International Longshoremen's and Warehousemen's Union, 5, 8, 146, 161–67, 168, 173–76, 183–84; and leadership positions, 165–67, 170, 189; and multilingual meetings, 131, 149, 164, 167, 170, 189, 242*n*22; prewar limitations of, 146–54, 188; and race-conscious election of leaders, 164–65; and rearticulation of race, 146, 188, 189; and strike of 1937, 105; and strike of 1940-1941, 124; and sugar strike of 1946, 168–74, 189; and united front, 149. *See also* Working-class interracialism
Issei, 261*n*106. *See also* Japanese
Izuka, Ichiro, 123, 175, 176

Japan: and citizenship, 95, 218*n*138; and protection of emigrants, 78, 79, 80, 81; and war with China, 100, 221*n*173; and World War II, 132–33
Japanese: and Americanization movement, 94–96, 99, 103, 146, 152, 153, 154, 157, 218*n*137; and cessation of migration, 34, 78; and concentration camps, 156, 245*n*63, 245–46*n*64; and employers' antiunionism, 123, 152–53, 230*n*93; labor resistance of, 28, 33–34; and manhood, 83–84, 216*n*105; and martial law, 8, 156–57, 209*n*23, 246*n*66; nationalism of, 94, 100, 155, 221*n*173; odds of skilled employment, 64, 64(table), 94, 99; as part of workforce,